CHINESE ENTREPRENEURSHIP AND ASIAN BUSINESS NETWORKS

This volume examines the business behavior of ethnic Chinese entrepreneurs in the People's Republic of China, Vietnam, Malaysia, Singapore, Indonesia and Australia whose business acumen and network connections (*guanxi*) have aroused great admiration and sometimes envy and discomfort. The book tries to dispel some of the (culturally biased) misperceptions about the business conduct of the ethnic Chinese in East and Southeast Asia such as their homogeneity, tribal image and socioeconomic exclusivity, the idea of Greater China as an exclusive, transnational Chinese business circle both within and outside China etc. It also illustrates the challenges, which the rapidly progressing integration of East and Southeast Asia's market cultures into the global market system pose, for ethnic Chinese entrepreneurs, their family businesses, conglomerates and network ties.

The contributors comprise sociologists, anthropologists, political scientists, economists and geographers from Germany, Denmark, the Netherlands, the United Kingdom, Singapore, Malaysia, Australia and the USA – all leading scholars on ethnic entrepreneurship, the Chinese overseas and Chinese (business) affairs in East and Southeast Asia. Most of the case studies are based on solid, indepth empirical research and will prove extremely useful for anyone wishing to understand what makes Chinese network capitalism tick and why it will continue to be a critical force of Asia's great transformation.

Due to its reflective agenda and multi-disciplinary approach, this book will be essential reading for those interested in East and Southeast Asia, development studies, Chinese (ethnic) entrepreneurship, business networks, management as well as socioeconomic change.

The publication of this book is made possible by a grant from the Faculty of Arts and Social Sciences, National University of Singapore.

Thomas Menkhoff is Practice Associate Professor at the School of Business, Singapore Management University, Republic of Singapore. **Solvay Gerke** is Professor and Head of the Department of Southeast Asian Studies, Bonn University, Germany.

CHINESE ENTREPRENEURSHIP AND ASIAN BUSINESS NETWORKS

Edited by
Thomas Menkhoff and
Solvay Gerke

Routledge
Taylor & Francis Group

LONDON AND NEW YORK

First published 2002
by Routledge, an imprint of Taylor & Francis
2 Park Square, Milton Park, Abingdon, Oxon, OX14 4RN

Simultaneously published in the USA and Canada
by Routledge
270 Madison Ave, New York NY 10016

Routledge is an imprint of the Taylor & Francis Group

Transferred to Digital Printing 2007

© 2002 Thomas Menkhoff and Solvay Gerke for selection and
editorial matter; individual contributors for their contribution

Typeset in Times New Roman by
Newgen Imaging Systems (P) Ltd, Chennai, India

British Library Cataloguing in Publication Data
A catalogue record for this book is available
from the British Library

Library of Congress Cataloging in Publication Data
Chinese entrepreneurship and Asian business networks / edited by
Thomas Menkhoff and Solvay Gerke.
p. cm.
'Some of the papers included in this monograph were presented at an international
conference ... entitled "Crisis management – Chinese entrepreneurs and business networks
in Southeast Asia", held at the University of Bonn ... in May 1999' – Ackn.
Includes bibliographical references and index.
1. Corporations, Chinese – Asia, Southeastern. 2. Business networks – China.
3. Business networks – Asia, Southeastern. 4. Chinese – Asia, Southeastern – Economic
conditions. 5. Corporate culture – China. 6. Corporate culture – Asia, Southeastern.
7. Entrepreneurship – China. 8. Entrepreneurship – Asia, Southeastern.
9. China – Foreign economic relations – Asia, Southeastern. 10. Asia, Southeastern – Foreign
economic relations – China. I. Menkhoff, Thomas. II. Gerke, Solvay.
HD2901 .C45 2002
338'. 04'089951–dc21
2002072685

ISBN 0-7007-1653-X
ISBN 0-415-33828-X

CONTENTS

List of figures   viii
List of tables   ix
List of contributors   x
Preface   xii
Acknowledgments   xv

PART I
Introduction   1

   Asia's transformation and the role of the ethnic Chinese   3
   THOMAS MENKHOFF AND SOLVAY GERKE

PART II
**Coping with change and crises – Chinese businesses
under siege?**   21

  1 **Asia's Chinese entrepreneurs between
     myth-making and renewal**   23
     THOMAS MENKHOFF AND DOUGLAS SIKORSKI

  2 **The unfinished agenda of the overseas Chinese**   43
     LINDA LOW

PART III
**Synergies between the Chinese diaspora and
Chinese business organizations in the People's
Republic of China and Vietnam**   63

  3 **A new alliance for profit: China's local industries and
     the Chinese diaspora**   65
     NOEL TRACY AND CONSTANCE LEVER-TRACY

CONTENTS

4 Chinese entrepreneurship and resilient national
   development: how "Web-based Chinese Management"
   can help the growth of China's multiple ownership
   economy   84
   KAI-ALEXANDER SCHLEVOGT

5 The role of private entrepreneurship for social and political
   change in the People's Republic of China and Vietnam   100
   THOMAS HEBERER

6 Private business and socio-economic network relations in
   the Chinese community in Ho Chi Minh City, Vietnam   129
   JAKOB LINDAHL AND LOTTE THOMSEN

PART IV
Chinese network capitalism and *guanxi* transactions
reconsidered   157

7 Chinese business development in Malaysia: networks,
   entrepreneurship or patronage?   159
   EDMUND TERENCE GOMEZ

8 Transnational entrepreneurship and Chinese
   business networks: the regionalization of Chinese
   business firms from Singapore   184
   HENRY W.-C. YEUNG

9 Personalism and paternalism in Chinese businesses   217
   TONG CHEE KIONG AND YONG PIT KEE

10 *Guanxi*: sentiment, performance and the trading of words 233
   YAO SOUCHOU

11 The globalization of Southeast Asia and rooted capitalism:
   Sino-*Nusantara* symbiosis   255
   WAZIR JAHAN KARIM

12 From a niche to a world city: barriers, opportunities and
   resources of ethnic Chinese businesses in Australia   267
   CONSTANCE LEVER-TRACY, DAVID IP AND NOEL TRACY

CONTENTS

PART V
Towards a comparative perspective of ethnic (Chinese) entrepreneurship   **293**

13   **Individualism and collective forms of business organisation: rural capitalists in India, Malaysia and Indonesia**   295
MARIO RUTTEN

PART VI
Looking back and forward   **319**

Towards a better understanding of Chinese capitalism and Asian business networks   321
THOMAS MENKHOFF AND SOLVAY GERKE

Index   331

FIGURES

4.1	The WCM model	85
4.2	Comparison of structural profiles between private enterprises and SOEs	87
4.3	Comparison of managerial practices between private enterprises and SOEs	89
4.4	Emphasis on Chinese culture	90
5.1	The magic triangle of change	100
5.2	Entrepreneur as a category in China	106
5.3	Deviance becomes policy: the case of the private sector	110
7.1	Oriental Holdings Bhd corporate structure	167
7.2	Public Bank Bhd corporate structure	170
7.3	YTL Corporation Bhd corporate structure	176
10.1	A ping-pong model of Chinese exchange	247

TABLES

I.1 The number of ethnic Chinese worldwide (in million) and as percent
of total population 5
1.1 Interconnections between Chinese businesses, economic
globalization and the Asian crisis 28
3.1 Sources of foreign capital in China (cumulative 1979–93,
percentages) 69
4.1 Mean difference tests for structural variables between private
and state-owned enterprises 86
4.2 Managerial differences between private enterprises and SOEs 88
4.3 Mean difference tests between private and state-owned enterprises
with regard to "emphasis on culture" 90
4.4 Mean difference tests for size of private and
state-owned enterprises 90
7.1 Malaysia: ownership of share capital (at par value) of limited
companies, 1969–95 (percentages) 162
7.2 Business activity and sub-ethnic identity of the largest Chinese
companies in Malaysia 164
7.3 Oriental Holdings Bhd: share capital, turnover and profit margins,
1984–95 (RM million) 166
7.4 YTL Corp Bhd: share capital, turnover and profit margins,
1991–6 (RM million) 172
7.5 YTL Corp Bhd: sectoral breakdown in terms of turnover
and pre-tax profits, 1995 (RM million) 176
8.1 Outward direct investment from Singapore by country,
1981–96 (in S$ million) 194
8.2 The historical geography of fifty-four Chinese business firms
from Singapore 195
8.3 Types of connections between transnational entrepreneurs
and host countries prior to overseas operations 197
8.4 Major problems faced and solutions by transnational
entrepreneurs from Singapore by region 198

CONTRIBUTORS

Chan Kwok-bun is Head and Professor, Department of Sociology, and Director, David C. Lam Institute for East-West Studies, Hong Kong Baptist University, Kowloon Tong, Hong Kong.

Solvay Gerke is Professor at the Department of Southeast Asian Studies, Bonn University, Germany.

Edmund Terence Gomez is Associate Professor at the Faculty of Economics, University of Malaya, Kuala Lumpur, Malaysia.

Thomas Heberer is Professor of Political Science/East Asian Politics at the Institute of East Asian Studies and the Institute of Political Science at Gerhard-Mercator University, Duisburg, Germany.

David Ip is Associate Professor at the Department of Sociology, University of Queensland, St Lucia, Brisbane, Queensland, Australia.

Wazir Jahan Karim is Professor of Anthropology at the Universiti Sains Malaysia, Penang and Director-General of the Academy of Social Sciences, Malaysia.

Constance Lever-Tracy is Senior Lecturer at the Department of Sociology, Faculty of Social Sciences, The Flinders University of South Australia, Adelaide, Australia.

Jakob Lindahl is a PhD Student at the Department of Geography and International Development Studies, Roskilde University, Denmark.

Linda Low is Associate Professor at the Department of Business Policy, Faculty of Business Administration, National University of Singapore, Republic of Singapore.

Thomas Menkhoff is Practice Associate Professor at the School of Business, Singapore Management University, Republic of Singapore.

Mario Rutten is Professor of Comparative Sociology of Asia at the University of Amsterdam and Head of the Branch Office Amsterdam of the International Institute for Asian Studies, The Netherlands.

Douglas Sikorski is Associate Professorial Fellow at the Department of Business Policy, NUS Business School, National University of Singapore, Republic of Singapore.

Kai-Alexander Schlevogt is President of the Schlevogt Business School, Germany, and Professor & Senior Research Fellow, Peking University, People's Republic of China.

Lotte Thomsen is a PhD Student at the Centre for Development Research, Copenhagen, Denmark.

Tong Chee Kiong is Associate Professor at the Department of Sociology, Faculty of Arts and Social Sciences, National University of Singapore, Republic of Singapore.

Noel Tracy is Associate Professor at the School of Political and International Studies, Flinders University of South Australia, Adelaide, South Australia, Australia.

Yao Souchou is Senior Lecturer at the Department of Anthropology, The University of Sydney, Australia.

Henry W.-C. Yeung is Associate Professor at the Department of Geography, Faculty of Arts and Social Sciences, National University of Singapore, Republic of Singapore.

Yong Pit Kee was a Research Assistant at the Faculty of Arts and Social Sciences, National University of Singapore, Republic of Singapore.

PREFACE

While trying to understand an object of inquiry be it a person, an ethnic group, a community or, in the case of this book, a Chinese business network, the social scientist typically begins by looking inside the object to discover its essence and then attributes its conduct, an outside manifestation visible to the observer, to such essence. We understand the externals by probing the internals – thus the strain, for example, to attribute Chinese entrepreneurship and business success (and, recently, failure) to culture, the so-called "supply side" of ethnic entrepreneurship (Chan Kwok-bun and Ong Jiu Hui 1999), be it ethnic solidarity, cultural values, ethnicity, and so on. In the field of Chinese immigrant entrepreneurship and business networks, this emphasis on culture is not without its critics. Two recent books, one in 2001 edited by Edmund Terence Gomez and Michael Hsiao Hsin-Huang (2001), and the other by myself in 2000 (2000), attempt a theoretical corrective of this emphasis on culture by advocating an added sensitivity to structure and context, the so-called "demand side" of ethnic business. Such a corrective, not surprisingly, proceeds by identifying the many myths and misconceptions of Chinese business networks in specific and Chinese immigrant entrepreneurship in general – and de-constructs them, piece by piece. The field is now in what Liu Hong (forthcoming) calls a "revisionist" mood – that of deconstruction, de-mystification, or de-glamorization of a "romance of ethnic Chinese business," if there is such a thing. The present volume edited by Thomas Menkhoff and Solvay Gerke joins the camp of the revisionists. This itself excites the field – a true witness to science being cumulative, self-reflexive and self-corrective.

Rarely a cultural or a structural explanation of any social object suffices by itself. In fact, Waldinger way back in 1984, some eighteen years ago, put forward an *interactive* explanation based on a series of industry case studies in New York – an outgrowth of a desire to integrate or fuse culture with structure, ethnic resources with opportunity structure, "supply" with "demand." In this approach, the demand for ethnic business and the supply of skills and resources *interact to produce* ethnic entrepreneurship, thus pointing to the artificiality of an either/or explanation of whether culture or structure shapes the trajectory of economic achievement. From the viewpoint of the process and history, culture and structure are often in a continuous dialectical interplay, thus nullifying any attempt to make a sharp division between the two. History articulates the dialectics of culture and structure. Without over-emphasizing it, there is a need to learn to think about the whole field dialectically. Of course, such a view is not new. It is a throwback to Yancey's (1976) idea of "emergent ethnicity." Ethnicity, if indeed useful to business, is typically "manufactured" in the host society rather than imported wholesale from the place of departure. Culture and, for that matter, identity, is rarely transplanted as is, but rather reproduced and produced, deconstructed and constructed, in exploitation of structural advantages as well as in adaptation to contextual constraints. Identity is often identity in context, *in situation*. Identity is about adaptation. Indeed, again thinking dialectically, we are better off focusing our analytical gaze at the exterior conduct of Chinese enterprises while doing their business in full view of the social milieu. In other words, their strategies as business conduct, or as what Giddens (1976) calls the "dialectic of control." This gaze at the exteriors has the promise of liberating us from the "black box of culture." At the very least, culture should be seen as a small culture, a much trimmed down fellow. Emergent immigrant culture is culture adapted. Dialectical thinking requires the researcher to be concerned with doing, not being. Ethnic entrepreneurship should always be seen as a social, collective response to structural constraints. Metaphorically, Chinese entrepreneurship is like a "toolbox," ever resourceful, always replenishing itself – one pulls out a tool depending on the requirements of the situation, but without necessarily abandoning the other tools.

Two things characterize the ethnic Chinese overseas: their subjection to discrimination and their over-representation (relative to the local people in the place of destination) in self-employment and entrepreneurship. There is in fact a good empirical literature that attempts to link the two phenomena. Among other things, in the future one may want to approach studies of Chinese business networks by *bringing back* into mainstream social science, research: on prejudice and discrimination, which has a rather long history in sociology and psychology; on economic sociology, which is relatively new; and, perhaps most significantly, on the sociology and psychology of race and ethnic relations – where there is an abundance of deep social theory as well as creative methodology. For example, the daily dilemmas of the Chinese in Southeast Asia do remind us of Georg Simmel's (1908) "stranger?" So close, yet so far away. The unity of nearness and farness, social distance and intimacy, is organized within the existential condition of Georg Simmel's stranger or Robert Park's (1928) marginal man. It is no wonder the ethnic Chinese entrepreneur is liked and disliked at the same time. This position of ambivalence is the Chinese's weakness as well as their strength, their fate as well as their choice, a deep paradox indeed. The point stressed here is to be diligent in avoiding the marginalization of research on Chinese business networks. Much is to be gained by returning to social theory and using theory actively. This book by Thomas Menkhoff and Solvay Gerke serves as a timely reminder.

The mood of a field of studies can often be detected by the language used. If we were to move away from a cultural bias that typically looks inward and backward, we must be careful in our usage of such words as bounded community solidarity, ethnic enclave or ghetto, family loyalty, or ethnicity, identity and race as understood conventionally. To put it graphically, the field perhaps requires an "opening out" and "opening up." Our gaze should be at the external character of the Chinese business networks and their modes of transactions and interactions with the milieu. In other words, the exterior conduct of commerce. Once we start doing this, we may begin to realize that the logic of commerce, Chinese or not, dictates a sharp sensitivity to the other, the non-Chinese, the larger, much larger social world out there beyond the narrow confines of family, clan, lineage, ethnic group, community, or what the journalists call "tribes." Reality is where attention is drawn, the social psychologist has long been told. This is particularly so in a rapidly globalized world where transnationality prevails. Chinese entrepreneurs are quickly becoming a significant force of social change, inside and outside China. The conduct of a Chinese merchant in terms of his integration into society is what really matters. As it happens, the many myths and misconceptions of Chinese businesses will begin to fall, one by one. And the field will then confidently move through the phase of deconstruction, and into that of integration.

Chan Kwok-bun
Head and Professor
Department of Sociology

Director
David C. Lam Institute for East-West Studies (LEWI)
Hong Kong Baptist University
Kowloon Tong
Hong Kong

References

Chan Kwok-bun (ed.) (2000) *Chinese Business Networks: State, Economy and Culture*, Singapore: Prentice Hall; Copenhagen: Nordic Institute of Asian Studies.

Chan Kwok-bun and Ong Jiu Hui (1999) The Many Faces of Immigrant Entrepreneurship. In R. Cohen (ed.), *The Cambridge Survey of World Migration*, Cambridge: Cambridge University Press, pp. 523–31.

Giddens, A. (1976) *New Rules of Sociological Method*, New York: Basic Books.

Gomez, E. T. and Hsiao, Hsin-Huang Michael (eds) (2001) *Chinese Business in South-East Asia: Contesting Cultural Explanations, Researching Entrepreneurship*, Surrey: Curzon.

Liu Hong (forthcoming) Paradigm Shift in Southeast Asian Chinese Business History? Some Preliminary Observations (in Chinese), *Journal of Oriental Studies (Dongfang wenhua)*, Center of Asian Studies: Hong Kong University.

Park, R. (1928) Human Migration and the Marginal Man, *American Journal of Sociology*, XXXIII, No. 6.

Simmel, G. (1908) The Stranger, *Soziologie*, Leipzig: Duncker and Humbolt.

Waldinger, R. (1984) Immigrant Enterprise in the New York Garment Industry, *Social Problems*, 32(1), 60–71.

Yancey, W. L. *et al.* (1976) Emergent Ethnicity: a Review and Reformulation, *American Sociological Review*, 41, 391–403.

ACKNOWLEDGMENTS

Some of the chapters included in this monograph were presented at an international conference sponsored by the Deutsche Forschungsgemeinschaft (DFG) entitled "Crisis Management – Chinese Entrepreneurs and Business Networks in Southeast Asia," held at the University of Bonn, Department of Southeast Asian Studies, Bonn, Germany, in May 1999. It was chaired by Solvay Gerke (University of Bonn), Hans-Dieter Evers (University of Bielefeld) and Thomas Menkhoff (National University of Singapore). The editors gratefully acknowledge the financial support received from DFG and the University of Bonn, as well as the Mayor of Bonn for hosting the conference. The editors are especially indebted to the National University of Singapore (NUS), Faculty of Arts and Social Sciences, for a grant towards the publication of this monograph. Thanks are also due to Professor Chan Kwok-bun (Hong Kong Baptist University) for his illuminating preface and Prof. Hans-Dieter Evers (Center for Development Research, University of Bonn), Associate Prof. Tong Chee Kiong (NUS), Associate Prof. Alan Chan (NUS), Associate Prof. Tan Ern Ser (NUS) and Mr Peter Sowden, Editor, RoutledgeCurzon, for administrative, editorial and other inputs, as well as the various contributors.

Part I

INTRODUCTION

ASIA'S TRANSFORMATION AND THE ROLE OF THE ETHNIC CHINESE

Thomas Menkhoff and Solvay Gerke

The ethnic Chinese – key drivers of Asia's transformation

Since the mid-1980s intra-regional trade and investment links in East and Southeast Asia have expanded rapidly with the shift of production by firms from Japan and new industrial countries to lower-cost, neighboring countries. Various new economic sub-regions such as Greater Guangdong (Guangdong, Fujian, Hong Kong, Taiwan), Greater Shanghai or the southern Growth Triangle involving the Riau Islands of Indonesia, the Malaysian state of Johor and Singapore, have emerged, capitalizing on regional economic complementarities. Another growth triangle is under construction, at least as a blueprint, the Northern Growth Triangle, linking southern Thailand with four Malaysian states (e.g. Penang, center for light industries and electronics, as the hub) and northern Sumatra in Indonesia. The ethnic Chinese from Hong Kong, Taiwan, Singapore, Malaysia or Indonesia are actively involved in these massive transformation and integration processes (Berger and Hsiao 1988; Hamilton 1991; Menkhoff 1993; Chan and Chiang 1994; Buchholt and Menkhoff 1996; Weidenbaum and Hughes 1996; Haley *et al.* 1998; Chan 2000).

The Chinese overseas

The ethnic Chinese in Southeast Asia and beyond are often described as *overseas Chinese* or Nanyang *huaqiao*. Nanyang means "Southern Ocean" and refers to the entire sub-continental and island countries of Southeast Asia and the surrounding seas where Chinese people came to live. *Hua* has been used by the Chinese to refer to China. The word *qiao* means "a short stay as a visitor" and mirrors the early, mainly nonpermanent, settlements of Chinese laborers, merchants and traders in Southeast Asia as indicated by the term "Chinese sojourners." The word *huaqiao* implies that all Chinese living outside China on a short-term basis have to be regarded as overseas Chinese. Given the differing circumstances faced by Chinese communities in Southeast Asia in terms of naturalization policies,

3

citizenship, length of settlement and so forth, it is apparent that the category "overseas Chinese" with its negative connotations such as their alleged orientation towards China as ancestral country, disloyalty towards their host societies and so forth has a weak conceptual basis: "What makes the term all the more unhappy is its implication that all Chinese were part of the Chinese nation, that remaining Chinese mattered, and that a special relationship existed between China and the overseas Chinese" (Pan 1998: 16).

Even the term "Chinese overseas" (*haiwai huaren*) has been criticized by some scholars as it perpetuates a China-centric standpoint in the study of Chinese communities in different parts of the world (Kwok 1999). It also ignores the large number of people of Chinese ancestry who have melted into other communities. All nations in Southeast Asia have special terms to describe the second-, third- or fourth-generation offspring of the first generation Chinese who often married indigenous women, integrating local life-styles and cultural traits of their host society into their own everyday life. The Chinese term for the Chinese of mixed parentage is *Ming-houng*. In the Philippines, the Chinese of mixed parentage are called *mestizos*, in Thailand *Luk-Chin* (children of Chinese), and in Malaysia *Baba*-Chinese. In Indonesia, children of mixed marriages are called *peranakan*, a term which refers to the descendants of early Chinese immigrants who have settled in Indonesia for several generations, adapting themselves to Indonesian culture.

How then can we define the Chinese with whom this book is mainly concerned? Some investigators have suggested self-identification as the defining criterion for the Chinese in Southeast Asia (Somers-Heidhues 1974: 7). However, this definition does not consider those Chinese who are – as formal citizens of a Southeast Asian country – regarded by others as Chinese despite their eventual contrary self-identification as members of the respective country. Wu and Wu (1980: 122) have defined ethnic Chinese as members of the ethnic Chinese community in the region: "... if they maintain a degree of Chinese cultural identity and think of themselves as Chinese, and if both the countries of their residence and third parties, including persons of other nationalities, regard them as Chinese." Our own conceptualization of ethnic Chinese in Southeast Asia follows that of Pan (1998: 15) who sees the Chinese overseas as "people who are Chinese by descent but whose non-Chinese citizenship and political allegiance collapse ancestral loyalties."

Misperceptions about Chinese businesses

There are several misperceptions about ethnic Chinese and their businesses, which need to be addressed. Contrary to popular stereotypes of ethnic Chinese communities in Southeast Asia as being homogenous entities, it has to be acknowledged that they are in fact very heterogeneous which complicates classifications (Wang 1978: 8; 1994). Scattered all across the globe (Table I.1), they possess different cultural, linguistic and religious peculiarities, habits, life-styles and worldviews and are exposed to different issues.

Table I.1 The number of ethnic Chinese
worldwide (in million) and as
percent of total population

Singapore	2.2	77.7%
Malaysia	5.6	28.0%
Brunei	0.041	15.6%
Thailand	6.3	11.5%
Cambodia	0.350	5.5%
Indonesia	3.8	2.7%
Myanmar	0.041	0.8%
Vietnam	1.1	2.0%
Laos	0.006	0.2%
United States	1.8	—
Canada	0.6	—
Africa	0.1	—

Various sources.

A stiff-necked stereotype of the ethnic Chinese (businessmen) is that they are all successful economic actors. Another often heard common-sense argument is that all the Chinese in Southeast Asia are rich; a notion that is continually enhanced by media reports featuring Asia's ethnic Chinese tycoons, their achievements and the capital they have accumulated. At the beginning of the 1990s, overall estimates put the "GNP" of "Asia's 51 m overseas Chinese," Taiwan and Hong Kong included, at $450 bn – a quarter larger than China's GNP. The liquid assets (not including securities) of "the worldwide community of overseas Chinese" were estimated to be worth $1.5–2 trillion (*The Economist*, 7/18/1992 and 11/27/1993).

It is often ignored that the Chinese entrepreneurs in Southeast Asia were frequently forced into business as a consequence of their trading minority status (Evers and Schrader 1994), that they do fail in business ventures, that there are significant disparities within Chinese communities etc. Both historical and contemporary studies on Chinese entrepreneurship tend to focus on the bright side of business and success stories rather than on its dark side (Backman 1999) or those who did not make it.

Another popular belief is that the ethnic Chinese in Southeast Asia and beyond are excellent (interwoven) net workers who have formed an exclusive regional Chinese network of companies, clans and villages linked by ties of blood and native place, which is part of the large global network of overseas Chinese businessmen (Kotkin 1992; Chang 1995). A related myth is the notion that the reliance on *guanxi*, personal connections and networking is a uniquely Chinese phenomenon without any dysfunctions and that respective strategies are aimed at embracing mainly the fellow ethnic Chinese (Menkhoff 1998). Constructs such as "greater China" or "the global Chinese tribe" are manifestations of such troublesome beliefs. As Pan (1998: 17) has stressed, the grandiose idea of greater China as a transnational Chinese business circle embracing all the ethnic Chinese, both within and outside China, "raises fears of Chinese expansionism and evokes suspicions about the loyalties of the overseas Chinese toward their countries of residence."

During the past 15 years or so, journalists, academicians and others have been actively involved in constructing the Chinese success story, ethnicity and otherness for different reasons (Dirlik 1997). Asia's rise was manifested in dozens of books aimed at understanding the role of the ethnic Chinese in Asia's great transformation (e.g. Cragg 1996). Looking back, it seems that certain aspects of Chinese businesses were overlooked or distorted. Reasons include the pitfalls of essentialism, orientalization, lack of comparative research on Chinese and non-Chinese entrepreneurs and their business organizations and so forth.

Some analysts are examining the subject with ideological sympathy, contributing to what anthropologist Yao (1997), one of the contributors of this volume, has called the "romance of Chinese business." One variant of this romance is to view Chinese entrepreneurial culture as a reflex of Chinese ethics, particularly Confucianism that is often treated as a black box. The eclectic culture of the Chinese merchants, the heterogeneity of the Chinese societies and sub-cultures in Asia, folk religious influences and other alternative sources of ethics such as Mahayana Buddhism or Christianity, discrepancies between religio-cultural values and norms on the one side and actual behavior on the other or the impact of rapid environmental change are seldom systematically addressed in the literature.

Some studies on Chinese businesses can be classified as potentially harmful if they are based on doubtful premises with negative (sometimes racist) connotations. The titles of publications such as "The Chinese Connection," "Tribes" or "The Chinese Diaspora Turns Homewards" propagate a socially and economically exclusive tribal image of the ethnic Chinese, which is not in line with Southeast Asia's empirical reality (Suryadinata 1997).

While such etiquettes may help to further a tendency among Chinese businessmen and other "Asians" towards self-orientalization (Said 1978) and global tribalism, it must be realized that they may provide certain interest groups with opportune arguments to blame the Chinese minority for economic crises or the lack of development progress and/or to justify political, cultural, socioeconomic and physical subordination. Indonesia, where the religious, social and cultural life of the local Chinese is affected by the pressure for social assimilation, is an illustrating case in this respect (Buchholt and Menkhoff 1994).

The economic dominance of certain strata of Indonesia's Chinese minority in trade, commerce and other sectors of the economy has often been highlighted as an important factor explaining the hostility towards them. It is widely believed that the ethnic Chinese who account for only about 3 percent of Indonesia's population of around 185 m, controlled about 70 percent of private domestic capital and 66 percent of the country's top 300 conglomerates (of whom 7 percent were Chinese-*pribumi* joint ventures) prior to the Asian crisis (*Straits Times*, 1/26/1994). While the accuracy of such data has been questioned (Wang 1999), it is obvious that such imbalances, whether real or imagined, can foster anti-Chinese sentiments and that they can easily exacerbate ethnic relations as the past has shown.

Due to their visible role in business and the failure to produce a substantial number of equally visible *pribumi* entrepreneurs, Indonesia's Chinese minority has often been a target of unrest and racial attacks. Victims of physical attacks and discriminatory actions are mostly petty traders, shop owners and small entrepreneurs, that is, those who are visible and seizable. As far as the pre-Asian crisis period is concerned, *cukongs* were safer due to their connections despite repeated critiques of the alliance by certain groups.

Indonesia's record of violent frustration riots (Medan 1994; Pekalongan 1995; Tasikmalaya 1996; Sulawesi 1997; Java and Sumatra 1998) illustrates the explosive character of global market expansion, material deprivation, ethnic prejudices, particularistic interests of strategic groups and the diminishing power and legitimacy of the nation state *vis-à-vis* economic globalization (Evers 1980). The almost unchecked rioting and looting in Jakarta in May 1998 in conjunction with Soeharto's decline constitutes the climax of these tensions. They left more than 1,000 dead, billions of dollars in damage and triggered an exodus of tens of thousands of ethnic Chinese and foreigners (*Straits Times*, 11/27/1998, 1/11/1999).

The events in Indonesia have spillover effects on intra-regional relations and indicate some of the challenges faced by the Association of Southeast Asian Nations (ASEAN) to develop a large and more coherent regional market. The Chinese from Taiwan, Hong Kong and Singapore constitute the largest investor group in the ASEAN countries (except for Singapore) whose economies are largely dominated by the ethnic Chinese. The centuries old fear of China, the awakening giant (Overholt 1993), also influences Chinese-indigenous relations and social attitudes towards the ethnic Chinese in Indonesia and other Southeast Asian nations (Wang 1999).

The increasing investments of the ethnic Chinese from Southeast Asia in their "ancestral country" China represents a potential source of envy and mistrust as well as the perpetuation of ethnic stereotypes. In the past, Indonesian media commentators have expressed concern about the investments of the Chinese Indonesians in Mainland China. Indonesian Chinese businessmen putting money into China have been accused of disloyalty, double loyalty or of promoting capital flight, although they were simply pursuing strategies most businessmen would pursue in order to create new value and to cope with risks arising from an uncertain social and political environment. The capital that the Indonesian Chinese are investing in China and elsewhere, critics argued, is urgently needed for domestic development.

In Indonesia, reservations against the ethnic Chinese ties with China and anti-Chinese sentiments are interwoven with the decades-old fear of China as an external (Communist) threat, China's former political activism in the region, prejudiced attitudes, discriminatory behavior and other factors. In future the situation might become even more complicated due to increasing Mainland Chinese competition in Asian and Third World markets and the forces of globalization.

The objectives of this monograph

In view of the many misperceptions about ethnic Chinese businesses in Asia and its potentially harmful effects, we believe that it is necessary to provide a balanced picture of ethnic Chinese entrepreneurship and business networks based on sober empirical facts rather than on imagination. Besides addressing a couple of theoretical and empirical gaps in the literature on the subject matter, the book is aimed at challenging the invulnerability myth of ethnic Chinese businesses by exploring the impact of the Asian crisis on Chinese firms in the region (Menkhoff and Sikorski) and the Chinese minority in one of Asia's foremost crisis economies, namely Indonesia (Low). Another goal is to counteract concerns about the "mysterious" collaboration between the ethnic Chinese in Southeast and Mainland China by providing empirical data on the actual investment patterns of the Chinese diaspora in the People's Republic of China and its rationale (Tracy and Lever-Tracy), as well as the interconnections and synergies created between the Chinese overseas and Mainland China's private entrepreneurs as well as state-owned firms (Schlevogt). In both China and Vietnam, private (Chinese) entrepreneurship has become a key driving force of socioeconomic and political change as demonstrated by Heberer, Lindahl and Thomsen. The critical examination of the popular "Chinese commonwealth and global tribe hypotheses" is another central concern of the monograph. Based on detailed case studies of large Chinese-owned companies in Malaysia, the chapter by Gomez challenges commonsense assumptions that culture and ethnicity are the main driving forces of successful Chinese entrepreneurship and network expansion in Asia. Yeung provides new insights into the corporate activities of transnational Chinese entrepreneurs from Singapore and their globalization efforts. Tong and Yong reveal the internal management and organizational patterns of Chinese enterprises *vis-à-vis* the institutional framework in which they are embedded, based on the case of a well-known Singaporean trading firm. Yao presents an alternative interpretation of the famous Chinese *guanxi* tactics, which are often essentialized in the mainstream literature on Chinese businesses. Wazir deconstructs the often-voiced socioeconomic exclusivity of Chinese businessmen and their networking strategies, by highlighting the significance of inter-ethnic entrepreneurial collaborations between Chinese and Malay business partners. Lever-Tracy, Ip and Tracy describe and assess the dynamic and integrated Chinese business community in Brisbane, Australia. Like many of the other authors of this monograph, they question the adequacy of conceptualizing these developments, exclusively, in terms of the emergence of an ethnic business enclave, advantaged by the social capital of bounded solidarity and enforceable trust. Rutten's chapter underlines the importance of comparative research on ethnic (Chinese) entrepreneurship by elaborating the many similarities of ethnic entrepreneurs in India, Malaysia and Indonesia. To sum up, the monograph can be understood as a timely attempt to re-examine many of the taken-for-granted assumptions about the strength and uniqueness of what has been termed Chinese capitalism, networks and business culture in the age of global market expansion.

The contributors comprise sociologists, anthropologists, political scientists, economists and geographers from Germany, the Netherlands, the United Kingdom, Singapore, Malaysia, Australia and the USA – all leading scholars on ethnic entrepreneurship, the Chinese overseas and Chinese (business) affairs in Asia Pacific.

More than two-third of the contributions are based on contemporary empirical research. Most authors do address – implicit or explicit – the challenges, threats and changes that globalization, global market forces and the Asian economic crisis imply for ethnic Chinese entrepreneurs, their family businesses, conglomerates and networks who have played a significant role in the regional economic integration of East and Southeast Asia (and, as some authors argue, increasingly in the context of global market expansion).

Several of the chapters included in this monograph were presented at an international conference sponsored by the Deutsche Forschungsgemeinschaft (DFG) entitled "Crisis Management – Chinese Entrepreneurs and Business Networks in Southeast Asia," held at the University of Bonn, Department of Southeast Asian Studies, in May 1999. It was chaired by Solvay Gerke (University of Bonn), Hans-Dieter Evers (University of Bielefeld) and Thomas Menkhoff (National University of Singapore).

Themes and contributions

Theme 1: coping with change and crises – Chinese businesses under siege?

The Asian crisis triggered by the devaluation of the Thai baht in 1997 justifies a discussion of its impact on the ethnic Chinese in Southeast Asia and their socioeconomic role. While empirical data on the consequences of Asia's new realism (a term which refers to the disruptions, hardships and changing mindsets produced by the Asian financial and economic crisis) on Chinese business are scarce, there is evidence that the economic downturn has changed the perceptions of business people, academicians and the general populace with regard to Asia's growth prospects, corporate sustainability, societal progress and the benefits of global capitalism. The financial troubles of Chinese-owned banks in Malaysia, ethnic violence in Indonesia, the relatively large numbers of bankruptcies in Chinese-dominated Singapore or the downsize of economic globalization in the form of currency devaluations, retrenchments, loss of income, increased poverty etc. at the height of the crisis were manifestations of these changing sentiments. During the past few years, concerns that the Asian crisis has exposed certain foundational defects of Asian economies such as poor regulation of the economy, insufficient financial transparency or stockholder accountability, nepotism, influence peddling etc. have globalized. This has serious implications for Chinese capital in the region as elaborated in the chapter by Thomas Menkhoff and Douglas Sikorski. Some Western management gurus and social scientists have argued that external environmental forces in combination with the Asian crisis make it necessary to revamp the traditional type of management and corporate governance of Chinese firms to ensure corporate sustainability in the age of globalization and that the institutional characteristics of Chinese businesses and how it is organized socially are contra productive in the age of global market expansion. Menkhoff and Sikorski examine some of these propositions in their chapter. They also point to the ongoing corporate restructuring activities of Chinese firms in Asia and discuss the future of Chinese capital in the region.

The Asian crisis has intensified prejudices and discriminations towards the ethnic Chinese, particularly in Indonesia as indicated by the violent anti-Chinese riots in May 1998 in Jakarta. Against this background, Linda Low suggests that there is an unfinished agenda of integration as far as Indonesia's ethnic Chinese minority is concerned. She feels that there is a certain amount of myth that the recent racial and religious riots in Indonesia are all communal and ethnic based. In a deep recession with growing poverty and income decline, race riots are often disguised forms of societal struggles that reflect the great divide between the poor and rich, and it is unfortunate that the groups are, respectively, the indigenous Indonesians and the ethnic Chinese. While socialization and politicization can engender racial integration, she argues that economics can be as powerful an instrument because it offers a practical policy tool to stabilize the environment to make racial integration and finishing the agenda more conducive. In turn, a virtuous circle is generated as racial, social and political stability propels the economy further. Putting the topic into a regional context, it is stressed that the enlarged ASEAN as a group cannot afford to muddle through any more, and that ethnic Chinese as a potent economic force should be appreciated and induced to play its rightful roles. Two open issues are raised and discussed: (1) whether overseas Chinese, with their capital, entrepreneurship, networks and proven track record can induce the recovery process in ASEAN economies and (2) whether race would be cast aside to allow competitive forces to reinstate themselves to make the ASEAN and Asia Pacific region dynamic and sustaining again? As the author concludes, racial issues will not go away so easily unless economic survival threatens, above all, sociopolitical differences.

Theme 2: synergies between the Chinese diaspora and Chinese business organizations in the People's Republic of China and Vietnam

The multiple interconnections between the Chinese diaspora, Mainland China and its neighbors in Southeast Asia, respective reservations, tensions and development potentials justify and necessitate a closer examination of this theme. There is a certain amount of mistrust and fear in some ASEAN countries towards booming China (which has extended its hegemony to Southeast Asia several times during the last centuries) although its economic take-off has boosted regional transactions and growth. China is perceived as a potential threat by some countries in the region and abroad due to its growing economic and military power.

With its vast domestic market and huge army of cheap labor, the "awakening giant" is getting more and more attractive for foreign investors. Partly due to increased FDI competition, foreign investments in Malaysia decreased significantly in the first part of the 1990s. Changes introduced in Indonesia's investment regime before the Asian crisis were partly made in response to China's increasing investment attractions and those of other emerging markets.

There are conflicting interpretations with regard to the increasing economic ties between the ethnic Chinese entrepreneurs in Southeast Asia (investments by the ethnic Chinese in Mainland China are believed to make up 80 percent of total foreign investment) and China. One group of observers puts emphasis on the negative consequences of associated developments such as a newly assertive Chinese regional identity, increasing ethnic tensions, network power etc. Another group stresses the expected positive consequences of this process such as economic gains from bilateral trade ties, joint projects and so forth. Indonesia, Malaysia and Singapore have taken different trajectories with regard to these issues as argued elsewhere (Menkhoff 1997). To exemplify the multiple interconnections between the Chinese diaspora and Mainland China and to understand the impact of change, we have included three chapters, which deal with associated issues based on contemporary empirical research.

The chapter by Noel Tracy and Constance Lever-Tracy presents findings of a survey sponsored by the Asia Research Center of Murdoch University and the East Asian Analytic Unit, Department of Foreign Affairs and Trade aimed at collecting empirical data on the development, amount and geographical distribution etc. of FDIs by the ethnic Chinese from other Asian countries in China. As the authors argue, the growing trading power of the Chinese economies coupled with the capital resources, industrial capacity and regional business networks of the Chinese diaspora means that any prospects for Japanese economic hegemony in the region are ruled out. If this was ever a realistic prospect, its time has long since passed. They see the strength of the Chinese diaspora in their ability to operate within and without China equally effectively. China's industrial renaissance has depended substantially on Chinese diaspora investment and entrepreneurship and will continue to do so for the foreseeable future. Equally, China's international trading position has relied heavily on the performance of the southeastern provinces, Guangdong and Fujian, and Chinese diaspora marketing channels in Hong Kong. As Tracy and Lever-Tracy argue, this is not going to change quickly. The idea that Shanghai can replace Hong Kong as the major financial and international trading center for China's ongoing economic revolution is essentially political wishful thinking. What makes Hong Kong so important for China is its critical mass of accumulated expertise and credibility. At the same time, China remains a principal outlet for investment capital for the Chinese diaspora and the principal means of increasing their industrial and trading capacities profitably. Provided the business environment, therefore, remains reasonably attractive, at least in some regions in China, and there is little reason to think it will not, then Chinese diaspora investment is likely to continue to flow in that direction.

11

Since the synergy created between China's economic reforms and Chinese diaspora entrepreneurship and capital has reshaped regional political economy in less than a decade, there is no reason to think it will not continue to do so, which will benefit the whole region.

According to Kai Alexander Schlevogt, there are particular synergies between the Chinese diaspora and Mainland China in the area of management, which can propel China's transition towards a socialist market economy and private sector development. Based on extensive empirical research in the People's Republic of China, he argues that the new stratum of private entrepreneurs has successfully readopted the traditional management model of the Chinese overseas characterized by flexible structural and managerial choices, emphasis on family-based traditional values and small company size. This "web-based management system" provides China's policy-makers, with a useful blueprint to reform and revitalize the ailing state-owned sector which could result in resilient economic growth within the framework of a new capitalist network economy. Besides exemplifying the exchange of ideas and other resources between Mainland Chinese economic actors and the Chinese diaspora, Schlevogt also speculates about the potential long-term consequences of this process, which may create a transnational platform for increasing China's political influence and projecting "oriental values" far beyond its national borders.

Thomas Heberer also deals with the important role of private entrepreneurs in the People's Republic of China as well as Vietnam who are seen as significant agents of political and social change. He interprets the ongoing privatization process in these countries as "bottom-up processes." In both economies the private sector is currently the most dynamic economic sector that has significant economic, social and political implications. Based on both primary and secondary data, he demonstrates the rapid emergence and features of this new societal stratum of entrepreneurs who are striving not only for social and political acceptance but also for larger social and political participation. One of Heberer's key arguments is that private entrepreneurship in both the transition economies is context bound and that it accelerates the process of social and political change by economizing politics, developing social stratification, social mobility and a change of values and attitudes. Heberer's chapter is based on several months of intensive fieldwork in both countries.

The chapter by Jakob Lindahl and Lotte Thomsen supplements Schlevogt's and Heberer's studies by focusing on the socioeconomic dynamics of the Chinese community in Vietnam's Ho Chi Minh City and its multiple connections to the outside world. The chapter reconstructs how the Viet *Hoa* community regained its economic position after the implementation of the so-called *doi moi* economic reform measures. The authors also explore how the different kinds of relations within and among Chinese-owned business firms and their external business partners in Taiwan and elsewhere are managed by the Viet *Hoa*. A key argument is that these relations have to be interpreted as adaptive and strategic responses to Vietnam's distinct historical development and present political and institutional framework. A particular challenge for Vietnam's private sector in general and the Chinese minority in particular are the changing and ambivalent signals sent out by policymakers and the ongoing market reforms. But as their analysis suggests, Vietnam's Chinese minority is increasingly being recognized as an important contributor to the country's economic development.

Theme 3: Chinese network capitalism and guanxi transactions reconsidered

Books such as "The Bamboo Network" (Weidenbaum and Hughes 1996) underline the strong interest of journalists, writers and academicians in ethnic Chinese network capitalism. The local, regional and transnational *guanxi* (connections) of the Chinese overseas and their talent to spin local, regional and global business webs, preferably based on long-term, non-contractual trust relationships with kinsmen are almost legendary (Menkhoff and Labig 1996; Tong and Yong 1998). Their *guanxi* capital, cultural ethos, language proficiency as well as their local and regional knowledge are believed to be of crucial importance in penetrating and integrating Asia's markets.

There is evidence that the economic transactions and social relationships between the peoples of China, Hong Kong and Taiwan have facilitated the regional integration of Greater China, lubricated by Chinese capital inflows from Southeast Asia (Herrmann-Pillath 1994; Tracy and Lever-Tracy in this volume). Four-fifths of Hong Kong's investments have been invested in China's Guangdong province where many Cantonese have relations. Many Taiwanese investors have interests in Fujian despite the political conflicts between both sides of the Taiwan Straits. A growing number of the ethnic Chinese from Southeast Asia are doing business with people, villages and provinces in China with whom and where they have personal connections (*guanxi*) due to locality (native place), kinship or classmate ties as well as linguistic and cultural commonalities. But to interpret such developments as evidence that all these net-workers are interwoven to form a regional Chinese network of companies, clans and villages linked by ties of blood and native place, which is part of the large global network of overseas Chinese businessmen (e.g. Chang 1995), is misleading.

Other erroneous notions about the traditional relational capitalism of ethnic Chinese can be summarized as follows: "kinship *guanxi* is an effective lubricant of Chinese business networks," "all Chinese tycoons are well connected which explains their business success" or "*guanxi* capital will catapult the overseas Chinese to world economic dominance." The chapters by Gomez, Yeung, Tong and Yong, Yao, Jahan Wazir Karim and Lever-Tracy, Ip and Tracy may help to correct such images by providing alternative and, as we believe, more accurate accounts of Chinese network capitalism and *guanxi* transactions.

Based on extensive secondary research, Edmund Terence Gomez examines how some of Malaysia's largest Chinese-owned enterprises have been developed despite working in an environment that has provided little support for their interests.

One of his main intentions is to challenge the hypothesis that common ethnic identity, often referred to as a form of the Chinese commonwealth involving a network of many individual enterprises that share a similar culture, is the main independent variable of Chinese business success and that it will facilitate the emergence of a dynamic and globally connected entrepreneurial community. In order to test these popular assumptions, three case studies are provided of the largest Chinese-owned companies operating in three different sectors of Malaysia's economy: the manufacturing-based Oriental Group, owned by the family of the late Loh Boon Siew; the Public Bank Group, owned by Teh Hong Piow, and its role in the financial sector; and the YTL Corporation Group, owned by the Yeoh family, and its involvement in construction and power generation. Gomez's conclusion is that entrepreneurial ability, competency, occupational experience and the use of class resources are more significant in explaining the success of Chinese entrepreneurship and the expansion of networks rather than ethnicity and culture *per se*.

Henry Yeung's chapter provides interesting empirical insights into the internationalization strategies of Chinese business firms from Singapore, in particular those well embedded in regional, social and business networks, and the important role of entrepreneurship in this process. Transnational entrepreneurship continues to play a crucial role in the regionalization of Chinese family firms from Singapore and other Southeast Asian nations, driven by two types of entrepreneurs: owner entrepreneurs and manager intrapreneurs. While owner entrepreneurs tend to exploit their social and business networks to take their businesses across national boundaries, manager intrapreneurs require substantial management control and autonomy bestowed on them by their headquarters in Singapore in order to put their entrepreneurial skills into practice in the host countries. Yeung's extensive data originate from a research project that covered 200 parent companies in Singapore and over fifty Singaporean entrepreneurs in Hong Kong, China and Malaysia.

The study by Tong Chee Kiong and Yong Pit Kee focuses on the organizational principles of Chinese firms. It seeks to understand the social foundations from which these principles were derived and argues that economic actions are embedded in social relations that both constrain as well as emancipate institutional behaviors. The chapter provides a detailed case study of the Lee Rubber Group of Companies, one of the largest and most influential rubber companies in Singapore, which later diversified into banking, manufacturing and trading. The chapter highlights the relevance and rationality of *xinyong* (trustworthiness) and *guanxi* (personal relationships) in the development of Chinese-owned family firms. Patterns of ownership, development and authority structures prevalent in these firms are also discussed. The authors argue that the tendency to emphasize *guanxi* and trust has to do with the centrality of personal control. The concern for personal control is most clearly demonstrated in intra-firm dynamics, where control is largely affected through restricting ownership to trusted, close *guanxi* relations. Kinship is the most prominent base for ownership control, with all strategic positions in the firm reserved for family members. As their data clearly show, the importance of *guanxi* in the development of a business goes beyond the family unit. Friends and ex-colleagues, for instance, are just as vital.

Yao Souchou presents a new and unique interpretation of the *guanxi* concept based on his research among Chinese traders in a small township in Sarawak, East Malaysia. Unsatisfied with conventional approaches to *guanxi*, which emphasize the practice of building economically and politically useful relationships upon existing social ties (thus signaling a perfect marriage of sociality and individual gain), he argues that *guanxi* as culturally inscribed in Chinese society represents a special case among a range of possible transactional outcomes. Working from the ideas of British philosopher Austen and anthropologist Appadurai, it is hypothesized that the cultural model of *guanxi* is always "diseased" when the mode of transaction is subject to the danger of rupture inherent in the very ideal of doing business the Chinese way. Instead of the harmonious blending of social pleasure and mutual benefits, what characterizes *guanxi* exchange among Chinese traders in the East Malaysian township is the "tension" in reconciling these twin objectives. *Guanxi* in Sarawak as in other Chinese communities is neither about social relationship nor about individual gain, but a dialectic relationship of the two. As the former does not give profit and while the latter offers only personal gain marked by competitive violence, it is the strategy aimed at harvesting the twin objects that typifies the cultural model of *guanxi*.

Jahan Wazir Karim challenges a particular myth about ethnic Chinese entrepreneurs, namely their socioeconomic exclusivity by stressing the significance of inter-ethnic business cooperation between Chinese entrepreneurs and Malay businessmen in Malaysia. Contrary to notions of Chinese and Bumiputera business cooperation as being characterized by low trust relations, her data underline the prevalence of trust and cooperation in these inter-ethnic business endeavors. She argues that the old Sino-*Nusantara* symbiosis prevalent in early forms of rooted capitalism is gradually giving way to one which is more typical of globalistic empires prevalent in late capitalism in the more developed West. The extensive network of small and medium sized enterprises and industries in Malaysia and elsewhere, which forms the backbone to trade and commerce in Southeast Asia, is seen to function as an important buffer in regional and global recessions.

One of the concerns of Constance Lever-Tracy, David Ip and Noel Tracy is that studies of overseas Chinese businesses have long been bedeviled by area and other boundaries as indicated by the large number of studies on the ethnic Chinese in Southeast Asia or, in particular, in the Western countries. In reality, the research subjects, small owners as well as billionaire tycoons, readily move their investments, their family members and themselves back and forth across the boundaries, facilitated by complex transnational networks. Against this background, the authors provide interesting insights into the emerging dynamic and integrated Chinese business community in Brisbane, Australia. The economic activity of the Brisbane Chinese is concentrated within Chinese-owned enterprises. A connecting core of the ethnic economy has continued to be provided by restaurants, the original niche, despite diversification. They have functioned as the major conduit into employment and into independence. They are internally articulated, with their own training mechanisms, ladders and hierarchies, their own norms and channels of information, and they are a focus for new forms of vertical integration capable of generating new supplier activities. There is also a rapid growth of firms mainly devoted to supplying ethnic business. The incipient enclave is, however, not exclusive. While there are very few for whom ethnicity is irrelevant to their business, there are scarcely any who do not also have external business dealings. Personalized trust matters, but can be extended beyond a narrow ascriptive group. More significant is the strength and growth of a group of international traders, who may have few links with other Chinese businesses in Brisbane but for whom their transnational networks, and their social capital in the Chinese diaspora, are the very foundation of their business. For all kinds of Chinese business in Brisbane, resources originating overseas, capital, experience, authentic products, networks are often crucially important and for some there were continuing inflows of capital, upgraded skills and newly migrating family and network members. The picture of a locally bounded and enclosed phenomenon conveyed in terms such as enclave and bounded solidarity do not allow for the growing importance of diasporas in a globalizing world. As well as being a group of enterprises tending to become an ethnic enclave, one might also think of Brisbane Chinese businesses, in some of its aspects, as a local fragment of a global whole.

Theme 4: toward a comparative perspective of ethnic (Chinese) entrepreneurship

For a long time, it has been argued that capitalism breeds best in a ground of individualism. Contrary to entrepreneurs in Europe, Asian entrepreneurs were generally thought to be culturally more inclined to operate along collective forms of business organization such as joint-family enterprises or ethnic (kinship) networks, a trait which was seen as one of the reasons for the lack of economic development in Asia and the insufficient competitiveness of Asian entrepreneurs *vis-à-vis* their Western counterparts. The growth of East Asia over the past few decades has challenged these notions. Numerous researchers started to put forward the antithesis by emphasizing organizational skills, co-operation, transaction cost advantages etc. as key explanatory factors of the economic success of Asian businessmen. Studies that are based on the network concept or the so-called flexible specialization approach state that collective forms of business organization are the key variable to development. To a large extent this approach follows the study of present-day small entrepreneurship in Europe, more in particular in Italy, whose success has been explained in terms of specific forms of economic co-operation at the firm and sector level (Grabher 1993; Perry 1999). What then are the real differences between Asian and European entrepreneurship?

One of the few scholars who has done extensive research on this issue is Mario Rutten (Rutten and Upadhya 1997) who contributed an interesting comparative study of rural entrepreneurs in South and Southeast Asia to this volume.

Rutten feels that both earlier and recent approaches to the study of ethnic and small business entrepreneurship are one-sided since they often discuss entrepreneurial behavior in terms of individualism versus co-operation, assuming that some groups are culturally more inclined towards co-operation than others. His research on rural entrepreneurship indicates that both types of entrepreneurial behavior are present within one group. It is not so much co-operation or individualism, which explains successful or unsuccessful entrepreneurial behavior, but the flexibility to adjust social and economic forms of organization to changing circumstances in terms of space and time. Rutten supports these hypothesis with three case studies of rural entrepreneurs in India, Malaysia and Indonesia who belong to three different communities: (1) large farmers-traders and owners of small-scale rural industries in central Gujarat, west India, almost all of whom belong to the middle and upper castes within the Hindu community; (2) Muslim owners of small and medium-scale iron-foundries in rural central Java, Indonesia; and (3) Chinese and Malay owners of combine-harvesters and workshops for agricultural machinery in the Muda region of north Malaysia. His Asian case studies are in line with the results of studies of entrepreneurs in Europe, which have shown that both individualism and co-operation have been important in the rise of industrial entrepreneurship. As a result, Rutten argues, notions of differences in entrepreneurial behavior between Asia and Europe have to be "reconsidered."

Bibliography

Backman, M. (1999) *Asian Eclipse – Exposing the Dark Side of Business in Asia*, Singapore: John Wiley and Sons.

Berger, P. L. and Hsiao, M. (1988) *In Search of an East Asian Development Model*, New Brunswick (USA) and Oxford (UK): Transaction Books.

Buchholt, H. and Menkhoff, T. (1994) *Huaqiao* – Die soziale Rolle der ethnischen Chinesen in Indonesien, *ASIEN – Deutsche Zeitschrift für Politik, Wirtschaft und Kultur*, No. 51, pp. 25–38.

——(1996) *Vom Wanderkrämer zum Towkay – Ethnische Chinesen im Prozeß der Modernisierung der asiatisch-pazifischen Region*, Schriftenreihe Internationales Asienforum, Band 8. Köln: Weltforum Verlag.

Chan, K. B. (ed.) (2000) *Chinese Business Networks – State, Economy and Culture*, Singapore: Prentice Hall.

Chan, K. B. and Chiang, C. (1994) *Stepping Out – The Making of Chinese Entrepreneurs*, Singapore: Simon and Schuster.

Chang, M. H. (1995) Greater China and the Chinese "Global Tribe," *Asian Survey*, 35, September, 955–67.

Cragg, C. (1996) *The New Taipans*, London: Arrow Books.

Dirlik, A. (1997) Critical Reflections on "Chinese Capitalism as Paradigm," *Identities*, 3(3), 303–30.

Evers, H.-D. (1980) Ethnic and Class Conflict in Urban South-East Asia. In H.-D. Evers (ed.), *Sociology of Southeast Asia*, Kuala Lumpur: Oxford University Press.

Evers, H.-D. and Schrader, H. (eds) (1994) *The Moral Economy of Trade. Ethnicity and Developing Markets*, London: Routledge.

Goldberg, M. A. (1985) *The Chinese Connection: Getting Plugged in to the Pacific Rim Real Estate, Trade and Capital Markets*, Vancouver: University of British Columbia Press.

Grabher, G. (1993) *The Embedded Firm – On the Socioeconomics of Industrial Networks*, London and New York: Routledge.

Haley, G. T., Tan, C. T. and Haley, U. C. V. (1998) *New Asian Emperors*, Oxford: Butterworth/Heinemann.

Hamilton, G. (1991) The Organizational Foundations of Western and Chinese Commerce: A Historical and Comparative Analysis. In G. Hamilton (ed.), *Business Networks and Economic Development in East and Southeast Asia*, Hong Kong: Centre of Asian Studies, University of Hong Kong.

Herrmann-Pillath, C. (1994) *Netzwerke und die Politische Oekonomie der Beziehungen zwischen Taiwan und der VR China*, Baden-Baden: Nomos.

Hicks, G. (1993) How Chinese Capital Changes the Scenario in Southeast Asia, *China Mail*, 6(4), 26–7.

Huntington, S. (1993) The Clash of Civilisations? *Foreign Affairs*, 72(3), 22–49.

Kotkin, J. (1992) *Tribes: How Race, Religion, and Identity Determine the Success in the New Global Economy*, New York: Random House.

Kwok, K.-W. (1999) The New "Global Chinese Community?" Paper presented at the 5th World Chinese Entrepreneurs Convention in Melbourne, Australia, October 6–9, 1999.

Landa, J. (1983) The Political Economy of the Ethnically Homogeneous Chinese Middlemen Group in Southeast Asia: Ethnicity and Entrepreneurship in a Plural Society. In L. Y. C. Lim and L. A. P. Gosling (eds), *The Chinese in Southeast Asia*, Singapore: Maruzen.

Menkhoff, T. (1993) *Trade Routes, Trust and Trading Networks – Chinese Small Enterprises in Singapore*, Bielefeld Studies on the Sociology of Development, Vol. 54 (edited by Prof. H.-D. Evers). Saarbrücken, Fort Lauderdale: Breitenbach Publishers.

—— (1997) China's Transformation and the Chinese Diaspora in Singapore, Malaysia and Indonesia (in German). In H. J. Wald (ed.), *Confucian Capitalism in East- and Southeast Asia*. Schriftenreihe der Zentralstelle fuer Auslandskunde (ZA), Deutsche Stiftung fuer Internationale Enwicklung (DSE), Vol. 25. Bad Honnef, Germany.

—— (1998) Chinese Business Networks – A Hypothetical Dialogue. In L. Pan (ed.), *Encyclopedia of the Chinese Overseas*, Singapore: Archipelago Press.

Menkhoff, T. and Labig, C. (1996) Trading Networks of Chinese Entrepreneurs in Singapore, *Sojourn – Journal of Social Issues in Southeast Asia*, 11(1), 130–54.

Overholt, W. (1993) *The Rise of China: How Economic Reform is Creating a New Superpower*, New York: Norton.

Pan, L. (ed.) (1998) *Encyclopedia of the Chinese Overseas*, Singapore: Archipelago Press.

Perry, M. (1999) *Small Firms and Network Economies*, London and New York: Routledge.

Rutten, M. and Upadhya, C. (eds) (1997) *Small Business Entrepreneurs in Asia and Europe: Towards a Comparative Perspective*, Delhi: Sage Publications.

Said, E. W. (1978) *Orientalism*, London: Routledge.

Somers-Heidhues, M. F. (1974) *Southeast Asia's Chinese Minorities*, London: Longman.

Suryadinata, L. (1997) *Ethnic Chinese as Southeast Asians*, Singapore: Institute of Southeast Asian Studies.

The Economist 7/18/1992: The overseas Chinese: A driving force, pp. 21–4.

The Economist 11/27/1993: China's diaspora turns homeward, pp. 27–8.

18

The Straits Times 11/23/1993: Ethnic Chinese, networking and where loyalties lie – Excerpts from SM Lee Kuan Yew's speech at the Second World Entrepreneurs Convention in Hong Kong.

The Straits Times 1/26/1994: Chinese and Indian "Tribes" will be Economic Powerhouses.

The Straits Times 6/17/1995: The ties that do not bind.

The Straits Times 12/14/1995: Indonesian Minister tells ethnic Chinese "Avoid taking part in overseas Chinese groups."

The Straits Times 11/27/1998: Why Chinese Indonesians must buy "social insurance."

The Straits Times 11/1/1999: Chinese Indonesians living in a state of siege.

The Straits Times 1/21/1999: Monopoly firms to pay fine or face jail.

Tong, C. K. (1991) Centripetal Authority, Differentiated Networks: The Social Organisation of Chinese Firms in Singapore. In G. Hamilton (ed.), *Business Networks and Economic Development in East and Southeast Asia*, Hong Kong.

Tong, C. K. and Yong, P. K. (1998) Guanxi Bases, Xinyong and Chinese Business Networks, *British Journal of Sociology*, 49(1), 75–95.

Wang, G. (1978) *The Chinese Minority in Southeast Asia*, Singapore: Chopmen Enterprises.

——(1994) The Culture of Chinese Merchants. In G. Wang, *China and the Overseas Chinese*, Singapore: Times Academic Press.

——(1999) China and Southeast Asia: Myths, Threats and Culture. EAI Occasional Paper No. 13, East Asian Institute, National University of Singapore, Singapore: World Scientific and Singapore University Press.

Weidenbaum, M. and Hughes, S. (1996) *The Bamboo Network: How Expatriate Chinese Entrepreneurs are Creating a New Economic Superpower in Asia*, New York: The New Press.

Wu, Y.-L. and Wu, C.-H. (1980) *Economic Development in Southeast Asia – The Chinese Dimension*, Stanford/Calif.: Hoover Institution.

Yao, S. (1997) The Cultural Limits of Confucian Capitalism. Paper presented at the Conference on Chinese Business in Southeast Asia, Institute of Advanced Studies, University of Malaya, Kuala Lumpur, Malaysia, June 23–25, 1997.

Yoshihara, K. (1988) *The Rise of Ersatz Capitalism in South-East Asia*, Singapore: Oxford University Press.

Part II

COPING WITH CHANGE AND CRISES – CHINESE BUSINESSES UNDER SIEGE?

1

ASIA'S CHINESE ENTREPRENEURS BETWEEN MYTH-MAKING AND RENEWAL

Thomas Menkhoff and Douglas Sikorski

Introduction

The Asian crisis provides a timely occasion to re-examine taken-for-granted assumptions about the strength and uniqueness of "Chinese" capitalism in the age of globalization, with its special networks based on various *guanxi* ties (Menkhoff and Labig 1996) and organizational behavior founded on Confucian family-oriented value systems (Redding 1990; Weidenbaum 1998). While some analysts believe that the malaise has revealed the "downside" of economic globalization and global market forces, others such as Madison (1998: 5) have stressed that it would be misleading to interpret the Asian crisis as evidence of the failure of global capitalism. Rather, it demonstrates the failure of capitalism to be "truly global." As Madison puts it, the crisis has exposed certain "foundational defects" of East Asian economies and their corporate sectors such as:

> ... poor regulation of the economy, lack of transparency in government bookkeeping, a corporate culture that valued neither financial trans-parency nor stockholder accountability, insider trading, low productivity and inefficient use of capital and labor, industries run less for the sake of turning a profit than for enhancing the power of their directors, over-reliance on export in relation to domestic consumer spending, over-guaranteed and under-regulated banks, soft bank lending practices and a dysfunctional relation to capital, even outright fraud on the part of major banks and financial institutions, opaque systems of cross-ownership, an incestuous relation between governments, banks and highly indebted companies (e.g. South Korea's chaebols), nepotism, cronyism, influence-peddling, and corruption, a reluctance on the part of the governments to let large floundering companies go bankrupt, a fail-ure, even, to have properly designed bankruptcy laws, labour market rigidity, a lack of democratic openness, an over-reliance on technocratic elites and a lack of social safety nets.

Such concerns have serious implications for the *modus operandi* of Chinese business and the reputation and future of Chinese capital, which has been one of the key drivers of rapid economic growth in the Asian region over the past three decades (Menkhoff 1993; Chan and Chiang 1994; Low 1995, 1997; Haley *et al.* 1998; Chan 2000).

This essay touches upon how the regional economic malaise has affected the businesses of the ethnic Chinese in Southeast Asia. It also sets about the task of deconstructing some of the many myths and generalizations concerning Asia's "new taipans" (Cragg 1996) that have been reproduced and perpetuated by both journalists and academicians due to the pitfalls of essentialism, orientalization, lack of comparative research on ethnic (Chinese) entrepreneurship and business etc. Popular myths include their relative invulnerability, homogeneity and socio-economic exclusivity as well as the notion that the formation and use of social relationship capital (*guanxi*) is a uniquely Chinese phenomenon (Mackie 1998; Wong 1998). Their ties and workings with *non-Chinese* are often downplayed or ignored. Overseas Chinese family business is referred to by Redding (1990) as an "enigma" because its workings are not transparent. Chinese culture, indeed the language itself, obscures the Chinese people from the rest of the world. Nevertheless, the overseas Chinese, in general, are certainly among the most multicultural and most mobile, of international ethnic groups.

These preliminary remarks should be sufficient to outline the major objectives of this chapter, namely (1) to illustrate some of the challenges that globalization and the economic crisis imply for ethnic Chinese entrepreneurs, their family businesses, conglomerates and networks, which have played a significant role in the regional/global economic integration of East and Southeast Asia (Kotkin 1992; Kao 1993; Yeung 1999, 1999a) and (2) to correct essentialist notions of Chinese businesses, which is inextricably linked with the logic of global capitalism rather than "Chinese" capitalism. In line with Dirlik's (1997: 334) proposition that the so-called Chinese capitalism is highly dependent on the functioning of the global economy and that it has been largely shaped by its requirements, we argue that culturalist explanations of Chinese economic success and business behavior are insufficient. "Not all Chinese businesses are successful. Not all successful businesses are Chinese" (Chan and Ng 2000).

The chapter is organized in the following way: the first part outlines some of the challenges of global capitalism and the Asian crisis for Asia's "new taipans," suggesting some aspects of Chinese business that may have contributed to the economic downturn and assessing the impact of the ensuing developments on Chinese firms in terms of management and corporate governance. The second part examines the need to revamp the "traditional" type of management, corporate governance and institutional characteristics of "Chinese capitalism" to ensure survival in the post-crisis era. It also provides a brief impact assessment of the economic crisis on Chineseness and the discourse on Chinese transnational identity. The final section draws some conclusions with regard to the future of Chinese capitalism in Asia.

24

Global capitalism and the Asian crisis:
new challenges for Asia's Chinese tycoons

The Asian crisis

The Asian financial and economic crisis of 1997–8 has delayed the envisaged Asian century and is seen by many analysts as an unexpected, startling revelation of the devastating power of economic globalization. As the Swiss-based World Economic Forum (WEF) pointed out in its Asian Competitiveness Report 1999, it would be wrong to interpret the Asian debacle as a particularly Asian crisis. Rather, it is an indicator of a "type of global crisis that reflects the rapid arrival of global capitalism, in a world not yet used to the integration of the advanced and developing countries" (quoted in *Straits Times*, 3/10/1999).

Spurred by IT innovations, new financial services and deregulation, huge global financial markets have recently evolved. The speed of movement, volume and volatility of short-term speculative capital flows have been blamed for triggering and exacerbating the regional financial problems. The currency crisis underlines the weaknesses of emerging markets and nation states *vis-à-vis* mostly unregulated global financial markets and the need for reforms at different levels as, for example, outlined in a "30-point plan to prevent a repeat of the Asian meltdown" developed by Harvard economist Jeffrey Sachs (*Straits Times*, 3/10/1999). But external factors are not the issue in this paper. Strong concerns have been expressed that certain "internal" institutional characteristics and practices may have contributed to the crisis.

In the past good governance has often been highlighted as one of the crucial causes of the Asian miracle (World Bank 1993). The state guaranteed political stability and helped to sustain investors' confidence and competitive wage levels. It ensured "sound" macro-economic fundamentals and used social engineering to distribute societal wealth more or less equally. The crisis may necessitate a re-evaluation of explanatory approaches of the Asian miracle, which put the state at center stage. How government policies aimed at (de-)regulating and monitoring financial markets and finance institutions are executed, how public enterprises are managed and supervised, how the political party system and its collaboration with the private sector is engineered in everyday life etc. plays a decisive role in understanding the evolution of the crisis.

Singapore's elder statesman, Senior Minister Lee Kuan Yew, believes that one of the root causes of the Asian crisis lay in weak institutions of government and corporate governance. In a speech at the Europe-Asia Forum in Singapore on February 1998 (MITA 1998), he stressed:

> … everyone overlooked the institutional and structural weaknesses in these economies. The corporate sector in Thailand, Indonesia and South Korea borrowed heavily, even recklessly … To compound the problem, local banks in these countries extended loans based not on feasibility of

projects, but on personal relations or political connections. The lenders were aware of the problem but accepted it as a way of business. Some even saw the presence of politically connected business partners as implicit government guarantees for the loans. They went along with the game.

Malaysian politicians have stressed the external faults of the international financial system. Nevertheless, Daim Zainuddin emphasized the need to take cognizance of internal weaknesses (in a speech at the 33rd annual general meeting of the Malaysian Malay Chamber of Commerce, having been appointed the new Minister of Economic Affairs with effect from June 25, 1998):

> Even though the primary cause of the current crisis can be attributed to external factors, we must also take cognisance of internal weaknesses that contribute to our exposure to external pressures... Strengthening corporate governance is very necessary... Unscrupulous market players must not be allowed to manipulate the market for their own greed. The regulatory framework must be strengthened.
>
> (*New Straits Times*, 6/29/1998)

Widely identified as one of the core triggers of Asia's rise, culture is a crucial intervening variable in the process of economic growth and development. Traits of business cultures and institutional characteristics such as the importance of personal relations in business, the particular social structure and imperatives of moral economies, the emphasis which is put on social network capital as collateral, risk assessment and so forth can explain some aspects of organizational behavior. But this is not to say that cultural or Asian values form the *root* cause of the dilemma (*The Economist*, 7/25/1998). For Asia-Europe Foundation executive director Tommy Koh, one of the early apologists of "Asian values,"[1] the Asian crisis is "a blessing in disguise" since it has taught important lessons, including to "ensure good corporate governance and abolish crony capitalism" (*Straits Times*, 12/20/1998).

Changing images of Chinese businesses

In the light of the recent developments, the image of Chinese businesses and associated stereotypes as being successful and powerful has changed. There is a growing body of literature whose themes refer to Chinese businesses as being "under siege" (e.g. Yeung 1999a). Ethnic Chinese family businesses and conglomerates are in many ways (and to a different degree) affected by the Asian crisis as the following extract of an interview with the research director of the European Institute of Asian Studies suggests:

> In the past, much of the drive in the Southeast Asian economies has come from very rich ethnic-Chinese groups that have been able to operate with

great flexibility, making financial decisions quickly but without much transparency. Their rapid response ability was one of the reasons for the successes of the Asian model, but now it's likely to disappear as international banks become less ready to support these groups without changes in their style of management to conform more to Western corporate norms. That's going to mean slower decision-making, but it's probably a positive correction.

(*Asian Wall Street Journal*, 2/6–7/1998: 12)

Others have argued that the Chinese business model built on connections (*guanxi*) and opaque finances might not be sustainable in the twenty-first century due to globalization, fierce competition, the increasing value of international brand names and so forth:

Ethnic Chinese families, who once enlarged their businesses in a price-driven acquisition fashion with no thought about Western buzzwords like synergy, are now looking to rationalize their portfolios. For some, it is a matter of necessity; for others, it is a chance to free up cash that could be used to snap up assets that better dovetail with their core businesses.

(Hiscock 1998: 23)

The "dark side" of *guanxi* (Backman 1999), overexposure to non-productive sectors (e.g. property), paternalistic management methods, resistance to modern notions of shareholder value and the demands of minority shareholders, pressures from the IMF, increased competition in the new economy, lack of credit, bankruptcies, dependence on Western technology, insufficient innovation and branding, legal–political insecurity, eroding strategic alliances with ruling power elites and ethnic conflicts represent some of the critical issues. Table 1.1 illustrates some of the effects of global market expansion and the economic downturn on Chinese business.

Lack of liquidity and creditworthiness at the firm level (as a consequence of non-performing loans, easy credit etc.) are probably two of the most critical consequences of the economic malaise. Besides the reluctance of international banks to provide business loans, Chinese firms in certain parts of Southeast Asia are directly or indirectly affected by the growing global presence of international credit rating agencies such as Moody's Investors Service Inc. or Standard & Poor's who assess the economic viability of national economies for foreign private and institutional investors. Since the outbreak of the crisis, foreign observers have criticized Asian firms for not being transparent enough (as demanded by foreign investors or financial institutions), which is seen as a function of family governance and top-down management systems prevalent in these firms. If the Chinese family business is a "family fortress" – with internal operations guarded against outsiders and poorly understood – modern market-based credit assessment becomes problematic.

The economic meltdown has given a boost to powerful global multilateral agencies such as the International Monetary Fund (IMF) whose reform packages

Table 1.1 Interconnections between Chinese businesses, economic globalization and the Asian crisis

Contributions to crisis	Impact of globalization	Impact of crisis
Borrowing based on *guanxi* rather than on project feasibility	Lack of credit by international lenders Growing significance of international rating agencies	No liquidity/credit-worthiness Non-performing loans, bankruptcies and forced mergers
Over-exposure to non-productive sectors such as property and stock markets		Unsold properties/no buyers/profit High import bills for components
	IMF threatens national sovereignty and monopolies	High debt, eroding monopolies and strategic alliances with power elites
	Opening of financial markets	More competition
Institutional characteristics such as personal networks	Network capitalism based on kinship ties and personalism limit economic options	Corporate sustainability not guaranteed New networks need to be developed
	Ethnic revivalism	Ethnic conflicts

and structural adjustment programs are threatening the national sovereignty of countries such as Indonesia and what is known there as *cukong cronyism* (Robison 1986). The traditional collusion between big businesses and the old ruling elite, as embodied in the infamous monopolies granted to both Chinese and indigenous conglomerates (with their protection from competition and special access to raw materials and government procurement), is a major focus of reform efforts. The country's economic crisis and the subsequently implemented policy changes driven by the IMF have drastically changed Indonesia's business environment. Domestic and international pressures to reform have intensified as indicated by new anti-monopoly laws and the promotion of *pribumi* cooperatives. The ongoing market reforms and deregulation measures have increased the competitive pressure dramatically, triggering change at different levels. This also implies the necessity to develop new network ties to business partners locally, regionally and globally with less reliance on traditional 'ethnically defined' business networks.

Changing perspectives on the post-crisis management

The Asian crisis, global market forces and the rapidly changing business environment represent big challenges for Asian corporations most of whom are small- and medium-sized enterprises (SMEs) owned and/or controlled by Chinese families (Tam 1977; Wong 1985; Tong 1991; Menkhoff 1993). So far, little systematic research has been conducted to assess the real impact of the crisis on these firms, their owners and employees and how management and lower-level employees cope with the tough business environment, pay cuts and retrenchments. Some hints are provided by a survey conducted by Adams and Vernon (1998) in Thailand aimed at examining how local firms adjust to the economic crisis.

The core objective of the survey was to find out how managers assessed the business climate before (mid-1995 to mid-1997) and during the crisis (mid-1997 to mid-1998) based on the following variables: "assessment of business environment before the crisis," "reasons for optimistic or pessimistic assessments," "ranking of problems they encountered in their businesses in 1995–6," "assessment of business environment since the 1997 crisis," "reasons for pessimistic (or optimistic) assessments," "degree to which businessmen are personally affected by the crisis" and "how they are actually affected" and "ranking of problems they encountered since the crisis."

Respondents identified a multitude of critical issues, reflecting the severity of the business conditions during the crisis. Financial problems, currency devaluation, declines in demand for products and services, dropped sales, delays in payment, reduction in purchasing power, fierce competition, high levels of accounts receivable, excess inventory, high interest rates, cash flow problems/lack of liquidity, collapse of the banking industry, access to cash and discontinued bank loans represented critical issues. Most companies dealt with the problems resulting from the crisis in a reactive way. "Solutions" comprised layoffs, decreased spending and lowering of prices, consolidation of operations, restructuring, cost containment, shut down of production lines, inventory reductions, salary cuts, change of investment plans, refocusing of corporate priorities, development of product, people and quality, focus on customers who have good credit, new business ventures, exploration of new markets overseas. Reactions to current difficulties appeared to outweigh strategic planning and proactive change management.

A survey on the impact of the regional economic crisis on Singaporean firms conducted by the Singapore Chinese Chamber of Commerce & Industry (SCCCI) in June 1998 (SCCCI 1998) revealed the following: 82.1 percent of the 312 respondents reported a slowdown in business since January 1998, 80 percent had their sales decline by more than 10 percent, 41.3 percent indicated that costs had increased by 10–25 percent, 43.9 percent said that high interest rates and charges were having a serious impact on their business and 56.4 percent of the respondents felt that interest rates were too high.

With regard to measures to counter the impact of the crisis, 50.3 percent of the survey participants reported that they had frozen wage increases, followed by 40.7 percent who diversified into other markets, 34.9 percent who scaled down operations, 32 percent who shelved projects, 21.1 percent who retrenched staff, 17.9 percent who opted for relocation of their businesses to cheaper premises, 17.6 percent who cut wages and 3.5 percent who closed down business operations.

Contrary to popular notions that small firms represent the backbone of most national economies in Asia and that they are strongholds in times of crisis, the relatively large number of bankruptcies indicates that the corporate sustainability of Chinese family firms cannot be taken for granted. According to Singapore's *Straits Times* (1/4/1999), 2,372 individuals went bankrupt in Singapore in the first 11 months of 1998 – 54 percent more than the same period in 1997 and 90 percent more than the whole of 1996. Most of the 269 companies wound up in 1998 were small – 36 percent or 96 companies had a paid-up capital in excess of $1 m, according to the Official Assignee (OA). Fifty-six construction firms were liquidated in 1998. No such firms were wound up in 1996, and only two went bust in 1997. Insufficient liquidity, increasing debts, cash flow problems, lack of demand, insolvency, bankruptcies and so forth exemplify the negative consequences of the downturn. Family feuds, succession problems, poor corporate governance, resistance to change etc. represent other challenges.

Based on the ascendancy of the Anglo–Saxon system of capitalism, Devinney (1998) has identified several weaknesses of Asian corporations such as the lack of (middle) management talent and transparency. For him, family governance and top-down patriarchal systems of corporate governance are 'antithetical' to modern equity-financed corporate structures that require coherent strategies instead of expansion based on opportunistic *guanxi* ties and government fiat, transparency of company's strategy to external scrutiny, accountable managers with strategy implementation skills, professionalism and clear procedures with regard to performance management, measurement and control. One of his conclusions is that Asian firms must change in order to survive the crisis and to be successful in the post-crisis era. Those who fail to implement world best practices will pay a high price. Another proposition is that Asia's traditional relational capitalism with its emphasis on frugality, authoritarianism and top-down management structures, relationships and trust 'will ultimately die' because it is inflexible and incoherent in terms of strategy. Devinney's essay calls into question the logic and sustainability of Chinese network capitalism.

Rethinking the logic of Chinese network capitalism

Chinese network capitalism between myth and reality

Books such as "Tribes" (Kotkin 1992) or the *New Asian Emperors* (Haley *et al.* 1998) underline the strong interest of journalists, writers and academicians in Chinese network capitalism.[2] Many analysts have stressed the powerful network connections of the ethnic Chinese businessmen and their ability to spin local, regional and global business webs, preferably based on long-term, non-contractual trust relationships. Their cultural ethos, language proficiency, local and regional knowledge as well as *guanxi* capital are believed to be of crucial importance in penetrating and integrating Asia's markets (Menkhoff and Labig 1996; Tong and Yong 1998). The economic transactions and social relationships between the peoples of China, Hong Kong and Taiwan have facilitated the regional integration of Greater China, lubricated by Chinese capital inflows from Southeast Asia (Herrmann-Pillath 1994; Tracy and Lever-Tracy in this volume). Four-fifths of Hong Kong's investments have been invested in China's Guangdong province where many Cantonese have "relations." Many Taiwanese investors have interests in Fujian despite the political conflicts between both sides of the Taiwan Straits. A growing number of overseas Chinese from Southeast Asia are doing business with people, villages and provinces in China with whom and where they have personal connections (*guanxi*) due to locality (native place), kinship or classmate ties as well as linguistic and cultural commonalities. One common, yet misleading hypothesis put forward by some scholars is that these net-workers are interwoven to form a regional Chinese network of companies, clans and villages linked by ties of blood and native place, which is part of the large global network of overseas Chinese businessmen (e.g. Chang 1995). Other popular notions about the traditional relational capitalism of ethnic Chinese can be summarized as follows:

"Kinship guanxi *is an effective lubricant of Chinese business networks"* Chinese family businesses are a "family fortress" and retain many of their characteristic attributes despite dynamic growth and change in size, technologies, products, services and markets. According to Landa (1983), *guanxi* based on kinship ties is of strategic importance in Chinese network construction and the formation of business alliances due to Confucian ideals that relatives should help and trust each other. The fact that many Chinese entrepreneurs in Southeast Asia married daughters of fellow villagers from Fujian or Guangdong (China) – who helped them to extend their business networks by introducing them to their "wealthy" relatives – has been put forward as another indicator for the centrality of kinship in Chinese business networking (Salaff 1982). Business based on kinship *guanxi*, so goes the main argument, helps to tap into other resourceful clusters of relationships and to lower transaction costs in turbulent business environments characterized by a lack of institutional safeguards against state indifference or hostility (Kowtha and Menkhoff 1995).

"Chinese tycoons are well connected" The self-identification of this special business class on the basis of race, language and culture has instilled in them an extraordinary capacity for cooperation that defines their uniqueness, creating a mutual support network. Ethnic Chinese billionaires such as Thailand's Dhanin Chearavanont, Malaysia's Robert Kuok, or Indonesia's Liem Sioe Liong, as well as Singapore's government-linked companies invested enthusiastically in China. In 1982 Dhanin's Charoen Pokphand Group opened China's first wholly foreign-owned enterprise in Shenzhen. His businesses in China range from petrochemicals to Kentucky Fried Chicken outlets. His good relationships in China make him one of the most attractive partners for foreign businessmen who want to penetrate China's market. "Sugar King" Robert Kuok, whose business empire comprises plantations, sugar refining, shipping, property, insurance and hotels,

was one of the first overseas Chinese investors in China. Kuok has good *guanxi* with the government in Beijing. He is an advisor on Hong Kong, and holds shares of the listed Hong Kong affiliate of China's state-owned investment corporation CITIC. One of his earliest regional business partners was Liem Sioe Liong's Salim Group. Besides Robert Kuok, Liem also participates in joint ventures with Thailand's agribusiness billionaire Dhanin Chearavanont. These commodity trader-turned-tycoons have transformed their family trading firms into pan-Asian business empires stretching from Asia to the United States, from Australia to Europe. The popular notion is that they form ethnic business networks based on mutual benefits and interpersonal trust that transcend Western or other attempts at networking.

"Guanxi capital will catapult the overseas Chinese to world economic dominance" With a combined gross domestic product estimated at between US$2 and 3 trillion, many analysts argued prior to the crisis that the global network of overseas Chinese would catapult Asia to world economic dominance in the twenty-first century. Chinese businessmen were seen as regionally/globally linked traders specialized in connections, cultural mediation and the movement of goods, technologies and services from one country to another.[3] According to Kotkin (1992), the ongoing globalization process and influx of new communication technologies such as video-conferencing systems, video telephony, telefax, electronic mail and data interchange for the transmission of trade, transport, customs, distribution documents and so forth have made regional and global business networking very efficient among the overseas Chinese. More and more Chinese trade associations are going online, following the launch of the World Chinese Business Network (WCBN) in December 1995, which provides data on more than 10,000 Chinese corporations from fifteen countries. The worldwide network of Chinese business associations represents a significant resource for companies to market themselves. Official association meetings and mutual visits as well as electronic networking through the Internet provides the opportunity to merge with other Chinese networks in the region and beyond.

"The Spirit of Chinese Capitalism" is posed as a unique model Asia's rise inspired the ideological construction of a unique "Chinese capitalism" operating in the region. Dirlik (1997: 307) has emphasized that the idea of a "Chinese variant of capitalism" was first propagated by non-Chinese in the United States, triggered by the fascination with China's reform policy, as well as economic crises in developed core countries juxtaposed with East Asia's economic success. Neo-Confucian values related to family, education and so forth were seen as key variables in Asia's rise. Scholars such as Kahn, Berger, Redding, MacFarquhar or Kotkin laid the foundation for "the new discourse on Chinese capitalism" and global networking initiatives such as the series of "World Conventions of Chinese Entrepreneurs."

In academia, this new interest manifested itself in conferences and publications on Chinese identity within the context of Chinese diaspora, "constituting affirmations of identity based on common origins" (Dirlik 1997: 308). A crucial outcome of these ideological activities is the bridging of the "many differences among Chinese and the invention of a new kind of unity and identity among Chinese populations around the globe in a process of re-sinification."[4]

Towards a better understanding of Chinese network capitalism

"The significance of kinship ties in forging interfirm connections is overestimated" Popular theories about the distinctive characteristics of ethnic Chinese networking along kinship lines are not always validated by empirical data. There is evidence that ethnic Chinese business networks based on kinship, clanship, territorial and ethnic principles have disintegrated since the post-war period (Yoshihara 1988; Menkhoff 1993; Menkhoff and Labig 1996). Nevertheless, images of such networks as exclusive systems of kin relationships and mafia-like connections persist. Family ties are important in business, Chinese or not Chinese, as far as the survival and internal organization of small businesses are concerned (Bechhofer *et al.* 1974; Zimmer and Aldrich 1987). However, the importance of such ties in forging interfirm connections (whether in the region or around the globe) is often overestimated for various reasons. The number of kinsmen with whom one can do business is limited. Kinship reciprocity tends to limit economic options (Wong 1988). Kinsmen often claim favors such as lower prices and/or delayed payments on the basis of kinship solidarity. At the same time, however, kinship is often created by transforming longstanding and reliable businesspersons into 'uncles' in accordance with the Chinese kinship system and sociocultural features (Menkhoff 1993). This form of *instant* kinship goes some way in enlarging business connections and in ensuring that trading partners behave within the rules of kinship as prescribed by the respective moral economy of trade.

Both Wong's (1988) study of Hong Kong enterprises and Menkhoff's (1993) monograph of small firms in Singapore suggest that kinship provides a weak framework for the external business transactions of Chinese enterprises:

> There is little evidence that a dualistic business ethic is prevalent or that honesty and trust are found only within the kin group while sharp practices reign without ... The inter-firm economic order ... is secured largely on non-kin solidarities ... forging business alliances through a conscious marriage strategy is hardly practical with the decline of the custom of arranged marriages and the inability of Chinese family heads to disinherit their children for disobedience ... the intensity of kinship reciprocity tends to limit economic options. Therefore it is invoked sparingly only when it suits one's ends ....
>
> (Wong 1988: 136)

"The importance of non-kin connections is underestimated" The evolution of Chinese conglomerates in Asia underlines how important *non-Chinese* connections

are in expanding business. A crucial factor in the success stories of Asia's tycoons is the formation of strategic alliances. Business partnerships with non-Chinese enabled some of them to build global empires. Malaysia's billionaire Robert Kuok was networking with Malay political leaders and Europeans before the term became a buzzword. Through a 30 percent-owned joint venture with French commodities giant Cie Commercial Sucres et Denrees in Paris, he is now the world's largest sugar trader.

Increasingly, the Chinese overseas are tapping foreign talent. Indonesia's Lippo Group, built by Lee Mo Tie (Mochtar Riady), invited American and Dutch finance groups into a strategic partnership that resulted in an Australian (Ian Clyne) becoming the new head – the first foreigner to head a local bank in Indonesia.

"The global network of the Chinese tribe: an imagined community" Mainstream analysts of Chinese businesses often fail to present satisfactory evidence and statistics that would chart the extent and value of synergy created by regional or global business networking. The idea of a tightly-woven global tribal network of ethnic Chinese based on mutual trust appears to be an outflow of stereotypical fantasy if one considers the heterogeneous nature of Chinese communities world-wide or the keen competition between Hongkongers or Singaporean Chinese. Furthermore, there are barriers towards their successful expansion into global markets, which require more research in order to assess their significance.

One handicap might be the paternalistic corporate governance of ethnic Chinese businesses with their centralized decision-making and opportunistic diversification strategies. This is regarded by some management experts as non-conducive to the utilization of funds and skilled manpower for technological innovation and product development (Carney 1998).

Impersonal Internet strategies may transcend the old personal networks. Initial business success of the Chinese overseas was based on their special contacts within their personal networks, but today the Internet provides instant and reliable information and communications.

Businessmen who rely on tribal networks and ethnic resources alone for the partners, capital, buyers and sellers do not fully utilize opportunities provided by the processes of regional integration and globalization. In an increasingly borderless world, which has more competitors than ever before, entrepreneurs who want to go global have to change their mentality. They have to "globalise their mind" and have to become "nationality less" to use a phrase by management guru Kenichi Ohmae (1990). Successful global corporations tend to be culturally more diverse due to the necessary adaptation to local conditions. Analysts agree that today's global managers must be cosmopolitan personalities who are comfortable with surprises and ambiguity, who value diversity and appreciate multicultural differences. Entrepreneurs with a "tribal mentality" are anachronistic in the age of information superhighways. The new generations of pragmatic Chinese entrepreneurs in ASEAN who have obtained MBA degrees at Western universities and/or who have worked for Western or Japanese companies would probably subscribe to this (Low 1997).

Cultural globalization implies that the persistence of "traditional" Chinese values as competitive advantages cannot be taken for granted. New value orientations emphasizing post-modern values, consumerism and more pleasure seeking life-styles may have negative effects on the competitive edge of ethnic Chinese and their networks. But of course modern ways are not only hedonistic! Many Chinese firms in Asia are seeing a management transition from traditional founding fathers to siblings often educated in the West where they picked up Western concepts of business administration that seeks to maximize shareholder (equity) value. Firms are also being forced by the crisis to seek outside help in management and finance (as in the case of Lippo, above).

Change management – corporate restructuring and new network configurations

Asia's financial and economic crisis has taught Chinese firms one lesson: the need to put more emphasis on core competencies, good corporate governance, change management and restructuring. Many large Chinese business organizations, which have been affected by the downturn, are now being restructured, a process that also implies changing network configurations.

A prominent example of downsizing is Indonesia's Salim Group, which holds stakes in many businesses from bread bakers in Singapore to cellular phone companies in China. It is now expanding overseas as its economic power at home disappears. In March 1999, it was reported that the company had signed a conditional deal to sell its entire 23 percent stake in listed United Industrial Corp (UIC) to Hong Kong-listed developer HKR International controlled by the Cha family for S$310.9 m as part of its restructuring efforts. According to Bloomberg News, the sale was expected to help Salim cut its massive debts part of which arose after the group's Bank Central Asia in Indonesia was made insolvent by massive runs triggered by the fall of former Indonesian president Soeharto, Salim's patron (*Straits Times*, 3/10/1999). On April 7, 1999, however, HKR called off the deal. A few days later, it was announced that Telegraph Developments Ltd (TDL), an affiliate of Chinese Filipino tycoon John Gokongwei's flagship company JG Summit Holdings had agreed to purchase the 23 percent stake of the Salim group in UIC for $310.87 m (*Straits Times*, 4/29/1999).

Another example is MBf Holdings in Malaysia that reported a substantial 1998 net loss hurt by declining consumer's demand for key products and services. The company disclosed that it had finalized its restructuring exercise that would see its main business activities streamlined into three core business areas: card and payment services, property and trading: "MBf is determined to move forward. In rationalising the group's operations, the company has decided to dispose of or wind down non-core and unprofitable businesses," the president of MBf's corporate services said (*Straits Times*, 3/11/1999).

The connection between the Asian crisis and changing network configurations is evidenced by the large number of foreign banks who have acquired controlling stakes in local (Chinese) banks. One prominent example is British bank Standard Chartered, which agreed to buy 75 percent of Thailand's Nakornthon Bank previously owned by the Wanglee family, becoming the third foreign owner of a Thai bank (*Straits Times*, 4/29/1999).

Chineseness, global capitalism, ethnic conflicts

Dirlik (1997: 311) has argued that there is a temporal coincidence of the rapid development of capitalism in Southeast Asia with the appearance of concerns for Chineseness and "Chinese capitalism," which he thinks is clearly linked with the structural conditions of global capitalism. He sees the discourse on Chinese transnational ethnicity and Chinese capitalism as a result of material activities made possible by the practices of global capitalism such as the transnationalization of production by transnational corporations (TNCs) and China's modernization policy. As he reads it, the Chinese diaspora is well positioned to be involved in transnational production flows, subcontracting and other global transactions. Due to their horizontal network relations, especially small Chinese businesses can take advantage of the new international division of labor in industrial East Asia:

> As Chinese businesses have been incorporated into the new production networks of transnational corporations, not only are the older networks likely to be transformed, but new networks need to be invented to answer the requirements of a new international division of labour. Subcontracting practices enhance the practice of networking.
>
> (Dirlik 1997: 310)

In view of abundant business opportunities in the region and anti-Chinese sentiments in certain parts of Southeast Asia, subcontracting practices are likely to enhance the interrelationships and ties among various Chinese populations, in what Dirlik calls the "ethnicization of production." Such a proposition reflects some of the myths surrounding the popular "bamboo network" idea. It also ignores the increasing number of joint ventures between Chinese and non-Chinese groups, TNCs etc.

The impact of the Asian crisis on the idea of an imagined pan-national Chinese community is difficult to assess at this point of time. One possibility is that Asia's downturn will be instrumental for deconstructing those images. The different effects of the crisis within the Asian region underline the heterogeneity of "Asia" in general and the different fortunes of ethnic Chinese businesses operating in Indonesia, Malaysia, Thailand, Singapore or Taiwan in particular. This might help to overcome stereotypes of ethnic Chinese as belonging to a "pan-national tribe with a common identity." The other possibility is that the mixture of prejudices, discriminations, scapegoating, institutional barriers and downsizing tendencies in some parts of the region will fuel tendencies towards re-sinification and ethnic tensions within Chinese communities and the nation states within which they live (Buchholt and Menkhoff 1994).

Thus, cultural and ethnic distinctions will not disappear quickly. While the increasing calls for more transparency in corporate governance and professional management are understandable and justified in view of skyrocketing non-performing loans, bankruptcies, insolvencies and associated hardships, the thesis that Chinese styles of management and networking will sooner or later converge into 'Western styles' has yet to be supported by empirical facts (Hamilton 1991; Woolsey-Biggert and Hamilton 1992; Hickson and Pugh 1995). As Redding (1998) has pointed out, Chinese firms sometimes combine Western structures of management with Chinese control structures. Examples of such hybrid forms are the Hutchison group under the helm of Mr Li Ka-shing or First Pacific headed by Mr Manny Pangilinan: "These are not pure types. They are not Chinese family businesses, and they are not Western-type multinationals. They take key characteristics from both."

Conclusion

This essay elaborates the challenges, threats and changes that globalization, global market forces and the Asian economic crisis imply for Chinese capital in the region. Several research questions and issues were raised, namely (i) how Chinese firms cope with the Asian crisis and associated business problems, (ii) to what extent a reinvention of Chinese corporate governance is necessary in light of the rapidly changing business environment, (iii) the strengths and weaknesses of Chinese network capitalism in the new global economy and associated myth-making processes, as well as (iv) the issue of Chinese transnational ethnicity and concerns for Chineseness in the age of globalization and ethnic resurgence.

The businesses of ethnic Chinese in Southeast Asia and beyond are exposed to a myriad of external influences, which trigger change. Redding (1998) has stressed that these forces are both "liberating" and "constraining." Liberating influences include access to new sources of capital, metropolitan world markets and new production technologies, IT and modern management techniques such as change management. One example, though the extent and social base are still little understood, is the increasing involvement of local Chinese companies as original equipment manufacturer (OEM) producers in global commodity chains (Dirlik 1997). Constraining influences include the disciplines of disclosure and the growing international concern over un-level playing fields, cartels, corruption, cronyism, lack of democracy and so forth, which have been identified by some observers as root causes of the economic malaise.

These external environmental changes and pressures might compel Asian corporations and conglomerates to revamp their system of corporate governance and to implement changes in terms of structure, technology, people or culture to ensure corporate sustainability in the post-crisis era and to uphold their legitimacy *vis-à-vis* Western business standards (Redding 1998). The cases of Indonesia's Salim group and MBf in Malaysia illustrate that processes of adaptation are inevitable for large firms seeking capital, technology and other access to the global marketplace.

The responsiveness of small- and medium-sized Chinese firms to the new forces of globalization remains to be seen. Many of these smaller organizations fail to implement modern quality/productivity management concepts such as continuous quality improvement (CQI) due to lack of management know how, poorly qualified staff and the organizational peculiarities of small family firms. The implementation of associated requirements seems to be incompatible with "old-fashioned power cultures" regardless of whether the underlying managerial culture is Chinese, Malay, Indian or German. Effective implementation requires continued communication and role modeling by knowledgeable top management, formal quality and other training, the setting up of QI teams, delegation of responsibilities to lower-level employees, benchmarking, formulation of key performance indicators, the integration of CQI priorities into budget and business plans as well as accountability for KPI performance and sufficient incentives. If adjustments are imposed, middle managers and lower-level employees are not always willing to go along with organizational changes. While there are many reasons why people resist change, paternalistic organizational cultures, authoritarian management styles and poor corporate governance are central explanatory variables (Menkhoff and Kay 2000). Regardless of size, strategy-development and centralized control remain the weak spots of most Chinese firms: "These are not normally given up, so whatever the organization grows to, it remains in its essentials a family possession, even under conditions of hybridizing ... They thus retain their inherent weaknesses, namely dependence on key individuals and fragility at times of succession, but this does not matter, because the system of Chinese capitalism as a whole remains robust" (Redding 1998).

The troubles of Chinese conglomerates in Indonesia exemplify the negative consequences of collapsed network alliances with non-Chinese business partners. In early 1999 Indonesia's parliament agreed to fine companies operating a monopoly by up to three times their annual profits and to put the owners in jail (*Straits Times*, 1/21/1999). Although the ruling is unlikely to have much impact since many listed companies are technically bankrupt, it symbolizes the changing structural conditions to which Indonesian Chinese entrepreneurs have to adapt.

Whether ethnic Chinese businessmen in Asia will rely less on network relationships and political–economic alliances in future will be dependent upon the nature of the institutional framework and structural forces in their respective host countries, which forced them to resort to such instrumental responses in the first place. Given its functionality, the slow pace of institutional change and the multiple causes of the economic meltdown, it is unlikely and to a certain extent illogical to assume that the Asian crisis will cause the "death" of traditional relational capitalism in the Chinese business world as Devinney's (1998) essay implies.

Despite the current tough business environment and the social challenges in Indonesia, Chinese capital will play a prominent role in the economic consolidation and further development of Asia.

Whether the issue of Chineseness and associated ideological activities such as the concept of a Chinese variant of capitalism will become less significant globally as a result of the crisis remains to be seen. Once Asia's downsizing process is completely reversed, it is likely that the pre-crisis discourse on the Asianization of Asia, the resurgence of the new Asian consciousness and so forth will continue. This would make cross-cultural, comparative research on ethnic (Chinese) entrepreneurship in the East and West and the utilization of new theoretical frameworks as requested by Rutten and Upadhya (1997) even more prevalent.

Notes

1 Prof. Koh interprets the debate over Asian values as a manifestation of East Asia's psychological and intellectual liberation from the Western dominance of the last 200 years.
2 Terms such as networking or network represent simple labels for a complex set of business strategies and choices, which are difficult to explore empirically. Networking, that is, the mobilization of resources through personal contacts and each other's ties, can be done in many ways: through ownership links, economic links of mutual cooperation, links formed through sharing of common directors, marital or friendship links (Tong 1991).
3 Ethnic Chinese are seen as effective cultural brokers between different cultural zones due to their cultural empathy. Their cultural capital, assets, linkages, entrepreneurial energy, passion for education and value system underpinning Chinese business behavior such as familism, trust, utilitarian discipline and high achievement motivation are believed to foster economic and scientific development critical to success in the global economy (Kotkin 1992).
4 According to Kotkin (1992), the evolution of a transnational economy and the rapid development of information and communications technologies are key factors that explain the rise of "global Asian tribes" such as the Indians and Chinese. The Little Indias and Chinatowns from London to Kuala Lumpur serve as important nodes in these "ethnically-based transnational economic networks."

Bibliography

Adams, F. G. and Vernon, H. (1998) How do Firms Adjust to Economic Crisis? The Case of Thailand, *Sasin Journal of Management*, 4(1), 1–5.
Backman, M. (1999) *Asian Eclipse: Exposing the Dark Side of Business in Asia*, Singapore: John Wiley & Sons.
Bechhofer, F. *et al.* (1974) Small Shopkeepers: Matters of Money and Meaning, *The Sociological Review*, 22(4).
Buchholt, H. and Menkhoff, T. (1994) Huaqiao – Die soziale Rolle der Ethnischen Chinesen in Indonesien, *ASIEN – Deutsche Zeitschrift für Politik, Wirtschaft und Kultur*, 51, 25–38.
Carney, M. (1998) A Management Capacity Constraint? Obstacles to the Development of the Overseas Chinese Business Family, *Asia Pacific Journal of Management*, 15, 137–62.

Chan, K. B. (ed.) (2000) *Chinese Business Networks – State, Economy and Culture*, Singapore: Prentice Hall.

Chan, K. B. and Chiang, C. (1994) *Stepping Out – The Making of Chinese Entrepreneurs*, Singapore: Simon & Schuster.

Chan, K. B. and Ng, B. K. (2000) Not all Successful Businesses are Chinese: Lessons from the Singapore Experience. In E. T. Gomez and H.-H. M. Hsiao (eds), *Chinese Business in South-East Asia*, London: Curzon Press.

Chang, M. H. (1995) Greater China and the Chinese "Global Tribe," *Asian Survey*, 35, September, 955–67.

Cragg, C. (1996) *The New Taipans*, London: Arrow Books, 1996.

Devinney, T. (1998) New Models for Asian Capitalism, *Asia Inc.*, October, 58–9.

Dirlik, A. (1997) Critical Reflections on 'Chinese Capitalism' as Paradigm, *Identities*, 3(3), 303–30.

Haley, G. T., Tan, C. T. and Haley, U. C. V. (1998) *New Asian Emperors*, Oxford: Butterworth/Heinemann.

Hamilton, G. (1991) The Organizational Foundations of Western and Chinese Commerce: A Historical and Comparative Analysis. In G. Hamilton (ed.), *Business Networks and Economic Development in East and Southeast Asia*, Hong Kong: Centre of Asian Studies, University of Hong Kong.

Herrmann-Pillath, C. (1994) *Netzwerke und die Politische Oekonomie der Beziehungen zwischen Taiwan und der VR China*, Baden-Baden: Nomos Verlag.

Hickson, D. J. and Pugh, D. S. (1995) *Management Worldwide – The Impact of Societal Culture on Organizations around the Globe*, Harmondsworth: Penguin.

Hiscock, G. (1998) Uncertain Future: Challenges Ahead for Ethnic Chinese Business Networks, *Harvard Newsletter*.

Kao, J. (1993) The Worldwide Web of Chinese Business, *Harvard Business Review*, March–April, 24–36.

Kenichi Ohmae (1990) *The Borderless World: Power and Strategy in the Interlinked Economy*, New York: Harper Business.

——(1995) *The End of the Nation State – The Rise of Regional Economies*, New York: Free Press.

Kotkin, T (1992) *How Race, Religion, and Identity Determine the Success in the New Global Economy*, New York: Random House.

Kowtha, Rao and Menkhoff, T. (1995) Tribes, Trust and Transaction Costs – A Preliminary Model of Trust Building in the Asian Context, Research Paper #95-07, Faculty of Business Administration, National University of Singapore.

Landa, J. (1983) The Political Economy of the Ethnically Homogeneous Chinese Middlemen Group in Southeast Asia: Ethnicity and Entrepreneurship in a Plural Society. In L. Y. C. Lim and L. A. P. Gosling (eds), *The Chinese in Southeast Asia*, Vol. 1, Singapore: Maruzen.

Lasserre, P. (1988) Corporate Strategy Management and the Overseas Chinese Groups, *Asia Pacific Journal of Management*, 5(2), 115–31.

Low, L. (1995) The Overseas Chinese Connection: An ASEAN Perspective, *Southeast Asian Journal of Social Science*, 23(2), 89–117.

——(1997) The Overseas Chinese – An Overlapping Generation Model. In H. J. Wald (ed.), *Konfuzianischer Kapitalismus in Ost- und Suedostasien*, Schriftenreihe der Zentralstelle fuer Auslandskunde (ZA), Deutsche Stiftung fuer Internationale Enwicklung (DSE), Vol. 25, Bad Honnef: DSE-ZA.

Mackie, J. (1998) Chinese Business Organizations. In L. Pan (ed.), *The Encyclopedia of the Chinese Overseas*, Singapore: Archipelago Press.

Madison, G. B. (1998) *Globalization – Challenges and Opportunities*. Working Paper. McMaster University, Ontario/Canada.

Menkhoff, T. (1993) *Trade Routes, Trust and Trading Networks – Chinese Small Enterprises in Singapore*, Bielefeld Studies on the Sociology of Development, Vol. 54 (edited by Prof. H.-D. Evers), Saarbruecken/Fort Lauderdale: Breitenbach publishers.

Menkhoff, T. and Labig, C. (1996) Trading Networks of Chinese Entrepreneurs in Singapore, *Sojourn*, 11(1), 130–54.

Menkhoff, T. and Kay, L. (2000) Managing Organizational Change and Resistance in Small and Medium-Sized Family Firms, *Research and Practice in Human Resource Management*, 8(1), 153–72.

MITA (1998) *Speech by Senior Minister Mr Lee Kuan Yew at the Europe-Asia Forum 1998* on 20 February 1998 at Shangri La Hotel, Singapore, Singapore: Ministry of Information and the Arts (MITA), Media Division.

Redding, S. G. (1990) *The Spirit of Chinese Capitalism*, Berlin: De Gryter.

——(1998) How Chinese is Chinese Business?, *The Straits Times*, December 20.

Robison, R. (1986) *The Rise of Capital*, Sydney: Allen and Unwin.

Rutten, M. and Upadhya, C. (eds) (1997) *Small Business Entrepreneurs in Asia and Europe: Towards a Comparative Perspective*, New Delhi: Sage Publications.

Salaff, J. W. (1982) Marriage Relationships as a Resource: Singapore Chinese Families. In S. L. Greenblatt, R. W. Wilson and A. A. Wilson (eds), *Social Interaction in Chinese Society*, New York: Praeger.

SCCCI (1998) *A Survey on the Impact of the Regional Economic Crisis*, Singapore: Singapore Chinese Chamber of Commerce & Industry.

Tam, S. (1977) Centrifugal Versus Centripetal Growth Processes: Contrasting the Ideal Types for Conceptualizing the Development Patterns of Chinese and Japanese Firms. In M. Warner (ed.), *Organizational Choice and Constraint: Approaches to the Sociology of Enterprise Behaviour*, Farnborough, Eng.: Saxon House.

The Economist 7/25/1998: Asian Values Revisited – What Would Confucius Say Now?

The Straits Times 11/28/1998: Salim Group Turns its Attention Around.

The Straits Times 12/20/1998: How Chinese is Chinese Business?

The Straits Times 1/21/1999: Monopoly Firms to Pay Fine or Face Jail.

The Straits Times 3/10/1999: Salim to Sell UIC Stake to HKR.

The Straits Times 3/10/1999: Asia in Need of "Social Software."

The Straits Times 3/11/1999: MBf Holdings' Net Loss Widens to $473 m.

The Straits Times 4/20/1999: No reason for Failed Deal.

The Straits Times 4/29/1999: No Tussle for Control of UIC.

The Straits Times 4/29/1999: Deal Reached for Nakornthon.

Tong, C. K. (1991) Centripetal Authority, Differentiated Networks: The Social Organization of Chinese Firms in Singapore. In G. Hamilton (ed.), *Business Networks and Economic Development in East and Southeast Asia*, Hong Kong: Centre of Asian Studies, University of Hong Kong.

Tong, C. K. and Yong, P. K. (1998) Guanxi Bases, Xinyong and Chinese Business Networks, *British Journal of Sociology*, 49(1), March, 75–95.

Tracy, N. and Lever-Tracy, C. (1997) A New Alliance for Profit – China's Local Industries and the Chinese Diaspora. In H. J. Wald (ed.), *Konfuzianischer Kapialismus in Ost- und*

Suedostasien, Schriftenreihe der Zentralstelle fuer Auslandskunde (ZA), Deutsche Stiftung fuer Internationale Enwicklung (DSE), Vol. 25, Bad Honnef: DSE-ZA.

Weidenbaum, M. (1998) The Bamboo Network: Asia's Family Run Conglomerates, *Strategy & Business*, 1st Quarter, (10), 59–65.

Wong, S.-L. (1985) The Chinese Family Firm: A Model, *British Journal of Sociology*, XXXVI, 58–72.

—— (1988) *Emigrant Entrepreneurs – Shanghai Industrialists in Hong Kong*, Hong Kong: Oxford University Press.

—— (1998) *Chinese Entrepreneurs as Cultural Heroes*. EAI Occasional Paper No. 3, Singapore: East Asian Institute.

Woolsey-Biggert, N. and Hamilton, G. (1992) On the Limits of a Firm-Based Theory to Explain Business Networks: The Western Bias of Neoclassical Economics. In N. Nohria and R. G. Eccles (eds), *Networks and Organizations – Structure, Form and Action*, Boston: Harvard Business School Press.

World Bank (1993) *The East Asia Miracle*, Oxford: Oxford University Press.

Yao, S. (1997) The Cultural Limits of Confucian Capitalism. Paper presented at the *Conference on Chinese Business in Southeast Asia*, Institute of Advanced Studies, University of Malaya, Kuala Lumpur, Malaysia, June 23–25, '97.

Yeung, H. W.-C. (1999) The Internationalization of Ethnic Chinese Business Firms from Southeast Asia: Strategies, Processes and Competitive Advantage, *International Journal of Urban and Regional Research*, 23(1), 103–27.

—— (1999a) Under Siege? Economic Globalization and Chinese Business in Southeast Asia, *Economy and Society*, 28(1), 1–31.

Yoshihara, K. (1988) *The Rise of Ersatz Capitalism in South–East Asia*, Singapore: Oxford University Press.

Zimmer, C. and Aldrich, H. (1987) Resource Mobilization Through Ethnic Networks – Kinship and Friendship Ties of Shopkeepers in England, *Sociological Perspectives*, 30(4), 422–45.

2

THE UNFINISHED AGENDA OF
THE OVERSEAS CHINESE

Linda Low

Introduction

There is no pretension to give a comprehensive and satisfying treatment of the proposed subject in one paper. The financial crisis and economic recession sweeping across Asia since July 1997 have compounded the political economy and social dimensions of ethnic relations. The situation is more acute in countries where gaps in income disparities and racial assimilation or integration remain, broadly interpreted as the unfinished agenda of the overseas Chinese. As the extant literature (Mackie 1992; Low 1995, 1997a; Suryadinata 1997; Pan 1998) provides the general historical background and insights into specific aspects of the overseas Chinese, this chapter focuses on the impact and ramifications of the Asian financial crisis. The section on "cultural dimensions in the Asian financial crisis" throws light on some factors pertaining to either Asian or Chinese values and practices. While acknowledging that socialization and politicization can engender racial integration, this chapter offers a thesis that economics can be as powerful given the hierarchy in Maslow's needs. It offers a practical policy tool to stabilize the environment to make racial integration and finishing the agenda more conducive. In turn, a virtuous circle is generated as racial, social and political stability propels the economy further.

Because overseas Chinese form only 3.5 percent of the population in Indonesia to represent one end of the unfinished agenda in Southeast Asia, a case study will be made of it in the section titled "the political economy of overseas Chinese in Indonesia." Counterfactual evidence and results as found in Malaysia, which has Chinese as one-third of its population, a formal New Economic Policy (NEP) and Thailand and Singapore at the other spectrum of integration will be offered in the section "the Chinese issue in Malaysia, Thailand and Singapore." While lessons may not be easy to generalize, a comparative analysis may help in an understanding of the issues and implications in a post-financial crisis Southeast Asia in the section "some generalizations and implications." As a ten-member strong entity when Cambodia finally takes its place in the Association of Southeast Nations (ASEAN), social and political stability would be as crucial as international competitiveness for the region to ratchet up the development ladder. Global conditions will be more competitive as sheer propinquity may drive China and the rest of East Asia into a potential rival bloc *vis-à-vis* ASEAN. The last section concludes with some prospects.

The cultural dimensions in the Asian financial crisis

Capital inflows as productive direct foreign investment (DFI) turned into speculative portfolio investment fuelling bubbles in the stock and real estate markets. Asian currencies appreciated with a stronger US dollar, which invariably forms a large component of their weighted basket of currencies. Traditional high interest rate and devaluation to offset speculative attacks of the currency undermined by herd instincts as market sentiments turned awry, caused banking and stock market failures as non-performing loans (NPLs) grew and asset prices collapsed. Massive reversal of capital flows, unhedged foreign loans under fixed exchange rate regimes and fragility of the banking systems obscured any gains from devalued currencies as the real sectors of the economy also suffered from deleterious high interest rates.

Even as the banking system is recapitalized and reformed with either assistance from the International Monetary Fund (IMF) and other international sources, the mood to lend and revitalize economic activities and trading in Thailand and Indonesia remains dismal. Malaysia's drastic capital controls (since eased by a system of graduated exit taxes) and exchange rate control may have stabilized the economy somewhat. But fresh capital inflows and investor confidence have been affected. Neither export markets nor domestic consumption are responding fast enough for all crisis economies. It is not an exaggeration that so long as Japan languishes in recession, Asia as a whole will find it immensely difficult to reflate. The United States' unusual state of economic euphoria can be fragile as its trade surplus and indebtedness grow. Excess capacity in ASEAN and China, which is under pressure from its own economic reforms despite its strong reserve and current account positions, cannot be easily absorbed by the United States or Europe alone.

The Asian financial crisis is as much caused by the malfunctioning of the globalized capital market as abetted by weak domestic macroeconomics and banking and financial systems that cannot withstand or adjust to the pressure of capital account liberalization. Political and state interference with the market process in the name of deregulation and privatization, building infrastructure and opening opportunities for local business has created an unhealthy chain of moral hazards. The phenomenon is quite invariant across the crisis countries starting with the trigger from Thailand, spilling over to Indonesia and Malaysia. The contagion spread to Singapore and the Philippines but they were relatively more robust for different reasons. While the city-state is more resilient because of its economic fundamentals and proactive policies, the Philippines was more chastened following the aftermath of the Marcos regime.

Over and above the basic causes, as much as Asian values typify the family as the social unit and has inspired hard work, thrift and high savings in the excessive state, a perverse form of ersatz and crony capitalism, has also been spawned. There is no logic or necessity that Asian values are intrinsically superior (Arogyaswamy 1998: 113–27). In fact, Asian values may degenerate into crony capitalism. Crony capitalism occurs when there is diversion of financial resources to particular individuals and families with political connections instead of resources being allocated under market efficient modes to promote long-term industrial development.

While Asian values may not necessarily be only Confucian or Chinese ones (Low 1997b), the hand of the Chinese is omnipresent. Coupled to indigenous Southeast Asian practices and political economy, the cultural dimensions in the Asian financial crisis may not be as innocuous. Ubiquitously, the super rich in business people in Asia are of Chinese origin (Hiscock 1997). Unsurprisingly, they are part of the overseas network whose linkages through clan, guild, village and dialect constitute an "invisible" but potent economic force, which almost rivals the gross domestic product (GDP) of the United States and Japan (see for instance, Seagrave 1995; Hodder 1996; Weidenbaum *et al.* 1996).

The common denominator and glue among the rich Chinese is the concept and practice of *guanxi* or in-tribal connections, which enables and expedites business deals seamlessly and effectively around the world. Unlike corporate connections as in Japanese keiretsus or Korean chaebols and business and political groups of pribumis and bumiputeras in Malaysia and Indonesia, respectively, the Chinese have their extended families, dialect, guild connections and *guanxi*.

As explained elsewhere (Redding 1990; Chirot and Reid 1997), immigrant overseas Chinese are intrinsically insecure in alien and hostile lands. They tended to be footloose as early sojourners (Low 1995, 1997a). Thailand is spatially nearer China and shares Buddhism and respect for the monarchy with their Chinese migrants and Singapore is overwhelmingly populated by the Chinese (over three-quarters). The Philippines dominated first by the Spanish then the Americans may be relatively neutral. Elsewhere, the degree of assimilation would be difficult in Muslim and Malay states as in Malaysia and Brunei or in culturally diverse and incompatible Indonesia. Being very pragmatic and practical, the overseas Chinese sought only to be economically free to go about their business and did not mind paying whatever monetary tribute to indigenous rulers for the license to do so. Neither were the overseas Chinese ambitious politically, which suited the colonial divide-and-rule policy as in British Malaya whereas neither the Portuguese nor Dutch in Indonesia cared very much for ethnic integration.

Politics and democratization in Southeast Asia tended to have authoritarian and charismatic leaders play a greater role than political party structures and institutions in maintaining stability and continuity (Sachsenroeder and Frings 1998). These include the People's Action Party (PAP) led by Lee Kuan Yew, the Golkar Party that supported the 32-year-old regime of Soeharto, the United Malays National Organization (UMNO) dominated by Dr Mahathir in his near two decade rule and the Democratic Party in Thailand. Thailand has differed somewhat with a wider array of prime ministers and coalition governments. Whether efficient soft authoritarianism in these Asian states satisfies Western notions of democracy remains a controversy. But with a growing middle-income class, universal education and greater awareness of alternative political cultures and system in an equally globalized political and economic context, the ground is changing everywhere in Asia politically.

Since generations of the overseas Chinese have settled and become nationals in their countries of domicile, their political participation has also grown even if a Chinese head of state in either Malaysia or Indonesia is still too premature. As they share an economic destiny, they would naturally want their contribution and inputs in the political and social system as well. Thus, from a state of merely supporting indigenous political masters in exchange for economic license to grow personal and national fortunes, the Chinese in Malaysia and Indonesia have developed political ties and aspirations in varying degrees.

Being more astute and savvy in business and commerce, the Chinese command proportions of income and wealth that are disproportionate to their representation in the population base. This is as much a commission by the Chinese as an omission by them and the ruling indigenous elites for not creating a more sustainable balance, especially in Indonesia. As long as high economic growth under the "miraculous" conditions since the late 1980s enlarged the national pie and improved poverty levels, the problems of non-integration remain masked and benign. In under a year, the Asian financial crisis has destroyed this cozy compact and revealed extreme income disparities as the recession shaved off income relatively more intensely and deeply among the low-income groups. Racial conspiracies tear at Asia's social fabric. There was a move by the overseas Chinese to make the ethnic riots in Indonesia a global Chinese issue, which has begun to raise China's concern in Southeast Asia (Suryadinata 1995; *Straits Times*, 7/30/1998 and *International Herald Tribune*, 9/12–13/1998).

The political economy of the overseas Chinese in Indonesia

Indonesia has achieved remarkable economic growth and was touted as a model of development among developing countries by the World Bank as recently as just before the crisis broke. Its GDP growth averaged 6.1 percent in the 1980s, rose to 7.6 percent during the period 1990–1995 and attained 7.8 percent in 1996 (Islam 1998: 2). Simultaneously, economic diversification was witnessed with the manufacturing sector growing at 10 percent on the average between 1985 and 1995 and accounted for a quarter of its GDP. Both gross investments and domestic savings enjoyed double-digit growth rates and only employment growth was less impressive; two-thirds of total employment remained in the informal sector. Just before the crisis, however, the growth in Indonesian exports was slowing down and a sharp reduction in rice production and impending rising food prices worsened the situation as a drought ensued.

With zero GDP growth, unemployment was projected to be 7.9 m in 1998 or 8.3 percent of the labor force, while a 5 percent contraction would raise the figures to 9.2 m or 9.7 percent, respectively (Islam 1998: 4–5). An alternative projection put the unemployed to be between 9.3 and 13.7 m in 1998 with the unemployment rate between 7.2 to 14.4 percent (Lee 1998: 40). These figures are the highest when compared to 2.0 m unemployed or 6 percent of the unemployment rate in Thailand for 1998, 0.4 m and 5.2 percent, respectively in Malaysia. The more likely outcome will be higher underemployment, as a sizeable segment of the population is still poor. Without unemployment and a national social security safety net, people cannot afford to be openly unemployed, underemployment standing at 41.5 percent in 1996 will increase with people working less hours than what is regarded as full time employment and even working longer hours for very low incomes.

The vulnerable groups will be the 22 m living below the official poverty line of whom approximately two-thirds were in rural areas. Poverty in Indonesia remains a predominantly rural and agricultural phenomenon, the incidence of poverty being highest among self-employed and wage-earning farmers in rural areas. The urban poor comprise those in agriculture, wage workers in manufacturing, construction and services. More will be pushed below the poverty line with the crisis, directly and indirectly, as a downward pressure on wages of those still employed will exacerbate poverty all round. Inflation will aggravate poverty further as prices of food and other essentials rise. While the self-employed farmers may fare better, the urban and rural poor wage earners will be affected. The statistics are blind with respect to gender and race. But more job loss in the manufacturing sector will logically affect more women and, relatively, more pribumis in farms and rural areas which is equally telling.

Totaling some 8 to 10 m, Indonesian Chinese may constitute only 3.5 percent of Indonesia's population (Javanese dominate at 45 percent followed by Sundanese at 14 percent) and there may be poor Chinese as well. But gross statistics constitute bad advertisements. These include the Chinese accounting for two thirds of Indonesia's private urban economy. They dominate networks for distribution of food and other essentials, control 65 percent and own 80 percent of assets of the top 300 conglomerates (in 1993). Of the largest top 10 corporations in Indonesia, nine are Chinese owned except for one by the Soeharto family, which is also very well connected with the infamous wealth of Liem Sioe Liong (Salim Group). The Soeharto family and Liem Sioe Liong are ranked in the ninth and eighteenth positions, respectively, among the top 100 billionaires in Asia with a net worth of US$6.3 and 4.5 bn, respectively (Hiscock 1997: 5).

The financial dynasty of the Soeharto children spreading over real estate, banking, industry, telecommunication, transport, media and many other sectors, is a paradox. Started as licenses or special contracts and prospered through the years and augmented by contacts from other Soeharto's associates, the first family's business empire was once rationalized as a counterweight to Chinese domination. In some areas, they are sufficiently well connected and powerful to break up inefficient monopolies and while they may have competed unfairly, they do not necessarily constitute bad economics.

Belatedly, in 1996, Soeharto called on all Indonesian individuals and corporations whose annual after-tax income exceeded 100 m rupiahs (US$43,000) to contribute 2 percent of their income to a special fund for Indonesian's 25 m poor (Hiscock 1997: 115). But as voluntary contributions were not forthcoming, a presidential decree in December imposed the 2 percent surcharge on wealthy taxpayers to fund the Sejahtera Mandairi Foundation overseen by the president himself. The tax may give a perception that Soeharto was critical of big business for not supporting voluntarily. But it was too small and too late a measure to do any good for the masses of neglected poor. Without a more seriously thought through and coordinated effort invoking the wealthy Chinese and pribumis including the Soeharto children, the nation in waiting (Schwartz 1994) is also one of missed opportunities (Robison 1997).

Unlike the programmed NEP in Malaysia, there is an unfinished agenda of assimilation in Indonesia. Sino-Indonesians are pressing for full and equal citizenship and access to participation at the same time that extremist Muslims are pressing to reduce the economic power of ethnic Chinese along NEP principles. As much as the NEP has created opportunities for corrupt and less transparent deals for the bumiputeras, the more corrupt bureaucracy in Indonesia would not be able to cope with a Malaysian-styled NEP to close the ethnic wealth gap. But when Malaysia eased foreign ownership by allowing overseas investors to own up to 51 percent of local retailers compared with the previous cap of 30 percent, the circumstance is more to prevent overall bankruptcy than anything ethnic in intent (*Asian Wall Street Journal*, 7/22/1998). Foreign investors may own up to 100 percent if they make Malaysia their regional distribution center. Rules under the NEP were liberalized to allow Chinese investors to take over some badly affected bumiputera companies.

An important policy change was in an Indonesian presidential decree on 16 September 1998, which stated that all government bodies would provide equal treatment and service to all Indonesians. It also eliminated state-sanctioned racial discrimination including the ban on usage of the term "pribumi" in all welfare formulation and organizations, programs or implementation of government coordinated activities (*Straits Times*, 10/8/1998). The decree will involve a review and revision of all laws, policies, programs and activities, especially the issue of business permits, finance, residency, education, health, employment opportunities, wage-setting and other employment rights.

However, according to Indonesian human rights activists, the laws are still unfair to the ethnic Chinese (*Straits Times*, 2/15/1999). Institutional and social discrimination is still visible because the government has not removed the legal basis for the discrimination. The decree has abolished all discriminatory practices only by a statement. The inertia is symptomatic of his administrative style in the belief that the decree will resolve problems or they will go away on their own. In practice, the vague decree has not been as widely circulated as expected and opportunities for corruption remains as ethnic Chinese try to bribe their way through formal and informal barriers to entry. Unwritten quotas in state universities and the civil service remain. Former President Habibie was trying to assure ethnic Chinese and stem capital flight as he met up with ten Chinese tycoons to alleviate their security concern (*Straits Times*, 7/27/1998). He has called the Chinese his ally as their capital and contribution to confidence in Indonesia in such trying times are clearly vital (*Asian Wall Street Journal*, 8/4/1998 and *Straits Times*, 8/5/1998).

Racial riots are not just directed against the ethnic Chinese, as clashes between the Muslims and Christians have been as violent and strong with incidents of lawlessness threatening to bring Indonesia to the brink of a social revolution. As many as 3 m lives may be at risk if this erupts according to Abdurrahman Wahid (*Straits Times*, 2/12/1999). A conspiracy theory has rationalized the rape incidents and racial hatred directed against the Chinese during the May 1998 riots that brought down President Soeharto, as part of the power struggle at the top involving even the military (*Far Eastern Economic Review*, 7/23/1998 and *Straits Times*, 9/4/1998).

Historically, the distrust of the Chinese began some three decades ago when an abortive Communist coup took place in Jakarta. The government in China may have given moral if not material support for that and the suspicion extended to the ethnic Chinese in Indonesia. This is especially when they continued to have remittances sent back to China and family and social ties remained. But long after they have given up thoughts of going back to the mainland and contributed to Indonesia's growth since, the Indonesian Chinese are beginning to question the basis for the continued hatred. They have not colonized Indonesia like the Dutch and having lived in such a state of siege, a rethinking has to be either they stand up for their rights or seek a new life abroad. Their decision will change the shape of Indonesia's future since the ethnic Chinese forms such a significant economic force (*Far Eastern Economic Review*, 7/30/1998 and *Straits Times*, 1/11/1999).

For those who are persuaded and convinced either by ex-President Habibie or how they see their options, they would have to finish the agenda of social integration. As a start, the Indonesian Chinese, both individuals and pressure groups have got together to form the Indonesian Chinese Reform Party to organize and involve themselves in the political process (*Far Eastern Economic Review*, 6/2/1998). This is long overdue and the inertia has been as masked by complacency with steady growth and progress as both the state and prominent Chinese too occupied with their respective agendas. The riots may have finally provoked the necessary action but the concern may also be whether it is too late and more distrust and disillusions have come with the riots and rapes.

Indonesia has an additional political and succession dimension personified by Soeharto. The turbulence and uncertainty in 1997, from catastrophic forest fires in Sumatra and Kalimantan to sociopolitical dissent in East Timor and Irian Jaya and wider problems of political liberalization, succession, economic decline and social tension may have overshadowed Indonesia's growth record faster than in

Malaysia. Being so much larger and diverse is an important challenge just as the much longer Soeharto regime and Soeharto family had deeper ruinous effects.

From the expulsion of Megawati Sukarnoputri from the Jakarta headquarters of the Indonesian Democracy Party (PDI) on 27 July, 1996, provoking the worst rioting in Jakarta, the rest of 1996 saw further unrest including ethnic violence. Racial violence erupted between indigenous Dayaks and immigrant Madurese in December in West Kalimantan (Kingsbury 1998: 164). The worst was, however, yet to come. In February 1997, the attack on a Roman Catholic church in Pontianak could have been due to inflamed Muslim passions. Jakarta was engulfed in more social and labor unrest as small traders vented their anger against local thugs and police on 27 January, 1997. This was followed by a riot on 31 January, 1997, in West Java's biggest textile factory and another strike and demonstration in Jakarta and Semarang on 22 April, 1997. Low-level regional unrest in East Timor, Aceh and Irian Jaya simmered from late 1996 to late 1997, and continued after the general elections.

The election campaign, which officially begun, on 27 April, 1997, was the most turbulent to date and election-related violence was focused in Central Java since late March. The worst violence occurred in Banjermasin in South Kalimantan on 23 May, 1997. As the final count in the 1997 parliamentary elections was announced on 23 June, 1997, that the Golkar Party won 74.5 percent, unhappiness with malpractice in running the elections and manipulation of the poll continued through June with rioting. On the basis of the May 1997 general elections results, the new parliament and the new People's Consultative Assembly (MPR), which meets every five years to elect the president and vice-president, initially had some impact in suspending the widespread unrest experienced between 1996 and 1997 as then president Soeharto was reaffirmed. But as the crisis continued abetted by the drought that brought on hunger and abject poverty, income disparity translated into racial, anti-Chinese sentiments and the situation worsened.

While short-term measures like promoting more labor intensive public sector infrastructure projects, targeted credit for self-employment and targeted food distribution and alleviation in other social areas as in education subsidies for children may help, more long-term policies cannot be avoided much longer (Booth 1998). While Indonesia has abundant labor resources, it cannot avoid a technologically more advanced and progressive world (Hill and Thee 1998). But such technological topics relegated to "second order" in importance and deserving of examination in an environment of political stability and economic growth, is as much an error of complacency as in policy mistakes. All micro, "single issues" as in technology, infrastructure, education and health policies, industrial policy, rural and regional development and poverty alleviation impinge on the macroeconomic and political picture. As an industrial latecomer, Indonesia should not neglect the evolutionary process of technology development and that clever intervention as witnessed in Taiwan and Korea can produce results.

Ethnic tensions have not bated in Indonesia since President Wahid has taken over from Habibie, if anything, they may have worsened as the economy continues in its tailspin with the much-needed economic, corporate and financial reforms in limbo. It is beyond the scope of this chapter to debate these issues here but needless to say, until the economy stabilize with political consolidation, the ethnic clashes seem as much a cause and effect.

The Chinese issue in Malaysia, Thailand and Singapore

The May 1969 riots in Kuala Lumpur caused a decisive poverty reduction and wealth redistribution policy through the NEP in 1972. It dictated certain limits for non-bumiputera ownership and equity share in companies, and other terms to favor the socioeconomic progress of the bumiputeras by certain time frames. With exhilarating economic growth and the ability to deliver large mega infrastructural projects, which were politically and nationally inspiring, the charisma of Prime Minister Mohamed Mahathir has created stability across all races. From an ultra Malay stand, as a consummate politician, he has mellowed to balance both intra-party and ethnic politics in the alliance of the ruling Barisan Nasional government as well as UMNO politics. His visionary yet earthy, commonsense philosophy has made him as inspiring in his 2020 vision for Malaysia as when he blamed heartless global speculators for decimating Malaysia's hard-earned national wealth (Haggard and Low 2000).

The dramatic growth enjoyed has spawned a growing middle-income class of Malay professionals and businessmen who joined those of the Chinese. Racial differences receded into the background as the economy managed to splendidly restructure the economy to more export-led industrialization, eradicated poverty especially rural poverty, improved income distribution and created wealth and assets more across-the-board than in Indonesia. However, it does not mean that Malaysia was spared of crony capitalism and nepotism as Mahathir's family business is not insignificant with complicated tie-ups with Chinese groups and individuals as well (Gomez and Jomo 1997). There is also a lot of UMNO interests in the commercial and industrial sectors, beginning with Daim Zainuddin, Finance Minister in the 1980s and again in 1998, he is the UMNO treasurer and a businessman first and last, despite his political and party positions (Gomez 1990, 1991, 1994).

At the onset of the financial crisis, Malaysia appeared to have less sociopolitical problems. It had the same symptoms in NPLs, crony capitalism, corruption and some recklessness in terms of higher exports aggravating import dependency and a relatively slow rate of human resource development as the economy remains at a low technology level. These oversights appear incongruent to boasts of mega national projects like the Multimedia Supercorridor (MSC) to promote applications in information technology.

Politics was fast turning what may have been an economic slowdown in Malaysia into a nasty recession as a political agenda about succession entered the fray in September 1998. A sudden political twist came with Anwar Ibrahim who was sacked as Deputy Prime Minister, a post he held since 1993 together with his other positions as Finance Minister and Deputy President in UMNO on 2 September, 1998. He was originally charged with misdemeanors ranging from bisexual promiscuity to leaking state secrets. As events unfolded during his trial since November 1998, support for him for Mahathir's mismanagement of his dismissal and arrest together with his inherent popularity as representing a very renaissance and cultured man who is also a devout Muslim waned as UMNO politics fell into disarray.

Anwar has supporters in Indonesia including his personal relations with former President Habibie and former Indonesian Finance Minister and adviser to Habibie, Mar'ie Muhammad. Anwar's think tank, the Institute of Policy Research, has strong links with Habibie's Centre for Information and Development Study. An Indonesian Committee for Solidarity was formed three days before Anwar's arrest on 20 September, 1998, with Nasir Tamara who is also a leading member in the Indonesian Association of Muslim Intellectuals nominally headed by Habibie. Anwar is also supported by the Muslim Indonesian leader Abdurrahman Wahid and Amien Rais both of whom played key roles in Soeharto's downfall in May 1998. Former managing director of IMF, Michael Camdessus, has also sought assurance from the Malaysian government on Anwar's alleged beating while in custody. Anwar was the chairman in the IMF Development Committee and was described by Camdessus as a very good finance minister (*Straits Times*, 10/6/1998).

Middle-class Malaysians had been radicalized by events in the weeks following Anwar's arrest as they discovered the art of street protests and reformasi but still not of the force of the students in Indonesia (*Jakarta Post*, 9/25/1998). Anwar's case probably benefited the Islamic opposition party PAS that adopted a religious gloss of injustice toward Anwar. It also enjoyed the defection of UMNO Malays who were increasingly confused and disillusioned by Mahathir's commanding style of politics. United in opposition to Mahathir, PAS and other more secular and multi-racial parties like Parti Rakyat, Chinese-based Democratic Action Party (DAP) and a dozen or so of Islamic non-government organizations (NGOs), have formed The Malaysian People's Movement for Justice (*Far Eastern Economic Review*, 10/8/1998).

Anwar's arrest came a day after Mahathir imposed exchange controls on 1 September, 1998. It was a masterly stroke of killing two birds with one stone as Anwar is an advocate of the free market and would not have abided the capital control and fixing the ringgit at RM3.80 to a dollar (Haggard and Low 1998). Other capital control measures include forcing foreign portfolio investment to remain in the country for at least a year, exports and imports must be paid in foreign currency, Malaysians need approval to invest more than RM10,000 abroad, Malaysians and foreigners who have ringgit accounts in Singapore and elsewhere have one month to bring the money back (estimated at RM100 m in cash held overseas and RM25 bn in offshore accounts), from 1 October, travellers in and out of Malaysia may not carry more than RM1,000, visitors cannot take out more foreign currency than what they brought in and finally, RM500 and RM1,000 currency notes were taken out of circulation.

A wider implication of this drastic political move is the repercussion on regional relations as Anwar's links with Indonesia's elite are too close for them to ignore the situation and the Philippines have also expressed concern. Former President Estrada has urged Filipinos to support Anwar, reminding them that Filipino hero, Jose Rizal, was a Malay and that an ASEAN observer team of parliamentarians be able to visit Anwar and attend his trial. Anwar's arrest was purportedly delayed to avert embarrassment with the Commonwealth Games on in Kuala Lumpur and Queen Elizabeth II in attendance. Similarly sensitive were ASEAN leaders attending the Asia Pacific Economic Cooperation (APEC) summit hosted by Malaysia a month after the arrest. Solidarity in ASEAN is tested with human rights charged among new and now old ASEAN members.

In particular, the near two decade rule under Prime Minister Mahathir has been compared with the 32-year rule of Soeharto in Indonesia in terms of autocratic control, nepotism and craving to perpetuate duration of regime. On the other hand, Malaysia has enjoyed a more dramatic growth and income distribution and generally satisfied racial aspirations of the bumiputras under the NEP. The theatrical political style of Mahathir is legendary, including giving Kuala Lumpur the highest building in the world and speaking out against the imperialism of developed countries. His theory of conspiracy alleging Jew financial George Soros of manipulating the currency crisis to punish ASEAN for admitting Myanmar as a member may have been over stretched. But his arguments against unrestricted capital movement in the capital account may bear some rethinking in emerging markets without the requisite institutional support and savvy as in developed economies.

The National Economic Action Council (NEAC) tasked to get Malaysia out of the crisis, formed in early 1998, chaired by Daim has proposed *inter alia*, a relaxation to allow non-bumiputras to hold a 100 percent stake in the manufacturing and construction sectors. This includes the Chinese who do not have to sell assets back when the economy recovers. But the 30 percent limit remains in strategic sectors including banking, cars, aerospace and shipping. Only eleven banks are fully foreign owned in Malaysia but the market value of bumiputras has fallen 54 percent and the overall bumiputra equity ownership in public-listed companies at market value has fallen from 29 to 27 percent in the last year since the crisis (*Straits Times*, 7/24/1998). While the government will not interfere, it notes that higher equity share by non-bumiputras or foreigners may not be widely accepted by the community.

Shutting down the offshore ringgit market in Singapore, borrowing from Japan and the World Bank and tapping the Employees Provident Fund (EPF) and state-owned Petronas, enabled Malaysia to avoid approaching the IMF. The original plan to recapitalize Renong Bhd via government-guaranteed bonds for government stakes in some of Renong's public sector projects was scuttled. It was feared as a precedent to the return of cronyism despite promises of no favored bailouts (*Straits Times*, 10/12/1998 and *Asian Wall Street Journal*, 10/9–10/1998, 10/12/1998).

Malaysia has been under pressure to substitute the austere capital controls with an exit tax, which would work like the Tobin's tax on speculators (*International Herald Tribune*, 1/23–24/1999, *Bangkok Post*, 1/23/1999, 1/26/1999 and *Asian Wall Street Journal*, 1/26/1999). It finally announced graduated taxes on capital gains, aimed at discouraging the outflow of foreign portfolio funds while attempting to encourage new inflows with no change on the peg of the ringgit (*Straits Times* and *Business Times*, 2/5/1999 and *Asian Wall Street Journal*, 2/5–6/1999). The complex levy system, memory of precipitous policy measures, which needed repeated clarifications of conflicting and confusing statements, are all too recent to attract new funds. All things considered, perversely, Malaysia's short experiment with capital controls may not have been altogether unsuccessful in stabilizing the volatilities. But the capital controls and subsequent decontrols have caused an exodus of foreign funds and sell-down by foreigners. The Kuala Lumpur Composite Index (KLCI) plunged 5.9 percent to 526.1, its largest one-day fall since 8 September, 1998, a week after the capital controls were announced (*Straits Times*, 2/9/1999).

Clearly, Malaysia is keen to attract fresh foreign investment and the World Bank's private equity unit, the International Finance Corporation (IFC), is reviewing whether to reinstate Malaysia to its benchmark emerging market index (*Straits Times*, 2/9/1999). Malaysia was the first country to be removed by the IFC Investible Index since it was started in 1993. The investment community may feel that Malaysia has broken the trust with capital controls. The other market-capitalized weighted stock indices calculated by Morgan Stanley Capital International (MSCI) has not reconsidered the reinstatement until there is sufficient evidence that the measures make Malaysia "truly investible." Still, sentiments in Malaysia are that the worst is over and with funds from the World Bank and Japan, the economy is likely to grow at double the 1 percent official growth forecast for 1999 (*Straits Times*, 2/10/1999).

All told, the role of Chinese as a historical legacy and source of income disparity as witnessed in Indonesia, seems less relevant or marginal in Malaysia. Mahathir has claimed that there are no more racial problems in Malaysia as the indigenous people had kept up with the ethnic Chinese, which is not like Indonesia at all (*Straits Times*, 2/10/1999). While Mahathir's rule may be getting less tolerable, the Malaysians are not as desperate as the Indonesians to rid themselves of their authoritarian leader. In fact, both cabinet ministers and the average Malaysian would want him to lead Malaysia into the new century (*Straits Times*, 2/16/1999).

Mahathir's actions may have been caused as much by the divisive UMNO party politics and agitation with Anwar's popularity. His subsequent delayed appointment of Badawi as his deputy in the government and UMNO may have allayed some fears of his desire to cling to power and his health. He seemed excessively overburdened with portfolios as Prime Minister, Deputy Prime Minister, Minister for Home Affairs and UMNO President in addition to being the Chairman of NEAC. In other words, the Chinese element had practically no significance to the current woes in Malaysia.

The same observation may be made of Thailand. In the first place, where Chinese is a minority, Thailand has assimilated them better than most of its ASEAN counterparts. Whatever crony capitalism, corruption and government involvement in business found in Thailand are no more vituperative as found elsewhere without any perverse Chinese factor. The same ill preparedness in the banking system with globalized capital flows, the incriminating evidence of the Nukul report on the ineptitude and sheer negligence of officials from the Bank of Thailand (BOT) and other government officials, the bubble economic effects and others are no less highlighted.

The Chinese factor may domestically be a non-factor in Singapore. But if the economic crisis and recession continues and deepens, social cohesion may return as an issue simply because of socioeconomic difficulties in the wake of higher unemployment as warned by Prime Minister Goh Chok Tong (*Straits Times*, 2/15/1999). Instead of less transparent family or party-affiliated companies, Singapore has another brand of enterprise in government-linked companies (GLCs). It may suffer from the same one-dominant party system and rule by the PAP since 1959. But the carefully engineered succession as Goh Chok Tong succeeded Lee Kuan Yew who remains as Senior Minister, in his own words as the "extra man on the team" (*Straits Times*, 1/30/1999), has generally worked. Singapore's response to the crisis has been to offer whatever assistance it can afford to give and neighbors such as Indonesia and Malaysia are comfortable to accept as well as restructure and reform particularly to open its domestic banking and financial sector to more foreign participation and competition.

In its regional efforts it has to be respectful of racial sentiments since it is predominantly Chinese. A couple of incidents affecting bilateral relations between Indonesia and Singapore are germane to the discussion. First, when former President Soeharto named Habibie as his vice president in February 1998, Lee Kuan Yew had remarked without naming Habibie that the financial market may be "disturbed" that the criteria and choice had been on the appointee's expertise in science and technology with high spending on such projects (*Asian Wall Street Journal*, 9/4/1998). Even as food and other supplies were brought over by Education Minister Teo Chee Hean and officials (*Straits Times*, 8/6/1998), then President Habibie did not see the friendship as falling under the category of "a friend in need is a friend indeed." To him, Singapore was just a "dot" in his office map much as he expected the wealthy city-state to have helped more.

A more grievous misunderstanding occurred as former President Habibie's mistaken notion was that there are no Malay officers in Singapore's Armed Forces, once similarly conjectured by Malaysia, and he called Singaporeans the real racists (*Straits Times*, 2/10/1999). This shows not just "big brother politics" but also dangerous connotations of intolerance of Singapore's success. Thus, while Singapore may have no domestic Chinese problems, its Chinese characteristics as perceived externally are perhaps not as benign.

In spite of its superlative efficiency based on international competitiveness, rule of law, overall good governance and relatively less corruption, Singapore is quintessentially a small, open city-state that needs the political goodwill of its much larger neighbors to give it both physical sustenance and economic space. As a virtual capital of the overseas Chinese, Singapore may not be as easily forgiven as being a safe haven whenever there is a capital flight due to political instability in nearby Malaysia or Indonesia, even if it did nothing to attract such refuge.

In truth, as part of its foreign talents policy, Singapore has indeed liberalized its immigration rules and regulations even if they were not directed to the overseas Chinese. From September 1, 1998, a new pass system was implemented by the new Ministry of Manpower (former Ministry of Labor) for all foreign workers, which featured a graduated approach (*Straits Times*, 7/25/1998). Top talents as in professionals, entrepreneurs, investors and talented specialists are welcomed together with their dependents extended to as distantly related ones such as parents and parent-in-laws. The privileges are less generous for the skilled and semiskilled categories. Further revelation of the six criteria for permanent residency for foreign talents based on a point system and the relaxation that Singaporean wives can sponsor their foreign husbands, were made (*Straits Times*, 2/10/1999). It may not be so much the context of the foreign talents policy as the timing of the offer: just when the ethnic Chinese are being victimized in Indonesia in July 1998, that is telling. Both outflows of capital and talents, which would also affect confidence in the source country like Indonesia, would deepen the problems with quality of friendship.

Some generalizations and implications

From the discussion of certain cultural and political economy factors in Indonesia, Malaysia, Thailand and Singapore, a few general observations may first be made. Indonesia appears to suffer the most from any historical remnants or baggage of the overseas Chinese. Elsewhere, even the term "overseas Chinese" as opposed to being just Malaysians, Thais or Singaporeans without the Chinese appendage has been implicitly withdrawn. That a presidential decree had to be made to stop pribumi as both a term and a policy in Indonesia reflects its desire and effort to remove the racial discrimination and stigma.

Indonesia would have been more successful in ridding itself of the Chinese racial factor had it not missed innumerable opportunities to eradicate poverty and improve income distribution as Malaysia wisely did with its NEP. Indonesia has enjoyed the bonanza of high oil prices and revenues and steady growth in the 1980s up to mid-1990s. Its Chinese community has also missed the opportunity of integrating itself more cohesively with the rest of the population. This is all the more important given its very small share in the total population, making its control over national wealth more glaring and alarming than in Malaysia.

It is truly an unfinished agenda for the Indonesian Chinese in more sense than one. They have also not sought more active political participation although Indonesian politics are not as open and democratic as the British legacies in

Malaysia and Singapore with a strong social and political role of its armed forces, Angkatan Bersenjata Republik Indonesia (ABRI). The Muslim groups and other NGOs are more numerous and dominant than any Chinese groups, which remain unorganized and diffused simply because the Chinese leaders and corporations have not seen themselves fit as getting involved in any ways other than business and commerce. They have helped neither their own communities nor the pribumis, simply to remain neutral and business-like above all.

The Malaysian NEP and philosophy may not suit Indonesia because of its racial arithmetic, greater diversity, regional spread and more widespread corruption. The colonial legacy from the British may have been more favorable in leaving a relatively more efficient public administrative system and core of civil servants and traditions. Despite its divide-and-rule policy, it may have perversely given each racial group an understanding of its respective role and standing and averted head-on collision and clashes.

With or without a formal pact as the NEP, the Indonesian politicians, policy makers and religious and social thinkers should not have left it all to the incumbent president to hold and unite the country by sheer charisma. Soeharto has consciously neither groomed nor nominated any successor until he was forced to hand over to Habibie just before he was ousted in May 1998. On the other hand, Mahathir had as many as four deputies and heirs-in-waiting to date and it is equally open to speculation who would ultimately succeed him. Whether being only 3.5 percent of the total population would have made it easier or more difficult for the Chinese in Indonesia to finish their unfinished agenda is a moot question at this juncture.

A common observation is that the overseas Chinese are much maligned and blamed as a socially disruptive group in both Malaysia and Indonesia. In reality, the social and political economy issues as well as the current financial and economic crisis are as much attributable to domestic macroeconomic fundamentals as crony capitalism, corruption and nepotism and the external financial system. But racial factors constitute a convenient whipping boy to mask, distract and disguise power factions as alleged in Indonesia when various groups were really agitating for Soeharto's downfall. Again, the Chinese themselves have not taken the necessary precautions to protect and absolve themselves.

In contrast to state-business, political party-business or family-business networks and links, a better model in government-linked companies as in Singapore may be touted. But being so small, uniquely Chinese dominated and with more than sufficient economic growth and wealth accumulation through public housing home ownership programs, its formulations are unlikely to be replicable elsewhere. Even with some special rights for indigenous Malays, especially through Mendaki in the earlier years, all privileges conferred are still based on meritocracy within the same race.

On the other hand Singapore has more to worry about its Chinese characteristics across countries in the region. That it is predominantly Chinese and has developed strong economic and business links with China through many public and private sector projects, may grant Singapore an identity badge that keeps it in a class of its own. "Big brother" politics and grudging admiration of its economic success are frequently translated into jealousies and suspicions even by big neighbors like Indonesia or relatively successful ones like Malaysia. As the Thai Chinese are so well assimilated in Thailand, they seem to have no problem dealing and working with Singaporeans.

What is patently clear is that the Chinese factor is less and less problematic the more economically successful state the is in ASEAN. Clearly, in terms of this thesis, Indonesia and Singapore stand, respectively, at the two ends of the spectrum. Growth without equity is as inadequate and even dangerous as a policy in the long run as seen in Indonesia. While Singapore is not altogether absolved of racial contagion effects just as it suffered such infections from the financial crisis, its sociopolitical foundations are stronger and more robust. Logic, consistency and a generally meritocratic society with highly selective elitism to nurture the crème de la crème have served Singapore well thus far. The Chinese community has completed its agenda in building Singapore as a racially harmonious and cohesive country. Much as the Senior Minister has expressed his concern that with half the population travelling abroad in any year, whether the Singapore society will remain intact, his worry has less to do with racial than wider cultural dilutions as social norms are being picked up from around the world (*Sunday Times*, 2/1/1999).

Conclusion

This chapter may conclude rather safely that economic growth with the necessary improvements to income distribution and equity may avert racial issues and problems associated with overseas Chinese seen as rich and obnoxious as they may have not bothered to assimilate themselves genuinely in the local communities. On one hand, the average Indonesian Chinese may argue that they have not been given the chance and opportunity to do so. On the other, the much richer and privileged Chinese billionaires have not seen the need to do so.

There have indeed been many missed opportunities in Indonesia for the unfinished agenda of the overseas Chinese. When it does recover from the financial and economic crisis as one nation, the pribumi Indonesians and Indonesian Chinese would have to seriously rethink how to avoid and avert the racial riots directed against the ethnic Chinese. The riots and atrocities witnessed in Indonesia throughout 1998 and continuing into 1999 may be based on racial disparities in general and the ethnic Chinese as a specific group. A conspiracy theory has claimed that the ethnic Chinese are used as an excuse and there were more intrinsic power struggles and factions instigating the racial disruptions and riots to bring down Soeharto. Whatever is the truth, the point remains that the Chinese are in a vulnerable position.

It may have been premature for Mahathir to pronounce that Malaysia has no more ethnic racial problems because every group has or at least had the opportunity to catch up with one another given the outbreak in ethnic tensions in March 2000 in

Kuala Lumpur. Still, Malaysia may come out of its economic difficulties more easily than extricating itself of UMNO politics and resolving the Malay disillusion with the party. With PAS waiting in the wings to capture UMNO dissenters and deserters, the situation is not that innocuous either as PAS is very traditionally Islamic and its politics have not changed in the last twenty years as UMNO has, as a more modern and mature political party. Alliance parties and political coalitions as in the Barisan Nasional is still the best formula for Malaysia. The Chinese have their rightful position and the Malaysian Chinese Association (MCA) will have to work harder to preserve Chinese support and trust as dissenters would head for the DAP.

Thailand and Singapore are relatively most successful in not having a Chinese issue at all. While Thai Chinese have neither a domestic nor external angle to worry about, Singapore has to be more sensitive and respectful of perceptions of its Chinese base by both Malaysia and Indonesia. But if the economic crisis continues and deepens, economic strains and stresses would also tear at social including ethnic fabrics as warned by the Prime Minister Goh Chok Tong (*Straits Times*, 2/15/1999). This may be a threat both domestically and externally as when racial revolutions brewing in Indonesia spill over to Singapore. While Malaysians may be more enlightened and professional in their thinking and deeds and are generally more affluent and content, Indonesians as a whole constitute a more volatile and potentially threatening group of over 200 m people. Its sheer size is sobering even if Singapore is best anchored on the rule of the law and international standards and practices in economic, political and foreign policies as well as in international relations.

The Asian financial crisis is the most challenging and widespread problem confronting ASEAN and will probably be with it for a little while more. If all affected countries stayed the full course of their economic reforms and structural changes, a leaner, more competitive and transparent region may emerge for ASEAN to stand convincingly and effectively as a group to counter or withstand competition from China and its hinterland in Northeast Asia. Ideally, such divisions should not be made or necessary. But so long as sovereign borders and identity prevails, countries will have to learn about economic cooperation and integration. Chinese *guanxi* may be adapted and refined to be Asian *guanxi* to create and expedite business deals around the region.

To learn from this crisis, politicians, policy makers and even academic researchers and thinkers must rethink strategies, options and opportunities together with the rest of the professionals and the more enlightened sectors. The enlarged ASEAN as a group cannot afford to muddle through any more and the ethnic Chinese as a potent economic force should be appreciated and induced to play its rightful roles. Only further research and studies can bear out whether the overseas Chinese with their capital, entrepreneurship, networks and proven track record can induce the recovery process in ASEAN economies. Would race be cast aside to allow competitive forces to reinstate themselves to make the ASEAN and Asia Pacific region dynamic and sustaining again is an intriguing problem.

Certainly, racial issues will not go away so easily unless economic survival threatens, above, all sociopolitical differences.

Bibliography

Arogyaswamy, B. (1998) *The Asian Miracle, Myth, and Mirage: The Economic Slowdown is Here to Stay*, Westport and London: Quorum Books.

Asian Wall Street Journal, Various issues.

Booth, A. (1998) *The Indonesian Economy in the Nineteenth and Twentieth Centuries: A History of Missed Opportunities*, London and New York: Macmillan and St Martin's Press.

Business Times, Various issues.

Chirot, D. and Reid, A. (1997) *Essential Outsiders: Chinese and Jews in the Modernisation of Southeast Asia and Central Europe*, Washington DC: University of Washington Press.

Far Eastern European Review, Various issues.

Gomez, E. T. (1990) *Politics in Business: UMNO's Corporate Investments*, Kuala Lumpur: Forum.

——(1991) *Money Politics in the Barisan Nasional*, Kuala Lumpur: Forum.

——(1994) *Politics in Business: Corporate Involvements of Malaysian Politics*, Townsville: James Cook University of North Queensland.

Gomez, E. T. and Jomo, K. S. (1997) *Malaysia's Political Economy: Politics, Patronage and Profits*, Cambridge: Cambridge University Press.

Hill, H. and Thee Kian Wee (eds) (1998) *Indonesia's Technological Challenge*, Canberra and Singapore: Research School of Pacific and Asian Studies, Australian National University and Institute of Southeast Asian Studies.

Haggard, S. (ed.) (2000) *The Political Economy of the Asian Financial Crisis*, Washington DC: Institute for International Economics.

Haggard, S. and Low, L. (2000) The Political Economy of Malaysia's Capital Controls. In S. Haggard (ed.), *The Political Economy of the Asian Financial Crisis*, Washington DC: Institute for International Economics, pp. 73–86.

Hiscock, G. (1997) *Asia's Wealth Club: A Who's Who of Business and Billionaires*, London: Nicholas Brealey.

Hodder, R. (1996) *Merchant Princes of the East: Cultural Delusions, Economic Success and the Overseas Chinese in Southeast Asia*, Chichester: John Wiley.

Islam, R. (1998) Indonesia: Economic Crisis, Adjustment, Employment and Poverty. Development Policies Department, Issues in Development, Discussion Paper 23, Geneva: International Labour Organization.

Kingsbury, D. (1998) *The Politics of Indonesia*, Melbourne and Oxford: Oxford University Press.

Lee, E. (1998) *The Asian Financial Crisis: The Challenge for Social Policy*, Geneva: International Labour Organization.

Low, L. (1995) The Overseas Chinese Connection: An ASEAN Perspective, *Southeast Asian Journal of Social Science*, 23(2), 89–117.

——(1997a) The Overseas Chinese: An Overlapping Generation Model. In H. J. Wald (ed.), *Konfuzianischer Kapitalismus in Ost- und Suedostasien*. Schriftenreihe der Zentralstelle fuer Auslandskunde (ZA), Deutsche Stiftung fuer Internationale Enwicklung (DSE), Vol. 25, Bad Honnef: DSE-ZA.

——(1997b) The Reculturisation of Asian Values for Development. In O. H. Cheong (ed.), *East Asian Economies: Sustaining Growth and Stability*, Kuala Lumpur: Institute of Strategic and International Affairs, pp. 29–50.

Mackie, J. A. C. (1992) Overseas Chinese Entrepreneurship, *Asia-Pacific Economic Literature*, 6(1), 41–65.

Pan, L. (ed.) (1998) *Encyclopedia of the Chinese Overseas*, Singapore: Archipelago Press.

Redding, G. (1990) *The Spirit of Chinese Capitalism*, Berlin: Walter de Gruyer.

Robison, R. (1997) Politics and Markets in Indonesia's Post-oil Era. In G. Rodan, K. Hewison and R. Robison (eds), *The Political Economy of South-east Asia*, Melbourne: Oxford University Press.

Sachsenroeder, W. and Frings, U. (eds) (1998) *Political Party Systems and Democratic Development in East and Southeast Asia*, Vol. I, Southeast Asia, Aldershot: Ashgate

Schwartz, A. (1994) *A Nation in Waiting: Indonesia in the 1990s*, Sydney: Allen & Unwin.

Seagrave, S. (1995) *Lords of the Rim*, London: Bantam.

Sunday Times, Various issues.

Suryadinata, L. (1995) *Southeast Asian Chinese and China*, Singapore: Times Academic Press.

——(ed.) (1997) *Ethnic Chinese as Southeast Asians*, Singapore: Institute of Southeast Asian Studies.

The International Herald Tribune, Various issues.

The Straits Times, Various issues.

The World Bank (1998) *East Asia: The Road to Recovery*, Washington DC: World Bank.

The World Bank (1999) *Global Economic Prospects and the Developing Countries 1998/99: Beyond Financial Crisis*, Washington DC: World Bank.

Weidenbaum, M. and Hughes, S. (1996) *The Bamboo Network: How Expatriate Chinese Entrepreneurs are Creating a New Economic Superpower in Asia*, New York: The Free Press.

Part III

SYNERGIES BETWEEN THE CHINESE
DIASPORA AND CHINESE BUSINESS
ORGANIZATIONS IN THE PEOPLE'S
REPUBLIC OF CHINA AND VIETNAM

3

A NEW ALLIANCE FOR PROFIT

China's local industries and the Chinese diaspora

Noel Tracy and Constance Lever-Tracy

Introduction

With hindsight, we can see that the opening of China to foreign investment was a crucial moment in the evolution of the Chinese diaspora as a major force in the international political economy. The importance for them of the opportunities resulting from economic reform in China were in providing profitable outlets for surplus capital, the means of industrial restructuring and the basis of exponential growth of their industrial capacity. On the Chinese side, we can now see that the Chinese diaspora have been one of the critical factors turning the southeast into the new powerhouse of China's economy[1] and the leader in export orientation and economic reform since 1985.[2]

Chinese diaspora enterprise is also one of the most important factors keeping the economic reform process in China going. This process, as it emanates from Beijing, is increasingly facing seemingly insurmountable difficulties. These are manifested in the mounting crisis in the finances of state industry, the obstacles to labor reform in the state sector for fear of creating mass urban unemployment, the difficulties of proceeding with price reform for fear of bankrupting state enterprises and undermining peasant incomes, the crisis in the banking system created by political directives to continue providing credit to state industries that have no possibility of repaying, and the danger of recurring inflationary pressures (*SCMP*, 7/12/1994: 11; *SMP*, 7/3/1994: M4).

At the same time as the macroeconomy has faced severe difficulties, the micro-economy, away from the major centres of political power, especially in the smaller cities, towns and villages of coastal provinces along the southeastern and eastern seaboard, continues to grow at a rapid rate. In these areas, what is apparent is that two forces at the heart of the continuing success of economic reform in China, township and village enterprises and Chinese diaspora entrepreneurship and investments, are increasingly business partners.

The Chinese diaspora are also increasingly the major factor in the access of goods manufactured in China to international markets, evidenced by the quite disproportionate volume of China's export trade that passes through Chinese diaspora marketing channels in Hong Kong on their way into world markets. Half of the exports from Guangdong in 1996 and two-fifths of the national total have come from foreign invested firms (CCSM, 1996: 8), a large majority of which involve the Chinese from Hong Kong and Taiwan and other parts of the worldwide diaspora of the ethnic Chinese living outside the mainland (CSY, 1996: 598–600).

It must be understood, however, that this growing relationship between the Chinese diaspora and China has few political connotations. They regard each other with considerable disquiet. The members of the Chinese diaspora fear policy changes and the possible consequences for their business of any struggle for succession or loss of control by Beijing. The Chinese authorities for their part are less than enamored with the increasing importance of the Chinese diaspora in the economy, the economic power that is flowing to the southeastern provinces substantially as a result of the Chinese diaspora investment, and the role models that they are providing. Even where the authorities in Beijing have set out to woo leading Chinese diaspora business leaders, the path to cooperation has not always proved smooth, with the latter abruptly withdrawing from large projects when faced with bureaucratic obstacles, and the former seeking to impose restrictions and controls, particularly on ownership and rates of return, which have proved unacceptable. In this respect there was a noticeable cooling in relations in 1994 following the introduction of new control measures at the end of 1993, which followed two years of increasing cooperation.

Chinese diaspora investment in China

There have been three waves of foreign investment in China since the economic reform process began in 1979.

The first wave was characterized generally by large expenditures by transnational energy companies on offshore oil and gas exploration in collaboration with central government ministries, and in hotels and tourist facilities.

The second phase began in late 1984 and reached its peak in 1988. This featured the movement of small- and medium-sized manufacturing firms into southern China via Hong Kong, in particular into the Pearl River Delta in Guangdong province and the Xiamen-Chuanzhou-Zhangzhou triangle in Fujian. This had been made possible by the opening of the Pearl River Delta and a number of open coastal cities to foreign investment in 1985. This movement subsided after 1988, initially as a result of central government measures to combat growing inflationary pressures, but later due to political concerns both about human rights and about the future of the economic reform process itself following the Tiananmen crackdown in 1989.

However, Deng Xiaoping's tour of the south in the spring of 1992, and his call for the rest of China to follow the economic restructuring taking place there, gave

66

impetus to a third wave, which had already shown signs of taking off in 1991 (Zhang and Tracy 1994: 1–2). This wave is still continuing.

This current wave has proved substantially larger and more sustained than the previous two. It has built on the momentum of the second, with an increased movement of small-, medium-sized and even some large-scale manufacturing enterprises into China. This time, while investment continues to be concentrated in the southeast, overseas investors are increasingly seeking opportunities further afield, particularly along the east coast, in Jiangsu, Zhejiang, Shanghai and Shandong, in the northeastern provinces, particularly, the Liaoning Peninsula, Tianjin and Beijing and even in some of the more remote interior provinces. At the same time a new interest became apparent at the start of the new wave, this time involving the larger regional conglomerates, in large-scale infrastructure projects and real estate developments. The rapid advance in industrial capacity, resulting from China's breakneck speed of economic growth, had created the need for a massive upgrading of infrastructure to overcome bottlenecks to further development in the form of power shortages and woefully inadequate transport and port facilities (Zhang and Tracy 1994: 1–2). While this interest in infrastructure waned in 1994 as a result of new government regulations, in particular those limiting the rate of return on power stations and ports to 15 percent, many projects had got underway under the old regulations and continued in progress.

The results of foreign investment

The results of these three waves of foreign investment are quite stunning. Direct foreign investment flows into China were only around US$370 m a year at the start of the 1980s but had risen to nearly US$2 bn by 1985 and nearly US$3.8 bn by 1989. After faltering briefly they took off again at a dizzying pace and in 1992 the inflow was nearly two and a half times larger than the previous year and the number of newly registered foreign-funded enterprises came to 1.3 times the total of the past thirteen years. By the end of 1992 there were 84,000 foreign-funded enterprises in China, with an accumulated realized foreign capital input of US$68.7 bn. By the end of 1993 the number of realized projects had doubled again to 167,500 with another US$25.8 bn in direct foreign investment coming in that year. In 1994 a further US$35 bn came in, up 40 percent on 1993, and another US$37 bn in 1995 (*SCMP IE*, 12/3–4/1994: B1; *SMP*, 7/3/1994: M4; *CSY*, 1996: 598). Estimates indicate that nearly US$20 bn came in during the first six months of 1996, 20 percent more than in the same period the year before. In 1993 the size of the average investment was only US$310,000 while the average foreign invested enterprise in the southeast employed around 150 workers (Zhang and Tracy 1994; *SCB*, 1993: 1; *Beijing Review*, 3/3/1994: 11, 14–20, 37; *SCMP*, 12/3–4/1994: B1).

These figures are historically unprecedented: no other developing country has received anything remotely like these sums in such a short time period. No less than US$38 bn had been invested in 1992 and 1993 alone and in the latter year

China received more foreign investment than any other country in the world bar the United States (*SCMP IE*, 12/3–4/1994: B1). Even this was exceeded by the more than US$70 bn invested in 1994 and 1995 (*CSY*, 1996: 598). In a more analogous comparison, foreign investment in China over five recent years has far exceeded that received by Indonesia (previously the largest recipient of foreign investment in developing East Asia) in the 25 years from 1967–92 (*The Australian*, 9/25/1992: 13; *Indonesia Development News*).

What is even more striking is that these massive investment flows have been dominated by a single and until recently little known source, the Chinese diaspora. They have out invested the economic superpowers, the United States, Japan and the European Union combined, by a factor of more than five to one, contributing well over 80 percent of both investment projects and capital invested since 1979. Furthermore, their proportionate contribution increased as the total inflow of capital also grew in the 1990s, from under 50 percent of the total in 1985 to more than 80 percent in both 1992 and 1993 (Chan and Zhu 1994: 14). Although this figure slackened slightly in 1994 and 1995, it still remained well over 70 percent (*CSY*, 1996: 598).

What is also particularly significant is that the Japanese are being out invested by the Chinese diaspora even in areas of traditional interest and influence in China's northeast. Japanese reports have lamented how Hong Kong and Taiwanese investors are far ahead of their Japanese counterparts in the number and size of projects in Dalian (*Nikkei Weekly*, 8/16/1993: 20). Even in Shanghai, which has been the prime magnet for the major Western and Japanese multinationals, Hong Kong and Taiwan remain the largest investors (SWB *FEW*/0356, 10/26/1994: WG/5; *Peng*, 1996: 3).

Table 3.1 shows the origin of foreign investment in China. A word of warning is, however, in order in interpreting these figures. There has been a marked tendency for the Chinese diaspora entrepreneurs, from whatever home base, to route their China investments through Hong Kong and to form companies there for that purpose. In the case of the Taiwanese, until recently, government restrictions on direct investment in the mainland made it necessary to invest through a third country and many continue the practice.

In the case of Chinese from Southeast Asia, the internationalization of their operations over the last decade has led in many cases to the opening of branch offices in Hong Kong, and some of the larger regional conglomerates from Singapore, Malaysia, Indonesia and Thailand have even established second headquarters there. Twenty-six of the top 200 companies on the Hong Kong stock exchange in 1995 were owned by Southeast Asian diaspora interests (Lever-Tracy *et al.* 1996: 107). This enables them to tap the Hong Kong capital market and to draw on its expertise in dealing with China. Raising money in this way enables them to spread their risks and protects them from the charge of capital flight from their home bases, where their status as an ethnic minority leaves them vulnerable.

Two of the largest Chinese diaspora investors in China, the Sino-Thai agribusiness group, Charoen Pokphand and the Sino-Indonesian Sinar-Mas group

Table 3.1 Sources of foreign capital in China (cumulative 1979–93, percentages)

Source country	Enterprises	Value of foreign direct investment
Hong Kong	63.7	69.1
Taiwan	12.3	9.3
Macao	2.5	2.8
Singapore	1.8	2.2
Thailand[a]	0.8	1.2
Sub-total[a]	81.1	84.6
US	6.9	5.4
Japan	4.2	4.8
Other sources	7.8	5.2
Total (%)	100.0	100.0
No.	167,500	US$68.7 bn

Sources: State Commerce Bureau, FDI in China: Analyses of Trends and Future Directions, 1993; International Trade News (MOFTEC), 5/16/1994, p. 1.

Note

a Investment in China from these countries is almost entirely made by the ethnic Chinese.

have both made their investments in China through their publicly-listed companies in Hong Kong. There are many other examples of the Southeast Asian Chinese directing investments in China through Hong Kong, including the Sino-Indonesian Liem and Riady families and the Dharmala group, the Malaysian Kuok, Hong Leong and Berjaya groups, Sino-Thai, Bangkok Land and the Singaporean, Far East Organisation, controlled by the Ng family (Lever-Tracy *et al.* 1996: chapter 7).

The overall figures for foreign investment in China are somewhat inflated by disguised "round tripping" mainland funds, returning to gain the benefits offered to foreign investors. On the other hand the official data also probably understates the proportion of foreign investment flowing from Chinese diaspora sources. While we can be fairly certain that there are few Western companies' investments hidden in what might be considered essentially Chinese sources like Hong Kong, because the Chinese authorities are very anxious to identify them, as they are worried about an over dependence on the Chinese diaspora, it is clear that investments from the smaller Chinese diaspora groups, for example, in North America and Australia are being hidden by inclusion in their country of origin. While Hong Kong's contribution is thus overstated in the official data, that of Taiwan and Southeast Asia and more distant sources is likely to be considerably understated. We can therefore reasonably conclude that the whole of the Chinese diaspora is engaged in the process of re-industrializing and modernizing China.

The southeast received some 55 percent of foreign capital in 1993 although this had slipped to 43 percent by 1995 as two other regions, the Yangtse Delta (with 25 percent in 1995) and the Bohai Gulf region (with 19 percent) were beginning to take on some prominence (*SSC*, 1996: 111). These latter two regions may be considered as being at roughly the same stage in their relationship with the Chinese diaspora as was the southeast before the latest wave of investment began in late 1991. Large numbers of relatively small investments are in place, and in favorable conditions these will grow quite rapidly, as they have done in Guangdong and Fujian. However, it is pertinent to note that the southeast, which contains the bulk of foreign investment, is also the source of the vast majority of the Chinese diaspora. The principal diaspora groups, the Cantonese, the Chiu-chow, the Hakka, the Hokkien and the Hainanese, all originate in Guangdong, Fujian or Hainan.

A survey of 400 foreign invested manufacturing firms, which we carried out in four areas in Guangdong and Fujian in 1991, found only six foreign investors who were not ethnic Chinese. Over a fifth of those in Guangdong and around a third of those in Fujian were from Taiwan (supporting the view that official figures under-estimate their presence). There were also twenty Southeast Asian Chinese and eleven American Chinese (who would be recorded in statistics just by country of origin).

Reasons for the Chinese diaspora investors' predominance in China

The generally poor performance of non-Chinese investment in China has not been from want of interest or effort. Non-Chinese investors have often reported the difficulties of operating in China whether Western, Japanese or Korean. Language barriers, incompatible management styles, unreliable workers who cannot be sacked, red tape and an unpredictable legal and regulatory environment have often been cited to explain their tardy entry Problems in dealing with the central authorities are legendary: negotiations dragging on interminably; new demands at the eleventh hour; the interventions of competing ministries and authorities; new conditions introduced retrospectively; the excessive costs of setting up in major centers, in particular in Shanghai and Beijing; and the unattractiveness of many of the joint-venture partners, many of them cash-strapped state dinosaurs, proposed by the authorities. Conflicts with workers and with the authorities have erupted and projects have been blocked or withdrawn (Lever-Tracy *et al.* 1996: 194). Western companies have still not overcome these difficulties, although there are signs that by the mid-1990s the Japanese are beginning to find their way around them (Peng 1996: 3).

How have the Chinese diaspora managed to avoid these severe difficulties?

First of all it is important to note that most Chinese diaspora investments are well away from the older established industrial areas with the majority in smaller cities, townships and villages where they have been able to deal with a much lower level of government. They can do this by keeping their initial investment small and so within the level of decision-making competence of the local officials. They have thus been able to avoid much of the bureaucratic red tape that covers the larger investments, by avoiding both central and provincial government scrutiny.

They have also tended to avoid entanglements with state sector companies and, as a result of the location of their investments, been able to recruit workforces that have little or no tradition of industrial employment or the iron rice bowl conditions that apply in the state sector.

This orientation away from the established industrial areas and from state sector companies has been crucial. Where Chinese diaspora investments have been made in places where the state sector is still strong or in joint ventures with large state companies or where the project is large enough or important enough to attract Beijing's interest, they have often fared little better than their Western or Japanese counterparts.

This is where the scale of the investment has become crucial, for it is often only possible to deal directly with the local government in the townships and villages if the initial investment is kept small. For a long time the size of projects within the local government competence was only US$1 m (it has now risen to US$10 m). Initially, small investments, however, could be multiplied, expanded or consolidated later. Many of these have grown rapidly, in some cases employing thousands of workers within a few years. Such township and village governments have generally improving finances and even the wealth to become foreign investors in their own right in some cases, and offer greenfield industrial sites.

Most Western and Japanese companies, on the other hand, make their initial contacts at the level of ministries, provincial government or the larger municipalities, like Shanghai, Beijing or Tianjin. All these have pressing problems of their own, in particular the need to find new sources of government revenue and to find joint-venture partners for ailing state companies under their control. They are therefore likely to strike hard bargains out of sheer necessity and thereafter to be constantly forced to seek new concessions. There are, of course, examples of profitable alliances with state sector companies, but going through official channels is fraught with danger and there are numerous traps for the unwary and inexperienced.

The ability of the Chinese diaspora to deal directly with local governments in the areas where domestic economic reform is at its strongest is at the heart of the Chinese diaspora success in China. It is also a clear illustration of one of the ways in which advantage has passed from scale to flexibility in the post-Fordist world.

Networks

The Chinese diaspora have been able to gain the advantage because operating flexibly and informally and on a small scale closely resembles their normal business practices. Chinese business tends to be conducted through a series of personalized networks based on friendship and trust, which are given substance by long-term relationships and reputation for trustworthiness and reliability, rather than in the open marketplace or in an institutional framework.

What makes these networks such an advantageous framework for doing business is their overlapping nature. There is not one Chinese diaspora network but many, based initially on things like language groups, clan associations or place of origin, or alternatively on old school or university friends, but given substance over time by business association. Business people are often members of more than one network and can pass members from one network to another; the new member frequently being accepted on the personal guarantee of the member introducing and vouching for them. The strength of these networks is also their capacity for extension to new members in new places.

Networks are an essential part of the Chinese diaspora success in China. Getting to the local official in a township or village, who can open the necessary doors, can be achieved through them. Connections within the diaspora, back to ancestral villages, towns and cities have thus suddenly become a critical business advantage. Once one person has established a good business and a personal relationship with local officials, there are few obstacles to new introductions. Local officials can introduce investors to known officials in other townships, who are part of their network. As long as nobody breaks their word, the extension of the network and its business advantages knows few limits. On the other side, as well as introducing new potential investors to the township, the established Chinese diaspora business people may assist the local township government with investments and bank credit in Hong Kong and beyond.

The enormous strength of the Chinese diaspora business networking is the ability to make horizontal linkages when the vertical hierarchical structures are not necessarily supportive of their business endeavors (Lever-Tracy et al. 1996). The inadequate legal system and the bureaucratic nightmare of negotiating with communist party officials, often unsure of their own or their superiors' attitude to economic reform, can thus be overcome in the same way as were discriminatory policies against Chinese businesses in Southeast Asia in the past.

It is this ability to utilize and more importantly extend networks, which explains the way the Chinese diaspora have been able to expand their operations beyond the home and ancestral villages, without the need to pass through and become entangled in official channels, and why the bulk of their investments can continue to be made well away from the major centers of political power. Their predominant position among foreign investors springs not from the size of their investments but from the sheer number and continuing multiplication of small and medium-sized investments throughout coastal China.

The China network of the Sino-Indonesian Oei family

One clear example of the way in which networks provide an advantage in China can be seen in the widespread operations of the Sino-Indonesian Oei family in China.

One network has led them back to their place of origin in Quanzhou in the Fujian province, where they now have extensive interests. A second network links the eldest son of the family, Oei Hong-leong, back to old comrades in adversity in other parts of China. Sent to University in China in the mid-1960s, he became caught up in the Cultural Revolution and as the son of bourgeois parents was rusticated to the countryside in Shanxi province. Fellow victims from the Shanxi experience, many of them now high-ranking party officials, constitute a crucial part of his network in China and have led his company, China Strategic Management, to extensive investments in Shanxi province, Zhejiang province and in Dalian, in Liaoning province (*Jetro China Newsletter* 102, January 1993).

This is a strategy that is very difficult for non-Chinese investors without personal connections to replicate. Even if a connection is made, credibility and reputation must then be built up and this takes time. It is clearly the ability of the Chinese diaspora to move quickly and decisively, on the basis of a past accumulation of trust, which is also part of their competitive advantage. Finally, insofar as most diaspora Chinese business remains based on personal entrepreneurship, when the right connection is made a decision can be made quickly between principals without the need to report back to superiors, a luxury that few Western or Japanese company executives are granted.

The surveys we conducted with almost entirely ethnic Chinese investors in Guangdong and Fujian bear out this argument. The ventures largely involved small investments, four-fifths of them under US$5 m (in total value, including the share of any Chinese partner) and with a majority under US$1 m in two of the four areas. Nearly half in three areas and two-thirds in the fourth employed fewer than 200 workers. While many investors were reported as being themselves of small or medium size, even large ones had chosen the route of small projects with 70 percent of larger investors in projects capitalized at under US$5 m and substantial minorities of them in projects of under US$1 m. That this was an investment strategy rather than an expression of their limited commitment, is indicated by the fact that most of these larger investors had more than one project in China, often in the same location.

The Chinese diaspora and economic reform in China

In the introduction we suggested that the Chinese diaspora has become a major factor in the continuation of the economic reform process in China, contributing to the development of the southeast as a powerhouse of economic growth and playing a central role in exports. Their impact on China has to be understood in terms of their partnership with and reinforcement of the forces for change in the localities. If the Chinese diaspora have been able to save the economic reform process, at least in part, from its own contradictions, it has been by bypassing the problems of the bureaucracy and the state sector and linking up with lower level authorities, who welcome their contribution to local job creation, access to technology and marketing channels. The success and contribution of the Chinese diaspora therefore depends as much on their ability to link up with other dynamic forces released by the decentralizing economic reform process as on their own entrepreneurial talents.

The township and village governments were encouraged to turn to industrial activity and to trade and profit from their products, after agricultural decollectivization in the late 1970s. At this level, below that of county government, they are not subject to central planning mechanisms (nor do they benefit from subsidies). Both productivity and production have increased more in such rural than in urban industry, and while in 1978 they accounted for only 9 percent of China's industrial output, this had risen to 19 percent in 1985 and then to 30 percent in 1990 and 42 percent in 1993 (Zweig 1991: 720; Yan 1995: 8–9). The outcome has been a substantial narrowing of the urban rural gap in wage levels, living standards and poverty rates (Chai 1992: 741; Zhang 1992: 86–87).

It is to those areas where the collective sector is most prominent, not only in the southeast but in Jiangsu, Zhejiang and Shandong, that the Chinese diaspora investment is now increasingly drawn. After Guangdong and Fujian, these three provinces had the largest numbers of foreign invested enterprises by the end of 1993 and in each case the pace of foreign investment had accelerated rapidly since 1992 (*SSC*, 1994:76). It therefore becomes clear why investment is drawn to these areas, as it was to the southeast rather than to those places that the Beijing authorities are most anxious to promote, in particular Shanghai and the industrial northeast. This is because of the availability of suitable business partners and local officials who can make their own decisions, admittedly within prescribed limits, without constantly having to worry unduly about higher authorities and their plans and constraints. Once the initial difficulties were sorted out, mostly involving mutual suspicion, the Chinese diaspora and local government officials made excellent business partners. The former are made up of essentially self-made men and women who make their own decisions, while the latter, recently granted previously unheard of autonomy, came in many cases to revel in their ability to make decisions based on rational criteria at the local level.

This is the strength of the partnership: decisions can be made quickly by those to be most closely affected by the outcomes. It is also noteworthy, and this comes from observation, that the quality of many mayors of local townships is quite outstanding and compares very favorably with officials at higher levels.

The Chinese diaspora are important for the local authorities in the first instance because they bring much needed employment to underemployed rural and semi-rural populations. As joint-venture partners they also provide the means of importing technology without the foreign currency constraint and the official permissions needed if local collective sector firms tried to do it independently. Also they often provide partners for local companies who have reached their limits based on domestic demand and existing technology, by providing the possibility of a new orientation towards export markets, which can take advantage of the economies of scale and the new partner's marketing channels. Foreign partners and an export orientation also mean an increasing emphasis on the quality of the product to meet international standards, which will also pay dividends in domestic markets in the future. Joint ventures with foreign partners also mean that the company is formally privatized and thus has to be managed according to market criteria, which permits internal reform of the enterprise.

Face to face interviews with managers of previously collective enterprise confirm the importance of all these factors. In Quanzhou, for example, local managers of previously collective (urban) enterprises now in joint ventures with Chinese diaspora entrepreneurs, repeatedly emphasized the importance, for the success of their business, of their new found freedom from city government restrictions on their ability to make rapid product line changes and on the gaining of export licenses. Last, the local economy gains from the wages paid to workers and the possibility of providing inputs to the new industries, while the local government gains from the taxes and fees for service paid by the new partnerships and wholly foreign-owned companies. Large numbers of small- and medium-sized investments in the locality also mean that none are strong enough to hold the local government to ransom in the way a large multinational might.

The role model for the emerging social forces in China, which the Chinese diaspora provide, should not be underestimated in any consideration of their contribution to the economic reform process. In a country that suffered from "gigantism" in the Maoist period, and in which the top 1 percent of firms still produces 34 percent of industrial output after 17 years of economic reform (down from 65 percent in 1985) (*CSY*, 1996: 401), the model of the small dynamic company that can compete effectively in world markets, provides a radical and appropriate departure from the past. It is appropriate because it provides a model that the emerging social forces unleashed by economic reform can hope to emulate. That they are already seeking to do so is now readily visible to the visitor to the more vigorous townships in the Pearl River Delta and is increasingly apparent in southern Fujian. As the Chinese diaspora spread into new areas, it is likely that this phenomenon will become more pronounced. It is also appropriate in that it suggests that the way forward for the ambitious is through self-help and initiative rather than through position and rank, thus helping to dispel some of the cultural baggage of the past.

The importance of the Chinese diaspora for the process of economic reform is also in carrying further into China the "Guangdong model," of decentralized economic development based on small- to medium-sized, labor intense manufacturing and an orientation to export markets. Such a model provides increased opportunities for the collective sector to increase production by re-orienting itself towards international markets and the improved quality of products that this necessitates. With increasing difficulties in the state sector, the process of economic reform and development itself appears to depend more and more now on the township and village enterprises and the foreign invested companies. Fortunately for China their increasing cooperation on a wider scale than the southeast already seems to be eventuating.

In our surveys we found that a substantial majority of investors were in joint-venture partnerships. What is of central importance for the ability of these diaspora investors to establish a synergy with the dynamic forces on the ground is the nature of the mainland partner chosen. Private partners were in fact found in only negligible proportions in two of the survey areas, in 13 percent of ventures in the third and in 50 percent in the SEZ.

The most common choice was a township or village enterprise owned by a local government, or such a local government body itself (at the level at which state plans and subsidies ceased to apply). In the three non-SEZ areas such bodies constituted over 70 percent of mainland partners. What is particularly noteworthy is that the larger investors had sought the same kind of partners. While 73 percent of the China partners of small investors were at the township and village level, this was also the case for 65 percent of larger investors. Even more striking was the avoidance by both large and small investors of partnerships with higher levels of government. Central or provincial government-owned enterprises or bodies as partners were negligible in three areas and only 13 percent in the SEZ, while even government bodies at city, district or county level were partners in under a fifth of the ventures.

This approach seems to have generally served its purpose well. Complaints about government inefficiency and bureaucracy featured quite strongly among respondents in the SEZ, which comes under the central government, despite its supposedly carefully fostered open environment for foreign investors. In the other three areas, however, such complaints were scarcely mentioned. On the other hand, such partnerships, even with the lowest levels of the local government, had given small as well as large investors access to loans from banks in China. Overall 48 percent of those with China partners and 42 percent with the township and village partners, but only 28 percent of the wholly foreign owned, had obtained such credit.

Impact of the China link on
the Chinese diaspora business world

The most obvious impact of the move into China for the Chinese diaspora is the enormous increase in their industrial capacity that has been made possible. At the end of 1993, Chinese diaspora-owned enterprises and joint ventures employed around five and a half million workers in Guangdong and one and a half million in Fujian (*FSY*, 1993: 357; 1994: 307; *SYG*, 1994: 327). With these southeastern provinces representing roughly half their capital investments in China, we could therefore reasonably project a workforce in China of 14 m at the end of 1993. With 1994 already shaping up as another bumper year for foreign investment, we could conservatively expect this number to have increased to around 18–20 m by the end of 1994.

Approaching this in another way, we could consider the case of Hong Kong. In 1985, just as the Pearl River Delta was being opened to foreign capital, the manufacturing sector employed 950,000, the highest figure on record. As a result of the movement of many manufacturing industries, particularly the more labor intense, into China, this figure had fallen to just under 500,000 in 1994. However, by the same time, the Hong Kong industry employed, at a conservative estimate, 4 m workers in Guangdong alone. The manufacturing capacity of Hong Kong's entrepreneurs has increased at least four fold in the last ten years, quite an enormous change. In addition there are 55,000 or so small local firms in Guangdong subcontracting to Hong Kong companies (Overholt 1993: 189–91). What is more, the export statistics show that they have won an increased share of the world markets for their increased output.

The effect on the Taiwanese has also been far from insignificant. With more than 20,000, largely manufacturing, firms operating in China, according to official data (probably a considerable underestimate), they must employ at least 3 m workers, doubling their industrial workforce and productive capacity in Taiwan itself. The move into China clearly represents much more than just a restructuring of the economies of Hong Kong and Taiwan, but also an enormous increase in total industrial capacity. The opening of China has permitted the Chinese diaspora to increase their productive capacity exponentially, and thus their relative position within world capitalism.

Hong Kong itself has indeed also been restructured to cope with the enormous increase in trade volumes pouring out of and into China since 1985. Based on the increases in the entrepot trade with China, Hong Kong has risen to the seventh largest trading economy in the world by the mid-1990s with an international trade volume of US$274 bn in 1993 (*ADB*, 1993: 166; *SCMP*, 11/5–6/1994: 11; *SWB FEW*/0352, 9/28/1994: WG/3). While banking, shipping, port and container and insurance services have multiplied, the most remarkable growth, has been in small marketing organizations: from around 14,000 in 1985 to more than 89,000 by the end of 1992 (*SCMP*, 7/2/1994: B2). The growth of employment in this sector, despite the small size of the average firm, 6–8 employees, has been more than enough by itself to offset the job losses in manufacturing in the same period. Basically, Hong Kong's manufacturing is now done in China while the "city state" concentrates on strategic planning, management, design, research and marketing and the services these require.

The movement of large sections of Hong Kong and Taiwan's economies into China and the fact that the products are essentially marketed via Hong Kong, raises a number of questions about the bases of political and economic analysis in this increasingly globalized world. The problem is that political and economic space no longer coincide and the nation state may not always be the most appropriate unit of economic analysis. Nowhere is this more apparent than in the relationship between the Chinese diaspora and China. The economies of China, Hong Kong and Taiwan increasingly overlap and it is not a particularly useful task to try to separate them. Certainly, what makes the least sense is to see them as three separate economies. The economic overlap between these three political entities is, however, only the most obvious and most rapidly developing example of what is happening elsewhere in the region.

The expansion of Singapore's economy into the Malaysian state of Johor and the Indonesian island of Batam is another clear example. The encouragement of growth triangles and even quadrangles suggests that even nationalist developmentalist states see the potential in allowing dynamic economies with surplus capital but which lack space and opportunities for further profitable and productive investments, to expand beyond political borders into adjoining regions. These offer space and new labor forces for entrepreneurs and work and opportunities for previously underemployed rural workforces. Economies can no longer be contained within national boundaries, but neither is globalization the uncontested playing ground of Western and Japanese transnational corporations.

If increased capacity has been a major outcome of the move into China so has increased scale. One of the major features of the last decade in East Asia has been the emergence of a large number of what can now only be described as transnational companies from the Chinese business world. Their entry into China has, of course, not been the only factor in this phenomenon but there can also be little doubt that it has been crucial in a substantial number of cases.

One of the most striking examples in this respect has been the rise of the Charoen Pokphand group. Emerging from Thailand into the regional economy in the mid-1980s, they are now among the largest investors in China with more than seventy operational projects. Their net revenue from these investments exceeds US$500 m per annum. They also have major investments in Indonesia, Taiwan and Hong Kong in the region, and in Turkey and the United States beyond. With three listed companies in Hong Kong they have used the opportunities presented by China's need for industrial modernization to diversify well beyond their agribusiness base in Thailand into motorcycle manufacturing, brewing, retailing, petrol refining and distribution and into telecommunications. The result is that the controlling Chearavanont family has come from relative obscurity to be ranked among the richest business families in the world by both Fortune and Forbes Magazine in the 1990s (*Time*, 5/10/1994; *BRW*, 7/25/1994).

Another emerging multinational is the Lippo Group. Until the mid-1980s its principal asset appeared to be its 17.5 percent holding in the Bank of Central Asia in Indonesia, which it managed for the principal shareholder Liem Sioe-leong. In 1984 it diversified into Hong Kong by acquiring the Hong Kong Chinese Bank from the Bangkok Bank Group for US$40 m. Since then it has grown into a major regional conglomerate with assets now exceeding US$2.5 bn. It has used its connections in the Fujian province to diversify into a major infrastructure contractor with several major projects underway, and to develop a large international tourist resort. Other China ventures outside Fujian include cement manufacturing, property development and a joint-venture bank. In Hong Kong its principal activities are property development and banking. In Hong Kong it has formed a number of powerful alliances: first with Li Ka-shing, now a minority shareholder in the Hong Kong group, and with two mainland organizations, China Resources, the trading arm of the Ministry of Foreign Trade (MOFTEC) and China Travel Service, with a view to regional cooperation. By 1994 it had seven companies listed on the Jakarta stock exchange and four listed in Hong Kong and an international organization with operations ranging from the United States to Australia (*Lippo Annual Report*, 1993; *Corporate International June*, 1994; *The Economist*, 7/16/1994: 63–4).

Champion Technology of Hong Kong represents a different kind of success story. Founded in 1987, it developed the world's first multilingual radio paging system and pager, now marketed under the brand name Kantone. It now operates paging networks in fifteen Mainland Chinese cities with more than 300,000 subscribers. It has recently entered a joint venture to extend its system to India and has acquired one of the British pioneers of paging services, Multitone. Its latest China joint venture involves moving into the development of two-way messaging in China using low-orbit satellites. Its rapid rise is due almost entirely to the China market, which in 1992 provided 88 percent of its revenue and the springboard for its launch into other markets (*Corporate International June*, 1994: 36–7).

While these few examples can do little justice to the numerous changes in the scale of operations among the Chinese diaspora groups, they are not untypical and we could have cited many other examples. Our own surveys of smaller ventures are in accord with this picture. Many of them had grown substantially since commencement and the longer they had been operating, the more this was the case. Seventy percent of the ventures had plans for further expansion and over 80 percent of investors interviewed expressed optimism about prospects in China. None were planning to withdraw or to contract.

What is perhaps most interesting is that despite all the fears in Southeast Asia about capital flight to finance investment in China, Chinese businesses throughout the region has seen an unprecedented boom since 1985, evidenced by economic growth rates, share flotations, acquisitions and new activities, including riding out the world recession of 1990–3 as though it never happened, and this precisely since China was effectively opened to foreign investment, clear evidence that both China and the regional economies are now feeding off each other.

Conclusion

In August 1994, the China News Agency in Taipei (CNA) announced that based on 1993 data, international trade conducted by the three Chinese economies, China, Hong Kong and Taiwan, accounted for 8.5 percent of world trade, up 1.1 percent in 1992. The data also showed that for the first time the international trade of the three economies had exceeded that of Japan. They also expected the three economies to control 10 percent of world trade by the end of 1994. Individually, the three economies ranked eighth (Hong Kong, 3.72 percent), eleventh (China, 2.62 percent) and fourteenth (Taiwan, 2.16 percent) in 1993 with trade totaling US$636 bn against Japan's US$602 bn (*SWB FEW*/0355, 10/19/1994: WG/3).

This growing economic integration, recognized and commented on by a very unlikely source, is a clear indicator that economics and politics are no longer seen as necessarily linked. The Taiwanese state is no closer to resolving its political differences with Beijing and therefore does not see this economic integration as implying even political rapprochement let alone unity. Likewise, Hong Kong's future usefulness to China will depend less on political integration than on continuing economic autonomy. The logic of seeing these three economies as no longer separate is increasingly evident even, in the case of Taiwan, to the Chinese state's most uncompromising political opponent. The fact that economic integration does not mean political integration, however, does not mean that this economic integration has no implications for the international political economy. The growing trading power of the Chinese economies coupled with the capital resources, industrial capacity and regional business networks of the Chinese diaspora means that any prospects for Japanese economic hegemony in the region are ruled out. If this was ever a realistic prospect, its time has long since passed.

The strength of the Chinese diaspora is their ability to operate within and without China equally effectively. China's industrial renaissance has depended substantially on Chinese diaspora investment and entrepreneurship and will continue to do so for the foreseeable future. Equally, China's international trading position has relied heavily on the performance of the southeastern provinces, Guangdong and Fujian, and the Chinese diaspora marketing channels in Hong Kong. This is not going to change quickly. The idea that Shanghai can replace Hong Kong as the major financial and international trading centre for China's ongoing economic revolution is essentially political wishful thinking. What makes Hong Kong so important for China is its critical mass of accumulated expertise and credibility. At the same time, China remains a principal outlet for investment capital for the Chinese diaspora and the principal means of increasing their industrial and trading capacities profitably. Provided the business environment, therefore, remains reasonably attractive, at least in some regions in China, and there is little reason to think it will not, then Chinese diaspora investment is likely to continue to flow in that direction. The synergy created between economic reform in China and Chinese diaspora entrepreneurship and capital has reshaped the regional political economy in less than a decade: there is no reason to think it will not continue to do so, to the benefit of the whole region.

9 April 2001

Postscript

With hindsight the authors are surprised by the extent to which the analysis presented here, and the trends described, have stood the test of time. Since it was written the Asian crisis has come and gone, Hong Kong has returned to China and major political turmoil has overturned governments around the region. Nonetheless, the Chinese economy and its exports have continued to grow despite the continuing problems of its state-owned sector, still driven by the dynamic alliance of the Chinese diaspora investors and local private and collective township and village enterprises.

Since we wrote, the entire East Asian region has been hit by a financial crisis which began in 1997, the consequences of which continue to grip parts of the region, particularly Japan and Southeast Asia. Throughout the crisis China remained a bastion of stability largely as a result of two factors: its strong external account reflected in export surpluses, FDI flows and foreign currency reserves; and the Keynesian-type policies pursued throughout the crisis by the government to ensure that domestic demand remained at reasonable levels. The result was that China maintained economic growth rates of 6–8 percent throughout the crisis and remained stable when much of the rest of the region had dropped into negative territory and near-depression economic conditions.

By the end of the decade, the Chinese state-owned sector was responsible for no more than 30 percent of industrial output (*China Statistical Yearbook*, 2000) and the need for its restructuring continued to exert pressure on the Chinese government. At the same time, the collective sector of town and village enterprises, the private sector and the foreign-invested sector, in which the Chinese diaspora-invested enterprises continued to contribute more than half of all new investment, continued to grow at rates above the national average.

In 2000, China's exports reached US$249 bn, having grown more than 27 percent in that year. While it is unlikely that this rate of growth can be maintained, China has now clearly established itself among the world's leading trade-oriented economies. What was more significant from the point of view of our analysis, was that the foreign-invested sector, which includes joint-ventures, contributed no less than 48 percent of this substantial total. Small domestic firms in the collective sector contributed more than 20 percent of the balance. With the southern provinces of Guangdong and Fujian producing close to half this total, it was also clear that the Chinese diaspora firms and their commercial allies in China were continuing to lead this export charge (*China's Customs Statistics Monthly*, 12, 2000).

A word needs to be added about the role of Taiwan both in the crisis and in China. Along with China, Taiwan was the only other East Asian economy to maintain positive growth throughout the regional crisis. What was more important, however, was the growing recognition of the massive industrial restructuring that had taken place in Taiwan. The IT industry had clearly become the key industrial sector by the late 1990s. Taiwanese corporations had also become key elements in the revival of the US computer industry, providing not only key components but also a large part of the research and design of new products. Another important factor was that Taiwanese entrepreneurs were starting to move substantial parts of their IT manufacturing to China. A large IT component industry composed substantially of Taiwanese firms, some 800 at the last count, was located in Dongguan in the Guangdong Province. This new industry complemented a domestic IT industry in nearby Shenzhen, this along with Beijing are the two key areas for IT

Research and Development in China. This transformation confirmed Taiwan as the technology center of the Chinese diaspora economy.

Notes

1 The surveys referred to in this chapter were funded by the Asia Research Centre, Murdoch University and by the East Asia Analytic Unit of the Department of Foreign Affairs and Trade (Australia). They were designed and analyzed by social scientists at Flinders University in South Australia and at the University of Queensland. The team worked in close cooperation with a group at the China Business Centre at the Hong Kong Polytechnic. Interviewers were professional social scientists from Chinese research institutes or universities with whom the team had had some contact in the course of their initial research. All had previous experience in conducting surveys. The four areas were chosen for their diversity and the presence of good contacts there. Within the areas respondents were chosen randomly from lists of foreign funded firms held by local government bodies. Findings have been published in East Asia Analytic Unit (1995) and in Lever-Tracy *et al.* (1996).

2 This paper was first published in 1997 in "Konfuzianischer Kapitalismus," a reader on the Chinese overseas compiled by Thomas Menkhoff on behalf of the German Foundation for International Development (DSE) (Wald ed. 1997). It is reproduced here without alteration, but with a short supplement at the end, which places it in the context of the changes of the last five years.

Bibliography

Primary sources in Chinese

CCSM (*China's Customs Statistics Monthly*).
CSY (*China Statistical Yearbook*). Various years.
FSY (*Fujian's Statistical Yearbook*). Various years.
International Trade News (MOFTEC).
SCB (State Commerce Bureau) (1993) *FDI in China: Analysis of Trends and Future Directions*, Beijing.
SSC (*A Statistical Survey of China*). Various years.
SYG (*Statistical Yearbook of Guangdong*). Various years.

Primary sources in English

The Australian.
ADB (Asian Development Bank) (1993) and (1994) *Annual Reports*.
Beijing Review.
BRW (*Business Review Weekly*).
Corporate International *Company Handbook – Hong Kong*. Various years.
East Asia Analytic Unit (DFAT, Australia) (1995) *Overseas Chinese Business Networks in Asia*, Canberra: AGPS.
The Economist.
Indonesia Development News.

Jetro China Newsletter.
Lippo Annual Report.
Nikkei Weekly.
SCMP (South China Morning Post).
SCMP IE (South China Morning Post International Edition Weekly).
SMP (Sunday Morning Post).
SWB FEW (Summary of World Broadcasts, Far East Weekly). Economic Series, BBC London.
Time.

Secondary sources

Chai, J. (1992) Consumption and Living Standards in China, *The China Quarterly*, 131, September.

Chan, M.-H. and Zhu, W. (1994) The Hong Kong–Taiwan–South Korea Factor in China's Exports and Its Impact. China Business Centre, Hong Kong Polytechnic, Working Paper No. 2 (in Chinese).

Lever-Tracy, C., Ip, D. and Tracy, N. (1996) *The Chinese Diaspora and Mainland China: An Emerging Economic Synergy*, Houndmills: Macmillan and New York: St. Martin's Press.

Overholt, W. (1993) *The Rise of China: How Economic Reform is Creating a New Superpower*, New York: Norton.

Peng, F.-C. and Chan, E. (1996) Japanese Spearhead Move to Yangtse Valley, *Sunday Morning Post*, 18 August.

Yan, S. (1995) Export-Oriented Rural Enterprises, *Jetro China Newsletter*, September–October.

Zhang, X. (1992) Urban Rural Isolation and its Impact on China's Production and Trade Pattern, *China Economic Review*, 3/1.

Zhang, X. and Tracy, N. (1994) The Third Foreign Investment Wave in Mainland China: Origins, Features and Implications. Asia Research Centre, Murdoch University, Working Paper No. 34.

Zweig, D. (1991) Internationalising China's Countryside: The Political Economy of Exports from Rural Industry, *The China Quarterly*, 128.

4

CHINESE ENTREPRENEURSHIP AND RESILIENT NATIONAL DEVELOPMENT

How "Web-based Chinese
Management" can help the growth of
China's multiple ownership economy

Kai-Alexander Schlevogt

Introduction

The overseas Chinese entrepreneurs are stars, but not well-known ones. Across generations of immigrants, they have produced sparkling economic wonders in many Southeast Asian countries. They control an enormous share of economic assets, which is disproportionate to their numbers, and managed to produce more billionaires per capita than any other ethnic group. Even during the Asian economic crisis, they fared better than many other businesses. Their success and pursuits are usually not well publicized. They prefer to operate in industries without glamor, engaging in businesses that other entrepreneurs avoid. Further they do not usually write their biographies, telling the world about their great achievements.

In contrast to the overseas success story, conventional wisdom tells us that the Chinese on the mainland are a different breed. We all know the images of the lazy factory worker in state-owned enterprises (SOEs) and the heaps of unwanted goods they produce. This casts into doubt ethnic theories of Chinese economic success.

Recently, the winds have changed in China. This article examines whether the emerging new private management model in Mainland China can help the growth of Mainland China's entire economy in a resilient fashion. The key point is that a new model that I call "Web-based Chinese Management" (WCM), read-opted from the overseas Chinese, will not only contribute to the further success of private enterprises, but can also be used to revitalize the ailing state-owned sector. These positive effects are not due to Chinese ethnicity *per se*, but stem from the combination of the behavior it generates and the right environment for such behavior to be successful. The result of the economic transformation might be a new capitalist order, called "network economy." Given that Chinese entrepreneurship can now prosper in an interconnected way both overseas and on the mainland, there is strong potential for a regional Chinese economic powerhouse to emerge, which might also have the political ability to project and enforce its political clout and Eastern values far beyond the motherland.

This article is organized in four sections. I will first discuss the readoption of the overseas Chinese organizational model on the mainland and its role in the development of the private and state sectors. Afterwards, I will elaborate on the emergence of a new capitalist order and transnational ethnic powerhouse, which may result from the transfer of ideas and other resources.

China awakens – the renaissance of traditional organization and culture in Mainland China

The web-based Chinese Management (WCM) theory

Recent research (Schlevogt 1999a, 2002) has shown that the new entrepreneurs in Mainland China have readopted a traditional Chinese organizational model, which I call "Web-based Chinese Management" (WCM) (Schlevogt 1999b). It closely resembles the model that is practiced in many overseas Chinese private businesses (Redding 1990; Hamilton 1991; Whitley 1994). It is characterized by distinctive structural choices and management practices, as well as an emphasis on traditional Chinese culture and small company size. The WCM model is illustrated in Figure 4.1. Its individual elements and empirical significance are discussed below.

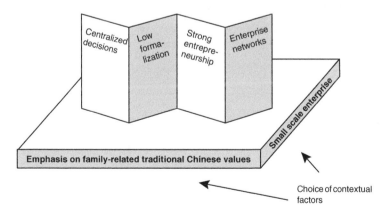

Figure 4.1 The WCM model.

Distinctive Chinese organizational structure

In terms of organizational structure, the WCM model has two distinctive characteristics: high centralization and low bureaucracy (compared to state enterprises).

High centralization There is a high degree of centralization of power in the hands of one autocratic entrepreneur. He is usually the founder and owner, a phenomenon that has been termed "dictatorship by the owner-manager" (Montagu-Pollock 1991: 23).

Low degree of bureaucracy The degree of formalization, specialization, standardization of control systems and integration is very low. In addition, there is a distinctive lack of a well-designed organizational hierarchy. Formal needs of control are less important, given that the CEO exerts personal control.

Empirical survey research comprising interviews with 124 CEOs in Beijing and Shanghai conducted by the author has revealed the structural distinctiveness of private enterprises in Mainland China (Schlevogt 1999a, 2001, 2002). Half of the random sample were state enterprises, the other half were private firms. The measures employed included well-validated structure scales from the Aston research (Inkson *et al.* 1970; Pugh and Hickson 1976) and extensions (Miller and Droege 1986), managerial measures (Khandwalla 1977; Venkatraman 1989), as well as several new scales measuring subcontracting relations and the emphasis on traditional Chinese values. Scales were standardized (the maximum score equals 100 percent). In terms of data collection, personal standardized interviews with key informants (Seidler 1974; Phillips 1981) were conducted. The majority of them (85 percent) were CEOs; the rest included several senior vice-presidents. The response rate was 79 percent. The results of the study (see Table 4.1) show that

Table 4.1 Mean difference tests for structural variables between private and state-owned enterprises

Structural dimension	Hypotheses for private enterprises	Findings from mean comparison					
		$\bar{x}$ Private (%)	$\bar{x}$ State (%)	$\Delta\bar{x}$	t-value	df	Result
Formalization	Lower	44.2	74.2	−30.0*	−6.4***	81	√
Specialization	Lower	62.5	77.7	−15.2	−2.8**	99	√
Control	Lower	62.6	66.7	−4.1*	−1.3	96	√?
Integration	Lower	47.5	64.7	−17.2	−5.1***	99	√
Centralization	Higher	63.2	57.6	5.6	2.2*	99	√

Notes
•$p < 0.05$; ••$p < 0.01$; •••$p < 0.001$ (two tailed).
* Levene's test significant, therefore inequal variance t-test used.
$\bar{x}$ = mean and $\Delta\bar{x}$ = mean difference.

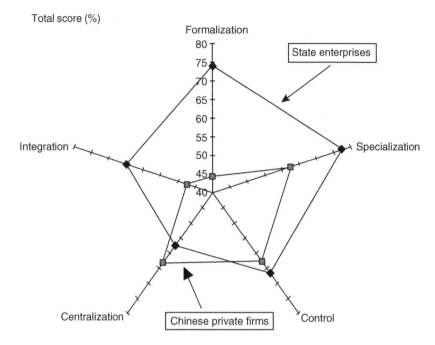

Total score (%)

Figure 4.2 Comparison of structural profiles between private enterprises and SOEs.

state enterprises are significantly more structured than private firms. The different profiles for private Chinese enterprises and SOEs are illustrated in Figure 4.2.

Distinctive Chinese management practices

With regard to management practices, WCM has two distinctive characteristics: strong entrepreneurship and intricate firm networks.

Entrepreneurship   Chinese private enterprises tend to follow proactive and aggressive strategies, and adopt a flexible leadership style and entrepreneurial decision-making.

Firm networks   The focal firms usually have extensive firm networks. They vary in their degree of formality. By "proliferating" or "spawning" instead of try-ing to grow in size, many Chinese enterprises facilitate close ties with family members, who might otherwise search for employment elsewhere.

Empirical research (Schlevogt 1999a, 2002) has largely supported the dis-tinctive managerial choices of Mainland Chinese private firms. The research methods were described above. Additional case studies underlined the existence of informal intricate webs, which could not be fully captured by the formal subcontracting scale alone. The results of the study are shown in Table 4.2 and illustrated in Figure 4.3.

Table 4.2 Managerial differences between private enterprises and SOEs

Managerial dimension	Hypotheses for private enterprises	Findings from mean comparison					
		$\bar{x}$ Private (%)	$\bar{x}$ State (%)	$\Delta\bar{x}$	t-value	df	Result
Aggressive strategy	Higher	61.2	55.4	5.8	1.3	99	√?
Analytic strategy	Lower	72.2	81.1	−8.9*	−2.1˙	83	√
Defensive strategy	Lower	63.2	78.7	−15.5	−3.6˙˙˙˙	99	√
Futurity strategy	Higher	61.8	68.5	−6.7*	−2.4˙	95	X
Proactive strategy	Higher	76.1	81.0	−4.9	−1.3	99	X
Risk strategy	Higher	44.7	47.5	−2.8	−1.0	99	X
Participative leadership	Lower	50.8	71.1	−20.3*	−4.0˙˙˙	89	√
Flexible leadership	Higher	68.2	66.5	1.7*	0.4	78	√?
Coercive leadership	Higher	59.3	48.8	10.5	2.7˙˙	99	√
Vertical communication	Higher	63.2	55.8	7.4*	1.4	85	√?
Adaptive decision-making	Lower	61.1	65.1	−4.0	−0.7	99	√?
Entrepreneurial decision-making	Higher	78.1	64.3	13.8	13.8˙˙	99	√
Planning decision-making	Lower	63.8	72.5	−8.7*	−1.7	87	√?
Subcontracting	Higher	34.8	31.3	3.5	1.2	99	√?

Notes
•$p < 0.05$; ••$p < 0.01$; •••$p < 0.001$ (two tailed).
* Levene's test significant, therefore inequal variance t-test used.
$\bar{x}$ = mean and $\Delta\bar{x}$ = mean difference.

Distinctive Chinese culture and small size

There are two additional contextual elements of WCM, which influence the structural and managerial choices of private Chinese enterprises. They include emphasis on Chinese cultural elements and small organizational size.

Emphasis on Chinese cultural elements   One distinctive characteristic of private Chinese enterprises is the emphasis on family-related values. They include respect for age and hierarchy, group orientation and the importance of trust-based relationships. It is not traditional culture in itself, which acts as an influencing factor, but the emphasis placed on traditional Chinese values by CEOs.

   Small size   Most Chinese private enterprises are relatively small, as measured, for example, by the number of employees and revenues. Their small size is usually not a function of the age of the business. The reason is the CEO's desire to keep the organization in the hands of his family, which would be difficult in the case of

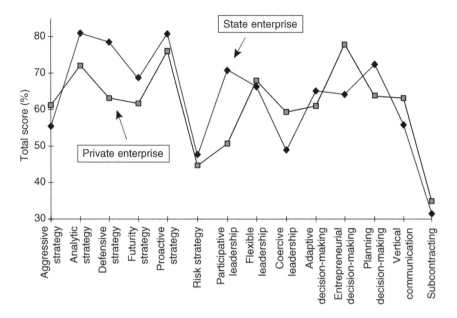

Figure 4.3 Comparison of managerial practices between private enterprises and SOEs.

uninhibited growth. Significant expansion would make it necessary to bring in outside professional managers and often investors, too.

The author's empirical study of Mainland Chinese enterprises supported the distinctiveness of these two contextual factors (see Tables 4.3 and 4.4). The results for culture are graphically illustrated in Figure 4.4. With regard to *guanxi*, further analysis showed that private enterprises emphasize family-based relations, while "simple" *guanxi* are important in SOEs as well. With respect to collectiveness, SOEs also emphasize belonging to the group (the work unit, Chinese: Danwei). The distinguishing feature of private enterprises is the emphasis on belonging to family-based groups. Table 4.4 shows that Chinese private enterprises were significantly smaller than their state-owned counterparts.

Using structural equation modeling, it could be shown that emphasis on Chinese culture was a potent factor influencing the organizational choices of private enterprises, but not those of state enterprises. It had a direct and indirect impact (via its negative association with size, which was in turn significantly related to organizational choices) on structure and management.

Performance implications of WCM

Despite its inherent disadvantages in terms of limits to the growth of the focal organization, which makes it less suitable for industries that require significant

Table 4.3   Mean difference tests between private and state-owned enterprises with regard to "emphasis on culture"

Aspect	Hypotheses for private enterprises	Findings from mean comparison					
		$\bar{x}$ Private (%)	$\bar{x}$ State (%)	$\Delta\bar{x}$	t-value	df	Result
Respect	Higher	84.2	76.7	7.5*	2.0˙	90	√
Guanxi	Higher	86.6	84.1	2.5	0.8	99	√?
Collectiveness	Higher	81.2	83.9	−2.7	−0.7	99	X

Note
$\bar{x}$ = mean and $\Delta\bar{x}$ = mean difference.

Table 4.4 Mean difference tests for size of private and state-owned enterprises

Aspect	Private enterprises					State enterprises					$\Delta\bar{x}$ (log)	
	$\bar{x}$	Med	s	log $\bar{x}$	s	$\bar{x}$	Med	s	log $\bar{x}$	s	t	df
Sales (million)	21	5	51	6.70	0.75	347	95	789	7.80	1.00	6.17˙˙˙	99
Employees	59	20	96	1.46	0.47	12,796	702	76,054	2.85	3.89	9.95˙˙˙	82*

Notes: Sales are denoted in Renminbi (RMB) Yuan.
$\bar{x}$ = mean, $\Delta\bar{x}$ = mean difference, Med = median, and s = standard deviation.

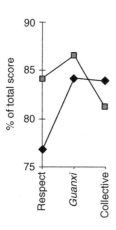

Figure 4.4 Emphasis on Chinese culture.

indivisible economies of scale, the WCM has been very conducive to the company performance of private enterprises on the mainland. So far, there has been only anecdotal evidence for this effectiveness. The author's empirical research (Schlevogt 1999a, 2002) showed for the first time that whereas SOEs destroyed economic value (measured as the spread between return on equity and cost of capital), private enterprises created value. There are three major reasons why private Chinese enterprises usually perform well in a highly uncertain and complex environment in which sensitivity to changing consumer tastes is vital and mass-specialization instead of mass-production important:

Social capital   Chinese family structures generate strong social capital. For the sake of the family, the Chinese study hard, work long hours, labor for less and make more sacrifices than non-family members would do. Since family members usually participate in the capital and are responsible for their own spin-offs, they have additional strong incentives to act as entrepreneurs and to work hard. There is also a strong degree of company loyalty in family members. They are likely to stay with the firm even when better paying opportunities arise elsewhere or at least support the family firms from overseas. Moreover, trust among family members allows for a high degree of secrecy in information-sensitive areas. In addition, conflicts with the "boss" are reduced because of culturally-grounded authority structures in the company that often reflect positions in the family.

Flexibility   There is a high degree of flexibility associated with small firm size, centralized leadership and national, as well as international lineage-based networks. In the Chinese family business, the CEO can make decisions quickly without the need to engage in extensive consensus-building exercises or frustrating authorization processes. Paperwork is negligible. No committee sessions have to be held. Spreadsheets are almost non-existent – calculations are performed in the head based on intuition and experience. Narrow compartmentalization is despised. Employees learn to perform different jobs and can be easily switched from one deployment to another. Subcontracting-based and other more informal enterprise networks help Chinese businessmen access resources quickly.

Cost-efficiency   Given that transactions with other enterprises in the network are based on good faith, transaction costs are very low. Due to the importance of "face," there are a lot of social checks and balances in the task environment to avoid cheating. Given the importance of networks that afford access to resources, investment into working capital and fixed assets is kept low. Because the Chinese entrepreneur is likely to focus on what he can do best, he is less likely to engage in activities for which he does not have the required skills or knowledge and that thus would be less profitable. The company itself incurs little overhead costs, since most transactions are performed outside the company. Thus, no elaborate administrative staff has to be fed. Due to the frugal spirit and mentality of the owner, expensive headquarters, corporate jets, or similar luxury items are rejected. Economy Class substitutes for Ritz-style service.

The emergence of entrepreneurial revolutionaries – WCM and the growth of the private economy

The growth of the private economy in Mainland China since the start of the Gaige Kaifeng (reform and opening) policy is spectacular. The "revolutionary" spirit of Chinese entrepreneurs serves as fuel. In the five-year period from 1994 to 1998 alone, the share of individually owned private enterprises in gross industrial output rose from 10.1 to 16 percent. In 1998, the number of individually owned private enterprises exceeded 6 m, demonstrating the enormous dynamism of this new class of enterprises. With a share of 76 percent in 1998, they accounted for the largest part of the enterprise population in China. Non-SOEs in general, and private enterprises in particular, are also an important engine of job creation. At year-end 1997, the township and village enterprises (TVEs) employed 91.6 m people (13.2 percent of the total workforce), urban collectives 28.8 m (4.1 percent), and urban private enterprises 7.5 m (1.1 percent). There were also 19.2 m self-employed individuals in towns (19.2 percent). Together, the sum of all newly created jobs – somewhat more than the total population of Russia – significantly exceeds the number of people employed in urban SOEs (110.4 m, or 15.9 percent of the total work force). The remainder of workers is rural labor.

The distinctive new management style – readopted in the newly established private Chinese enterprises and reminiscent of overseas Chinese management – *ceteris paribus*, explains the inherent dynamism in the private sector and can well account for much of its resulting rapid growth over time. I thus advocate a microeconomic explanation for the growth of private enterprises, demonstrating the importance of management for economic development. Such a microeconomic explanation seems to be warranted given that factors in the macroenvironment, which in the past has been rather constraining and sometimes even outright hostile, cannot be thought of as fueling the rapid growth. It clarifies how private enterprises were able rather quickly to fill the void of pent-up demand, growing like cactuses in the desert with little outside water. They achieved this growth by spinning intricate enterprise networks, not by growing the focal organization, integrating vertically and horizontally through web links.

The distinctive features of WCM are conducive to enterprise and job creation, as well as enterprise prosperity. The model helps navigation in unstructured, uncertain and complex situations, and to harness the full power of human potential. Centralized charismatic leadership by the owner-dictator results in high speed of decision-making, great flexibility, and clear accountability. Informal structures and entrepreneurial leadership allow for dynamic adaptation to new opportunities. Small company size reinforces this agility. The emphasis on traditional Chinese values, especially familism, creates valuable social capital, which, among other things, helps to reduce costs. This is because the strong ownership incentives lead to a focus on profitability, achieved through responsible housekeeping and efficient cash-management. The implicit contracts are also highly useful in substituting for formal contracts under situations of uncertainty. (Formal contracts would always remain incomplete under such circumstances, because it is impossible to specify all contingencies in advance.) Extensive enterprise webs make it possible to leverage resources from other participants and serve as a seedbed for enterprise and job creation.

I expect that the importance and success of private Chinese enterprises will further increase in the future. The government would be well advised to nurture private enterprises, fostering their continuous growth by removing political constraints instead of necessarily through activist promotion. One example of a trend that will favor their increasing significance is the advent of the Internet in China. With 374 m expected users by the end of the year 2005, it may become the largest net market in the world (*China Daily Business Weekly*, 1999). The Internet is a great economic democratizer in many fields since it levels the playing ground and empowers individuals and small companies. The latter are in an excellent position to take advantage of the new opportunities in a flexible manner, and become the major players on the virtual battleground. Nevertheless, a certain number of private enterprises will fail, mainly when they expand too rapidly without using sophisticated analysis and an appropriate professional governance structure, which large companies need.

Opportunities for public innovators – WCM and SOE reforms

In contrast to the rosy picture of private economic development, Chinese SOEs encounter great difficulties. Useless assets, unwanted products, surplus labor, triangular loans and tremendous losses are piling up. Given the theoretical fallacy of Western macroeconomists' suggestions, their historical failure, as well as the new empirical evidence generated by the author of this study, it is timely to reevaluate current growth and reform policies and devise new ones. While maintaining macroeconomic stability, I suggest to target policies at the micro-level, by applying the WCM to SOEs. This represents cross-fertilization from the private to the public sector. Private firms will spur SOEs to improve, so that they may face private head-to-head competition.

The key leverage point of Chinese economic reforms is upgrading the human capital in the form of Chinese enterprise leaders and their employees, as well as creating organizations that emulate the ingenuous dynamics of private firms. Instead of just dumping unsuccessful SOEs, reformers should restructure their organization, transform their managers into entrepreneurs, and convert stockpiled products into bestsellers. All this means taking charge, rolling up the sleeves, and doing real things instead of "remote controlling" from Harvard or MIT. In this way China can control its destiny, finding the right solutions to its own problems and avoiding disastrous experiments, which in the worst case can cost it its sovereignty and survival as a nation. Focusing on microeconomic issues as the main policy lever is a new approach in theory and practice, replacing or at least complementing the former domination by "culture-free" macroeconomists. Here are the combined WCM elements, which are worth transferring to state enterprises:

Instilling entrepreneurial leadership One of the main virtues of private enterprises, which explains their dynamism and profitability, is their strong charismatic leadership and high degree of entrepreneurship. Thus, one key element of China's economic reforms would be to inject more intrapreneurship into SOEs, which then could become similarly dynamic as private firms. With regard to implementation approaches, as I have discussed elsewhere (Schlevogt 1999, 2002) there are various new ways for how entrepreneurship can be infused into companies that are not family-owned. Further, the quality and accountability of managers is another very important aspect in the success equation. To evaluate the value of a business, an assessment of managerial competence is more important than any sophisticated spreadsheet analysis – this is the experience from venture capitalists investing into new uncertain and complex technologies and businesses. Alas, it is also the scarcest resource in China (Schlevogt 2000). Systematic in-house and external management training, competence sourcing through alliances and joint-ventures, mentorship programs, role modeling, and best practice codification will help SOEs to create and nurture the invaluable business leaders, capable of developing smart strategies, designing excellent organizations, and inspiring employees.[1]

Creating strong enterprise webs The second important aspect of private Chinese management – proliferation into enterprise webs instead of growth in company size – is more difficult to emulate for SOEs. A potential approach would be to "carve out" various divisions of large integrated conglomerates, list them on the stock market, and thus expose them to outside market controls. The corporate center could still sell its services to the carved-out units. Similar to family-owned private Chinese enterprises, the individual units would be small in size and un-bureaucratic in their organization. They may link up with each other in horizontal and vertical webs and integrate with other outside companies and networks into "industrial clusters" (networks of networks). Certain industries, because of economies of scale, require a large minimum efficient scale. Due to technical reasons, it might be impossible to break up individual units. As a consequence, webs will not be an option in such a situation. In view of the inherent limits to growth in private enterprises, state sponsorship might be necessary to provide the required large amounts of capital for these sectors. Moreover, in cases of rampant overcapacity, it might also be necessary for the state to merge businesses into larger units through horizontal integration.

Accumulating valuable social capital A distinctive feature of WCM is the set of implicit contracts based on traditional cultural values. They are an excellent control and motivating device, making it possible to dispense with many more formal structural arrangements. This is an important element to be transferred to SOEs. Given the absence of strong family ties, the creation and inculcation of values in state enterprises has to be a more conscious design effort. One approach is building a strong corporate culture that replicates traditional Chinese (Confucian) values. The culture might be disseminated through centers of excellence that spread corporate identity symbols and codified practices, and role model behavior. Singapore is an excellent example of how traditional Chinese values can be (re-)implanted into the minds of people. Shenzhen-based

Pingan Insurance is an illustration of a large shareholder's company in which the visionary leader has implemented a complete Chinese-style corporate culture system.

The resilient network economy – WCM and the development of a new capitalist order on the mainland

Nurturing the WCM in private firms and extending it to SOEs can give rise to a new capitalist order on the mainland, which I call the "network economy." Given that through its intricate coordination and control mechanism it enables flexible and rapid adaptation to change, WCM makes the macroeconomy as a whole stronger, more adaptable and robust. Using their decentralized resource allocation mechanisms, private Chinese enterprises have helped to absorb and quickly overcome external economic and other shocks, increasing the resilience of the national economy as a whole. Due to its dynamism and flexibility, it not only creates and maintains employment, but also cushions shocks better than rigid bureaucratic modes. Resources can be switched easily within the network; there is no need to dismiss workers whenever a crisis happens. Supply can easily be adjusted to rapidly changing demand; there is no "stickiness" in the management processes. Economies of scales and scope can be attained through networking – without heavy investment in fixed assets by one single integrated firm. Flexible specialization replaces mass production. The model's lack of core rigidities thus may lessen the impact and occurrence of business cycles and lead to sustained high quality growth. It is thus a great blueprint not only for an organization, but also for the whole economy, a great vision for both the microeconomic as well as the macroeconomic levels. It is highly relevant for Western countries as well, which increasingly have to cope with more uncertainty and complexity.

The short-term economic crisis in Asia did not change the fundamental economic reality underlying the success of the model. On the contrary, the distinctive characteristics of private enterprises, among other macroeconomic factors such as controls on capital flows and currency fluctuations, helped to shield China from this highly infectious disease. For several reasons, its impact might have been much worse without the flexible networks. First, their flexibility has made it easy for enterprises to absorb the external shocks and readjust their product portfolios, for example, to changing demands in export markets. Second, the private sector, because it is mainly self-financed, did not suffer the negative impact of huge (short-term foreign) loans. These may endanger the economy when nervous investors call back their funds. Private enterprises thus had a balancing effect on the high (long-term and domestic) loan exposure of SOEs. Third, the overall enthusiasm spread by the successful development of private enterprises may have helped to sustain consumers' and investors' confidence at least in the short-run, avoiding runs at banks and immediate dramatic slumps in consumption and investment. This gave leaders the time to deal with some structural problems, such as rampant overcapacity and bad loans, which are similar to other Asian countries. Had these problems not been offset by strong confidence, they would have served as "dry wood," which, once ignited, would have sufficed to turn into a forest brand. If anything should halt China's long-term growth, in my view, it will be the lack of sufficient skilled human resources, not short-term economic woes, such as deflationary tendencies resulting from overcapacity (Schlevogt 1999d), which of course need to be addressed, too. One small company, which has already started to tackle the human capital challenge at least in terms of matching people, is Zhaopin.com (zhaopin means recruitment). It helps companies and individuals to match skills with opportunities in a virtual labor market.

Mainland China and the Chinese diaspora – a transnational ethnic powerhouse?

The transfer of management ideas and other resources from the overseas Chinese back to the mainland exemplifies the synergetic effect of a greater cooperation between China and the Chinese diaspora. The visible and invisible ties may lead to the emergence of a transnational, ethnic Chinese powerhouse. The traditional, pre-revolutionary Chinese management practices together with the associated emphasis on traditional family-based values that "left" China to be spread across the overseas Chinese diaspora, has returned to the mainland. Whereas previous discussions suggested that this management model is practiced only by the overseas Chinese, my research has shown that it can also once again be found in Mainland China, in the newly founded private Chinese family enterprises. Previous accounts proposed that because the communists took over the reign and suppressed private economic activity, the traditional management model had vanished from the Chinese motherland. These accounts, however, missed the dramatic changes in the wake of the economic reforms. The new legalized stratum of private businesses readopted age-old Chinese management practices and used them for modern economic warfare. It is important to note that this was not destined to happen by pure default. Other routes would have been possible. For example, the knowledge of the old management style might have been lost. Or, overseas practices could have been used in a radically changed form. Alternatively, after years of political influence on the mainland, people might have rejected the family-based leadership model, considering it "reactionary." They might have looked exclusively to the West for the Nirvana of management. That this did not happen, demonstrates dramatically the eternal springs of the Chinese cultural treasure and the confidence and belief the Chinese have in it, which despite bordering on obstinacy, is one of their greatest assets.

The readoption of the traditional Chinese management style and cultural values in the People's Republic of China (PRC) partly results from the influence of the overseas Chinese companies, their ideas, management expertise, enthusiasm, and capital. The Chinese diaspora represents the most important "foreign" investor group in Mainland China. The greatest part of foreign direct investment into the mainland comes from overseas Chinese pockets, which set up joint ventures and buy equity stakes in mainland companies. In the neighborhood of Hong Kong alone, they employ millions of people. Taiwan is equally active, engaging in economic integration despite political tensions with Beijing.

We thus witness a spiritual and monetary reunion of the Chinese diaspora and Mainland China. In my view, a new Chinese economic and political empire is taking shape. For the first time in Chinese history, it is invisible and transnational and does not assimilate other states – at least in the short-run. Changes of epic proportion lie ahead. When the empire emerges, the world will hold its breath. The new transnational ethnic powerhouse might give China the opportunity to spread its political influence and its values around the world, such as the importance of family and care for the community. It might thus act as a powerful counterbalance against the "universal" Western model of diminishing family values and increasing individualization. An ethnic "empire" also runs counter to the propagated trend of increasing "globalization" and emergence of a "stateless" state. It is even possible that the invisible empire becomes highly visible. There are many rumors on the mainland about the mistreatment of ethnic Chinese in Southeast Asia, for example, in conjunction with Indonesia's anti-Chinese riots in May 1998. In future ethnic strifes a nationalist mainland government might want to secure the life of the overseas Chinese by military means representing another turn in the complex interrelationships between China, its neighbors in Southeast Asia, and the ethnic Chinese living there.

Conclusion

This article discussed the readoption of a traditional Chinese organizational model in Mainland China and the (potential) impact on its economy and political power. I first showed that the distinctive overseas Chinese style, which I integrated into a "WCM" model, has returned to the People's Republic. The new breed of Chinese entrepreneurs once again uses flexible structural and managerial arrangements, and emphasizes traditional cultural values and small company size. These structural design choices and management practices are similar to what we know from anecdotes and fragmented qualitative research on overseas Chinese family businesses. Distinctive structural design choices that resound well with fragmented, overseas Chinese descriptions are the autocratic "godfather" style – the personalistic and paternalistic rule of their owners. There is also a strong similarity in the captain's disdain for all written documents, rules, procedures, organizational charts, and other "German inventions." In a figurative sense, he acts according to the truth that what the world really needs is more love and less paperwork! Love is extended in the form of the pater familiae's cherishing of family traditions and family relations, based on Confucian principles. There is also a lot of emotional capital (such as affection) and social capital invested in the countless personal and enterprise networks spun by the great Webmaster, both in the mainland and abroad. The Chinese webscape has been in place before Netscape. However, the Chinese entrepreneurs displays less love and mercy for competitors whom he eagerly combats by means of entrepreneurial strategies. The flexible and charismatic leadership epitomizes what were previously thought to be the exclusive traits of the "typical overseas Chinese manager."

As a powerful value creation engine, WCM is a key driver of rapid economic development, largely accounting for the unprecedented growth and dynamism of the private sector since the reforms that were implemented after the Cultural Revolution. WCM can also be used to instill entrepreneurship and transfer flexible structures to the ailing state sector. The success is not due to ethnicity *per se*, but is a function of Chinese management behavior generated by it, plus the right circumstances that allow it to flourish (even though initially in a very constrained way).

The process of reconnecting and merging overseas and Mainland Chinese ideas and interlocking resources on the basis of mutual interests and shared destinies can help to build a new economic and political order. At the macroeconomic level, the emergence of a Chinese network economy represents a new form of capitalism. A mighty bulwark against external shocks, it is a blueprint to deal flexibly and resiliently with environmental uncertainty and complexity. The increased collaboration between the Chinese diaspora and the Mainland Chinese motherland may also provide the fabric for building a new powerful ethnic body – both a political and economic entity – with the potential for protecting Chinese interests in a hostile and constraining environment, as well as projecting Chinese political influence and values far beyond the PRC. Entrepreneurs and their ideas can thus act as a new mighty force of political, economic, social, and cultural change.

This article is only a first tentative step towards understanding the present entrepreneurial landscape in China and imagining future national and transnational Chinese developments (both economic and political ones) that are interrelated with entrepreneurship. Subsequent research will have to analyze more closely the nature of linkages between the overseas Chinese and the mainland. Such research should examine, for example, which channels are used for transferring ideas and other resources, how these channels operate and which channels are most effective. Other studies have to analyze whether the increasing economic and cultural ties are likely to be used for spreading Chinese political and social influence.

Note

1 Improving these leadership elements is of key importance for certain private enterprises as well, which fall into the trap of growing beyond control. Even private entities sometimes engage in meaningless expansion projects because they do not know how to assess opportunities in the environment, appraise projects and develop strategies and organizations (Schlevogt 1999c). The rampant overcapacity of privately developed office space and residential housing are memorials in concrete of this failure.

Bibliography

China Daily Business Weekly 8/29/1999. Internet users, p. 5.

Hamilton, G. (ed.) (1991) *Business Networks and Economic Development in East and Southeast Asia*, Hong Kong: Center of Asian Studies, Hong Kong University.

Inkson, J. H. K., Pugh, D. S. and Hickson, D. J. (1970) Organizational Context and Structure: An Abbreviated Replication, *Administrative Science Quarterly*, 15(3), 318–29.

Khandwalla, P. N. (1977) *The Design of Organizations*, New York: Harcourt Brace Jovanovich, Inc.

Miller, D. and Droege, C. (1986) Psychological and Traditional Determinants of Structure, *Management Science*, 31(4), 539–60.

Montagu-Pollock, M. (1991) All the Right Connections, *Asian Business*, 27(1), 20–4.

Phillips, L. W. (1981) Assessing Measurement Error in Key Informant Reports: A Methodological Note on Organizational Analysis in Marketing, *Journal of Marketing Research*, 18 (November), 395–415.

Pugh, D. S. and Hickson, D. J. (1976) *Organization Structure in Context: The Aston Programme I*, Westmead, Farnborough, Hampshire, England: Saxon House.

Redding, S. G. (1990) *The Spirit of Chinese Capitalism*, Berlin: De Gruyter.

Schlevogt, K.-A. (1999a) *Inside Chinese Organizations: An Empirical Study of Business Practices in China*, Parkland, FL: Dissertation Publisher (ISBN: 1-58112-045-1).

—— (1999b) Web-based Chinese Management (WCM) – Toward a New Management Paradigm for the Next Millennium?, *Thunderbird International Business Review* (formerly: The International Executive), 41(6), Nov/Dec, 655–92.

—— (1999c). Fortune Blesses only Successful Development. *China Daily*, September 29. p. 4.

—— (1999d). Deflation Necessitates Micro-adjustments in China. *China Daily*, October 8. p. 4.

—— (2000) Developing International Management Education in Emerging Markets for the 21st Century: Challenges and Solution Blueprints for Chinese Universities and their Global Educational Web-Partners. *Second Asia Academy of Management Conference, Conference Theme: Managing in Asia – Challenges and Opportunities in the New Millennium*, December 15–17, Singapore.

—— (2001) The Distinctive Structure of Chinese Private Enterprises: A Comparison between the State and Private Sector, *Asia Pacific Business Review* 7(3), 1–33.

—— (2002) *The Art of Chinese Management*, New York: Oxford University Press.

Seidler, J. (1974) On Using Informants: A Technique for Collecting Quantitative Data and Controlling Measurement Error in Organizational Analysis, *American Sociological Review*, 39 (December), 816–31.

Venkatraman, N. (1989) Strategic Orientation of Business Enterprises: The Construct, Dimensionality, and Measurement, *Management Science*, 35(8), 942–62.

Whitley, R. D. (1994) Dominant Forms of Economic Organization in Market Economies, *Organization Studies*, 15(2), 153–82.

5

THE ROLE OF PRIVATE ENTREPRENEURSHIP FOR SOCIAL AND POLITICAL CHANGE IN THE PEOPLE'S REPUBLIC OF CHINA AND VIETNAM

Thomas Heberer

Introduction

Analyses of the transformation process in Eastern Europe refer sometimes to a 'magic triangle' (Figure 5.1), meaning the development of a market, of 'autonomy' (private ownership) and 'restructuring'. The last term refers to economic adaptation to the market and the formation of an entrepreneurship (Dietz 1993: 170–2). A similar magic triangle is also the initial stage in the process of social change in China and Vietnam, which has significant consequences for social structures (changes in values, institutions and elites). Taking the new private entrepreneurship as an example, restructuring and its political and social consequences are investigated. Unlike in Eastern Europe, restructuring in China and Vietnam is not a top-down process, but mainly a spontaneous, bottom-up one.

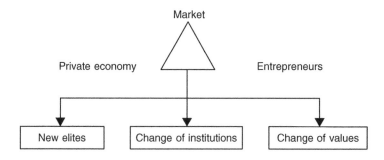

Figure 5.1 The magic triangle of change.

100

Entrepreneurs as social actors

Until quite recently, entrepreneurship was not an issue in China and Vietnam. Only since the revival of private economic activities and their subsequent momentum have new entrepreneurs begun to emerge. The role of entrepreneurs in the process of political and social change has up till now largely been neglected in academic literature (Oesterdiekhoff 1993: 66–70). Neither in economic, sociological or political science theories have entrepreneurs been seen to play a significant role. This may be due to the influence of the classic economists (A. Smith, Ricardo), of neo-classics or of Marxism, in which either individual actions, for example, by entrepreneurs, are held to be of little relevance, or entrepreneurs as a social group are regarded as a negative factor (Pierenkemper 1979: 9–14; Werhahn 1990: 17–20; Berghoff 1991: 15–20). Central functions were attributed to overall mechanisms like the market, investment or profit maximization, rather than to individuals or groups of individuals. The structuring and organizing factor is then completely neglected here.

To begin with I will define just what should be classified under the term entrepreneur and which specific characteristics the new entrepreneurs in both countries display.

In economic terms, the ideal-type entrepreneur is regarded as an active homo economicus who as an owner plans an enterprise, successfully founds it and/or independently and responsibly leads it with initiative, whereby [he] takes personal risks or capital risks (Wirtschaftslexikon 1984: 1768–69). Purely through the semantics of the word itself he is an 'acting object', whereby entrepreneurial activity sets a dynamic economic process in motion. Joseph A. Schumpeter, one of the most important entrepreneurship theorists, attributes creative, innovative behaviour and leadership qualities to entrepreneurs. Their function is to recognize and exploit new possibilities in the area of the economy. He also points out that the entrepreneur acts more by ambitions than by intellectual aims and frequently has to defend himself from accusations of deviant and antisocial behaviour (compare Schumpeter 1923, 1987: 149–51).

The economic side of entrepreneurship (compare the economic theory of entrepreneurship, Casson 1982) however does not reveal anything about its social and political role. If – in line with the new system theory – one assumes enterprises to be 'complex interwoven systems of events' (Ruegg-Sturm 1998: 3), whose collective activities produce processes of change, then it becomes clear that entrepreneurs are actors who are substantially involved in forming and influencing this system. At the same time they do not act in a vacuum, but are embedded in structures of social relations and therefore are not autonomous but act within a social environment. Social relationships are a necessary prerequisite for successful business dealings. In order to fulfil economic functions, social and political commitments are required, particularly if founding and leading an enterprise is regarded not as an event but as a process (Birley 1996: 20). Because of this process-like nature, the entrepreneur must act above and beyond the purely economic sphere, in order to maintain, develop and expand the enterprise. The Marxist definition of profit orientation as the key characteristic of entrepreneurship does not go far enough. First, profit is not an end in itself, but is – according to Georg Simmel (1994: 412) – simultaneously a 'centre of interest' that 'develops its own norms' and thereby takes on a controlling function. Second, psychic profits (Lavoie 1991: 39), that is, non-monetary incentives such as social recognition, are very important to entrepreneurs. In addition, in order to provide security and risk minimization for the entrepreneur several factors are required: a legal framework, the creation of individual contacts with politicians, banks and authorities, and organization in interest groups in order to achieve advantageous situations in economic, legal and political spheres *vis-à-vis* the state (precisely these activities can be characterized as political). The entrepreneur therefore has interests that reach far beyond the economic sphere, even if they do serve to secure his economic activities. As an interest actor he therefore also promotes economic and social change. Werner Sombart referred to the capitalist entrepreneur (as opposed to the landowning entrepreneur) as being 'decidedly subversive and a re-organiser', because he breaks with old conventions and gears the current economic system to completely new aims (Sombart 1987: 837). At the same time, he has a well-developed desire for power in the form of his enterprising spirit, which seeks to conquer all areas, not only in business but also in state spheres (Sombart 1987: 327–8; Schumpeter 1987: 155).

The question arises whether Schumpeter's ideal-type entrepreneur is also the typical entrepreneur in China and Vietnam, especially since the 'Western' entrepreneur is usually regarded as an autonomous individual (in the terms of the philosophy of the Enlightenment) (compare Schumann 1992: 13). Here we will refer to entrepreneurs as those who have founded and now run private enterprises or those who have taken over state-owned or privately owned businesses, which they now on the whole manage and develop independently.[1] This already demonstrates a great deal of innovation, as these are largely people who have left the secure state sector and now find themselves on economically, politically and socially risky, or even deviant ground. Kirzner (1978, 1983, 1985, 1989: 21–2) and Codagnone (1995: 64) have shown that entrepreneurial alertness, that is, recognizing and reacting to market signals, even to weak ones, is more important than technical innovation. Chances and gaps in the market should be quickly recognized and exploited in times of difficult and turbulent markets and poor economic conditions.[2]

It follows then that the transitional phase in China and Vietnam requires particularly flexible private entrepreneurs. It is the task of the relatively new entrepreneurship to contribute to the development of an as yet incomplete market system. In order to do this, they must amass a great deal of knowledge and create considerable social connections, along the lines of 'one makes the market work by working in the market' (Reid 1993: 242). Competence and knowledge however are not enough. Precisely in a situation where there is a lack of legal security, where private entrepreneurs are still subjected to some degree of economic, social and political discrimination, and where interest groups cannot openly act as pressure groups, the significance of informal structures such as social connections and networks is particularly great. This is also true for the primary aim of the entrepreneur, the desire or yearning for prosperity and the development of the enterprise, and also for another central factor in entrepreneurship: risk. Both require not only economic but also social and political safeguards.

Let us outline the area of action in which enterprises have influence: entrepreneurship allows a higher degree of autonomy, freedom to take decisions, independence and responsibility for oneself, and also implies a leadership function. The field of activity is also integrated in a tight web of social relationships. The entrepreneur in China and Vietnam is not organized in the usual work units (Chinese: Danwei), but is active, despite all the bureaucratic restriction, in the marketplace. And here he takes independent decisions; here he has a larger degree of social space. This freedom creates a specific attitude to business and makes the entrepreneur *per se* into an actor who more or less consciously tries to expand his room to manoeuvre, not only in business but also in social and political spheres, in which he of course also has to act. Therefore, he has the function of an actor who in the first instance expands his own scope for action, but by doing this at the same time expands society's scope for action *vis-à-vis* the state. If the state restricts the entrepreneur's room to manoeuvre, the economic results of the market deteriorate and economic growth is reduced. For this reason, the economic policy maker, the state, has little interest in introducing too great a restriction on the entrepreneur.

A summary of the most important results of our surveys and interviews shows great similarities between the entrepreneurs in China and Vietnam:

- One of the most important factors in the decision to become an entrepreneur was the desire for more independence and responsibility for oneself, which also indicates a desire for more individual and social room to manoeuvre. The percentage of those who expressed this wish was higher in more developed regions than in poorer areas. In the latter the desire for higher income and an improvement in living conditions was more significant. Other factors like access to capital, social connections (good relations with functionaries) and market chances also played a part in the decision. Self-fulfilment was one of the most important aims in life mentioned (in both countries over 70 per cent).
- Most of the entrepreneurs had previously been employed as functionaries or as managers (in state-owned enterprises). Particularly in South and Central Vietnam the proportion of entrepreneurs from families of former 'class enemies' (members of the old regime, 'capitalists') and the ethnic Chinese was high.
- The enterprise concept is influenced by traditional paternalistic ideas. Over 80 per cent wanted to see their enterprise as 'one big family' in which the 'father' (the entrepreneur) looks after the employees, who then work for the enterprise with unselfish devotion.

- Large majorities were in favour of implementing market economy structures and freedom of economic development as a prerequisite for modernization. They saw entrepreneurs as social role models and pioneers.
- The enterprises are very closely linked with the local authorities, which however leads to high costs (corruption, 'donations'). Without good social connections most entrepreneurs believe it would be very difficult to run their business. However, high percentages of those asked were critical about the way the Party and local government work. Only a quarter said they were satisfied with the Party's work. The others said that the Party was bureaucratic and not very efficient and a hindrance to their business. In both countries over 70 per cent agreed that it was necessary to establish legal security and political participation for entrepreneurs. In China there was a significantly greater percentage that spoke out in favour of entrepreneurs becoming involved in politics. This was less in the sense of individual activity and more concerning the creation of entrepreneur networks and interest groups. Absolute majorities were in favour of setting up non-state entrepreneur associations, even if they then primarily had to co-operate with the Party and the state. Nevertheless more than a third was of the opinion that such associations should function as interest groups *vis-à-vis* the state.
- Criticism of the political system was more outspoken in Vietnam than in China. Considerably more entrepreneurs there regarded the current situation as a transitional phase on the way to a more democratic system. Dissatisfaction with constant political fluctuations by the Party leadership may encourage this tendency. Chinese entrepreneurs were more strongly in favour of strong political leadership (93 per cent) than those in Vietnam. However, they then demanded of that leadership that it should introduce legal security and more freedom and individual rights.
- One must however take into account that there were also differences, in some cases significant ones, between regions and between urban and rural areas. Additionally, in Vietnam the replies varied significantly between the North and the South, due to very different socializations, while replies from China were much more homogenous.

In general, this study revealed that the new body of entrepreneurs is not only interested in the social and political processes of change, but is also actively trying to shape them. In no way do entrepreneurs consider themselves to be actors on the economic stage alone. They also consider themselves to be political ones, a fact which is documented both by their high degree of interest in political matters, and by their desire for a say in political decision-making. In both cases, over 70 per cent supported the necessity for instituting a system of legal security and political participation. In China, however, a considerably higher percentage held the view that entrepreneurs should take an active part in politics, especially by forming independent entrepreneur interest organizations. In both countries, the influences of the market economy and the privatization process are already producing a perceptible change in the power structure at the local level that is affecting both the party and government institutions in equal measure, for the economic success of the entrepreneurs erodes the power of the party, whose ideology is no longer so firmly rooted as it used to be, and that of the government, too. On the one hand, the entrepreneur needs assistance and political protection in a complex political environment where uncompromising support of the private sector is lacking. Among the various ways of achieving such protection are membership of the communist party at the local level, networks of contacts via friends or relatives to party and administrative cadres, and the suborning of these cadres.

On the whole, even this rough summary of the results of our study shows that the new entrepreneurship is not only interested in processes of social and political change, but is actively seeking to further this aim. Moreover, these results show the transformatorial potential of entrepreneurs in China and Vietnam, which essentially consists of the following patterns:

- they generate a dynamic economic process and economic innovations, thus initiating processes of social change;
- they contribute to the establishment of a market system and they reinforce market thinking;
- their actions lead to a stricter separation of state and economy;
- they are by no means merely profit-oriented. Non-monetary incentives such as social prestige and acceptance are important as well. The realization of economic objectives demands at the same time social and political engagement and influences political input and output;
- their strong interest in economic security and risk minimization requires the establishment of social connections and networks, a legal framework as well as the organization of interests in special associations in order to create advantageous conditions for business. Thus, entrepreneurs may act as protagonists for a legal system;
- they prefer a higher degree of personal freedom, individualism, autonomy and self-responsibility;
- their actions engender a change of the social structure;
- their specific consumption behaviour and life style influence the change of values and attitudes;
- they disregard old patterns and thus change not only values, but also institutions.

On the whole one can assume the following socio-political aims of private entrepreneurs in China and Vietnam:

- Desire for political and financial security and legal protection.
- Rejection of dominance by and preferential treatment of state ownership and distributional structures.
- Aversion to constant attempts by the Party and state to interfere in business.

Entrepreneurs in official discourses in China and Vietnam

The debate about entrepreneurs in China and Vietnam is comparatively new, since until recently entrepreneurs simply did not exist. In the 1950s the terms 'capitalist' and 'bourgeois' were commonly used, which branded them as antisocialists and therefore placed them outside society. As economic reforms were introduced, individual small-scale businesses and eventually private enterprises began to emerge. Previously, since the conversion of private enterprises to state-ownership in the 1950s, enterprises had been managed by twosomes consisting of the business director and Party Secretary. This fact still influences the discussion today in which the term 'entrepreneur' is often only used for managers or directors of state-owned companies (Li Junjie 1997).

Only as economic reforms were introduced at the end of the 1970s did small-scale entrepreneurs (individual businesses) begin to emerge, followed in the second half of the 1980s by larger 'private enterprises' (see Figure 5.2). The following diagram shows the changing evaluation of entrepreneurs right up to the reinterpretation of the term as 'traditional' (Chinese) or 'socialist' entrepreneurs.

The discussion about the rather neutral term 'entrepreneur' has only recently begun. Initially in China the term 'agricultural entrepreneur' was common, which

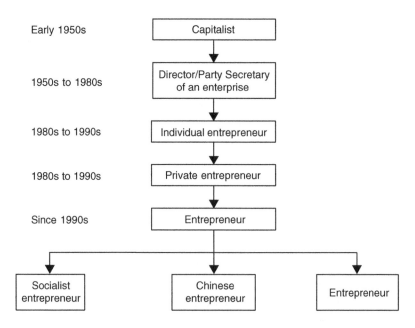

Figure 5.2 Entrepreneur as a category in China.

was used to denote successful rural managers and entrepreneurs. They were described as 'representatives of advanced productive forces in the countryside' and in the 'new socialist village', 'the forerunners of the development of commodity production', and 'fighters against poverty in the countryside' (Wang and Chen 1985). In 1997 in an essay in Jingji Yanjiu, the most important Chinese economics journal, the term 'entrepreneur' in Schumpertian usage was the subject of debate for the first time. It also contained indications that an entrepreneurship was beginning to develop again in China (Xu Zhijian 1997). As far back as 1994 the entrepreneurship was described in an essay as the national economy's 'most valuable resource'. This stratum of society should be encouraged and aided and the necessary conditions, such as economic, political and legal equality, created to stimulate their development. The essay continued that the state sector should no longer receive preferential treatment and that intellectuals should be encouraged to take up entrepreneurial activities (Wei and Sun 1994). In the same vein the Zhongguo Gongshang Bao wrote that it was an 'honour' to be an entrepreneur, running a business was a 'heroic act', even if it had to admit that it was a decidedly stony path that led to entrepreneurship on which many would fail (Yu Shaowen 1997).

A contribution in the sociological journal Shehuixue Yanjiu found that there was indeed a stratum of entrepreneurs in China, whereby the term 'stratum' was not meant ideologically (like a 'class') or pejoratively (like the 'exploiting class'), but referred to a 'living resource' that was developing in a process of social change and as the product of the very market economy which it serves (Li and Li 1996; Wang Xiaodong 1996; Wei and Xu 1996; Zhou Shulian 1996; Mi and Gao 1997: 42–6; Wang Qinghai 1997). Here it becomes clear how much the economization of politics is undermining the ideological base: the category 'class' is losing its meaning and is giving way to the apparently neutral term 'stratum'. Already in 1994 an economist had suggested that all managers of enterprises regardless of the form of ownership should be referred to as 'entrepreneurs' (compare Huang Rutong 1994: 26–7). At the end of 1997 a new journal entitled 'Entrepreneur' (*Qiyijia*) was founded. In the first announcement of its release the central organ of the Communist Party of China, *Renmin Ribao* ('People's Daily'), declared it was a journal 'which might change your fate' (Renmin Ribao, 27/10/1997).

Because the politico-economical delineation between Chinese and 'Western capitalist' entrepreneurs is becoming increasingly difficult, the Chinese entrepreneur is treated as a specifically Chinese phenomenon. A book published in 1997 claimed that Chinese entrepreneurs differed from their Western counterparts through their own 'special, particularly Chinese, characteristics': they were 'reformers', 'heroes' and acted in the interest of social requirements and in order to improve social prosperity in China (Liu Yong 1997: 1–2). Another author described the difficulties caused by the term 'entrepreneur' in China and proclaimed Chinese entrepreneurs to be 'socialist entrepreneurs', because, he said, they contribute to both the 'material' and 'spiritual civilization of socialism'. Unlike Western entrepreneurs they should fulfil two criteria: they should be innovators and also possess political qualities (Yuan Baohua 1997: 5).

An article in the *Renmin Ribao* also recognized an ideal-type entrepreneur very different from that described by Western economic theories. 'As far as political and ideological qualities are concerned, (...) he should resolutely adhere to the party line, its guidelines and policies and state legal regulations'. He should be able to hold his own in business, be hardworking, he should 'fulfil his public duties in an honest and upright way, work hard and live modestly, readily perform services to society and co-operate with leadership groups [of the Party and the state] in the public interest'. In terms of the job, entrepreneurs were expected to have leadership, organizational and coordination qualities, to show market flexibility, to take part in further training measures on modern entrepreneurial and management matters, and to be able to orient themselves on national and international markets. More qualified entrepreneurs should be trained, the conditions and environment for entrepreneurial activities should be improved and the state should help them. On the other hand, the article insisted that entrepreneurs should be kept more under control because of the high concentration of power in their hands and because power automatically corrupts (Qiu 1997).

Traditional Confucian ideas which suggest that entrepreneurs should act in the interest of state and society – under a certain measure of control – while in a corporatist way integrated into existing structures and who conform to paternalistic socialist conceptions are combined here with concepts concerning adaptation to modern global economy structures and qualities, neglecting, however, the innovation factor. The 'Chinese' as well as the 'Vietnamese' entrepreneur should be a 'patriot', that is, should identify himself with the political system and its values.

The socio-economic constellation in both countries produces two further entrepreneurial characteristics: first, a significant intermixing of functionaries and entrepreneurs, that is, cadres who have become entrepreneurs and vice versa. This results from several factors: the form of business ownership and the fact that appointments in those enterprises are made by higher-level administrative bodies (state and collective-owned enterprises); an interest in increased income (income from business is far higher than that from administration or party jobs); the opportunities that are open to functionaries because of their good connections and integration in networks. Second, to overcome legal insecurities and run their business successfully, entrepreneurs have to get involved in politics. Involvement in politics often takes the form of joining the Communist Party, or alternatively becoming a member of a committee or body, which may function as a kind of public protection (People's Congresses, Political Consultative Conferences, mass organizations). Functionaries or those with close connections to functionaries are in this respect certainly in an advantageous starting position (Cheng and Sun 1996). However the proportion of party members among private entrepreneurs is comparatively high (while the proportion of party members in the entire population was 4.8 per cent in 1997, it was

15.8 per cent among entrepreneurs according to a 1 per cent sample taken in 1996) (Zhang, Li and Xie 1996: 179; *Gongren Ribao*, 8/7/97).

While the debate in China is becoming increasingly positive in its attitude towards entrepreneurs, in the discussion in Vietnam the extreme positions are diverging more and more. Unlike in China, the private sector is officially referred to as 'the private capitalist sector' and private entrepreneurs are called 'private capitalists' (Guanli Shijie, op. cit. *Far Eastern Economic Review*, 6/11/1997: 28). In 1994 an essay claimed that because of the development of the private sector and foreign investors, the 'bourgeoisie' and the proportion of 'capitalists' were increasing in number. It continued that they would produce their own ideology and demand to have their say in politics. The state should therefore keep them more strictly under control (Political Report 1996: 115). On the one hand then, private entrepreneurs are virtually declared to be anti-socialist, but at the same time their potential is to be used to develop the economy. The political implications of this classification seem to be more important, namely political control, surveillance, distrust and administrative arbitrariness towards entrepreneurs, since the party leadership sees them as capitalist and hence regressive, backward-looking elements. As the declared aim of the Party is still socialism, capitalism is expressly rejected and the class struggle between socialism and capitalism manifests itself in all areas of society (Tien 1996: 33–4; Trong 1996: 5–11).

The state of privatization and entrepreneurship in China and Vietnam

China

What does private economic activity at present include? Let us first refer to the registered official private sector, shown in the figures from 1999:

- 31.6 m 'individual businesses' (enterprises with less than 8 employees, *getihu*) with 62.41 m staff and workers;
- 1.51 m registered 'private enterprises' (enterprises with more than 7 employees, *siren qiye*) employing 20.22 m (*Zhongguo Gongshang Bao*, 31/5/2000).

Moreover, the private sector in 1996 already contained the following segments (no newer data available):

- 25.83 m private rural enterprises with a work-force of 72.78 m people;
- 120,000 private scientific-technical enterprises (*minying keji shiye*) employing 2.91 m people;
- 220,000 enterprises (joint ventures or run with foreign capital) employing 25.01 m workers and staff members.

In 1999 there were at least 59.28 m enterprises with a work-force of 183.33 m people in the private sector. If we add the informal sector, namely unregistered private enterprises, family member helpers, persons with a second job that yielded the majority of their income, as well as the great number of enterprises with a state or collective status though in fact being private (especially in rural areas) and joint stock companies, it is possible that at present there are at least 250–280 m people working in the private sector. This figure is equivalent to more than 35 per cent of the work force, although it does not include any kind of the mixed forms of ownership, state and collective enterprises run quasi-privately (krypto-private activities), nor letting and leasing, even though the letting of public enterprises by contract has to be regarded as a form of privatization.

The initial starting point for the development of the private sector was poverty in the countryside (Figure 5.3). Already in the middle of the 1970s, that is, several years before the first political reforms, a spontaneous shadow economy developed, particularly in poor areas. As a consequence many 'free' markets

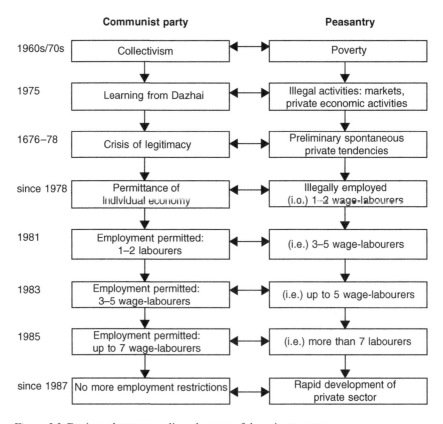

Figure 5.3 Deviance becomes policy: the case of the private sector.

developed, which at that time were considered illegal. During the economic crisis in the second half of the 1970s, the pressure from the countryside grew and some provinces (Anhui, Sichuan) tolerated this development. The return to family economy led to the revival of the private small individual business sector in 1979, as in the countryside it eventually led to redundancy for 150–200 m workers (according to Chinese data) who had no access to urban job markets or to the state sector. The only place where they could be absorbed back into the workforce was the informal sector, that is, self-employment. To begin with, it remained forbidden to employ workers as waged labour. However, as more and more small businesses employed 'family' or 'relatives', waged labour became standard. Hesitatingly the state allowed first the employment of two, then five and finally seven workers during the first half of the 1980s. The real state of affairs was, however, always one step ahead of the decisions made by the state. The development of the private sector was no longer under control, especially since the advantages it offered in terms of employment, providing consumer goods and income for local communities were very obvious. In June 1988 the State Council decreed the 'Provisory Regulations for Private Enterprises in the People's Republic of China'. The employee limits were removed and with them the main restriction on the development of the private sector.[3]

Vietnam

Despite considerable collectivization and nationalization of the North-Vietnamese economy in the 1950s and 1960s, peasants retained a certain degree of economic autonomy (Werner 1984: 48; Porter 1993: 44). In Hanoi, the capital of North Vietnam and later of the whole of Vietnam, private companies did business to a limited extent, mostly in the tertiary sector (Le Ngoc Hung and Rondinelli 1993: 9).

In contrast to northern Vietnam, after 1975 a considerable proportion of the South Vietnamese economy remained outside state control: 'At the end of the 1970s collective and privately owned industry operating outside the plan still accounted for close to 40 per cent of industrial output' (Le Ngoc Hung and Rondinelli 1993: 22). The planned and collective economy was obviously not accepted by the South Vietnamese population, which had been educated in the ways of the market economy for years by massive American influence lasting from the 1950s to the middle of the 1970s. The academic literature even describes official tolerance of the informal, private sector, for example, in trade and small businesses, before 1986, since in this way state companies could be provided with input-goods (Andreff 1993: 519; Dinh Qu 1993: 533). The economic crisis of 1978–81 led to a great increase in the number of people taking up secondary jobs, for which state materials and goods were often 'put to one side', for example, building materials and machines from state companies were 'borrowed' for private jobs (Beresford 1989: 183). In addition to this shadow economy, which at least in the South was quite extensive, a grey area in the form of lease contracts between state or collective companies and private households or individuals emerged, which was allowed substantial economic room to manoeuvre.

Among the most important reform measures introduced since 1986, which supported the further development of the private economy, was a government decree on enterprises (state, collective and private) in 1988. This decree was the first to create a legal basis for entrepreneurial activities, which already existed to an extent in the private sector. It also contained three decrees from the Council of Ministers concerning the collective, household and the private economy. Household economy (or house or home economy) consisted of all private secondary jobs done by workers, peasants and civil servants. Private economy on the other hand was defined as any private business activity considered as a person's main job (Südostasien aktuell, 5/1989: 248; Economic Sectors 1992: 81).

Parallel to the extension of the private sector through the founding of new companies, the state sector was restructured leading to a reduction in the number of state companies from around 12,000 to 6,310 by the end of 1995 and down to 5,790 by the middle of 1997. While some of the companies were closed at the local level, the majority simply seem to have been combined into larger companies. Over a million jobs have been lost through this measure, which have to be compensated for by the private sector (General Statistical Office 1996a: 41; *Straits Times*, 27/9/1997). Despite this apparently impressive restructuring, the Vietnamese government still does not have a clear privatization or reform programme for the state sector. There has been some very hesitant equitization of some state companies, but until now it has remained unsuccessful.

There has been some 'spontaneous' privatization in Vietnam. A large number of state companies have been contractually handed over to the managers with few conditions attached. Those who managed to make profits without state subsidies were able to become rich very quickly. Additionally, state assets from these enterprises were often redirected into private companies owned by the managers or their families (compare Weltbank 1996: 63 and Kolko 1997: 56–60). For this reason, it is these managers who are resisting the legal privatization process suggested by the World Bank, as they would then lose control of the state assets, which they have acquired for free and therefore would make no more private profits. This is also the reason why until 1995 only 19 of a total of 6,000 state companies had applied for privatization and only three of those have actually gone through with the plan (Kolko 1997: 59–61).

The total of officially registered limited companies, private businesses and joint-stock companies at the end of 1996 was 30,090; there were 1.88 m small or family businesses and 7,179 state enterprises.[4] Ronnas (1998: 1) gives different figures (1996: 2.2 m household enterprises, 20,000 private enterprises, 8,300 limited liability companies and 190 joint-stock companies). The differences between these figures show how difficult it is to express the situation in figures, as the different estimates reflect different political opinions.

As far as determining the quantitative extent of private business activities is concerned there are similar difficulties in Vietnam as in China. It is not possible to estimate the extent of the shadow economy, which consists on the one hand of secondary jobs and on the other hand of illegal if not criminal operations like smuggling and so on. Le Dan Doanh, head of the renowned Institute for Economic Management (CIEM) in Hanoi, estimates that in 1996 over 1 m non-registered private companies were trading in Vietnam.

As in China, false registration is a central problem, which is widespread among collectively owned companies and small businesses alike. Although they should long since have been registered as private companies because of their size (20, 30 or 50 workers) and capital assets, many entrepreneurs refuse to re-register because it would, for example, move the company into a higher tax bracket. Many state and collectively owned companies exist as such only nominally. In reality they hardly differ from private companies. In some Vietnamese statistics the collectively owned sector is already classified with the private sector (compare *Vietnam Economic Times*, February 1998: 15).

In terms of personnel the two sectors are also very closely interlinked. At least 39 per cent of entrepreneurs had previously worked as employees or managers in state and collective companies. In this area too one finds a striking difference between North and South Vietnam. From the 39 per cent mentioned above, nearly half came from North Vietnam and less than a third from the South. Connections, that had been made while previously working in the state or collective sector, have been kept up after founding private companies and contribute in this way to the close links between the different sectors of the economy in northern Vietnam. The closer links between the state and the private sector in northern Vietnam reflect the historically different development of the economy in the different parts of the country with decades of socialist structures in the North. On the other hand, private enterprises compete with state enterprises.

In both countries, privatization began as a spontaneous process, initially among peasants in the countryside. As well as widespread rural poverty before there were any reforms, other factors were also important: the peasants' strong desire for private property and family-based management forms; a certain autonomy the peasants enjoyed *vis-à-vis* the state; the peasants were not integrated in the state social welfare system; and the fact that the political leadership tolerated and ideologically accepted private activities as long as they did not involve employing workers as waged labour and therefore exploitation. The acceptance of private economy, however, turned out to be a Pandora's box, because private business activities almost automatically lead to employment of waged labour. Private business activities by peasants were easier for the political elite to tolerate because the peasants were not the main actor in the socialist remodelling of the country, unlike the workers. The primary aim in both countries was industrialization and socialization in urban areas, while the agricultural sector – according to prevailing opinion – should have become less and less important as industrialization progressed. In all socialist countries it was the cities and the urban economy, and above all large industrial concerns, that were regarded as the crucial sector for the dominance of socialist management. Liberalization and privatization processes that began in rural areas could therefore be tolerated more easily because they did not appear to threaten the Communist Party's real base of power, that is, industry and cities (see Milanovic 1989: 66–7).

Entrepreneurs as a category in China and Vietnam

The owners of private enterprises in both countries can be divided into the following groups:

- Small individual businesses (traders and skilled manual workers who run their own business alone or with support from members of the family)
- Small businesses with a limited number of waged-labour workers
- Large-scale entrepreneurs
- Suppliers of capital or shareholders who are in fact owners but do not work in the enterprise itself

Entrepreneurs are not a single, homogenous group. There are entrepreneurs running large-, medium-sized and small businesses, there are entrepreneurs whose origins lie in the local Party or state bureaucracy (cadres) who have significant connections, and those without such contacts. Werner Sombart distinguishes between 'powerful' and 'cunning' entrepreneurs. The 'powerful' ones come from bureaucratic origins and can count on the power potential to which they have access thanks to their previous jobs (cultural capital, connections, networks). The 'cunning' entrepreneurs act more as 'conquerors' and tend to rely on their entrepreneurial trading potential (compare Sombart 1987: 839). There are 'push' entrepreneurs who have become self-employed because they were dissatisfied with the working conditions in their previous employment, and there are 'pull' entrepreneurs who are attracted to the business of being an entrepreneur with its social and financial opportunities and have given up their previous job for this reason (see Amit and Muller 1996). One could classify entrepreneurs according to the different reasons for choosing self-employment, for example, (a) making use of market opportunities and incentives (mostly in urban areas and more developed regions); (b) blocked prospects of upward mobility; (c) privileged chances (privileges, social connections) for members of the political elite and sub-elite (particularly at the local level); (d) survival strategies (the unemployed, pensioners) (similarly Fang Li 1998: 87–8). Finally, social strata within the entrepreneurship should not be overlooked. Another alternative categorization would be by means of area of trade or industry, or origin: from a family business, from a political and administration-based network of connections, or from a business background (business enterprise or business administration). Each of these groups has its own status, which among owners is based on business success, level of education, social connections and (particularly in rural areas) achievements for the community (job creation, financial support for public projects, raising the local standard of living).

Private small businesses are run mainly by people for whom the state-collective sector and agriculture offer no suitable occupation or income. In urban areas these tend to be the unemployed, pensioners, the disabled and those with a criminal record, in the countryside it often affects peasants. These are mainly people with little education who come from the lower strata of society. Self-employment in the informal sector is, as in other developing countries, the only economic alternative. In recent years increasing numbers of workers have been leaving struggling state-collective companies, which can no longer guarantee their workers a minimum suitable wage or social package. Some of the smallest businesses are monetarily very strong, but they consume most of their income. Political uncertainties stop them from investing larger sums. The small group who do re-invest tend to develop into large businesses.

The large-scale entrepreneurs (in the 'private sector') are in a quite different situation to that of managers of small enterprises. The second Chinese 1 per cent sample of private entrepreneurs in 1995 and our own investigations showed the following trends for China, which incidentally are very similar to those in Vietnam:

- two-thirds were between 31 and 45 years old;
- 18.4 per cent had been to the university or polytechnic (the figure for the entire population according to the 1990 census was 1.9 per cent), only 0.3 per cent were illiterate (for the entire population the figure is around 22 per cent);
- the initial capital was in most cases the person's own income and savings (90.6 per cent) or that of relatives and friends (70.6 per cent). The majority of the companies were founded by one (56.1 per cent) or by two or three (28.8 per cent) suppliers of capital;
- 24.2 per cent of the urban and 17.3 per cent of the rural entrepreneurs had been functionaries before becoming entrepreneurs (the dominant job group);
- 58.6 per cent of the urban and 35.3 per cent of the rural entrepreneurs came from the public sector (state and collective-owned companies);
- 22.3 per cent of the urban and 11.2 per cent of the rural private entrepreneurs' fathers were functionaries, 23.3 per cent of the urban and 13.3 per cent of the rural spouses were functionaries, 26.0 per cent of the children (urban; rural 19.2 per cent), 39.1 per cent of close relatives of urban entrepreneurs as compared to 26.4 per cent of the rural ones and 46.2 per cent (urban) compared to 42.2 per cent (rural) of their friends were cadres (Zhang, Li and Xie 1996: 144–62);
- the occupation of the father (whether previously or at present) obviously plays an important role: research findings have shown that a considerable

proportion of entrepreneurs' children also become self-employed (Wu and Lin 1998: 73);

- the annual income for 60.7 per cent of the entrepreneurs was between 10,000 and 100,000 yuan, 12.7 per cent had more that 100,000 yuan (for comparison: the per capita income in 1995 was 3,893 yuan in urban areas and 1,578 yuan in rural ones) (compare Zhongguo tongji nianjian 1997: 291);
- at 17.1 per cent the percentage of party members was above average (for the whole of China it is around 5 per cent) (see Zhang *et al.* 1996: 144–62).

Large-scale rural entrepreneurs in both countries are on the whole former officials, technicians, qualified workers from various areas, people with relatively high levels of education or experience, and people with good personal connections with bureaucracy. On the whole this stratum is financially quite well off and it has been forced to re-invest in order to survive economically. The number of employees per company is continually rising, as is the number of enterprises, leading to a well-off entrepreneur stratum.

Unlike in the small, individual business sector, the new industrial entrepreneurs in China and Vietnam are not from the lower class, but mostly from the local sub-elite (former managers in state-owned and collective-owned enterprises, rural party functionaries), the immediate surroundings of the local elite (relatives of cadres), the lower middle stratum (blue collar workers, purchasing agents and sales representatives in state factories, successful individual entrepreneurs), also partly from political 'fringe groups' who were prevented from participating in social upward mobility (former 'class enemies' and their family members). This contradicts the opinion of Western social scientists that had come to the conclusion that brigands and buccaneers were the 'original' entrepreneur-type (e.g. Sombart 1987: 25–6). The observation that in post-socialist societies it was often talented individuals from the lower classes who became rich during the transition from the planned to the market economy, and who did so by no means entirely legal where fortunes were often amassed by private acquisition of state property (compare Sievert 1993: 237), is only partly valid for China. Such people can mostly be found in trade, in small individual businesses and in the shadow economy. However, the small business and shadow economy sectors should be regarded as the training ground where ongoing managers of large private enterprises can cut their teeth. Comparisons between different countries show that during massive changes in the economy, society and basic values, it is also members of the upper class (including the local upper class) who become entrepreneurs, first, because they are in a position to understand the changes taking place due to their knowledge of social relations and activities. Second, they wish to maintain their traditional role despite the changes, and third, they are distinctly market oriented anyway (compare Hoselitz 1963). In China and Vietnam, it is functionaries and their relatives who are contributing in this way to social change and to the economization of politics.

Socio-political impact of privatization: social change

Socio-political change, or to use a more familiar term, social change does not refer to mere alterations within the respective economic, political or social sub-system, but means change to the social structures of a system, or rather to the whole system itself. Social structures constitute 'regularities', such as role behaviour, values, organization patterns, social stratification and so on (compare Zapf 1992: 365). Social change is therefore a highly complex and comprehensive process, which is difficult to cover in its entirety in empirical analysis. We have therefore concentrated on the following central aspects:

- *Social stratification and change in elites, or rather the development of a new elite* Leading officials (administration, Party) represent the political elite, whereas upwardly mobile private entrepreneurs can be seen as the new business elite. There is some, limited, exchange of personnel between the political and the business elite, in particular in the form of cadres joining the business elite. Additionally, in the course of privatization processes there is a degree of overlap between the two elites as some cadres are simultaneously also involved in private business. As far as the social strata are concerned, there are differences between the pre-reform period and the reform period. Before the reforms began, the organization of the social strata was based mainly on political criteria, in that party membership and cadre rank were conditions for membership of the elite and that those who were considered to be 'class enemies', such as former landlords, rich peasants and their families, were in the lowest social stratum. Increasingly today, the organization of strata is more strongly based on economic premises.
- *Institutional change* The most visible change is in the personnel, the conception and the functions of institutions. The existence of the private sector requires institutions too, to gear themselves to the requirements of the market. Cadres have to have the relevant specialist knowledge to meet these new expectations. Parallel to this development, new institutions and organizations are emerging, some which represent the interests of private entrepreneurs (interest associations).
- *Change in values and attitudes* The private economy requires on the one hand particular values and attitudes, and on the other hand it changes the attitude to previous values and the ranking of existing values. All in all a sort of 'economization' of the value system is taking place, which apparently has already got as far as partly de-ideologizing the political ideology.

The rapid and comprehensive economic change that is happening in both countries at the moment has effects on both society and politics and brings about social change (for a detailed account see Heberer 1993; and Heberer/Taubmann 1998). The process of change was not intended by the political leadership in either country, neither could it simply be kept under control. The most striking change is the development of a new business elite from below. It consists mostly of entrepreneurs, who have become rich in the course of the privatization process. Because of differing market opportunities, a gap in incomes has developed that has led to a polarization of society. Recent research findings by Chinese and Vietnamese sociologists reveal drastic differences in income in both rural and urban areas.

In the early stages of privatization processes this prosperous group of entrepreneurs is the most important, but it is by no means the only social actor involved in social change. In the long term this elite will contribute to institutional change, which will eventually, also reach the political system, starting with the lower levels of the bureaucracy. Entrepreneurs are pushing their way into the bureaucracy in order to obtain competitive advantages. And their access to the bureaucracy is all the easier, the more functionaries move into private business for economic reasons (compare *Gongren Ribao*, 12/1/1992).

This then becomes a necessary condition for the development of a new political elite that can itself set off a new modernization drive, as experienced by the NIC-states in East Asia. In these countries the state or rather the bureaucracy was able to realize its higher aim of modernization despite considerable social resistance (Buerklin 1993; Henderson 1993). In contrast to the business elite, the state has the advantage that particularistic interests, for example, economic ones, can be channelled into a higher aim and if necessary it can use force to do so. This can only happen if a new business elite exists and if the conventional type of bureaucracy has undergone change, since a rigid, inflexible political system will hardly be able to implement change. Some researchers already assume the development of a new 'hybrid' class consisting of cadres from the administration and private entrepreneurs from rural areas (Unger 1994: 52–9).

Simultaneously, the ability of the state and Party to keep control is reduced and at least at the lowest level their interests are no longer adequately represented. In some provinces in China this process of change has apparently already progressed so far that in particular in the countryside a dualism of political and economical power exists (compare the study of Shue 1990 on China's Guanghan county). Private entrepreneurs are increasingly participating in formal institutions. According to Chinese research in 1995, 14.2 per cent of private entrepreneurs were members of the People's Congresses and 33.9 per cent were members of the Political Consultative Conferences (Hu and Zhu 1996: 38).

This development is very worrying for the political leadership. A document from the 'United Front Department' of the CCP's Central Committee required Party committees to keep an eye on private businesses, because private entrepreneurs were buying votes to get elected in local People's Congresses or were buying political advocates in Party committees and parliaments (*Dangdai* (Hongkong), 15/6/1994).

On the other hand officials are using their position to enrich themselves by creating advantages for private enterprises, that is, via corruption. This form of corruption seems to have become very widespread during the privatization process, as is demonstrated by the continual discussions on the subject in China and Vietnam (China aktuell, April 1994: 413–14. On Vietnam see Fritsche (1991: 4); Sjöberg (1991: 16); *Südostasien Informationen,* 1/1994: 28).

As a result of the economic privatization process, new interest groups with strong desires for political participation have emerged. Entrepreneurs are beginning to organize the representation of their interests in associations. Economic interests can in this way have a direct political effect, in that they could lead to a liberalization of economic policy (prices etc.). In the medium term this can result in the desire to have a say in politics, which is already partially manifesting itself in the desire of private entrepreneurs for party membership and a position in the bureaucracy.

In both countries a significant change in values and attitudes is underway. This is true, for example, of the attitude to wealth or prosperity. Unlike in the pre-reform period, in which wealth was considered indicative of exploitation, today prosperity is seen as a desirable and worthwhile aim in life. In China, Deng Xiaoping introduced the slogan that first of all at least part of the population should become rich. The Chinese mass media are full of reports about individuals' quick-growing 'prosperity'. Luxury items, new electrical goods, expensive hobbies etc. are accordingly fast becoming the new status symbols (Young 1991; China aktuell, January 1994: 46).

The pursuit of profit has apparently reached such a high level of acceptance that in comparison other values are losing importance. Sociologists in both countries have observed that in particular the family, one of the most important and basic social units, is suffering in the course of this change of values. Many parents hardly spend any of their time bringing up their children because they are too busy earning money (*Far Eastern Economic Review*, 13/1/1994: 71). Similarly, more and more school pupils are playing truant in order to make financial gains (Pfeifer 1990; Tran Trung Dung 1991: 14; China aktuell, February 1994: 176).

However, the social security offered by employment in the state sector still seems to attract people. This seems to be true for both countries, where the insecurity of the state sector has risen significantly in recent years due to company closures. For example, in a survey at five universities and polytechnics in Hanoi 85 per cent of the students still expressed a preference for employment in the state sector (Le Ngoc Hung and Rondinelli 1993: 17).

According to the Vietnamese Ministry of Labour, the positive opinion of the wealthy is accompanied by a certain animosity towards the poor who have not managed to profit from the reforms (*Far Eastern Economic Review*, 13/1/1994: 71).

An increased consciousness of oneself as an individual rather than as part of a collective is particularly noticeable among the generation of those born after 1970. A survey of Chinese school pupils in 1993 showed that nearly 50 per cent of those asked placed their own individual interests above those of society, and 60 per cent said that the organization of their future depended on their own efforts. The interviewers concluded as a result that there is a tendency to prioritize one's own well-being (China aktuell, February 1994: 187).

On the whole the early stages of such a comprehensive, far-reaching process of change lead to disruptions in the social order and lack of orientation. The old order is corroded and shaken to the core, but has not yet been replaced by a new, generally accepted order. Both economic and the subsequent socio-political change therefore first of all leads to destabilization and furthers the differentiation and polarization (social, regional).

Conclusion

Society differentiates itself in the sense of the above-described social change. Privatization from below, including the establishment of small enterprises, facilitates the process of change and thereby the 'quiet revolution from below'. This process does not automatically lead to a breakdown of the political system but erodes it in its present form.

In this context, the decisive question is whether a middle class will develop out of this new economic elite that might direct economic and political changes and thus lead the process of democratization. Barrington Moore's slogan 'no bourgeoisie, no democracy', having apparently been proved by the developments in Taiwan and South Korea, is today also applied to China and Vietnam. There is hope that in the long run a process of democratization will be generated by market development, private economy, more autonomy in society with regards to the state, the change of elites, the rise of independent interest groups and the formation of a 'middle class'.

The term 'middle class' refers to a new middle stratum, that is, to groups such as private entrepreneurs, employees in higher- or medium-level positions, civil servants, a great part of the intelligentsia as well as to independent professions that are once again to be found in increasing numbers. In China and Vietnam, the greatest hopes are focused on entrepreneurs, the stratum that is growing most quickly and is the wealthiest and most influential.

There are a number of reasons for but also against this supposition. A group has in fact come into existence whose protagonists, larger-scale private entrepreneurs and managers of big firms, pursue common economic interests and goals. This group has particular ideas regarding social development as well as an interest in participating in politics, though the policies of restriction and control by the bureaucracy might remind one of a 'blocked middle strata', that is a mobility-oriented group hindered by structural barriers that are part of the traditional system of power (Senghaas 1994: 71). From the opposite point of view this part of the middle stratum seems to be a heterogeneous group without common interests (Hsiao 1993: 9; Wank 1993: 295–300; MacDonald 1995: 56). Some commentators argue that private entrepreneurs are mostly persons with a low level of education and little social prestige who are only interested in an 'economic democracy', allowing them to establish and run enterprises, but not in a political democracy (Bruun 1993: 3–4). As a stratum they are said to be too weak, compared to the Party leaders, to be able to start political processes of change (An Chen 1993: 363–4; Zheng Yongnian 1994: 258).

Actually, the middle stratum consists of heterogeneous groups, such as persons with and without property, people with independent occupations, employees, and party functionaries as well as people not belonging to the Party, intellectuals and persons with a low level of education. The common features, however, are that they are mainly people with a higher degree of education, training or occupational experience, who want to freely develop their activities, who are interested in social advances and who, because of their work, have developed self-confidence, which allows them to strive for more participation. That does not mean, however, that this group in each case acts unanimously. On the basis of an interest-coalition, though, it tends towards common action.

In my opinion, it is not correct to argue that entrepreneurs in the large-scale private sector in general have a low educational standard. That applies more to people engaged in the small business sector. Furthermore, private entrepreneurs possess entrepreneurial abilities and experience that also have to be regarded as a factor of education. This also applies to the managers of non-private enterprises. The argument that private entrepreneurs were only interested in economic democratization is based on a static attitude. In view of their occupational activities, the economy should be their main interest. For stable business activity it is necessary to have equal opportunities (just as in the state-collective sector), a secure legal position and reliable business conditions. Open political actions, however, such as being drafted as a candidate in elections, or being opposed to the general political direction, might negatively influence not only business but may also have adverse personal consequences for the actors. On the other hand being organized in interest associations, being active in parliaments and other institutions are clear signs of political activities. Critics of political abstinence often wrongly compare political activities in both countries with those in democratic societies. As far as the social prestige of larger-scale private entrepreneurs is concerned, in rural regions it is already quite high and in urban areas it is increasing.

Entrepreneurship in both countries is still at a very early stage. The characteristics of traditional middle strata are not yet fixed, such as, for example, being safely embedded in the social establishment of power, prestige and income. In so far as their life-style, behaviour, convictions and the way others perceive them create a distinction between the entrepreneurs and other groups, this would, already, indicate the formation of a new social stratum. The successful major entrepreneurs possess a marked group consciousness that clearly places them apart from others. They are aware of their economic clout, and are not afraid to voice their interest in co-determination in matters affecting economic policy, especially through the medium of entrepreneurs' associations, whose political influence is currently concentrated on the formulation of proposals and draft bills relating to economic policy.

Although the entrepreneurs do not yet constitute a class, they are nevertheless already that what we call a strategic group: they exercise an important function in political development and change, project themselves as an organized pressure group with political negotiating power, and are able to enforce their desires at the strategic level. The organizations representing their interests have strategic knowledge, strategic planning capacity and the ability to implement the plans at their disposal. The appearance and behaviour of the members of the group can create social values and produce social change. The activities of the entrepreneurs are not yet being guided by strategies aimed at changing the system, but at gaining political influence and forming group structures. Hence, it is at all events true to speak of strategic action. In both China and Vietnam, the entrepreneurs as a body are striving to achieve a higher degree of co-determination and capacity for shaping their affairs. The word 'strategic', however, does not refer only to their activities, but also to their significance for political developments in a society (see Heberer 2001; as far as the concept of Strategic Groups is concerned, cf. Evers 1997 and 1999; Evers/Schiel 1988).

As I have shown, entrepreneurs develop a great variety of interests and activities that go beyond purely economic matters. That does not mean, however, that they are the only group to change the political system. For that a broader coalition of interests is necessary. They contribute, though, to a fundamental change from below. That is why one should not talk of the blocked middle strata, because the entrepreneurs contribute to the dissolution of the the traditional system and its limitations, and the state as well as the bureaucracy will be less and less able to block this strategic stratum. However, one should always keep in mind that private ownership is not sufficient to turn the middle stratum into a strong power. It is also necessary to establish a legal system that protects and promotes entrepreneurs. Interest groups are a great help in legally securing this business condition while economic legal security is at the same time a step towards political legal security.

Though Chinese and Vietnamese entrepreneurs do not have much in common with the European bourgeoisie at its early stage, one cannot deny that a more comprehensive privatization of economic activities has led to more motivation (due to economic reforms), mobility and the demand for radical social change. These circumstances have also had an effect on privatization in other sectors.

Notes

1 Manager of state-owned and collective-owned enterprises, that is, the sphere of 'intrapreneurship' (innovative managers). Compare Carsrud *et al.* (1986: 367–8).
2 Codagnone is referring to post-socialist societies.
3 For this development see Heberer (1989). The Private Enterprises Law in: *Renmin Ribao*, 29/6/1988.
4 Information from Do Minh Cuong, Nguyen Minh Tu and Tran Duc Vinh at the DED Regional Conference in Hanoi, 25–28 October 1996.

Bibliography

Amit, R. and Muller, E. (1996) Push- und Pull-Unternehmertum, *Zeitschrift für Klein- und Mittelunternehmen*, 2, Band 44, 90–103.

An Chen (1993) *Democratic Experimentation under Party Dictatorship: A Study of China's Political Reforms 1979–89*, PhD Thesis, Ann Arbor.

Andreff, W. (1993) The Double Transition from Underdevelopment and from Socialism in Vietnam, *Journal of Contemporary Asia*, 4, 515–31.

Beresford, M. (1989) *National Unification and Economic Development in Vietnam*, New York: MacMillan and St. Martin's Press.

Berger, B. (1991) *The Culture of Entrepreneurship*, San Francisco: ICS Press.

Berghoff, H. (1991) *Englische Unternehmer 1870–1914*, Göttingen: Vandenhoeck & Ruprecht.

Birley, S. (1996) Start-up. In P. Burns and J. Dewhurst (eds), *Small Business and Entrepreneurship*, Houndmills, Basingstoke, London: MacMillan, pp. 20–39.

Bruun, O. (1993) *Business and Bureaucracy in a Chinese City. An Ethnography of Private Business Households in Contemporary China*, Berkeley: Institute of East Asian Studies, Center for Chinese Studies.

Bürklin, W. P. (1993) *Die vier Kleinen Tiger, die pazifische Herausforderung. Hongkong, Singapur, Südkorea, Taiwan*, München: Wirtschaftsverlag Langen Müller.

Carsrud, A. L., Olm, K. W. and Eddy, G. G. (1986) Entrepreneurship. Research in Quest of a Paradigm. In D. L. Sexton and R. W. Smilor (eds), *The Art and Science of Entrepreneurship*, Cambridge/MA.: Ballinger, pp. 367–78.

Casson, M. (1982) *The Entrepreneur: An Economic Theory*, Oxford: Robertson.

Cheng, Y. and Sun, Y. (1996) Lun Zhongguo qiyejia de shuangzhongxing (On the Ambivalence of Chinese Entrepreneurs), *Caijing Wenti Yanjiu* (Studies on Problems of Finance and Economics), 12, 42–44.

Codagnone, C. (1995) New Entrepreneurs: Continuity or Change in Russian Economy and Society? In B. Gracelli (ed.), *Social Change and Modernization*, Berlin, New York: de Gruyter, pp. 63–82.

Dietz, R. (1993) Eigentum und Privatisierung aus systemtheoretischer Sicht. Ein Beitrag zur Theorie der Transformation, Sonderdruck (Reprint-Serie/Wiener Wirtschaftsvergleichendes Institut).

Dinh Qu (1993) Vietnam's Policy Reforms and Its Future, *Journal of Contemporary Asia*, 4, 532–53.

Fang Li (1998) *The Social Organization of Entrepreneurship: The Rise of Private Firms in China (Diss.)*, Ann Arbor.

Far Eastern Economic Review, Hongkong, Various issues.

Fritsche, K. (1990) Arbeitsmaschinen, nicht Menschen waren gefragt. Vietnamesische Gastarbeiter in Osteuropa, *Südostasien Informationen*, 2, 15–18.

——(1991) Die Herrschaft der Partei bleibt unangetastet. Zu den Grenzen vietnamesischer Reformpolitik, *Südostasien Informationen*, 4, 4–5.

Gabler Wirtschaftslexikon (1984), 11, Auflage, Wiesbaden: Gabler.

Gao, S. and Chi, F. (eds) (1996) *The Development of China's Nongovernmentally and Privately Operated Economy*, Beijing: Foreign Language Press.

General Statistical Office (1996a) *Kinh Te – Xa Hoi Viet Nam, 10 Nam Doi Moi (1986–1995). Impetus and Present Situation of Vietnam Society and Economy after Ten Years of Doi Moi*, Hanoi.

General Statistical Office (1996b) *Nien Giam Thong Ke 1996. Statistical Yearbook*, Hanoi.

Gongren Ribao (Worker's Daily), Beijing, Various issues.

Heberer, T. (1989) *Die Rolle des Individualsektors für Arbeitsmarkt und Stadtwirtschaft in der Volksrepublik China*, Bremen (Bremer Beiträge zur Geographie und Raumplanung 18).

Heberer, T. (1993) *Transformation des chinesischen Systems oder sozialer Wandel? Eine Untersuchung zum Verhältnis von ökonomischen, gesellschaftlichen und politischen Wandlungsprozessen.* Berichte des Bundesinstituts für ostwissenschaftliche und internationale Studien, 28, Köln.

——(1996) Die Rolle von Interessenvereinigungen in Autoritären Systemen: Das Beispiel Volksrepublik China, *Politische Vierteljahresschrift*, 2, 277–97.

——(2001) *Unternehmer als Strategische Gruppen: Zur sozialen und politischen Funktion von Unternehmern in China und Vietnam*, Hamburg: Institut für Asienkunde.

Heberer, T. and Taubmann, W. (1998) *Chinas Ländliche Gesellschaft im Umbruch. Urbanisierung und sozio-ökonomischer Wandel*, Opladen: Westdeutscher Verlag.

Henderson, J. (1993) The Role of the State in the Economic Transformation of East Asia. In C. Dixon and D. Drakakis-Smith (eds), *Economic and Social Development in Pacific Asia*, London, New York: Routledge.

Hoselitz, B. F. (1963) Entrepreneurship and Traditional Elites, Explorations in *Entrepreneurial History*, 1, 36–49.

——(1969) *Wirtschaftliches Wachstum und Sozialer Wandel*, Berlin: Duncker & Humblot.

Hsiao, H.-H. M. (ed.) (1993) *Discovery of the Middle Classes in East Asia*, Taipei: Institute of Ethnology, Academia Sinica.

Hu, Y. and Zhu, Y. (1996) Siying jingji de fazhan yu Zhongguo shehui jiegou bianqian (Development of Private Economy and Change of China's Social Structure), *Changbai Luncong* (Changbai Analyses), 6, 38–40.

Huang, R. (1994) Siying jingji lilun zuotanhui zongshu (Overview on a Conference on Theories of Private Economy), *Jingjixue Dongtai* (Economic Trends), 5, 26–7.

Huang, W. (1996), *Zhongguo de yinxing jingji* (China's Shadow Economy), Beijing: Zhongguo shengye chubanshe.

Kirzner, I. M. (1978) *Wettbewerb und Unternehmertum*, Tübingen: Mohr.

——(1983) *Perception, Opportunity, and Profit: Studies in the Theory of Entrepreneurship*, Chicago: University of Chicago Press.

——(1985) *Discovery and the Capitalist Process*, Chicago: University of Chicago Press.

——(1989) *Discovery, Capitalism, and Distributive Justice*, Oxford, New York: Blackwell.

Kolko, G. (1997) *Vietnam. Anatomy of a Peace*, London, New York: Routledge.

Lavoie, D. (1991) The Discovery and Interpretation of Profit Opportunities: Culture and the Kirznerian Entrepreneur. In B. Berger (ed.), *The Culture of Entrepreneurship*, San Francisco: ICS Press, pp. 33–52.

Le Ngoc Hung and Rondinelli, D. A. (1993) Small Business Development and Economic Transformation in Vietnam, *Journal of Asian Business*, 4, 1–23.

Li, C. (1997) Dangqian jingji chengfenlei he suoyouzhi goucheng de tongji wenti (Statistical Problems of Current Economic Categories and Ownership Structures), *Jingji Yanjiu* (Economic Studies), 7, 63–7.

Li, D. and Li, J. (1996) Wo guo qiyejia xianzhuang fenxi yu zhiyehua qiyejia peiyu jizhi yanjiu (Analysis of the Current Situation of the Entrepreneurs in our Country and Studies on Mechanisms for Professionalization and Training of Entrepreneurs), *Qiye Guanli* (Enterprise Management), 5, 30–1.

Li, J. (1997) Guanyu qiyejia zhiyehua de sikao (Considerations on Professionalization of Entrepreneurs), *Zhongnan Minzu Xueyuan Xuebao* (Journal of the Central-South Nationalities Institute), 4, 127–9.

Liu, Y. (1997) Zhongguo qiye shounao (Chinese Leading Entrepreneurs), Zhuhai: Zhuhai chubanshe.

MacDonald, K. M. (1995) *The Sociology of the Professions*, London, Thousand Oaks, New Delhi: Sage.

Mi, J. and Gao, D. (1997) Qiyejia jieceng de shehuixue hanyi (The Sociological Meaning of an Entrepreneurial Stratum), *Shehuixue Yanjiu* (Sociological Studies), 4, 42–7.

Milanovic, B. (1989) *Liberalization and Entrepreneurship. Dynamics of Reform in Socialism and Capitalism*, Armonk, London: Sharpe.

Nguyen van Thanh and Tran Thi Tuyet Mai (1993) Rural Employment Creation in Vietnam: Present Situation and Solutions. In The Development Strategy Institute of the State Planning Committee/The Rural Development Institute of the Chinese Academy of Social Sciences/Stockholm School of Economics (eds), *Rural Development: An Exchange of Chinese and Vietnamese Experiences*, Hanoi.

Nguyen Xuan Oanh (1991) Vietnam's Economic Reforms. Shifting to the Market, *Indochina Report*, January–March, 1–15.

Nguyen, Minh Tu (1996) Erste Diskussion über den unstrukturierten Wirtschaftssektor in Vietnam, Manuskript, Beitrag zur DED-Regionalkonferenz Asien, Hanoi 25–28.10.96.

Oesterdiekhoff, G. W. (1993) *Unternehmerisches Handeln und gesellschaftliche Entwicklung. Eine Theorie unternehmerischer Institutionen und Handlungsstrukturen*, Opladen: Westdeutscher Verlag.

Pfeifer, C. (1990) Bis Zum Kater unter den Tigern ist es noch weit. Ergebnisse und Probleme Einer Sozialistischen Entwicklungsstrategie in Vietnam, *Südostasien Informationen*, 4, 8–11.

——(1991) *Konfuzius und Marx am roten Fluß. Vietnamesische Reformkonzepte nach 1975*, Bad Honnef: Horlemann.

Pierenkemper, T. (1979) *Die Westfälischen Schwerindustriellen 1852–1913. Soziale Struktur und unternehmerischer Erfolg*, Göttingen: Vandenhoeck & Ruprecht.

Political Report of the Central Committee to the Eight National Congress (1996), *Vietnam – Social Sciences*, 4, 103–20.

Porter, G. (1993) *Vietnam. The Politics of Bureaucratic Socialism*, Ithaca: Cornell University Press.

Qiu, B. (1997) Zaojiu gao suzhi de qiyejia duiwu (Training a Contingent of High Quality Entrepreneurs), *Renmin Ribao*, 24 July 1997.

Renmin Ribao (People's Daily), Beijing, Various issues.

Reid, G. C. (1993) *Small Business Enterprise. An Economic Analysis*, London, New York: Routledge.

Ronnas, P. (1998) The Transformation of the Private Manufacturing Sector in Vietnam in the 1990s. Working Paper Series in Economics and Finance No. 241, Stockholm School of Economics.

Rüegg-Sturm, J. (1998) Neuere Systemtheorie und unternehmerischer Wandel, *Die Unternehmung*, 1, 2–17.

Schumann, D. (1992) *Bayerns Unternehmer in Gesellschaft und Staat 1834–914*, Göttingen: Vandenhoeck & Ruprecht.

Schumpeter, J. A. (1923) Unternehmer. In L. Elster, A. Weber and F. Wieser (eds), *Handwörterbuch der Staatswissenschaft*, Bd. VIII, Jena: Fischer, pp. 476–87.

—— (1936) *The Theory of Economic Development*, Cambridge/MA.: Harvard University Press.

—— (1987) *Beiträge zur Sozialökonomik*, Hg. Stephan Böhm, Wien, Köln, Graz: Böhlau.

Senghaas, D. (1994) *Wohin driftet die Welt?*, Frankfurt/M.: Suhrkamp.

Sexton, D. and Smilor, R. W. (eds) (1986) *The Art and Science of Entrepreneurship*, Cambridge/MA.: Ballinger.

Shue, V. (1990) Emerging State-Society Relations in Rural China. In J. Delman, C. S. Ostergaard and F. Christiansen (eds), *Remaking Peasant China. Problems of Rural Development and Institutions at the Start of the 1990s*, Aarhus: Aarhus University Press, pp. 60–80.

Sievert, O. (1993) Probleme des Übergangs von einer sozialistischen zur marktwirtschaftlichen Ordnung. In W. Dichmann and G. Fels (eds), *Gesellschaftliche und ökonomische Funktionen des Privateigentums*, Köln: Deutscher Instituts-Verlag, pp. 207–42.

Simmel, G. (1994) *Philosophie des Geldes*, Frankfurt/M.: Suhrkamp.

Sixth National Congress of the Communist Party of Vietnam (1987). Documents, Hanoi.

Sjöberg, Ö. (1991) Wirtschaftsreform in Vietnam, *Südostasien Informationen*, 4, 13–16.

Sombart, W. (1969) *Die vorkapitalistische Wirtschaft*, 1, Halbband, Berlin: Duncker & Humblot.

—— (1987) *Der moderne Kapitalismus*, 3 Vols, München, Berlin: Duncker & Humblot.

Stuchtey, T. (1994) *Privatisierungsstrategien im Transformationsprozeß Mittel- und Osteuropas*, Frankfurt/M.: Lang.

Thang Tran Phuc (1994) Tendencies of Change in the Vietnamese Social Class Structure in the Present Transitional Period, *Vietnam – Social Sciences*, 2, 3–9.

Tien Tran Huu (1996) Society – Class Relationship in the Transitional Period to Socialism in Vietnam, *Vietnam – Social Sciences*, 3, 29–35.

Tran, Duc Vinh (1996) Daten zum 'unstrukturierten' (informellen) Sektor in Vietnam, Manuskript, Beitrag zur DED-Regionalkonferenz Asien, Hanoi 25–28.10.96.

—— (1997) Überleben Jenseits der Planwirtschaft, *DED-Brief*, 3, 20–2.

Tran, H.K. (ed.) (1992) Economic Sectors in Vietnam, *Situation, Tendency and Solutions*, Hanoi: Thpong ke.

Tran Trung Dung (1991) Rette sich, wer kann [Interview] *Südostasien Informationen*, 4, 14.

Trong Nguyen Phu (1996) Socialist Orientation and the Path to Socialism in Vietnam, *Vietnam – Social Sciences*, 4, 3–11.

Tuan Nguyen Ngoc, Long Ngo Tri and Phuong Ho (1996) Restructuring of State-Owned Enterprises Towards Industrialization and Modernizing in Vietnam. In N. C. Yuen, N. J. Freeman and F. H. Huynh (eds), *State-Owned Enterprise Reform in Vietnam. Lessons from Asia*, Singapore: Institute of Southeast Asian Studies, pp. 19–37.

Unger, J. (1994) Rich Man, Poor Man: The Making of New Classes in the Countryside. In D. S. G. Goodman and B. Hooper (eds), *China's Quiet Revolution. New Interactions Between State and Society*, Melbourne: Longman Cheshire pp. 43–63.

Wang, D. and Chen, C. (1985) *Dangdai nongmin qiyejia* (Current Peasant Entrepreneurs), Zhengzhou: Henan renmin chubanshe.

Wang, Q. (1997) Guanyu zhiye qiyejia peiyu de jige wenti (On Some Questions of Training Professional Entrepreneurs), *Liaoning Daxue Xuebao* (Journal of Liaoning University), 1, 66–9.

Wang, X. (1996) Lun wo guo qiyejia zhiyehua de jiben silu, zhongdian yu nandian (Basic Ideas, Main Points and Difficulties in the Professionalization of Entrepreneurs), *Zhongguo Renmin Daxue Xuebao* (Journal of Chinese People's University), 5, 15–17.

Wank, D. L. (1993) *From State Socialism to Community Capitalism. State Power, Social Structure, and Private Enterprise in a Chinese City* (Diss.), Ann Arbor.

Wei, J. and Xu, Y. (1996) Zaojiu zhenzhengde qiyejia jieceng (Create a Real Entrepreneur Stratum), *Guanli Qianyan* (Management Front), 4, 34–8.

Wei, Z. and Sun, A. (1994) Lun wo guo qiyejia jieceng de peiyu (On Cultivation of a Stratum of Entrepreneurs in our Country), *Jingji Wenti Tansuo* (Discussion of Economic Problems), 10, 25–7.

Weltbank (ed.) (1996) *Weltentwicklungsbericht 1996: Vom Plan zum Markt*, Washington, DC.

Werhahn, P. H. (1990) *Der Unternehmer. Seine ökonomische Funktion und gesellschaftspolitische Verantwortung*, Trier: Paulinus.

Werner, J. (1984) Socialist Development. The Political Economy of Agrarian Reform in Vietnam, *Bulletin of Concerned Asian Scholars*, 2, 48–55.

Wischermann, J. (1994) *Ein Land zwischen Sozialismus und Kapitalismus – wohin steuert Vietnam?*, Schriften und Dokumente zur Politik, Wirtschaft und Kultur Vietnams, Nr. 4, Berlin: Deutsch-Vietnamesische Gesellschaft.

World Bank (ed.) (1995) *Bureaucrats in Business*, Oxford: Oxford University Press.

Wu, C. and Lin, J. (1998) Chengshi jumin de shehui liudong (Social Fluctuation of Urban Inhabitants), *Zhongguo Shehui Kexue* (Social Sciences in China), 2, 71–81.

Xu, Z. (1997) Chuangxin lirun yu qiyejia wuxing zichan (Innovational Profit and Invisible Assets of Entrepreneurs), *Jingji Yanjiu* (Economic Studies), 8, 47–50.

Young, S. (1991) Wealth but not Security. Attitudes Towards Private Business in China in the 1980s, *Australian Journal of Chinese Affairs*, January, 115–37.

Yu, S. (1997) Qiyejia yu quanli zhihuihua (Entrepreneurs and Wisdom of Rights), *Zhongguo Gongshang Bao*, 6/11/97.

Yuan, B. (1997) Ying zao shehuizhuyi qiyejia chengzhang de lianghao huanjing (Create Good Conditions for the Emergence of Socialist Entrepreneurs), *Qiye Guanli* (Enterprise Management), 192, 5–8.

Yuen, N. C., Freeman, N. J. and Huynh, F. H. (eds) (1996) *State-Owned Enterprise Reform in Vietnam. Lessons from Asia*, Singapore: Institute of Southeast Asian Studies.

Zapf, W. (1992) Wandel, Sozialer. In B. Schäfers (Hg.), *Grundbegriffe der Soziologie*, Opladen: Leske & Budrich, pp. 365–70.

Zhang, X., Li, D. and Xie, M. (1996), *Zhongguo siying jingji nianjian* (Yearbook of Chinese Private Economy), Beijing: Zhonghua gongshang lianhe chubanshe.

Zheng, Y. (1994) Development and Democracy: Are they Compatible in China?, *Political Science Quarterly*, 2, 235–60.

Zhongguo Gongshang Bao (China's Industry and Commerce Daily), Beijing, Various issues.

Zhongguo siyou qiyezhu jieceng yanjiu ketizu (1994) (Project Group for the Research of Private Entrepreneur Stratum in China), Wo guo siyou qiye de jingying zhuangkuang yu siyou qiyezhu de quanti tezheng (Economic Situation of Private Enterprises and Group Characteristics of Private Entrepreneurs), *Zhongguo Shehui Kexue* (Social Sciences in China), 4, 60–76.

Zhongguo Tongji Nianjian (China's Statistical Yearbook) (1998), Beijing: Zhongguo tongji chubanshe.

Zhou, S. (1996) 1995 nian Zhongguo qiyejia duiwu fazhan pingshu (Development of a Contingent of Chinese Entrepreneurs in 1995), *Jingji Guanli* (Economic Management), 2, 37–9.

6

PRIVATE BUSINESS AND SOCIO-ECONOMIC NETWORK RELATIONS IN THE CHINESE COMMUNITY IN HO CHI MINH CITY, VIETNAM

Jakob Lindahl and Lotte Thomsen

Introduction

The ethnic Chinese are important actors in Southeast Asia (Lim and Gosling 1983; Limlingan 1986; McVey 1992; Weidenbaum and Hughes 1996; Yeung 1999). Very little research has been done on their socio-economic role in contemporary Vietnam[1] one of about twenty countries in the world that has embarked on programmes directed at a transition from a planned to a market economy (Lee and Reisen 1994). The Chinese (Viet *Hoa*) minority played a significant role in pre-colonial and colonial Vietnam, and also in independent South Vietnam. Among other things, the Viet *Hoa* were employed as tax collectors and go-betweens for the French colonialists. When the Viet *Hoa* area of former Saigon, Cholon, was established in the beginning of the eighteenth century, it soon became a centre for private trade. Gradually, a considerable network of social and economic institutions, centred in Cholon and lead by different Chinese speech groups, was built up to support the Viet *Hoa* population in general and the business community in particular. However, the end of the Vietnam War in 1975 changed this picture dramatically. The implementation of communism in the entire unified country caused a clampdown on private business, starting with campaign X1 aimed at eliminating capitalist and go-between activities. According to Amer (1991), the campaign had a strong ideological character and was not an ethnic purge. Yet, it hit the Viet *Hoa* community hard, especially the business community in the south. All property owned by the community was nationalised, and the Viet *Hoa* social and cultural activities were forbidden. Since the campaign was not considered entirely successful, a more intensive follow up campaign (named X2) was initiated in 1978. The remains of the Viet *Hoa* business community were largely destroyed, and some 30,000 business people and 150,000 of their relatives were sent to re-educational camps in the so-called New Economic Zones. When Vietnam went to war with China one year later, the Viet *Hoa* minority was denounced as the society's 'fifth colon'. Between 60 and 70 per cent of the refugees – often referred to as the so-called boat people – were in fact Viet *Hoa* (Amer 1991).

In recent years attempts have been made to integrate the estimated 964,000 Viet *Hoa* (who represent about 1.5 per cent of Vietnam's total population) more deeply into society (Duong 1994; Khanh 1997). This paper argues that these are clearly associated with the *doi moi* (renovation) economic reform policy initiated in 1986, and the recognition that the ethnic Chinese are valuable contributors to the country's economic development.

Today, the Viet *Hoa* constitute around 13 per cent of the population in Ho Chi Minh City (HCMC) (Khanh 1997). They belong to five different Chinese speech groups[2] and mainly live in Cholon where the old rice storehouses still flank the river to remind spectators of the community's most important source of wealth in former times. Speech group temples, and also more recently established Viet *Hoa* institutions like the Viet *Hoa*,[3] *Phung Hung* and *Phung Nam* banks, the Viet *Hoa* Construction Company and the Industrial Association of District Five, are located within a short range. HCMC is by far Vietnam's most important economic centre, where 40 per cent of the country's total industrial output is generated (General Statistical Office, 1997; EIU, 3rd quarter 1998). The Viet *Hoa* community has experienced a remarkable re-emergence of economic activity, which is estimated to account for 30–50 per cent of all commercial activities in the city. In 1996, 19 per cent of private enterprises in HCMC were owned by the Viet *Hoa* (*General Statistical Office*, 1997; *Japan Economic Newswire*, 1997).

In examining[4] the Viet *Hoa* business community, one wonders how this minority population has re-established its economic position given the fact that only a short time ago many of its members had left the country. This chapter therefore intends to reflect upon a variety of causal explanations with regard to the dynamics in Cholon. One also wonders to what extent these dynamics are similar to or different from that in other Southeast Asian Chinese communities. This question can only be briefly touched upon in this chapter. Similarities are constituted by certain economic rationalities, which influence Chinese economic behaviour. It is widely argued that Chinese interfirm networks are built on personal relationships (*guanxi*), and that the individual firm's position in the network depends on the owner's credit and trustworthiness (*xinyong*)[5] (e.g. Redding 1990; Menkhoff 1992, 1997; Hamilton 1996, 1997; Numazaki 1996). According to Chen (1995), Chinese culture is relation-oriented, rather than individually or collectively oriented. Therefore, this chapter will deal with all kinds of interpersonal relations[6] and illustrate how they are managed within, among and outside Viet *Hoa* business firms (see Yeung 1994, 1998). Differences relate to the specific historical development as well as distinct policy frameworks of their host countries to which Chinese businesses had to adapt strategically.

Re-emergence of the private sector in Cholon

Most enterprises in Cholon were closed down or nationalised after 1975. However, many reopened almost immediately afterwards. Some were sufficiently small to be registered as households, while others joined to form cooperatives in accordance with the communist ideology. The Viet *Hoa* cooperatives were commonly established between family members and friends who had *guanxi* before Vietnam's reunification. By that, each family enterprise kept on working as an independent (yet cooperating) production unit. One respondent explains how this strategy of adapting to the planned economy, on the one hand, and maintaining enterprise autonomy, on the other, eased the readjustment to the emerging market economy in the 1980s:

> I and my friends made a cooperative on paper. We established a production line, where A made knitting work, B made dyeing and C made sewing. Therefore, doing business was very easy when we separated into individual enterprises after the *doi moi*. Even before that time, Viet *Hoa* enterprises were private in reality. It was only on paper that they were cooperatives.

It is therefore not surprising that many Viet *Hoa* enterprises were established before the overall boom of Vietnam's private sector by the mid-1990s (see Mallon and Irvin 1998). Several firms were established in the very first stages of the reform measures in the beginning of the 1980s. They reregistered as private businesses between 1988 and 1991 when most of the new enterprises in Cholon opened, coinciding with the official recognition of the private sector. In December 1990, the Private Enterprise Law and Company Law established the sector's legal basis (Mallon 1999).

The relatively fast rise of the private sector in Cholon was further encouraged by investments from the overseas Chinese from Taiwan, Hong Kong and Singapore, especially in garments, textile and plastics. This was supported by two initiatives of the Vietnamese government, namely the implementation of economic reforms that stabilised the economy and opened it to foreign investment, and in the form of a very direct appeal to the Viet *Hoa* and the 'compatriat *Hoa*' during an official meeting in Cholon in 1987:

> On the behalf of the Vietnamese Communist Party leaders; I call upon the compatriots of Vietnam, especially the Viet *Hoa* in this city to do business – industry as well as commerce (...) I also call upon the compatriot Hoa (overseas Chinese, added by JL and LT) who do business in this city and are acquainted with the Viet *Hoa* (...) to come here to contribute capital and machinery together with the *Hoa* in this city in order to rebuild HCMC as well as the Vietnamese country (...) shoulder to shoulder with the Vietnamese (...). To build up our county into a civilized, powerful and wealthy one. You compatriot *Hoa*, with your abilities, let us do business well.
>
> (Duong 1994: 169)

Together with their overseas relations, the Chinese community was suddenly considered as a potential rescuer of the national economy. Specific locations in the Tan Thuan, Binh Hung *Hoa* and An Ha export processing zones were made available for local and Chinese enterprises from other Asian nations. Consequently, investments from the tiger economies increased spectacularly. From 1988 to 1995, they constituted 41.2 per cent of Vietnam's total foreign direct investments (FDI) (IMF 1996). According to informants, about half of them were located in the HCMC area, largely canalised though networks to Viet *Hoa*-owned enterprises that benefited from the growing demands for consumer goods domestically (Nestor 1995; Nguyen 1996). Taking into account that outward investments, for instance from Taiwan, are estimated to be ten times higher than the country's registered outward FDI, the actual amounts of investments in Cholon from these countries were presumably much higher (Klintworth 1995). It has also been estimated that the Viet *Hoa* community in Cholon receives US$ 500 m of remittances each year, that is, more than 10 per cent of total FDI received by Vietnam annually (EIU Country Profile 1999–2000).

Today, most Viet *Hoa* enterprises operating in the textile-to-garment sector are small- and medium-sized enterprises (SMEs). As most of Vietnam's private textile and garment enterprises, they mainly produce labour-intensive garments and small-scale textiles (Norlund *et al.* 1995; Tran 1996). The ethnic Chinese who originate from Guangdong own most of the SMEs. Traditionally, they are the most powerful speech group in Vietnam, which dominated the garment and textile sector before 1975 (Khanh 1991). Most of the Viet *Hoa* entrepreneurs are men. Very few studies deal with the very presence of female Chinese entrepreneurs (see Tracy *et al.* 1996; Hefner 1998) who represented 20 per cent of our respondents. This clearly calls for more research and raises new and interesting questions, which will be partly discussed in the following section.

Authority and control systems in the Viet *Hoa* enterprises

The Viet *Hoa* intrafirm organisation corresponds to the general patterns of Chinese family business (e.g. Redding 1990). Ownership and management do overlap while the control system is centralised, personalised and authoritative. As an informant explained, this is legitimised by what is widely believed to be the Chinese Confucian culture:

> We live after a Confucian law, where everybody has to know who is the leader. In the enterprise, the leader decides what to do, there are no discussions. Everybody can show their ideas, but he always decides.

A relatively low degree of trust in non-kin employees means that delegation of control to middle management is very rare. When it does exist, it is limited to family members or relatives who supervise smaller parts of the production and who in turn are recontrolled by the top manager. By that, only he is familiar with the entire production process and indispensable. The importance of the family in terms of employment does not necessarily mean nepotism. Normatively speaking, there is consensus that all employees should be professionally qualified to gain positions in the enterprise and that family membership is not an unconditional quality. A larger footwear producer, a local family-owned firm, is a case in point. Most of its skilled managers were recruited from outside the family circle in line with the growth of the firm. With about 2,000 employees, it is by far the largest enterprise in our study. The day-to-day head of the entire enterprise group is a Vietnamese who has been a close friend of the family for a long time. Still, ownership and overall strategic decisions are kept in the family.

Like in other Chinese communities, the control system of the Viet *Hoa* firms is simple. This organisation contributes to the enterprises' competitiveness, which is a significant advantage especially in the garment industry where quick adjustments to sudden changes are essential. Entrepreneurs do emphasise flexibility as a key feature in production. As far as the internal enterprise organisation is concerned, they largely connect it with a high degree of product specialisation and the ability to change to other – though similar – products overnight. The size of the labour force, which comprises mainly female Vietnamese and ethnic minorities from rural areas, can be adapted in line with seasonal and conjunctional demand fluctuations to reduce costs. Flexibility is further reinforced by the fact that the manager is commonly an autodidact or informally trained based on the traditional tutor system.[7] He does not always act 'rationally' according to statistics or analytic methods, but mainly based on experience (and sometimes intuition), which is believed to be a key feature of the decision-making ability of the ethnic Chinese entrepreneurs worldwide (Redding 1990).

Nevertheless, the traditional management system of the Viet *Hoa*, which relies almost entirely on the experience of one or few persons, is not without weaknesses. It contrasts significantly with the dynamics and innovation, which could for instance be created by work team-based production patterns. The younger generation of the Viet *Hoa* entrepreneurs do to some extent question the value of Chinese management systems. On the one hand, they commonly wish to maintain Chinese cultural values, especially those constituting interfirm cooperation, which they connect to competitiveness. On the other, they do not perceive the personification and authority of intrafirm management systems as single-valued advantages. The son of one respondent expresses this dilemma very clearly:

> The Viet *Hoa* way of doing business has advantages as well as disadvantages. The advantage is that we can hide our know-how from others and control the whole enterprise by ourselves. But actually, that is as well the disadvantage. It means that others cannot make use of the know-how, and that enterprises cannot develop to a bigger scale. I hope this will change in the future, like in Taiwan. The Taiwanese used to have small enterprises too, but they developed. I hope that the *Hoa* community will do the same.

The relatively static intrafirm strategies are reinforced by the overall conditions in the textiles-to-garment industry: garments are labour-intensive and thus first of all competing on wages. In those subsectors of the textile industry, which have potentials for introducing more dynamic strategies, Cholon enterprises are impeded by national and international entry barriers, for example, competition from favoured SOEs in Vietnam and international tariffs.

Loyalty between employers and employees seems low in the Viet *Hoa* enterprises, for example, compared with the traditional lifelong mutual commitment in Japanese enterprises (Whitley 1992). It is chiefly a question of 'everyday loyalty', proved by obedience and correct work performance. Workers are generally regarded as disloyal if they jump to another enterprise to work but not if they establish their own business. On the contrary, the employer often supports such initiatives economically (Tong and Yong 1998), thus contributing to the relatively fast re-emergence of Viet *Hoa*-owned business in Vietnam. This phenomenon reflects a general understanding of one's need to have one's own business. A manager explained that he advised his workers 'not to work for me forever'. In the future they must develop themselves. 'I used to be a worker myself, but now I am the boss. They must try to follow my example'. As informants pointed out, it is also part of the manager's long-term strategy to accumulate 'credit slips' by supporting former employees who will have to repay him along the road to fulfil the norms of reciprocity. In addition, they are likely to become part of his *guanxi*, commonly as trusted subcontractors, in the future. Male managers usually support male employees while female managers often support women. However, there were no examples of this form of assistance across gender in our sample, only some tendencies to cross ethnicity and to support Vietnamese workers.

Risk management in an uncertain environment

Enterprises' growth strategies deal with risks and uncertainties, and they are characterised by a large extent of adaptability to the policy framework. Most small enterprises follow consolidating strategies. They concentrate production in garments, and they rarely raise formal bank loans. This is a question of taking precautions to protect the family property, whereas they usually rely on their own resources or obtain loans from family members or friends. This practice is partly determined by the policy framework. Vietnam's state and private enterprises are still caught in a 'transitional gap' (Gates and Kumssa eds. 1997), which is an outcome of conflicting incentives and signals of Vietnam's market reforms. Official credits are largely allocated to SOEs while private SMEs are limited by their lack of pawning possibilities. As a consequence, they are left with loans that run on short-terms and high interests (World Bank 1995; Román 1997; Mallon 1999).

Especially larger enterprises follow a more opportunistic diversification strategy (Hamilton 1997) to obtain production flexibility and capacity utilisation, for example, through intrafirm sourcing of orders so as to reduce risks connected to sector-specific crisis or recessions. In addition, the strategy aims to avoid attracting authorities' attention to the actual size of the enterprise and the profits made. In Vietnam, large-scale private economic activities commonly result in reinforced control and harassment. According to Mallon (1999: 174), 'disincentives to move beyond small-scale relate to the continuing policy and administrative bias against the private sector, and to poorly developed market institutions in Vietnam'. The diversification is cyclical and involves that entrepreneurs own at least three enterprises simultaneously. When one enterprise reaches a certain size, another is opened, sometimes in another sector. Production orders and employees are partly transferred to the new enterprise. Meanwhile, a third 'sleeping' enterprise is established and put on a standby. If attention is not fully distracted from the first enterprise, it is closed down. As the diversification is ongoing, the total number of production units grows while each of them remains small. Consequently, conglomerates are created in secret and the private sector policy framework is bypassed.

Structures of interfirm relations in the global textile-to-garment industry

To be involved in all kinds of networking is symptomatic for the Viet *Hoa* enterprises. Small enterprises – usually with less than thirty employees – often subcontract for SOEs, which are otherwise obliged to buy raw materials from state suppliers and to use other SOEs as subcontractors at fixed prices, generally exceeding the market price. Therefore, small orders are often concurrently delegated to private enterprises, which have lower labour costs to increase profits. These Viet *Hoa* enterprises either gain raw materials from the SOE or buy them at local markets where they are commonly purchased by the manager who is responsible for the quality of the finished products. The quality, and by that the origin, of raw materials is determined by requirements at the market destination. Commodities for the domestic or Eastern European market are produced by using local supplies while supplies of commodities to EU, which demands higher product quality, are largely imported from Taiwan or South Korea. Contracts between the Viet *Hoa* subcontractors and SOEs are formalised, but the Viet *Hoa* enterprises have maintained a certain degree of autonomy, which is largely manifested in control over the means of production. Between orders from the SOE, the managers are able to subcontract for other enterprises or produce for the domestic market, where sales are generally distributed through *guanxi* and sold by family or trusted friends. The garments from the SOE-subcontracting are partly sold domestically, partly exported in two kinds of global commodity chains,[8] corresponding to Tran's (1996) findings on Vietnam's participation in the global textile-to-garment industry.

First, Vietnam's textile and garment exports were generally redirected from the COMECON, especially towards the EU market in the early 1990s following the collapse of the Eastern bloc. As the *doi moi* had initiated a market-based export industry, a trading agreement was formed between Vietnam and the EU in 1992

(Toan and Nhan 1997). Access to this market for export garments is obtained through global commodity chains, commonly controlled by EU buyers[9] who generate so-called triangle manufacturing: Vietnamese SOEs subcontract for South Korea, Hong Kong or Taiwan enterprises that re-export the commodities to EU. Since the Vietnamese government attempts to develop a state-driven textile industry mainly relying on state-owned garment enterprises as partners, SOEs are clearly in the lead in the 'War of Quotas' in which enterprises struggle to get hold of the coveted EU export quotas. Therefore, private enterprises are often left in a vacuum, subcontracting for SOEs. A respondent explains how the large and medium sized Viet *Hoa*-owned enterprises sometimes use SOE-cooperation to bypass quota restrictions and purchase quotas from SOEs:

> When I need quotas to pass an order to Europe, I ask a state enterprise to sell for me. I ship my products in their name. State enterprises in a bad situation sell their quotas to get money.

Second, many relations to Eastern Europe have been re-established since this market regained buying power by the mid-1990s. In these networks, trade is not controlled by big European buyers. It is neither passed through nor made dearer by East Asian intermediaries, and thus it generally adds more value to Vietnam than the EU-chains. However, trade is commonly based on national bilateral agreements whereas SOEs play the lead in Vietnam (Tran 1996).

Subcontracting for Taiwanese enterprises is by far the most widespread transnational cooperation in which the Viet *Hoa* firms participate, among other things because other dominating investors (first of all South Korea and Japan) tend to invest in joint ventures with SOEs. The results of this study contradict Tran's (1997) findings in that 40 per cent of the garment producing enterprises embraced are directly related to Taiwanese enterprises without inclusion of Vietnamese SOEs. It is not clear whether the private enterprises in Tran's research are Viet *Hoa* or Vietnamese-owned enterprises. Therefore, it is uncertain whether this inconsistency is due to ethnicity, that is, that the Viet *Hoa*-owned enterprises depend less on state intermediaries than the Vietnamese because of personal relations to the tiger economies.

The Viet *Hoa* firms' networking with the Taiwanese is approached in at least three different ways, and is characterised by different degrees of formalisation.

(1) Larger enterprises often subcontract formally for Taiwanese enterprises, which for their part subcontract for European or US buyers. An example concerns ten Viet *Hoa* enterprises (of which two were included in our sample), which were all established immediately upon the garment sector's general shift towards Western markets, and which subcontract for the same Taiwanese Adidas sportswear producer. The Taiwanese control and coordinate production orders, providing high-speed sewing machines, capital, raw materials and management know-how. Commodities produced in Cholon are delivered to Taiwan from where 80–90 per cent are re-exported. All activities are coordinated from the regional head

quarters in Hong Kong. According to a representative of Adidas International, the Taiwanese control the enterprises that subcontract for them in Vietnam 'down to the bottom line':

> Almost all Adidas enterprises in the region are Chinese owned, and if they live up to the requirements of our quality standards, they can do business, as they prefer.

The Viet *Hoa* Adidas subcontractors stress that they are fettered by seven-year formal contracts, which include restrictions against producing non-Adidas commodities, and a price per piece on half the market price.

(2) SMEs, commonly established immediately upon the opening of private enterprises' possibility to export directly in 1991, often subcontract informally for Taiwanese enterprises. Their structural patterns correspond largely to those of formal subcontracting relations, for example, in the sense that raw materials, machinery and capital are provided by the Taiwanese.

(3) Very few large-scale Viet *Hoa* firms have established joint ventures with Taiwanese partners. The larger footwear producer mentioned earlier was the only firm in our sample, which had done so. FDI to Vietnam is otherwise heavily weighted towards joint ventures, but the majority are with SOEs (Kokko 2001; Mallon and Irving 2001). The Taiwanese transfer new technology and know-how to the firm, which has maintained its autonomy as far as day-to-day operations and long-term planning are concerned. Commodities are mainly sold at the domestic market and exported to Southeast Asia, EU and Eastern Europe.

Entrepreneurs who take part in national or transnational networking as described above, typically participate in more horizontal associational networks in Cholon concurrently. These are loosely bound ad hoc-agreements based on *guanxi*, which may help to increase profits by rising capacity utilisation and pro-duction flexibility through agreements to share labour force, machinery etc. By that, even small enterprises are able to carry out large orders. Those ten Cholon enterprises, which are subcontracting for Adidas, for example, have organised an associational network to disengage from the formalities in the Adidas cooperation and to gain bargaining power in relation to the Taiwanese. Another example is a textile cooperative, which consists of ten enterprises, all owned by members of the Guangdong speech group and forming an entire production line. This coop-erative is not related to any specific SOE but is allowed to cooperate with differ-ent SOEs on market terms. The cooperative structure has been maintained to secure access to subcontracting orders through SOEs. Similarly, a garment enter-prise, which was dissolved as a cooperative in 1991, has maintained cooperation between its former production units in a full textile-to-garment production line.

The economic rationalities of the Viet *Hoa* networking

The Viet *Hoa* entrepreneurs generally attach fundamental importance to *guanxi*, informal network relations and trust. This clearly increases their competitiveness as it encourages flexibility, efficiency and speed in transactions. As one respondent pointed out, even large transaction orders are often agreed upon over the telephone and carried out without the use of formal contracts:

> We do business on *xinyong* and the customers just tell me how many kilos they need, and I then supply. So, very often, when we have orders worth thousands of dollars, we can just say OK, and agree on only 5, 7 or 10 days of delivery.

Guanxi-dynamics can be understood as a form of social capital that is – as opposed to other forms of capital – accumulated in the relation between two persons (see Coleman 1988; Ostrom 1994). Entrepreneurs often refer to their personal relationships to other businessmen as long term. They might be lifelong or even passed on from one generation in a family to the next. On the other hand, concrete interfirm relations are usually relatively short or based on ad hoc-agreements. *Guanxi* is so to speak the interpersonal network relations between managers of enterprises, not between the enterprises as such. As close *guanxi* is constantly cultivated through mutual help, visits, business dinners, etc., cooperation between the enterprises is re-established fast and as required.

Some specific components of *guanxi* are repeatedly stressed by the Viet *Hoa* entrepreneurs as important cornerstones. Reciprocity norms and rules have to be strictly obeyed, demanding that prices, date of delivery and quality agreed upon in network cooperation should be kept. A high turnover combined with a low profit pr. commodity is usually strived for since 'profit is not always the most important factor to get a good reputation, and to make trust', as expressed by one respondent. As he explains in the following, it is considered a wise strategy to sell at a low price to realise capital fast, on the grounds that Vietnam's political and economic climate is still unstable:

> We have a motto in doing business; We think that selling a teapot on half the price is better, if we get the money immediately. That is better than getting a higher profit, and having to wait a long time to get the money back.

Capital involved in business deals is considered as 'sleeping', while cash is 'awake', opening up the possibility of realising new business opportunities whenever they emerge.

The literature on the Chinese overseas often emphasises that interfirm cooperation is culturally determined, and thus not market-oriented. Yet, Chinese economic rationalities and market forces are arguably interacting rather than diverging dimensions in Viet *Hoa guanxi* relations and do not exclude cost considerations. It might, on the one hand, be agreed to pay a small overcharge in a short period to cultivate relations to regular suppliers. On the other hand, it is considered perfectly 'natural' to change to a cheaper supplier if the regular exceeds the market price. What this general acceptance really means is that prices agreed upon usually correspond to the market price. Cooperation is adapted to the norms of *guanxi* and is also economically rational, and by that the relation's harmony is maintained.

Female entrepreneurs generally find it more difficult to 'pull *guanxi*' than their male colleagues. They unambiguously connect this with the male-dominated business environment. The paternalistic culture sets rules for female behaviour, which hinder their participation in those social activities where *guanxi* is usually built. A female entrepreneur explains the difficulties of women to develop *guanxi* because women are not always able to fulfil the norms of reciprocity:

> Men have big business, women only small. That is because of Chinese tradition. Men have better relations, because they take part in social activities. Men can drink at business parties and with government relations. That is an important opportunity, because very often the contract is signed right at the party table. A man can have good relations with his trading partners. He can offer cigarettes, lunch and dinner. All these things belong to the public relation area. Having relations is always difficult, but easier for men.

Therefore, some female entrepreneurs in Cholon organise their own *guanxi* based on speech group affiliation. The network is a forum for mutual assistance, exchange of information, business cooperation, arrangement of charity and study trips.

Expansion of network relations

Guanxi is generally based on a common reference, namely predetermined relations (see Chen 1995), which include the cardinal relations in the core family, relations between relatives and inherited speech group relations. Interfirm relations are characterised by a much larger degree of trust in non-kin than intrafirm relations, and also established intentionally beyond speech group relations, usually through a go-between. The go-between increases security in the expanded network, as his participation means that the newcomers are not only bound in honour to each other, but also to him (or her), as explained by an informant:

> For Viet *Hoa* written agreements do not have much validity in protection. This may be a sign of suspiciousness. The best security, when you do something with somebody, you are not familiar with, is if he is already related to your own business partners or colleagues. An introduction from your own business partner is not only an introduction, but also a security.

As relations are constantly being expanded, they are gradually transformed into a complex network, which is not limited to the family and speech group, but embrace strictly professional relations that are nevertheless still informal and based on trust. The closure of the community reduces risks in local network cooperation as it enables collective sanctioning. It eases access to information on potential partners' *xinyong* and *mianzi* (prestige), and by that his prosperity, social position and also his ability or willingness to play by the rules. Every Viet *Hoa* businessman's *xinyong* is said to be known by the entire business community due to its closure:

> In Cholon everybody knows each other. If I trust a person, I give him money. If a person has good *xinyong*, he obviously also has good money, everybody knows that. Viet *Hoa* have our own business regulations, which you cannot know about, because they are not in writing.

The Viet *Hoa* firms' transnational cooperation is most often directed towards Taiwan. The Viet *Hoa* cannot afford to be especially selective in respect to the attraction of foreign investment. Several respondents stated that it as an 'easy solution' to cooperate with the other Chinese. By that the rules of cooperation are clear, cross-cultural problems are avoided and cooperation is smooth, flexible and profitable. Those whose cooperation with Taiwanese is informal generally take up a much more sympathetic attitude than the Viet *Hoa* Adidas contractors. Several features could be pointed out to explain this, perhaps most obviously the fact that the Taiwanese partners in the informal networks simply turned out to be 'better' by sheer coincidence. Yet, the Viet *Hoa* entrepreneurs themselves solely emphasise culturally related reasons, most importantly that cooperation with other overseas Chinese is supposed to be informal and based on ad hoc agreements. They express strong feelings about the importance of preserving the family business' autonomy and the freedom to use local subcontractors and produce for other markets, when required. In the Adidas chain, the Viet *Hoa* contractors do not see the relation to the Taiwanese partner as *guanxi*. They emphasise that these relations – especially the fact that they are formalised by the Taiwanese – do not come up to their confident expectations of cooperation with the other Chinese. As one informant explained, formalisation violates social obligations and is generally perceived as an indication of lack of trust: 'Confucianism tells every Chinese to keep promises. A verbal promise is valid for everybody, and to ask somebody to give a written promise is to underestimate the person'. Since the Viet *Hoa* entrepreneurs expected cooperation with the Taiwanese to take a certain turn, they entered the Adidas commodity chain totally uncritically. This has very likely reinforced the disadvantages and hierarchical power structure of these relations. Consequently, at least one Viet *Hoa* firm involved in the Adidas commodity chain has opened one more enterprise to regain some control over business activities. It exports directly to Europe without Taiwanese (or state) intermediaries. The family's two enterprises cooperate horizontally as far as the formal restrictions in the Adidas chain allow. Thus, orders are outsourced from the Adidas producing enterprise to the new enterprise but not vice versa. An additional benefit of this strategy is that each enterprise does not exceed the 'critical size' of private enterprises in Vietnam. Other respondents involved in the Adidas chain also emphasise preferences to subcontract directly for European partners. It is important to notice that although the Viet *Hoa* businessmen more generally give priority to cooperate transnationally with the other overseas Chinese, they clearly also balance this disposition rationally against other, though limited, possibilities. Cooperation with non-Chinese would preferably be formalised, as this is (as opposed to cooperation with Taiwanese) recognised to include higher risks. It is considered difficult to form a correct estimate of the partner's trustworthiness when relations cannot be frequently cultivated. Another problem is that business people from other cultures do not necessarily act by the rules of reciprocity. This recognition of formalised cooperation can also be interpreted to indicate that the Viet *Hoa* entrepreneurs are, at least to some extent, open towards 'new' modes of cooperation and willing to transcend their ethnicity. Lever-Tracy *et al.* (1996) have stressed a similar tendency among the overseas Chinese in Australia to operate both formally and informally, depending on what seems rational in a specific situation.

Credit systems in the Viet *Hoa* interfirm relations

A well-established *guanxi* involves the possibility to obtain informal credit through different traditional Chinese credit systems, which increase the participating enterprises' competitiveness. Rules of credit in interfirm transactions are unwritten, but their essence is as follows. The refund arrangements depend on the profitability and transferability of a given commodity. If a person buys metal goods on credit he must guarantee to return 80 per cent of their value if he goes bankrupt as the transferability of metal goods is slow. If he buys garments, 60 per cent of the value must be payed back, while medicine only obliges one to 40 per cent. Goods sold on credit are returned without interests as explained by one respondent, 'because the lender already gets a high profit for long time – that is just a Viet *Hoa* law'. The Viet *Hoa* entrepreneurs often establish their first business with goods or capital obtained on credit, for example, from other speech group members who take their chances giving credence to them. They use the confidence they were shown strategically to prove their trustworthiness. As they repay the debt, the norms of reciprocity are fulfilled and the groundwork for a new *guanxi* is laid. A respondent explains:

I have an experience myself: in 1957 I produced plastic things, so then, I was very poor. I could only afford to buy 5 kg supplies at the time from the supplier, and he always asked: 'Why do you only buy 5 kg, and not the 22 kg contained in the package?' He was very tired of splitting the package, and decided to give me credit. The next time I got a whole

> package of 22 kg. He did not know my name, my address or my *xinyong*,
> he just trusted me. I paid for 5 kg and got the rest of the 22 kg on credit.

The respondent repaid his debt when the goods were sold, and the amounts of supply he received on credit steadily increased parallel with the degree of trust between him and the supplier. Likewise, he increased his own *xinyong* by refunding the debt punctually, and the two men built up a *guanxi* of long standing. When the supplier's large-scale enterprise was nationalised after 1975, the respondent was finally able to repay the favour that had a significant impact on his own career. He offered the former supplier entrance in the cooperative that he himself had joined in the difficult post-unification years.

Rotating credit systems, *hui*, are commonly used by the Viet *Hoa* businessmen who need investment capital (see Barton 1977, 1983). They are usually established by one businessman (the so-called *hui*-owner) to raise capital for different kinds of investments. He invites a group of people, for example, relatives, speech group members or colleagues, to participate with the same amount of capital monthly. The *hui*-owner usually receives the total amount the first month after which the system rotates so that the other participants are recipients one after the other. *Huis* are highly flexible, rent-free and have simple procedures. They often provide the only opportunity for the Viet *Hoa* SMEs to gain capital. In this informal system, they do not need to pawn real property as security, just their *xinyong*, as stated by a respondent:

> The owner of the *hui* has to know all the other persons. He would not ask persons he does not trust to take part in the *hui*. A *hui* is a form of renting money without interest, but with a high responsibility (…) the owner also has to have a good *xinyong*, as the others must have a reason to trust him.

On the face of it, it is risky to be a *hui*-owner as it includes granting for all participants. According to Barton (1977), the ethnic Vietnamese' *huis* are characterised by formality and high interest rates, and they are commonly controlled by professional moneylenders. The high risks of *huis* and associated mechanisms do partly explain why they are officially prohibited in Vietnam. It seems that policy makers are very hesitant to legitimise such non-state investment possibilities in order to maintain control over the private sector. The real degree of risk within the context of trust-based, low-rent Chinese *huis* in Cholon is relatively low. A Cholon entrepreneur is very unlikely to arrange or participate in a *hui* without carefully checking the trust and creditworthiness of the other participants, and also his own financial situation, as failure would simply put him 'out of business'.

A formal and an informal variant of the traditional Chinese partnership, *hegu* (Numazaki 1996; Hamilton 1997), does also exist in Cholon. In the former, two or more investors register as owners of one enterprise. Profits and control of the day-to-day business are distributed according to the amounts of capital invested by each person. One informal strategy, which is most commonly used, is a form of credit in interfirm relations. Person A invests as a sleeping partner in person B's enterprise to get a share of the profits, but rarely any influence. Because of the problems connected to owning large-scale private enterprises or private business groups in Vietnam, *hegu*-investment is one strategy used by the prosperous Viet *Hoa* business people to keep low profiles. As one respondent explains, when talking about a leader of her speech group, investments are spread to diversify risk and conceal actual wealth:

> He is very, very wise, because although he has much money, he does not want to invest alone, but he invests or contribute the capital to other people. He does not want to reveal himself as a rich man.

Therefore, receiving *hegu*-investments is common for SME-owners, usually from leaders of their respective speech groups or through go-betweens. In this way investment is spread throughout the Viet *Hoa* community in a variety of overlapping networks, which in turn increases enterprises' access to capital and their possibilities to invest in new opportunities more generally.

Speech group associations in Cholon

The importance of formal and informal Chinese business associations has often been emphasised in different Southeast Asian economies (Lim 1983; Omohundro 1983; Wickberg 1988; Hodder 1996). In Cholon, they were allowed to reopen in 1989 on the condition that they function solely as social temple associations as traditional Chinese *bangs* were considered a relic of the past capitalist south. Their structure and functions nevertheless correspond to the traditional *bang's*, whereas they will be referred to as *bang* in this chapter. *Bangs'* social activities, which were traditionally aimed at members of the speech group, are to some extent altered to include all Vietnam's ethnic groups today. They comprise building of schools in remote areas or the support of flood victims in the Mekong delta. This change in target groups is intentional rather than compulsory as it helps to restore the legitimacy of the *bangs* and also of the Viet *Hoa* community as such. Each of the five speech group *bangs* are managed by a board of about fifty persons, elected in secret by members of the speech group every four years. The board nominates a president and also five vice-presidents who attend to the legally affiliated institutions, for example, free-of-charge schools and hospitals, and act as substitutes for the president. The president is always among the speech group's most powerful men, that is, the most prosperous and well reputed. His position implies that he has considerable power and extensive *guanxi* locally, nationally and internationally.

In the Viet *Hoa* community *bangs* have different functions, compensating for the lack of institutional capabilities in the surrounding society. A foundation financed by charity aims to support entrepreneurial activities for poor members of the speech group by providing, for instance, sewing machines or cyclos. Credit is provided without interest, as the richer members of the speech group are encouraged to support such activities by the fact that it increases their *mianzi*. Therefore, *bang* is a proper forum for businessmen to 'be in evidence', to improve their position in the community, and not least to establish and cultivate business relations. A respondent explains that it is a definite advantage for him to be a member of the association as it improves mutual assistance:

> In the *bang*, I can make good relations to other people and do business with them. We make friends, and when we have problems, we help each other. We also help each other to understand regulations. Being a member has many advantages. For instance, Viet *Hoa* never advertise for workers, they just introduce good workers to each other.

Another respondent explains that he chose his subcontractor in the *bang* to be sure that deals are honoured. He stresses that the most reliable information on other businessmen's *xinyong* is gained through the *bang*:

> I have *xinyong* if the *bang* considers that I have. *Xinyong* depends on the *bang*. If a person thinks he has *xinyong* himself, it is not a good thing. It is something that the *bang* must consider.

Bangs' business functions are somehow blurred but they clearly involve credit, investment and subcontracting arrangements. First, several respondents mentioned that they have personal relations to a 'credit person', usually the president or a vice-president of their respective *bangs*. The Viet *Hoa* managers can ask the 'credit person' who has considerable *mianzi* and *xinyong* to organise a *hui* to raise capital. As the 'credit person' is trusted unconditionally, he can easily gather a group of participants to form a *hui* and to generate large amounts of money. Second, investment can be approved from *bangs'* investment funds, which have recently been re-established. These funds comprise overseas venture capital but also capital generated locally in enterprises affiliated to the *bang* but registered in the name of members of the board as explained by an informant:

> Nowadays, each *bang* has established their own business. The board members never operate officially on the behalf of the *bang*, but for themselves. The *bang* is not allowed to do business, so he or another member establishes business with the purpose of getting money to support the *bang*.

Third, the Viet *Hoa* managers can ask members of the board to contribute portfolio capital as silent investors in their enterprises, and last, the *bangs* act as an intermediary partner between the Viet *Hoa* and the overseas Chinese from other Southeast Asian countries. In the latter case, the *bang* redelegates orders either to local enterprises, which can fulfil the investors demands, or to its own affiliated enterprises, commonly using other local enterprises as subcontractors. A respondent explains how his own subcontracting for the *bang* is established ad hoc if he lives up to quality standards:

> If the *bang* has some work or an order, they can give me a small part. The first time, they only give me a small part to see, if I have good quality products. The customer report back to the *bang* that I have, and that gives me good prestige. Or the *bang* itself sees that I have good quality products. That gives me good prestige as well.

With *bang* as the intermediary and guarantee, cooperation among the ethnic Chinese businessmen in Vietnam and beyond becomes non-contractual and trust-based. Speed in transactions is increased while costs are lowered. However, some of the Viet *Hoa* entrepreneurs complained that *bang* certify and guarantee members' product and transaction quality but not necessarily those of foreign businessmen and investors. Therefore, local enterprises are sometimes jeopardised by the *bang* and become fettered by unsatisfactory overseas relations, which are informal and ad hoc. Associated business disputes are considered difficult to dissolve by the Viet *Hoa* entrepreneurs as not only their own but also *bang's* prestige and relation to the overseas investor are at stake.

Speech group *bangs* as driving forces behind professional institutions in Cholon

While each speech group *bang* supports the formation of interfirm networks based on the speech group's pre-existing trust and thus promotes its own interests, they also cooperate. Since the government banned *bangs* after Vietnam's reunification, the Viet *Hoa* business community was forced to change its strategy. Therefore, each speech group on the one hand maintained its legal and also illegal activities within the framework of the *bang*. On the other hand, the five *bangs* are the driving forces behind a network of related institutions, all constituting conducive conditions for the Viet *Hoa* enterprises. These institutions comprise different industrial organisations, perhaps most importantly the Association of Trade and Industry whose functions largely correspond to those of the former Chinese Chamber of Commerce, which coordinated the community's joint economic activities until it was banned after the reunification. The Association of Trade and Industry is managed by the leaders of the five *bangs* and established in cooperation with the Vietnamese state, whereas it is the official guardian of all private (Viet *Hoa* and Vietnamese) economic activities in Cholon.

The Association of Weaving, Clothing, Knitting and Embroidery organises around 200 (largely Viet *Hoa*) textile and garment enterprises with the purposes of distributing information on and influencing regulation and assisting interfirm networking. In addition, private enterprises are supported economically through the association's linkages to Viet *Hoa*-owned banks, which re-emerged by the mid-1990s, especially the Viet *Hoa* Bank which is one of the biggest private corporations in Vietnam (Backman 1995: 85).

The Viet *Hoa* Bank was established in 1992 by investments from about fifty persons – largely the Viet *Hoa*. It comprises all speech groups but is evidently closely related to the Teochew. Most of the stockholders are Teochew, and business meetings are often held in the Teochew *bang*. A respondent refers to a meeting between the bank and the Viet *Hoa* entrepreneurs, while explaining how the bank receives the overseas Chinese venture capital, and lends it to the Viet *Hoa* entrepreneurs as portfolio investments:

> Viet *Hoa* Bank gets money from foreign countries. The leader of the bank told us that we could lend money for new machines. We can get 60 per cent of the amount for the investment in new machines. Money for raw materials he can lend us a 100 per cent (...). The credit can be payed back in six to ten years. Sometimes with no interest, or at least only 0.8–1.2 per cent because the money is overseas money invested to make business. It is not the bank's money.

The Viet *Hoa* Bank has a significant impact on the competitiveness of the Viet *Hoa* enterprises. According to several sources, it applies different rent-rate policies to the Vietnamese and Viet *Hoa* enterprises, respectively. Capital raised overseas, for example, with interest to be paid at the rate of 6 per cent yearly are lent to Vietnamese-owned private enterprises with high interest. Associated profits are used to finance soft loans to the Viet *Hoa*-owned enterprises and guarantee revenue to the overseas portfolio investor. Trusted Viet *Hoa* entrepreneurs can get access to credits from the bank through their respective speech group *bangs*. It is important to note that this possibility does not relate to enterprise size or gender but to ethnicity, 'good relations' and trust. A female entrepreneur, for example, stressed that her good relations to the president of her speech group *bang* enabled her to obtain a loan for the purchase of new technology. An owner of a small enterprise explained that he received a loan because of a good *xinyong*. Difficulties to obtain such bank loans usually arise if *guanxi* is lacking with the consequence that one is obliged to use official channels, which are often impenetrable.

Changing power relations and political legitimacy in the Viet *Hoa* community

After Vietnam's reunification in 1975 and along with the deteriorated relations between the Viet *Hoa* community and the communist central government, internal power relations in the Chinese community altered. This was clearly connected to differences between the respective speech groups' political preferences during the Vietnam War. After the war, the central government installed the Viet *Hoa* (mainly Teochew) who had taken part in the South Vietnamese resistance at central positions in government organs that were established to be occupied with the Viet *Hoa* minority. Simultaneously, Guangdong lost their former position in the community in favour of the Teochew. As a consequence, the present Chinese Business Department of HCMC is dominated by Teochew, largely a ramification of the Viet *Hoa* Resistance, and institutionalised as a subdivision of the Peoples Committee of HCMC. The director of the Department is a Teochew himself and is known to be one of the most powerful persons in Cholon. The department's purpose is to ease the government's regulation of the Viet *Hoa* minority, but also to inform the government on requests from the community, which commonly aims at obtaining influence on business regulations. The Teochew speech group's central position in this department secures its good relations to the surrounding (Vietnamese) society, not only in the Peoples Committee of HCMC, but also nationally. The president of the Teochew *bang* is also the vice-president of the increasingly influential Vietnam Father Land Front, which has some of the countries most prosperous (private and state) businessmen among its members. The power gained through closure to the political élite has in turn strengthened the Teochew speech group's position in the Viet *Hoa* community, for example, in terms of influence in the Viet *Hoa* Bank and the different industrial organisations. However, it has also enhanced their legitimacy and has brought economic prosperity to the entire Viet *Hoa* community. An often mentioned example is the construction of the Anh Dong Market in the late 1980s, which was a prestige project selected by the authorities to show that the *doi moi* was successful and able to attract foreign investors. It was, however, a close call as the Singapore investors retired from the project after one year of negotiations. They considered the project as too risky and Vietnam's business climate as unstable. Subsequently, the five speech group *bangs* jointly established the mighty Viet *Hoa* Construction Company whose surplus is channelled to the community through the *bangs*. One respondent explains how the construction company is considered a lever for the entire community:

> (...) the Viet *Hoa* Construction Company is the biggest Viet *Hoa* corporation. They own Viet *Hoa* Bank. The purpose of the construction company is for all speech groups to get together and get capital for Viet *Hoa* business in HCMC and South Vietnam.

The An Dong Market project was finished in 1989 and is said to have had significant political importance. It was the biggest construction project carried out by domestic private investors since the country's reunification, and it clearly improved the local and overseas Chinese' trust in the economic reforms. Since the construction proved successful, it in turn positively affected the emerging reintegration of the Viet *Hoa* minority.

Personal business-state relations are a crucial part of the institutional framework for the Viet *Hoa* enterprises. Though the utility of such extra firm relations is commonly stressed by entrepreneurs, their forms and modalities differ according to enterprise size. Small enterprises' relations are generally limited to local or regional authorities, and commonly aimed at escaping problems connected to enterprise establishment or the day-to-day running of the business. They are usually established and cultivated through payoffs, resulting in some winking at bureaucratic processes or bending of legislations. Since these relations are not necessarily characterised by reciprocity and do not involve any cooperation, they are rarely perceived as *guanxi* but rather as harassment. Large- and some medium-sized enterprises depend on personalised relations to state representatives, which helps to gain reliable information on regulations and the necessary export quotas for the EU market. Entrepreneurs who fail to gain quotas are often compelled to break contracts with foreign investors or change exports towards quota-free markets. These relations are commonly perceived as *guanxi* although the authorities are predominantly ethnic Vietnamese. Therefore, 'special relationships' are not only predetermined and established intentionally across speech group lines. They transcend ethnic – and not least ideological – boundaries when necessary. Yeung (1994: 482–3) has pointed to extra firm relations as a means of legitimising private economic activities. The most obvious example is Kong whose owner is not a member of the Communist Party but of the Vietnam Fatherland Front through which he has personal relations in the government and the communist party. The motivation for establishing such relations is clearly not ideological but aims at improving individual economic interests, and also the overall conditions for the private sector. Kong promotes itself as a 'good example for the private sector', especially by showing consideration for working conditions and consequently has '(…) not been subject to any government inspection during the 15 years the enterprise existed' (one of Kong's managers). Further it is rumoured that some of the investors in the Kong group are in fact government representatives whose patronage serves for protection. Presently, there are no indications that extra firm relations lead to further polarisation between the rich and poor Viet *Hoa*. This is in contrast to Koon's (1992) findings on intra-communitarian stratification in Malaysia, a situation that is, according to Koon, largely due to the Chinese elite's upgrading of relations to Malay government representatives on behalf of the speech group and wider community. In Cholon, speech group relations are scarcely toned down although networking and institution building are based on other references as well. On the contrary, the Viet *Hoa* elite is closely related to the community to which it contributes significantly, both economically and socially.

Conclusion

This chapter suggests that the dynamics in the Chinese community in Cholon has to be understood as one of personal relations, which are managed within, among and outside the Viet *Hoa* business firms. These in turn interact with Vietnam's policy framework and market reforms, which are characterised by divergent signals towards the private sector. Nevertheless, it is clear that the Viet *Hoa* community and its relations to the Chinese overseas are presently regarded as important contributors to Vietnam's integration into the regional economy.

The Viet *Hoa* community responded fast to the economic reforms, and thus its (re)establishment has proven to be successful. Its network of speech group associations and related professional institutions definitely compensates for the lack of institutional capacity in the surrounding (Vietnamese) society. The Viet *Hoa* enterprises' access to (otherwise limited) credit through different Chinese credit systems is crucial for their competitiveness. While the degree of trust to non-kin is relatively low in intrafirm relations, it is high in interfirm relations, which are rationally motivated and established intentionally. Thus, the simple management structure within enterprises promotes fast responses to market changes, and a broadly defined and well-established *guanxi* secures flexibility in interfirm transactions.

Business-state relations that legitimise private economic activities are necessitated by the policy framework to secure enterprises' access to converted export quotas, information, etc. These relations transcend *guanxi* and ethnic boundaries. Since competitiveness sometimes depends less on know how than on know who, uneven opportunities are likely to be the result. On the other hand, 'personalised regulation' clearly enables some Cholon entrepreneurs to be more competitive and to increase their own position in the Chinese community. Yet, they also contribute to the increasing legitimacy and prosperity of the entire Chinese community.

Notes

1 For historical analyses see Barton (1977, 1983); Stern (1985); Ungar (1988); Amer (1991, 1996); Khanh (1991, 1997); and Duong (1994).
2 Guangdong comprise 56.5 per cent of the Viet *Hoa* population, Teochew (34 per cent), Fukien (6 per cent), Hainanese (2 per cent) and Hakka (1.5 per cent) according to Khanh (1991: 30–1).
3 As we found out during our fieldwork in 2000/2001, both the Viet *Hoa* Bank and the Viet *Hoa* Construction Company – which were important institutions in 1996 when we first collected data for this chapter – have been closed due to internal fraud. The consequences of this scandal for the Viet *Hoa* community are not known at this point in time.
4 Data were collected through qualitative interviews with twenty-one Viet *Hoa* entrepreneurs who own Cholon-based enterprises in the textile-to-garment (including footwear) industry. Moreover, a selected group of fourteen informants who were holding leading positions in the community such as the Viet *Hoa* speech group associations (*bang*) and industrial organisations was interviewed. Follow-up interviews were carried out in each group. The names of respondents, enterprises and informants have been either excluded or disguised to maintain confidentiality.
5 *Xinyong* should be understood both as trustworthiness, credit and credibility (Barton 1977, 1983; Menkhoff 1992).
6 Yeung (1994, 1998) has stressed that firms are often atomised in economic geographic network analysis for two (overlapping) reasons. First, network analysis commonly focuses too narrowly on the structural features of networks, not on their underlying socio-spatial organisation. Second, intra- and extrafirm relations are largely overlooked.
7 In the tutor system, a son is trained in his father's enterprise or in a enterprise belonging to relatives or friends of the family. In the latter case, the purpose is to avoid differential treatment of the son. A respondent explains that it is considered 'necessary for

him to work his own way to the top, which is too easy in his father's enterprise, as being strict with your own son is difficult'. After having finished the training, the son is integrated into the father's company, e.g. as a supervisor. In cases where the family owns more enterprises, he becomes responsible for the day-to-day running of a particular business unit.

8 The global commodity chain approach is based on the world systems theory. Global commodity chains (GCCs) are 'networks of labour and production processes, where the result is a finished commodity' (Hopkins and Wallerstein 1986: 159). GCCs are lead by 'firm leaders', and chains consist of several 'nodes' each of which have a particular function in transforming an object from raw materials to an article of consumption (Gereffi and Korzeniewicz 1994).

9 Buyer driven commodity chains are controlled by large retailers and brand names owners, who decentralise the manufacturing in subcontracting networks around the world. The buyers do not manufacture but manage the production networks. Typical industries are garments, footwear and low value consumer electronics (Gereffi 1994).

Bibliography

Amer, R. (1991) *The Ethnic Chinese in Vietnam and Sino-Vietnamese Relations*, Kuala Lumpur, Selangor: Forum.

——(1996) Vietnam's Policies and the Ethnic Chinese since 1975, *Sojourn, Journal of Social Issues in Southeast Asia*, 11(1), 76–104.

Ampalavanar-Brown, R. (1998) Overseas Chinese Investments in China: Patterns of Growth, Diversification and Finance: The Case of Charoen Pokphand, *The China Quarterly*, 155, September, 610–36.

Appelbaum, P. R. and Christerson, B. (1997) Cheap Labour Strategies and Export-Oriented Industrialization: Some Lessons from the Los Angeles/East Asia Apparel Connection, *International Journal of Urban and Regional Research*, 21(2), 202–17.

Appelbaum, P. R. and Gereffi, G. (1994) Power and Profits in the Apparel Commodity Chain. In E. Bonacich, L. Cheng, N. Chinchilla, N. Hamilito and P. Ong (eds), *Global Production: The Apparel Industry in the Pacific Rim*, Philadelphia, PA: Temple University Press.

Backmann, M. (ed.) (1995) *Overseas Chinese Business Networks in Asia*, East Asian Analytical Unit, Department of Foreign Affairs and Trade, Australia.

Barton, C. G. (1977) *Credit and Commercial Control: Strategies and Methods of Chinese Businessmen in South Vietnam*, Ithaca: Disputats.

——(1983) Trust and Credit: Some Observations Regarding Business Strategies of Overseas Chinese Traders in South Vietnam. In L. Y. C. Lim and P. L. A. Gosling (eds), *The Chinese in Southeast Asia. Vol. 1. Ethnicity and Economic Activity*, Singapore: Maruzen Asia.

Bonacich, E., Cheng, L., Chinchilla, N., Hamilton, N. and Ong, P. (eds) (1994) *Global Production: The Apparel Industry in the Pacific Rim*, Philadelphia, PA: Temple University Press.

Chen, M. (1995) *Asian Management Systems, Chinese, Japanese and Korean Styles of Businesss*, London: Routledge.

Chen, X. (1994) The New Spatial Division of Labour and Commodity Chains in the Greater South China Economic Region. In G. Gereffi and M. Korzeniewicz (eds), *Commodity Chains and Global Capitalism*, London: Praeger.

Christerson, B. and Appelbaum, R. P. (1995) Global and Local Subcontracting: Space, Ethnicity, and the Organization of Apparel Production, *World Development*, 23(8) 1363–74.

Colman, S. J. (1988) Social Capital in the Creation of Human Capital, *American Journal of Sociology*, 94, 95–120.

Deyo, C. F. (1983) Chinese Management Practices and Work Commitment in Comparative Perspective. In L. Y. C. Lim and P. L. A. Gosling (eds), *The Chinese in Southeast Asia. Vol. 1 Ethnicity and Economic Activity*, Singapore: Maruzen Asia.

Deyo, F. C. and Doner, R. F. (2001) Introduction: Economic Governance and Flexible Production in East Asia. In F. C. Deyo, R. F. Doner and E. Hershberg (eds), *Economic Governance and the Challenges of Flexibility in East Asia*, Lanham, MD: Rowman & Littlefield Publishers.

Dobson, W. and Chia, Y. S. (eds) (1997) *Multinationals and East Asian Integration*. Joint Publication by International Development Research Centre (Canada) and Institution of Southeast Asian Studies (Singapore).

Duong, M. (1994) *The Hoa Society in Ho Chi Minh City after 1975, Potentials and Development*. Nha Xuat Ban Khoa Hoc Xa Hoi. Ho Chi Minh City: The Toyota Foundation.

Economic Intelligence Unit (1998) *Vietnam 3rd Quarter 1998*, London: EIU, Redhouse Press.

——(1998) *EIU Country Profile 1998–1999*, London: EIU, Redhouse Press.

Fforde, A. Vylder, Og D. (1996) *From Plan to Market: The Transition in Vietnam 1979–1994*, Boulder, CO: Westview Press.

Fukuyama, F. (1995) *Trust. The Social Virtues and the Creation of Prosperity*, London: Penguin Group.

Gates, C. L. and Kumssa, A. (eds) (1997) Transition of Asian, African and European Economies to the Market and Socioeconomic Dislocations. In *Proceedings of the Workshop on the Socioeconomic Problems of Transnational Economies*, 30–31 July 1997. Nagoya, Japan: UNCRD Proceedings Series: No. 24.

Gates, C. L. and Truong, D. H. D. (1994) *Foreign Direct Investment and Economic Change in Vietnam – Trends, Causes and Effects*. NIAS Report No. 20, Copenhagen: Nordic Institute of Asian Studies.

General Statistical Office (1997) *Vietnam In the Open Door Time*, Hanoi: Statistical Publishing House.

Gereffi, G. (1994) The Organization of Buyer-Driven Global Commodity Chains: How U.S. Retailers Shape Overseas Production Networks. In G. Gereffi and M. Korzeniewicz (eds), *Commodity Chains and Global Capitalism*, London: Praeger.

——(1996a) Global Commodity Chains: New forms of Coordination and Control among Nations and Firms in International Industries, *Competition and Change*, 4, 427–39.

——(1996b) Commodity Chains and Regional Divisions of Labour in East Asia, *Journal of Asian Business*, 12(1), 75–112.

Gereffi, G. and Korzeniewicz, M. (eds) (1994) *Commodity Chains and Global Capitalism*, London: Praeger.

Granovetter, M. (1985) Economic Action and Social Structure: The Problem of Embeddedness, *American Journal of Sociology*, 91, 481–510.

Hamilton, G. G. (ed.) (1996) *Asian Business Networks*, New York: Walter de Gruyter.

——(1997) Organization and Market Processes in Taiwan's Capitalist Economy. In M. Orru, N. W.-Biggart and G. G. Hamilton (eds), *The Economic Organization of East Asian Capitalism*, London: Sage.

Harianto, F. (1997) Business Linkages and Chinese Entrepreneurs in Southeast Asia. In T. Brook and V. H. Luong (eds), *Culture and Economy. The Shaping of Capitalism in Eastern Asia*, Michigan: The University of Michigan Press.

Hefner, R. W. (ed.) (1998) *Market Cultures: Society and Values in the New Asian Capitalisms*, Singapore: Institute of Southeast Asian Studies.

Hernø, R. (1998) *Vietnam's Network Capitalism – Clientilist Institutions and the Emerging Private Sector*. Paper presented at the FAU Seminar, March 5–7, 1998, Denmark: Grenå.

Hodder, R. (1996) Merchant Princes of the East. *Cultural Delusions, Economic Success and the Overseas Chinese in Southeast Asia*, Chichester: John Wiley & Sons Ltd.

Hopkins, T. and Wallerstein, I. (1986) Commodity Chains in the World-Economy Prior to 1800, *Review*, 10(1), 157–70.

International Monetary Fund (IMF) (1996) *Vietnam. Transition to a Market Economy*, Washington, DC: IMF.

Jesudason, J. V. (1997) Chinese Business and Ethnic Equilibrium in Malaysia, *Development and Change*, 28, 119–41.

Jomo, K. S. and Gomez, E. T. (1997) Rents and Development in Multiethnic Malaysia. In M. Aoki, H. Kim and M. Okuno-Fujiwara (eds), *The Role of Government in East Asian Economic Development. Comparative Institutional Analysis*, Oxford: Clarendon Press.

Kao, J. (1993) The Worldwide Web of Chinese Business, *Harvard Business Review*, March–April, 24–34.

Khanh, T. (1991) *The Ethnic Chinese and Economic Development in Vietnam*, Singapore: Institute of Southeast Asian Studies.

——(1997) Ethnic Chinese in Vietnam and Their Identity. In L. Suryadinata (ed.), *Ethnic Chinese as Southeast Asians*, Singapore: Institute of Southeast Asian Studies.

Klintworth, G. (1995) *New Taiwan, New China. Taiwan's Changing Role in the Asia-Pacific Region*, New York: Longman, St. Martin's Press.

Kokko, A. (2001) Trade and Industrial Policy Reform in Vietnam. The Challenge of Continuous Change. In C. Brundenius and J. Weeks (eds), *Globalization and Third World Socialism: Cuba and Vietnam*, Houndmills: Palgrave.

Koon, P. H. (1992) The Chinese Business Elite of Malaysia. In R. McVey (ed.), *Southeast Asian Capitalists*, Ithaca, New York: Cornell University, SEAP.

Lee, C. H. and Reisen, H. (eds) (1994) From Reform to Growth. China and other Countries in Transition in Asia and Central and Eastern Europe, Paris: OECD, Development Centre Documents.

Leung, S. (ed.) (1996) *Vietnam Assessment. Creating a Sound Investment Climate*, Singapore: Institute of Southeast Asian Studies and Richmond: Curzon Press.

Lim, L. Y. C. and Gosling, P. L. A. (eds) (1983) *The Chinese in Southeast Asia. Vol. 1. Ethnicity and Economic Activity*, Singapore: Maruzen Asia.

——(eds) (1983) *The Chinese in Southeast Asia. Vol. 2. Identity, Culture & Politics*, Singapore: Maruzen Asia.

Lim, L. (1992) The Emergence of a Chinese Economic Zone in Asia, *Journal of Southeast Asian Business*, 8, 41–6.

——(1996) The Evolution of Southeast Asian Business Systems, *Journal of Asian Business*, 12(1), 51–73.

Limlingan, V. S. (1986) *The Overseas Chinese in ASEAN: Business Strategies and Management Practices*, Pasig: Vita Development Corporation.

Liu, H. (1998) Old Linkages, New Networks: The Globalization of Overseas Chinese Voluntary Associations and its Implications, *The China Quarterly*, (155), September, 582–609.

Low, L. (1995) The Overseas Chinese Connection: The ASEAN Perspective, Southeast Asian, *Journal of Social Science*, 23(2), 89–117.

Luoc, D. V. (ed.) (1997) *Vietnam's Policy of Trade and Investment*, Hanoi: Institute of World Economy.

Mallon, R. (1999) Experiences in the Region and Private Sector Incentives in Vietnam. In S. Leung (ed.), *Vietnam and the East Asian Crisis*, Cheltenham (UK): Edward Elgar.

——(1998) Vietnam: Consolidating the Market Transition. Paper presented at the Workshop on *Globalization, Changing Paradigms and Development Options in the Third World: Cuba and Vietnam*, Centre for Development Research. Copenhagen, 11–13 June, 1998.

Mallon, R. and Irvin, G. (2001) Systemic Change and Economic Reforms in Vietnam. In C. Brundenius and J. Weeks (eds), *Globalization and Third World Socialism: Cuba and Vietnam*, Houndmills: Palgrave.

McVey, R. (ed.) (1992) *Southeast Asian Capitalists*, Ithaca, NY: SEAP, Cornell University.

Menkhoff, T. (1992) Xinyong or How to Trust Trust? Chinese Non-Contractual Business Relations and Social Structure: The Singapore Case, *Internationales Asienforum*, 23(1–2), 261–88.

——(1997) The Social Organisation of Global Ethnic Trading Networks. In H. M. Dahlan, J. Hamzah, A. Y. Hing and J. H. Ong (eds), *ASEAN in the Global System*. Bangi, Malaysia: Penerbit Universiti Kebangsaan.

Menkhoff, T. and Labig, C. (1995) Towards an Understanding of Chinese Business Networks in Asia-Pacific – The Singapore Case, *Internationales Asianforum*, 26(3–4), 343–64.

Nestor, C. (1995) Spatial Patterns of Foreign Joint Venture Investment in Vietnam, 1988–1993. Paper prepared for the Conference on *Vietnam – Reform and Transformation*, Centre for Pacific Asia Studies, Stockholm University, 31 August–1. September 1995, Stockholm.

Nguyen, T. D. (1996) Foreign Direct Investment in Vietnam. In S. Leung (ed.), *Vietnam Assessment. Creating a Sound Investment Climate*, Singapore: Institute of Southeast Asian Studies and Richmond: Curzon Press.

Numazaki, I. (1986) Networks of Taiwanese Big Business: A Preliminary Analysis, *Modern China*, (12), 487–534.

——(1996) 'Cross-Family Partnership' as the Principle of Chinese Business Organization: A Historical and Cross-Cultural Analysis. Paper presented at the *International Workshop on Chinese Business Connections in Global and Comparative Perspective*, Beijing 10–12 September.

Nørlund, I., Gates, C. L. and Dam, V. C. (eds) (1995) *Vietnam in a Changing World*, Copenhagen: Nordic Institute of Asian Studies and Richmond: Curzon Press.

Omohundro, T. J. (1983) Social Networks and Business Success for the Philippine Chinese. In L. Y .C. Lim and P. L. A. Gosling (eds), *The Chinese in Southeast Asia. Vol. 1 Ethnicity and Economic Activity*, Singapore: Maruzen Asia.

Ong, A. (1999) *Flexible Citizenship. The Cultural Logics of Transnationality*, Durham and London: Duke University Press.

Ong, A. and Nonini, D. (eds) (1997) *Ungrounded Empires – The Cultural Politics of Modern Chinese Transnationalism*, London: Routledge.

Orru, M., W.-Biggart, N. and Hamilton, G. G. (eds) (1997) *The Economic Organization of East Asian Capitalism*, London: Sage.

Ostrom, E. (1994) *Social Capital, Self-organization, and Development*, Cambridge: Cambridge University Press.

Ramamurthy, B. (1998) *The Private Manufacturing Sector in Vietnam: An Analysis of the Winners*. The Economic Research Institute, Working Paper No. 251, August, Stockholm.

Redding, S. G. (1990) *The Spirit of Chinese Capitalism*, New York: De Gruyter.

Román, L. (1997) An Institutional Challenge – Transition in the Vietnamese Banking Sector. In B. E. Beckman, E. Hansson and L. Roman (eds) *Vietnam Reform and Transformation*, Center for Pacific Asia Studies, Stockholm, Sweden: Stockholm University.

Sayer, A. (1984) *Method in Social Science – A Realist Approach*, London: Routledge.

Sayer, A. and Walker, R. (1992) *The New Social Economy: Reworking the Division of Labour*, Cambridge: Blackwell.

Smith, A. D. (1996) Going South: Global Restructuring and Garment Production in Three East Asian Cases, *Asian Perspectives*, (20)2, 211–41.

Stern, M. L. (1985) The Overseas Chinese in the Socialist Republic of Vietnam, 1979–82, *Asian Survey*, XXV(5), 521–36.

Storper, M. and Scott, A. J. (1992) *Pathways to Industrialisation and Regional Development*, London: Routledge.

Storper, M. and Walker, R. (1989) *The Capitalist Imperative: Territory, Technology and Industrial Growth*, Oxford and New York: Blackwell.

Taplin, M. I. (1994) Strategic Reorientations of U.S. Apparel Firms. In G. Gereffi and M. Korzeniewicz (eds), *Commodity Chains and Global Capitalism*, London: Praeger.

Toan, T. T. and Nhan, T. H. (1997) Vietnam and the Process of Integration with World Trade Organizations and Blocs. In D. V. Luoc (ed.), *Vietnam's Policy of Trade and Investment*, Hanoi: Institute of World Economy.

Tong, C. K. and Yong, P. K. (1998) Guanxi Bases, Xinyong and Chinese Business Networks, *British Journal of Sociology*, 49(1), 75–96.

Tracy, L. C., Ip, D. and Tracy, N. (1996) *The Chinese Diaspora and Mainland China. An Emerging Economic Synergy*, London: Macmillan Press.

Tran, Angie Ngoc (1996) Through the Eye of the Needle. Vietnamese Textile and Garment Industries Rejoining the Global Economy, *Crossroads*, 10(2), 83–126.

Tu, J-H. (1997) Taiwan: A Solid Manufacturing Base and Emerging Regional Source of Investment. In W. Dobson and Y. S. Chia (eds), *Multinationals and East Asian Integration*, Ottawa: International Development Research Centre and Singapore: Institute of Southeast Asian Studies.

Ungar, S. E. (1988) The Struggle over Chinese Community in Vietnam, 1946–1986, *Pacific Affairs*, 60(4), 596–614.

Weidenbaum, M. and Hughes, S. (1996) *The Bamboo Network: How Expatriate Chinese Entrepreneurs are Creating a New Economic Superpower in Asia*, New York: The Free Press.

Whitley, R. (1992) *Business Systems in East Asia-Firms, Markets and Societies*, London: Sage.

——(1996) Business Systems and Global Commodity Chains: Competing or Complementary Forms of Economic Organisation? *Competition & Change*, 1, 411–25.

Wickberg, E. (1988) Chinese Organizations and Ethnicity in Southeast Asia and North America since 1945: A Comparative Analysis. In G. Wang and J. W. Cushman (eds), *Changing Identities of The Southeast Asian Chinese since World War II*, Hong Kong: Hong Kong University Press.

Wong, S.-L. (1985) The Chinese Family Firm: A Model, *British Journal of Sociology*, 36, 58–72.

World Bank (1995), *Vietnam Poverty – Assessment and Strategy*, Report No. 13442-VN, January 23, Washington, DC: World Bank.

World Bank (1995) *Vietnam. Economic Report on Industrialization and Industrial Policy*, Report No. 14645-VN, October 17, Washington, DC: World Bank.

Yeung, H. W.-C. (1994) Critical Reviews of Geographical Perspectives on Business Organisation: Towards a Network Approach, *Progress in Human Geography*, 18(4), 460–90.

—— (1997) Critical Realism and Realist Research in Human Geography: A Method or a Philosophy in Search of a Method? *Progress in Human Geography*, 21(1), 51–74.

—— (1998) *Transnational Corporations and Business Networks. Hong Kong Firms in the ASEAN Region. Routledge Advances in Asia Pacific Business*, London and New York: Routledge.

—— (1999) Under Siege? Economic Globalization and Chinese Business in Southeast Asia, *Economy and Society*, 28(1), 1–29.

Part IV

CHINESE NETWORK CAPITALISM AND *GUANXI* TRANSACTIONS RECONSIDERED

7

CHINESE BUSINESS DEVELOPMENT IN MALAYSIA

Networks, entrepreneurship or patronage?

Edmund Terence Gomez

Introduction: key concepts

Since the early 1990s, it has been argued that Chinese enterprises work along "networks" that lend it flexibility and power (see e.g. Redding 1990; Kotkin 1993; East Asian Analytical Unit 1995; Weidenbaum and Hughes 1996). Most of these studies promote the Weberian view that the "spirit" of the ethnic Chinese enterprise is founded in belief systems. Ethnic networks have reputedly emerged as an avenue for co-ethnics, who are minorities in a country where the state has been hostile to the development of their economic interests, to cooperate in business for mutual benefit. Chinese capital is conceptualized primarily as intra-ethnic networks, based on cooperation and trust, to help reduce transaction costs.

More nuanced theoretical conceptions of "networks" in business merit review. Putnam (1993), for example, argues of the existence of natural, preexisting "embedded" networks, based on trust and reciprocity, which constitutes a form of social capital within a particular society or community. On the other hand, Sabel (1992) argues of the artificial creation of "strategic" networks, that is, an instrumental tool involving subcontracting, information sharing etc., devised to reduce transaction costs and enhance profitability.

However, the overwhelming attention on the ostensible business networks among the Chinese-owned enterprises in Southeast Asia has diverted attention from other important concepts that are useful for explaining this community's form of capital development. Based on my research on the largest Chinese companies in Malaysia (see Gomez 1999), I would argue that among the important concepts that are more useful for understanding Chinese enterprise are entrepreneurship (Schumpeter 1943; Barth 1967), class resources (Light and Bonacich 1988), firm development and organization (Chandler 1962, 1977; Williamson 1975; Penrose 1980; Porter 1985, 1990), and patronage (Gomez and Jomo 1997).

There is a need to utilize these concepts as my detailed profile of a number of Chinese-owned companies and their growth conceptualized within the economic development of Malaysia, revealed heterogeneity of business styles. These differences were due to a number of factors, including state policies, resources available to these businessmen, the entrepreneurial endowment of individual businessmen and their access to state patronage through links with influential government leaders. In most cases, a combination of factors has contributed to the growth of major Chinese-owned firms. These factors include a productive use of experience gained in an industry before venturing into business, entrepreneurial deployment of resources generated from an initial investment in a company, and a rather focused approach to one trade rather than diversifying into any area of business that appeared potentially profitable. "Class resources" (Light and Bonacich 1988), including educational qualifications, access to funds and business experience, have been useful in explaining why some of the Chinese have managed to develop their enterprises. In some cases, class resources as well as entrepreneurial traits, such as the ability to correctly predict market trends and take risks by investing in a potentially lucrative opportunity, have proved crucial.

Chinese businesses in Malaysia

During the 1930s, Chinese migration to Malaya was curbed with the introduction of strict immigration laws. Such legislation has influenced the extent to which co-ethnics have continued to depend on one another economically as Chinese migration was one factor that had helped sustain a strong sense of ethnic – and sub-ethnic – identity among Chinese businessmen during the colonial period. For example, during the colonial period, Chinese Chambers of Commerce, trade associations and sub-ethnic associations, like the Hokkien, Hakka and Cantonese Associations, were important avenues through which the Chinese could act collectively for mutual benefit (see Heng 1988). The most prominent Chinese organization that was formed in the colonial period was the Malayan Chinese Association (MCA), which became the main partner of the United Malays' National Organisation (UMNO) in the multi-party ruling coalition, the Barisan Nasional (National Front). The MCA, formed in 1949 by some of the country's leading Chinese businessmen as a means to protect their economic interests in the post-colonial period, was probably the first major Chinese institution that transcended sub-ethnic barriers, though its elite-based leadership could not secure cross-class support. Presently, however, there is growing evidence that such Chinese trade organizations no longer serve as important "interest groups" through which representations can be made to the government concerning members' problems (see Jesudason 1997). Diminishing Chinese support for these organizations reflect, among other things, this community's heterogeneity, divided by place of origin, sub-ethnicity and social and class background. Generational change also helps account for the diminishing support for such organizations, as the local-born Chinese are less inclined to participate in them.

Even among the sub-ethnic Chinese groups, collaborative business ties are diminishing. The best example of sub-ethnic Chinese business cooperation was the establishment in 1932 of the Singapore-based Oversea-Chinese Banking Corporation (OCBC), a product of the merger of three Hokkien-owned banks. The Hokkiens, who have a long tradition of trade in business, had emerged as one of the largest Chinese entrepreneurs in Malaya and Singapore. The OCBC was formed during the Great Depression when these Hokkien banks, badly affected by the economic crisis, merged their banking activities to form an enlarged institution that remains one of the leading Chinese-owned banks in Asia.

Yet, OCBC was also the nucleus of three other major banks in Malaysia. Three men formerly in the employ of OCBC would break away to establish Malayan Banking Bhd (Maybank), MUI Bank Bhd (now renamed the Hong Leong Bank) and Public Bank Bhd. Maybank, Malaysia's largest bank in terms of deposits and capitalization and founded by Khoo Teck Puat, is now under the control of the state, while the founder of the MUI Bank, Khoo Kay Peng, lost control of the bank to another Hokkien Quek Leng Chan. Teh Hong Piow, who founded Public Bank, is the only former OCBC employee who remains in control of a bank in Malaysia.

Among the Chinese-owned banks in Malaysia, apart from the Hong Leong Bank and Public Bank, are the Ban Hin Lee Bank Bhd, Southern Bank Bhd and Pacific Bank Bhd, all controlled by Hokkiens.[1] Following the financial crisis in East Asia in 1997, the Malaysian government intensified its drive to get the country's numerous banks to merge to form larger enterprises with a bigger asset base that could make a greater impact in the local and global financial market. While a number of banks have begun to implement mergers, none of the Chinese-owned banks have entered into negotiations to achieve this goal.

State policies have had a profound impact on the Chinese enterprises, though none as much as the New Economic Policy (NEP) introduced in 1970, after the race riots of 1969 which was attributed to the inequitable distribution of corporate wealth among ethnic communities. The NEP was a twenty-year plan to achieve national unity by "eradicating poverty," regardless of race, and by "restructuring society" so as to achieve inter-ethnic economic parity between the indigenous Bumiputera (or "sons of the soil"), especially the Malays, and the predominantly Chinese non-Bumiputeras.[2] The NEP's second objective, the restructuring of society, was unquestionably the main emphasis of the policy. In 1969, the Bumiputera share of corporate wealth (by individuals and government trust agencies) amounted to a meager 2.4 percent. Chinese equity ownership stood at 27.2 percent, while more than 60 percent of the remaining equity was under foreign ownership (see Table 7.1). To fulfill the NEP objectives, the government increased public sector expenditure, particularly to fund trust agencies and the growing number of government-owned enterprises participating in business activities. Between 1957 and 1986, the number of public enterprises had increased from a mere ten to 841.

Increased state funding for public enterprises and trust agencies allowed them to go on a massive acquisition drive. This acquisition drive was aided by a 1975 government ruling that each public-listed company had to ensure that a minimum 30 percent of its equity was allocated to Bumiputera agencies or individuals. Apart

Table 7.1 Malaysia: ownership of share capital (at par value) of limited companies, 1969–95 (percentages)

	1969	*1970*	*1975*	*1980*	*1985*	*1990*	*1995*
Bumiputera individuals and trust agencies	1.5	2.4	9.2	12.5	19.1	19.2	20.6
Chinese	22.8	27.2	na	na	33.4	45.5	40.9
Indians	0.9	1.1	na	na	1.2	1.0	1.5
Nominees companies	2.1	6.0	na	na	1.3	8.5	8.3
Locally-controlled companies	10.1	—	—	—	7.2	0.3	1.0
Foreigners	62.1	63.4	53.3	42.9	26.0	25.4	27.7

Source: *Seventh Malaysia Plan, 1996–2000.*
Note: na, not available.

from this, public enterprises incorporated wholly-owned companies to venture into most areas of business and established joint ventures with Bumiputera, non-Bumiputera and foreign companies. In many cases, public enterprises merely acquired between 20 and 50 percent of equity in companies for investment purposes. Inevitably, affirmative action endeavors aroused non-Bumiputera dissatisfaction with the NEP. These fears were exacerbated to the extent that public enterprises encroached into economic sectors in which the Chinese had been prominent, particularly banking, property, construction and manufacturing.

Another outcome of the 1969 riots was the formation of the Barisan Nasional, a multi-party coalition that UMNO created in 1970 comprising most key opposition parties, after the Malay party nearly lost power in the 1969 general elections. The UMNO secured hegemony over the Barisan Nasional while the MCA's influence in the coalition diminished with the incorporation of parties that had Chinese support. When the MCA leaders were also evidently deprived of their traditional control over key ministries, Finance and, Trade and Industry, the Chinese businessmen lost a degree of confidence in the ability of the Chinese party to protect their interests in the government. Under the UMNO hegemony, the party arguably was compelled to engage in selective patronage in favor of the Bumiputeras. The emergence of a new Malay business class was strengthening the regime's hold on power and leading to a consolidation of economic and political power in the UMNO.

To ameliorate Chinese concern over the UMNO hegemony and the implementation of the NEP, the MCA was able to consolidate its ethnic Chinese identity through promotion of the "corporatisation movement," to secure mass Chinese support by endeavoring to protect the community's economic interests in the face of growing state and Malay capitalism. The corporatisation movement was an attempt to get the Chinese companies to overlook narrow clan divisions and cooperate in business. The movement also involved structural reforms to small-scale businesses and a modernization of their family-run management techniques (see

Yeoh 1987). When the MCA incorporated a major holding company, Multi-Purpose Holdings Bhd (MPHB), to pool Chinese resources ostensibly to venture into business to protect and advance Chinese capital, the party project was, initially at least, a phenomenal success. The MCA even managed to obtain for the first time the support of the working class Chinese who were convinced that the party had found a means to protect and develop Chinese economic interests (see Gale 1985; Yeoh 1987; Gomez 1994). The MPHB, however, led by MCA politicians, soon ran into problems and was burdened with huge debts. In the event, the MPHB was taken over by Kamunting Bhd, owned by a local Chinese family.

Since 1981, after Mahathir Mohamad was appointed Prime Minister, significant political and economic changes have transpired. Arguably, greater concentration of power in the hands of the executive has marked Mahathir's tenure. The Prime Minister is driven by a desire to achieve fully developed nation status for Malaysia by 2020, as well as to create a new class of internationally recognized Bumiputera capitalists. Mahathir consolidated his position in government in the late 1980s, seeing off a threat to his position by the influential former Finance Minister Razaleigh Hamzah. Afterwards, he was able to concentrate on achieving his development agenda for Malaysia without too much fear for his own political position. For the Prime Minister, the dynamic, entrepreneurial Bumiputera class he wished to create had to develop the capacity to compete and perform in an international business environment. Thus, a new breed of Malay and Chinese businessmen emerged as major corporate players during the NEP decades.

However, the uncertain future of Malay politics means that Chinese groups can never be totally sure of the consequences of the UMNO factional rivalry, particularly in view of the unclear succession line following the dismissal and jailing of Mahathir's heir apparent, Anwar Ibrahim. The perceptions of UMNO members that state economic privileges and benefits were accorded to Chinese businessmen continue to rankle, and how this issue is addressed by the future UMNO leaders struggling to consolidate their positions is obviously a matter of considerable concern to the Chinese businessmen. In these circumstances, in order to continue to accumulate and ascend most big Chinese capitalists in Malaysia may be well advised to accommodate well-connected Malays. It had long been a practice for even medium-scale Chinese companies to seek Bumiputera investors and appoint them as directors of their enterprises to qualify for certain privileges established by the NEP in land ownership, government contracts, and other Bumiputera incentives.

On the other hand, the UMNO-dominated government has also found it necessary to accommodate Chinese capital. Following a severe recession in the mid-1980s, the government recognized the importance of Chinese – and foreign – capital for sustaining growth and promoting industrialization; the recession also highlighted the need to check the activities of rentier capitalists. A similar trend was clear in the recession in 1998 after the financial crisis. Before the financial crisis, the Prime Minister saw the opening up of China's economy as offering potentially lucrative business ventures for Malaysian capital. This appears to have encouraged the Prime Minister's call for greater business cooperation between

Table 7.2 Business activity and sub-ethnic identity of the largest Chinese companies
in Malaysia

Company	Activities	Controlling shareholder	Sub-ethnic group
Genting Bhd	Gaming, leisure, plantations, power generation, property development, manufacturing	Lim Goh Tong	Hokkien
YTL Corporation	Construction, manufacturing, power generation, property development	Yeoh Tiong Lay	Hokkien
Public Bank	Gaming, financial services	Teh Hong Piow	Hokkien
Berjaya Group	Manufacturing, telecommunications, media, wholesaling, financial services, property development	Vincent Tan Chee Yioun	Hokkien
Jaya Tiasa Holdings	Manufacturing	Tiong Hiew King	Foochow
Kamunting Corporation/ Multi-Purpose Holdings	Construction, gaming, investment holding, property development	T. K. Lim	Hokkien
Hong Leong Group	Finance, banking, manufacturing, property development	Quek Leng Chan	Hokkien
Kuala Lumpur Kepong	Plantations, property development, manufacturing	Lee Loy Seng family	Hakka
Malayan United Industries (MUI)	Manufacturing, retailing, hotels, property development, media, education services	Khoo Kay Peng	Hokkien
Perlis Plantations	Manufacturing, hotels, commodity trading, shipping, plantations, property development	Robert Kuok	Foochow
Ekran	Construction, trading, timber extraction, property development	Ting Pek Khiing	Foochow
MBf Capital	Finance, property development	Loy Hean Heong family	Foochow
Tan Chong Motor	Manufacturing	Tan family	Hokkien
Lion Corporation	Manufacturing, retailing, motor assembly, construction, telecommunications	William Cheng	Teochew
Oriental Holdings	Manufacturing, hotels	Loh Boon Siew family	Hokkien
Hap Seng Consolidated	Manufacturing	Lau Gek Poh	Cantonese

the Chinese and Malays. At the Second Fujianese World Chinese Entrepreneurs Convention held in Malaysia in 1996, the Prime Minister said, "Malaysian Fujianese's close connections with their fellow-provincials in different corners of the world will help promote the business and investment opportunities in Malaysia" (quoted in Hong 1998). This pattern of development has influenced the nature of inter-ethnic business cooperation, suggesting a more level playing field between the two communities, even though this may not be the case in reality. The Prime Minister's desire to push Malaysia towards a fully-developed nation status and his recognition of the potential Chinese contribution to this goal has led to greater economic liberalization and the inclusion of Chinese capital into the national development aspirations.

At the end of 1990, Chinese equity had doubled from 22.8 to 45.5 percent (see Table 7.1). During the NEP period, a number of new Chinese capitalists had also emerged, among them Vincent Tan Chee Yioun, Khoo Kay Peng, William Cheng Heng Jem, T. K. Lim and Ting Pek Khiing. My study of the 100 largest public-listed companies in Malaysia in 1996, in terms of capitalization, revealed that at least 40 percent of these firms were controlled by the Chinese (see Table 7.2).

A number of other important points emerge from Table 7.2. First, a majority of these Chinese firms are owned by Hokkiens – or Foochows, a variant of the Hokkiens – suggesting that some form of intra sub-ethnic networking may have contributed to the rise of these companies. Second, a large number of these Chinese-owned enterprises are involved in manufacturing, suggesting that these businessmen are not mere rentiers but have a productive dimension to their form of business. Table 7.2 also indicates that the Chinese are involved in a range of activities including finance, gaming, hotels, plantations, construction, property development, retailing and media. The case studies below will provide some insight into the factors that have contributed to the development of Chinese capital in Malaysia.

Case studies

Loh Boon Siew and Oriental Holdings Bhd

Loh Boon Siew was a member of the MCA, establishing his reputation in business before independence was achieved in 1957; by 1992, three years before his death, he was reportedly Malaysia's second richest businessman, with corporate assets worth approximately RM1.8 bn (approximately US$0.3 bn) (see *The Star*, 5/19/1992). Born in Fukien province in China in 1916, Loh came to Malaya with his father at the age of twelve. Having very little formal education, Loh started out as a mechanic. At the age of eighteen, Loh set up his own workshop, and by the following year he had saved enough to purchase a fleet of eleven buses, operating through his Penang Yellow Bus Company Sdn Bhd. Within three years, the thriving company had a fleet of forty-one buses. By this time, apart from the

Penang Yellow Bus Company and his mechanic shop, Loh had ventured into the sale of used cars, spare parts, batteries and tyres. Loh also secured the franchise to distribute the British-made Aerial motorcycles in the northern regions of Malaya. During the Japanese Occupation of Malaya, most of his buses were confiscated; after the war Loh restarted these businesses rapidly expanded (*Malaysian Business*, January 1974; *The Star*, 11/20/1985; *The Sun*, 12/19/1994).

In 1958, during a visit to Japan, Loh's attention was drawn to Honda motorcycles. That year, his family company, Boon Siew Sdn Bhd, secured the franchise to be the sole distributor of Honda motorcycles. It was the first Japanese-made motorcycle in Malaya. The Japanese were then trying to break into the Malayan motor vehicle distribution industry that was controlled by the British. After a rather lukewarm start, demand increased appreciably, and by the mid-1970s Honda had captured 60 percent of the motorcycle market. Loh's distribution network soon expanded to Singapore and Brunei. In 1969, as the demand grew, Loh set up a plant in Penang to assemble Honda motorcycles, through his Kah Motor Co. Sdn Bhd. Later, Kah Motor secured the franchise to also distribute Honda motorcars and commercial vehicles. Kah Motor was originally the sole agent for Toyota cars, but relinquished this franchise in 1966 in favor of the Honda franchise.

Through his association with Honda, Loh came to national prominence, under the ambit of his main public-listed company, Oriental Holdings Bhd, incorporated in 1963 and quoted publicly in 1964. Honda cars are assembled by Oriental Assemblers Sdn Bhd,[3] in which Oriental Holdings has a 65.94 percent stake; the Honda car assembly plant in Johore was bought from General Motors in 1980. The assembly and distribution of Honda motorcycles and cars have yielded a significant portion of the turnover and profits of the Oriental Holdings group (see Table 7.3). In the motorcycle distribution market, however, competition has increased with the introduction of other Japanese motorcycles, particularly the Suzuki and Yamaha, distributed by the Lion group and the Hong Leong group, respectively (*Malaysian Business*, 6/16/1988).

Oriental Holdings owns the entire equity of Kah Motor, which has been consistently registering profitable turnovers. In 1995, for example, it registered a turnover of RM1,509m, compared to RM1,566m in 1994. Kah Motor has local and foreign-incorporated subsidiaries involved in a myriad of activities,

Table 7.3 Oriental Holdings Bhd: share capital, turnover and profit margins, 1984–95 (RM million)

	1984	*1985*	*1986*	*1987*	*1988*	*1989*	*1990*	*1991*	*1993*	*1994*	*1995*
Paid-up capital	100.2	100.2	100.2	100.2	100.2	100.2	100.2	120.2	144.3	144.3	144.3
Turnover	489.6	298.5	247.4	318.3	na	na	1155.1	1246.5	1527.9	2060.3	2413.6
Pre-tax profit	65.4	32.6	10.5	23.3	57.0	125.2	259.3	254.1	214.8	310.9	353.9

Sources: Malaysian Business, 6/16/1988; *KLSE Annual Companies Handbook*, 21(4), 1996: 70.

including motor dealing and repair, motor vehicle distribution, property development and hotels. Oriental Holdings has concentrated much attention on manufacturing, diversifying its range of motor component parts. The group's wide range
of manufacturing subsidiaries manufacture motor engines and a range of motor
vehicle components including seats, shock absorbers, clutches, brakes and
speedometers; the group is also heavily involved in the manufacture of plastic
component parts.[4]

Oriental Holdings' car assembly, component parts and plastic manufacturing
activities contribute a major portion of the group's total earnings. In 1995, for
example, it was estimated that the motor division contributed a 65 percent share
of the group's total earnings, while the autoparts and assembling divisions contributed another 6 and 7 percent, respectively. This sector is expected to generate
further earnings for the Oriental Holdings group since the government intends to
reduce the import content of material used in the automotive sector (*The Sun*,
6/17/1996). The plastic division, which manufactures plastic parts for the automotive industry, as well as the electrical and electronic industries, contributed
another 11 percent. Oriental Holdings also has an interest in companies that
manufacture steel products in China.

Following Loh's death, his daughter Cheng Yean took over as Chairman of
Oriental Holdings, while Loh's son-in-law, Wong Lum Kong, was appointed the
Managing Director. Another of Loh's children, daughter Say Bee, is also a Director
of the company. In terms of its shareholding structure, Loh's family companies
collectively own almost 52 percent of Oriental Holdings' equity – Boon Siew Sdn
Bhd (43 percent), Penang Yellow Bus Company (5.3 percent) and Loh Boon Siew
Sdn Bhd (1.2 percent) (see Figure 7.1). There are no prominent Bumiputeras in
Oriental Holdings' board of directors.

The business operations of the Oriental Holdings group also indicate that it has
not been privy to any concessions from the state. Nor have any of the companies

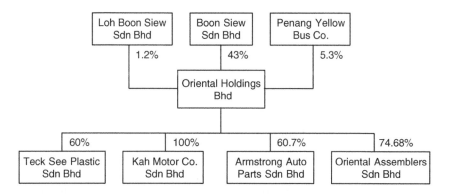

Figure 7.1 Oriental Holdings Bhd corporate structure.
Source: *KLSE Annual Companies Handbook*, 21(4), 1996: 65–9.

in the Oriental Holdings group worked with well-connected Bumiputera businesses even though Loh was an active member of the MCA, and was once the Deputy Chairman of the Penang MCA. Loh's case provides further credence to the view that the MCA's participation in the government has not significantly benefited major companies owned by the MCA leaders since the 1970s implementation of the NEP, which arguably reflects a declining influence by the MCA in government.

In terms of links with other Chinese companies, Loh was also a Director of the Southern Bank and Tasek Cement Bhd, in which he had a 10 percent stake. Lim Goh Tong, who owns the gaming concern Genting Bhd, was also a Director of the Southern Bank, which was seen as a Hokkien bank. Despite their common interests in the bank, and although Loh and Lim are Hokkien, there were no major business deals involving the two. Other shareholders of Tasek Cement have included Quek Leng Chan of the Hong Leong group, a Hokkien originally from Singapore, but here too, there are no major business links involving the companies in these groups.

Loh proved himself to have been quite entrepreneurial. Loh has clearly built on his early experience as a mechanic. This had helped him identify the potential impact of Honda motorcyles in the Southeast Asian market. The intermediary role that Loh had played between the British and the local economy in the distribution of motorcycles in the colonial period held him in good stead in the immediate post-colonial period when he secured the franchise to distribute Honda vehicles. Taking the risk of securing the franchise and distributing Japanese-model motorcycles during a period when the market was controlled by British-made models, he was eventually able to pioneer Japanese involvement in this sector.

From the role of a trader, Loh later moved into the assembly of motor vehicles. Further vertical integration was achieved when Oriental Holdings began to manufacture component parts. A historical review of Loh's business style suggests concentration on vertical integration in the motor vehicle industry despite the diversified nature of his business operations. Loh has worked closely with foreign companies, establishing links with the British and then the Japanese, and managed to gain expertise from them to develop independently. Meanwhile, the Japanese have probably also benefited from the distribution network that Loh managed to create in the country and region. Interestingly, in the distribution of motorcycles, Oriental Holdings' main competitors are other ethnic Chinese, including Quek Leng Chan and William Cheng of the Lion group.

Teh Hong Piow and the Public Bank Bhd

Teh Hong Piow, the son of a poor migrant from China, was born in Singapore in 1930. At the age of twenty, after completing his secondary education, Teh joined the OCBC as a clerk to support his family; he rose quickly to become a sub-accountant. In 1960, he joined the newly established Maybank as one of its senior executives, securing within four years the post of general manager. Teh was, however, affected by an acrimonious feud within Maybank involving its original shareholders. In 1965, at the young age of thirty-five, he applied for and secured a banking license and became the youngest Managing Director in full control of a domestic bank (*Investors' Digest*, May 1987; *Malaysian Business*, 8/1/1987).

The award of this license to Teh was significant as government leaders were then under increasing pressure from UMNO members to ensure more distribution of wealth to Malays, implying that the Chinese were receiving too many concessions from the state. Bank Bumiputra Bhd, the state-owned bank, established to promote the development of Malay capital, was established in the same year as the Public Bank. Teh has never disclosed how he managed to secure the banking license though he has admitted, "Getting a banking license in those days wasn't easy. But with the help of friends and connections, we managed to secure one" (quoted in *Malaysian Business*, 8/1/1987). The first chairman of the Public Bank was Nik Ahmad Kamil, an UMNO member who had served as *Mentri Besar* (Chief Minister) of Kelantan, Speaker of the *Dewan Rakyat* (House of Representatives) and Malaysian ambassador to the United Nations, the United States, Australia and the United Kingdom.

Public Bank, currently the largest Chinese-owned bank in Malaysia, was incorporated on 30 December 1965, started operations on 6 August 1966, and secured a public listing on 6 April 1967. Along with the Public Bank, Teh incorporated a finance company, Public Finance Bhd, which was publicly listed on 21 December 1966. Although Teh used Public Bank's profits to diversify, moving into property development – the bank's original RM2 m capital base was reportedly secured through the profits he had made from property development (see *Far Eastern Economic Review*, 10/3/1991) – this diversification phase soon ceased. Teh would later say: "I came to the realization that it was not wise to go into different types of business enterprises just for the sake of diversification. I believe that in order to do well, one should concentrate on the business which one knows best" (*The Star*, 10/24/1985).

The Public Bank grew rapidly. Between 1966 and 1996, Public Bank's paid-up capital increased from a mere RM12.750 m to a phenomenal RM826.097 m (*KLSE Annual Companies Handbook*, 21(4), 1996: 628–9). By 1996, the Public Bank had 155 branches, including one in Hong Kong, Sri Lanka and Laos as well as a representative office in China and Myanmar. The bank is planning to expand its involvement in Southeast Asia, moving into Thailand, the Philippines and Indonesia. The Public Bank started as a thirty-two-staff operation; by the early 1990s, the group had approximately 4,500 employees (*Malaysian Business*, 9/1/1999, 8/1/1996). Public Finance has seventy-two branches and is one of the country's leading finance companies. In its thirty-year history, the Public Bank group has never declared a loss, even during the mid-1980s economic recession.

Public Bank's growth strategy has been described by one senior bank official: "Our primary market is small-to-medium businesses, those involved in trade and manufacturing, or cottage industries. About one-third of our customers are large corporate clients, and the other two-thirds small-to-medium-sized businesses" (quoted in *Far Eastern Economic Review*, 10/3/1991). Having established some success in the Malaysian market, Public Bank has turned its attention abroad. In Vietnam, the Public Bank is trying to create a niche among the ethnic Chinese there, and when Public Bank took over the JCG Finance Company Ltd in Hong Kong, it catered primarily to small Chinese businesses and the colony's 74,000-strong Filipino community (*Far Eastern Economic Review*, 10/3/1991).

In Malaysia, apart from banking and finance, Public Bank is involved in leasing and factoring, stock broking and futures trading, trustee services, offshore

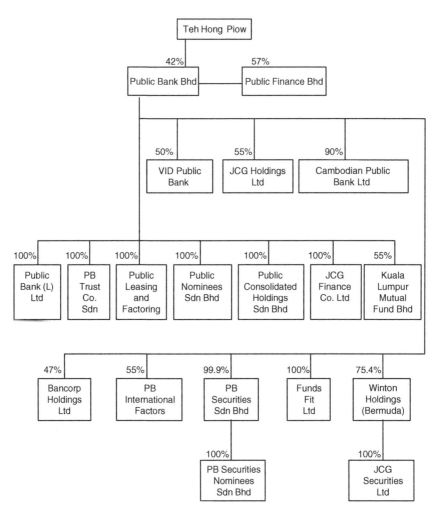

Figure 7.2 Public Bank Bhd corporate structure.

Sources: *KLSE Annual Companies Handbook*, 21(4), 1996: 628–39; *Malaysian Business* 9/1/1991.

banking and unit trust services. Among its main overseas acquisitions is the Hong Kong-based JCG Finance, which is also involved in the securities industry. Public Bank (Labuan) Ltd was established to move into offshore banking. Public Bank (Labuan) was used to acquire a 40 percent stake in Bancorp Holdings in New Zealand, a merchant and investment-banking group. Public Bank has a 55 percent stake in the Singapore-based PB International Factors (*Malaysian Business*, 9/1/1991; see also Figure 7.2).

The growth of Public Bank may have been enhanced because Teh has made it a point to conform to and implement state policies. For example, Teh claimed that his response to the NEP was to make it a point to study and follow all the government policies (see *Malaysian Business*, 9/1/1991). In 1982, Public Bank was granted "Approved Status" by the Ministry of Finance for meeting all of Bank Negara's (the central bank) priority lending guidelines and for fulfilling the NEP's Bumiputera ownership and employment quotas (*Malaysian Business*, January 1983). Public Bank has a reputation in the Malaysian market for being conservative and prudent (see *Malaysian Business*, 8/1/1996). Teh has also stressed this point: "We have continuously been able to contain our incidence of non-performing loans as well as being effective in our loan recovery. Thus, as at December 31, 1995, non-performing loans represented only 1.7 percent of the gross loans and advances. This is well below the industry average of 5.1 percent" (quoted in *Malaysian Business*, 8/1/1996).

There is no evidence of major business ties between Teh and well-connected Malay businessmen, nor are there any prominent Bumiputeras on the board of directors of Public Bank. This suggests that by conforming to the NEP regulations and steering clear of controversy,[5] Teh may have enhanced his ability to retain control of Public Bank and pursue an aggressive growth strategy. The fact that Public Bank has concentrated its activities in the financial sector appears to be another reason why the bank has managed to do well.

Francis Yeoh and the YTL Corporation Bhd

The Yeoh family has a long history of involvement in the construction industry and controls YTL Corporation Bhd. The Chairman of the company, Yeoh Tiong Lay, was born in Malaysia in 1930. He was the son of a timber merchant, Yeoh Cheng Liam, a migrant from China who was actively involved in construction through his company Yeoh Cheng Liam Construction Sdn Bhd. Tiong Lay was not professionally qualified when he went into business on his own at the age of twenty, though he probably gained much business experience working with his father. Tiong Lay would, however, later secure professional qualifications from the United Kingdom and Australia, which conferred upon him the title of "Chartered Builder" (*The Diplomat*, February 1986).

Through his company, Syarikat Pembenaan Yeoh Tiong Lay Sdn Bhd, Tiong Lay began business modestly, securing his first contract in 1950 to construct two police explosive magazines in two states in Malaysia. The company eventually went on to construct some of the largest buildings in the national capital, including the headquarters of two foreign banks, Citibank and the Hongkong & Shanghai Bank, and of the Malaysian-controlled multinational, Sime Darby Bhd (*The Diplomat*, February 1986; *Malaysian Business*, 2/16/1994).[6]

In 1984, Tiong Lay gained control of Hong Kong Tin plc, a nearly moribund tin-mining company. Through a spate of shares-for-assets swaps and rights issues, Tiong Lay injected a few subsidiaries owned by his family company, Syarikat Pembenaan Yeoh Tiong Lay – including YTL Cement Sdn Bhd, Batu Tiga Quarry Sdn Bhd and Yeoh Tiong Lay Brickworks Sdn Bhd – into the public-listed company, which was renamed Hong Kong Tin Corporation (M) Bhd. In 1988, Hong Kong Tin also implemented a reverse takeover of Syarikat Pembenaan Yeoh Tiong Lay; the quoted company was then renamed YTL Corporation Bhd (*Malaysian Business*, 1/16/1992). YTL Cement Bhd, Malaysia's largest ready-mixed concrete manufacturer, is another company in the YTL Corp group, which was publicly listed in 1993, though on the second board of the Kuala Lumpur Stock Exchange (KLSE). In mid-1997, YTL Corp also listed YTL Power International (YTLPI) Bhd, the largest independent power producer (IPP) on the stock exchange (*The Edge*, 3/17/1997). Although YTL Corp had established a reputation as a contractor for turnkey projects by the end of the 1980s, the company still remained a relatively small construction, property development and manufacturing concern; in terms of market capitalization, the company's paid-up capital was just about RM73 m in 1991 (see Table 7.4).

Yeoh Tiong Lay has seven children, all of whom were educated abroad and have secured professional qualifications. All seven third-generation Yeohs are directors of YTL Corp. Tiong Lay is the Chairman of the company, while his eldest son, Francis Yeoh, who is currently primarily responsible for the management of the YTL Corp group, is Managing Director; second son Seok Kian is the Deputy Managing Director. The largest shareholder of YTL Corp, with a 48 percent stake, is Tiong Lay's family holding company, Yeoh Tiong Lay & Sons Holdings Sdn Bhd. Yeoh Tiong Lay (as Chairman) and Francis Yeoh (as Managing Director) also lead public-listed YTL Cement, while three of Yeoh's other children sit on the board of this company. YTL Corp holds 53.32 percent of YTL Cement's equity (*KLSE Annual Companies Handbook*, 21(2),

Table 7.4 YTL Corp Bhd: share capital, turnover and profit margins, 1991–6 (RM million)

	1991	*1992*	*1993*	*1994*	*1995*	*1996*
Paid-up capital	73.08	90.37	90.51	109.20	178.99	179.18
Turnover	302.70	455.58	489.59	583.99	1025.40	1600.00*
Pre-tax profit	30.95	42.81	52.72	71.81	231.26	356.00*

Source: *KLSE Annual Companies Handbook*, 21(2), 1996: 257–66.

1996: 262, 595–9). Yeoh Tiong Lay & Sons Holdings' company records indicate that the shareholders and directors of this private investment and property holding company, which was incorporated on 31 January 1979 and has an issued capital base of RM40.720 m, are all members of the Yeoh family. This shareholding pattern reflects the strong emphasis on family control of the YTL Corp group, with the Yeohs forming the core of the group's management.

Bumiputera participation in the YTL Corp amounts to 16.29 percent, of which only 0.68 percent is held by Bumiputera individuals and 1.39 percent by Bumiputera nominees. The armed forces' provident fund, the Lembaga Tabung Angkatan Tentera (LTAT), is the main Bumiputera shareholder, with a 13.21 percent stake. Total Bumiputera equity participation in YTL Cement is 16.22 percent, of which Bumiputera individuals, including nominees, account for a third, or 5.16 percent; LTAT is the largest Bumiputera equity holder with 8.86 percent equity in YTL Cement (*KLSE Annual Companies Handbook*, 21(2), 1996: 595–9). There are no prominent Bumiputeras among YTL Cement's directors.

YTL Corp has benefited from some major government projects. In 1990, the company was awarded a RM840 m contract to design and develop twelve hospitals as part of the government's plans to create a nationwide rural healthcare network. The company also secured the contract to build a RM112 m airport in Sibu, Sarawak. YTL Corp has also been awarded two projects in the state of Perak, a low and medium cost privatized housing scheme and a 120 ha light industrial park (*Business Times*, 11/26/1993).

It was, however, in 1992, that YTL Corp gained much prominence when it became the first company to be awarded an independent power producer (IPP) license worth RM2.5 bn by the government; YTL Corp had submitted plans to the government to construct two power plants. The government-controlled privatized electricity company, Tenaga Nasional Bhd, then had power plants in the two sites proposed by YTL Corp, and had its own plans to build new plants to raise power generation (*Malaysian Business*, 6/16/1992). The license was for a privatized build-operate-own (BOO) project involving the construction and operation of two gas-fueled electricity-generating plants in the states of Terengganu and Johore (*The Star*, 10/25/1993). The project involved the sale of electricity to Tenaga over a 21-year period, sealed through a power purchase agreement. Though more IPP licenses were to be issued to other companies, the contracts ensured guaranteed minimum sales at high prices that ensured YTL Corp of profitable income for the duration of the 21-year contract.

The license was awarded in 1993 to YTL Power Generation Sdn Bhd, in which YTL Corp had a 50 percent stake. The other shareholders of YTL Power Generation, which had an initial paid-up capital of RM300 m, were Tenaga (20 percent) and the government's Employees Provident Fund (10 percent), while the remaining 20 percent equity was split between the British-based construction company John Laing plc, Mayban Ventures Sdn Bhd and a Bumiputera company

Bara Aktif Sdn Bhd[7] (*The Star*, 9/15/1994). To handle the operations and maintenance of the two power plants, YTL Power Services Sdn Bhd was incorporated. YTL Corp owned 51 percent of this company's equity, while the remaining 49 percent stake was held by the German-based power equipment supplier, Siemens AG; however, YTL Corp has a buy-back option for Siemens' stake in YTL Power Services, exercisable after six years (*Malaysian Business*, 2/16/1994).

Apart from the sale of electricity to Tenaga, YTL Corp was expected to benefit from the IPP in a number of ways. First, YTL Corp's main subsidiary, Syarikat Pembenaan Yeoh Tiong Lay, was expected to make a profit of approximately RM200 m from the turnkey construction of the two power plants. Second, the management fees from operating the plants were another source of income. Third, since YTL Power Generation was expected to be listed, extraordinary gains were anticipated when a portion of the YTL Corp's stake in the company was sold (*The Star*, 11/7/1994). The contract would also provide the YTL group with a recurrent earnings flow, with an expected total income of at least RM1 bn for the duration of the IPP contract. Since YTL Corp was expected to provide 20 percent of Tenaga's generation capacity, with electricity consumption growth estimated at an average 10–12 percent during the 1990s, and given Malaysia's rapid industrialization program, which caused the demand for power to rise, YTL Corp's involvement in electricity supply was expected to provide the company with a significant portion of the group's profits (see *Malaysian Business*, 2/16/1994). The IPP project was completed in September 1995, well ahead of the scheduled completion date. As expected, just a year later, in June 1996, YTL Corp recorded a massive increase of 54 percent with pre-tax profits of RM356 m on sales of RM1.6 bn (*Far Eastern Economic Review*, 12/26/1996).

Not unexpectedly, since this power generation activity proved profitable (see Table 7.4), YTL Corp hoped that this project would be a stepping-stone to becoming an international power supplier. According to Francis Yeoh: "In future, Malaysia could be the regional center of power exchange with links to Singapore, Thailand and further" (quoted in *The Star*, 9/15/1994). Subsequently, in 1994, Francis Yeoh secured a contract to supply electricity to Singapore, and in 1996, a US$600 m power deal in Zimbabwe, which involved the acquisition of a power plant and the development of two new power-generating units at the plant (*Far Eastern Economic Review*, 12/26/1996; *The Star*, 4/4/1997). YTL Corp has similar deals in Thailand and China, and is exploring possible power supply projects in the Philippines, Vietnam and India (*The Star*, 4/4/1997). In October 1996, YTL Corp tried unsuccessfully to take over 80 percent of Consolidated Electric Power Asia (CEPA), the power supply subsidiary of the Hong Kong-based Hopewell Holdings, controlled by Gordon Wu (*Asiaweek*, 12/6/1996). The takeover was seen by YTL Corp as an opportunity to create a YTL-controlled pan-Asian power giant, while the Prime Minister's view of the unsuccessful takeover attempt was that it was "a very good deal that got away" (quoted in *The Edge*, 3/17/1997). The government's investment holding company, Khazanah Holdings, had agreed to provide YTL Corp with RM1 bn as financial backing for the takeover (*Asiaweek*, 12/6/1996).

In May 1997, YTL Corp announced its plans to list YTL Power International on the main board of the KLSE, which was expected to help the company raise around RM2 bn. Apart from the contracts secured in Singapore and Zimbabwe, YTL Power International's subsidiaries and associate companies will include YTL Power Generation, a 30 percent stake in Teknologi Tenaga Perlis (Overseas) Consortium Sdn Bhd, which is to supply power to Thailand's Electricity Generating Board, and a 51 percent stake in YTL-CPI Power Ltd, that is to own a 60 percent stake in a joint-venture company, Nanchang Zhongli Power Co. Ltd, formed in China; the other members of the joint-venture are Jiangxi Provincial Power Electric Corp and Jiangxi Provincial Investment Corp (*The Edge*, 4/14/1997). YTL Corp is expected to hold 59 percent of YTL Power International's equity, while the other major shareholders are expected to include three state-linked enterprises, Khazanah, the EPF and the government-controlled Tenaga, an indication of the strong government endorsement of YTL Power International's expected forays abroad (*Business Times*, 3/11/1997; *The Star*, 4/4/1998).

YTL Corp's emphasis on developing an overseas market, both in terms of building power plants and electricity supply, is suggestive of an ability to build upon the experience gained from developing the IPPs locally. It is also unlikely that the company would secure any more IPP contracts in Malaysia, as power generation has become increasingly competitive. By 1997, at least five IPP contracts had been issued and a contract awarded for the privatized construction of a major hydroelectric dam in Sarawak, the Bakun Dam, which would also generate electricity for the peninsula.

YTL Corp has gone on to develop even closer ties with the government, working with a number of other state agencies in different sectors. The company is in a joint venture with the government's Urban Development Authority (UDA) to build apartments and office towers on prime land in KL's golden triangle. In 1994, YTL Corp also reached an agreement with the government's railway company, Keretapi Tanah Melayu (KTM) Bhd, to develop 1.4 m sq ft of prime land in Brickfields, also in the federal capital (*Business Times*, 12/19/1994). YTL Corp entered into joint-venture property development projects with a number of state development corporations (SEDCs); this has given the company access to lucrative housing development projects on land owned by the state governments (*Malaysian Business*, 2/16/1994). With Pasdec Corporation Sdn Bhd, a company owned by the Pahang state government, YTL Cement formed a joint venture, Pahang Cement Sdn Bhd, to construct a 600,000 tonne fully-integrated cement manufacturing plant near the state capital, ostensibly to catalyze the industrialization of the eastern corridor of the peninsula (*Business Times*, 11/26/1993).

YTL Corp's management has attributed its diversification to the increasing competitiveness of its mainstay, construction; moreover, they claim that the gross profit margins of between 5 and 7 percent from construction projects are neither lucrative nor contribute much to net asset growth (see *Malaysian Business*, 2/16/1994). This has contributed to the group's move into the hotel industry, giving it access to land, building its own hotels and developing its asset base. Apart from power generation, the other sectors that the group is concentrating on are manufacturing (primarily through YTL Cement) and property development (see Figure 7.3). Construction and manufacturing continue to be major contributors to the group's revenue, but even the company's directors acknowledge that the "earnings contribution" from the two power plants "will underpin the Group's long term growth" (quoted in *KLSE Annual Companies Handbook*, 21(2), 1996: 262; see Table 7.5). According to one estimate, at least 70 percent of the group's earnings will come from its power supply arm, allowing earnings from the sector to provide the capital required to finance further group expansion (see *Asiamoney* November 1994). This indicates the importance of the IPP contracts to the future development of the group.

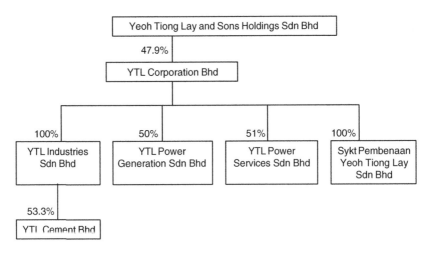

Figure 7.3 YTL Corporation Bhd corporate structure.
Source: *KLSE Annual Companies Handbook*, 21(2), 1996: 259–62; 596–7.

Table 7.5 YTL Corp Bhd: sectoral breakdown in terms of turnover and pre-tax profits, 1995 (RM million)

Sector	Turnover	Pre-tax profit
Construction	469.3	72.2
Manufacturing and trading	178.9	25.4
Property development and management services	90.7	23.6
Power generation	286.5	110.0

Source: *KLSE Annual Companies Handbook*, 21(2), 1996: 266.

The company's rapid growth, in terms of capitalization, profits and turnover, is attributable to the IPP contracts secured from the government in 1993 (see Table 7.5), systematic moves towards acquiring new technology and other factors. For example, after obtaining the IPP license, YTL Corp established ties with the German-based firm, Siemens, to implement the project. YTL Corp hopes to take over the running of the power plants in future once it has learnt the technology from the Germans. Similarly, to implement another major project secured from the government, involving the construction of twelve rural health care nucleus hospitals, YTL Corp has teamed up with the British-based construction company, John Laing plc. With YTL Corp's professionally qualified management, led by Yeoh Tiong Lay's children (referred to as "the cabinet"), the company's ability to obtain and develop technical expertise and competence augurs well. Diversification rather than specialization in construction alone appear to have been facilitated by new government-provided opportunities, as its older activities faced increasing competition.

Conclusion

The case studies reveal that different factors have influenced the pattern of growth of these three large Chinese-owned companies. The key common factor, however, among all three businessmen that has influenced the growth of their companies was their entrepreneurial ability, that is, the ability to spot an opening in the economy and venturing early into that field. For example, in the case of Loh, he recognized the potential for distributing Japanese-model motorcycles in Malaya. Although Loh was the first businessmen to distribute Japanese-model motor vehicles in Malaya, in spite of the competition he then faced from British-model distributors, he had a head start in this sector after the demand for British-model vehicles began to decline. Yeoh was the first businessmen to venture into power generation, before competition in this sector emerged. Yeoh's early entry in this sector allowed him to secure a very favorable deal to supply electricity to the government's privatized power distributor, Tenaga. Teh had recognized that rather than challenging established banks for the same market in Malaysia, he concentrated his efforts on creating a niche for Public Bank by servicing SMEs, which are primarily Chinese-owned.

There are important differences between the men leading these three companies. While Loh was a migrant from China, Teh and Yeoh Tiong Lay were born and grew up in a multi-racial environment. YTL Corporation is presently led by a third generation Yeoh. While Loh and Yeoh Tiong Lay had no major ties with the Malay political elite, Teh did depend initially on political ties to secure a banking license though he appears to have developed Public Bank independent of political patronage. Francis Yeoh appears to have the most significant links with the Malay political elite.

All three men were privy to certain class resources that helped them build up their enterprises. Loh had much experience as a mechanic that proved crucial in helping him recognize the potential of Honda motor vehicles. Teh's long employment with two major banks, the OCBC and Maybank, was probably instrumental in helping him develop Public Bank. Yeoh Tiong Lay came from a background of involvement in construction and also secured some professional qualifications that enabled him to develop his interests in this sector. Yeoh's children, including his eldest son, Francis Yeoh, were also professionally qualified which facilitated YTL Corp's entry into power generation; more importantly, they also have the capacity to acquire technology through joint-ventures and then develop their enterprise in this sector independently in an international environment.

Loh, who managed to develop his enterprise independently of state patronage, had established a reputation in business during the colonial period and immediately after, before the emergence of Malay hegemony over the state. Francis Yeoh and Teh had access to some state patronage that was crucial for getting them licenses in the banking and power generation sectors, but both businessmen showed a capacity to build on the original rent they secured without much more state support. While Yeoh did receive some backing from the government in his attempt to develop his power generation business abroad, since securing the power supply license, he has shown a capacity to develop "know-how" independently.

There is little evidence that Loh, Teh and Yeoh Tiong Lay (and his son) have seen the need to exploit common ethnic identity to promote their business interests, particularly after 1970 following the implementation of the NEP. In fact, since 1970, competition among the Chinese for state rents appear to have increased. Intra-ethnic business networking, in the form of joint ventures, subcontracting, or exchange of information, does not figure in any of the ventures undertaken by these three Chinese corporations. Although all three men are Hokkiens, a sub-ethnic community that has a history of business cooperation, there is no evidence of any significant business links in their corporate ventures. All three companies were established by individuals acting alone without the partnership of other ethnic Chinese or even with sub-ethnic Hokkien support. There is also little evidence that these men secured financial help from the other Chinese or Hokkien-owned banks to get started in business. Nor is there any evidence that these men depend on Hokkien-owned banks to finance their business deals, even when they venture abroad. For example, YTL Corp depended more on the state for financial backing in its attempt to build its power generation business internationally. Although Loh has a stake in the Southern Bank with some other Hokkien businessmen, there is no evidence that he has depended much on co-ethnic ties to develop Oriental Holdings. Both Loh, during the immediate post-colonial period, and YTL Corp, during the 1990s, have worked with foreign companies in an attempt to acquire know-how to develop their enterprise. There is little evidence that Public Bank has been able to create a niche for itself by securing the business of Hokkien-owned companies, even after Malayan Banking was taken over by the state. Rather, there appears to be much competition among Chinese-owned banks, including those owned by Hokkiens, like the Ban Hin Lee Bank, MUI Bank (now the Hong Leong Bank) and Southern Bank.

During the NEP decades, the government did bypass Chinese capital by incorporating foreign capital in important sectors, particularly in manufacturing and heavy industries (see Jomo 1994). However, even during the NEP period, those companies that had conformed to state directives, especially to ensure at least 30 percent Bumiputera equity participation in their enterprise, have found that there were avenues to develop their businesses. During the 1990s, as the Prime Minister intensified his drive to develop the Malaysian economy, there has been an attempt by the state to support local businessmen, regardless of ethnicity, who are capable of becoming internationally competitive. Following the 1997 financial crisis, the state has intensified its endeavor to involve Chinese capital, especially the SMEs, in its attempt to revive the economy. Economic crises in Malaysia, including the mid-1980s recession and the 1997 financial crisis, have reminded the government of the importance of Chinese capital in the local economy.

In terms of business style, all three companies have a core activity, though only the Public Bank is very focused on developing its interests and expertise in the financial sector. While Loh's Oriental Holdings has diversified extensively, the YTL Corp has been concentrating primarily on construction and power generation, but has seen the need to diversify in view of the competition in both industries. All three companies developed a reputation in a particular field, with YTL Corp and Oriental Holdings showing evidence of developing vertically integrated manufacturing capacity in their primary business, construction and auto assembly, respectively. While Loh attempted vertical-style growth by acquiring a company already involved in manufacturing, Yeoh and Teh have shown a proclivity to develop companies from scratch. None of these three groups has been built up through a myriad of shares-for-assets swaps, takeovers and reverse takeovers, a form of corporate development used by a number of Chinese capitalists in Malaysia.

In terms of organizational structure, Oriental Holdings and YTL Corp, both now run by the children of these companies' founders, have remained family-owned enterprises, a trait seen as a "Chinese" form of capital control. YTL Corp and Oriental Holdings are still family-run companies in that family members are responsible for policy making. The Public Bank remains under the control of the founder, Teh, and there is little indication that he is grooming his children to eventually take over this company. There is some evidence that the Public Bank may eventually come under managerial control in Chandler's sense, that is, where the family business gives way to modern business enterprise run by managerial experts (see Chandler 1977). However, in spite of the family ownership of Oriental Holdings and YTL Corp, there has been some professionalization of management, with the appointment of qualified non-ethnic Chinese to senior management positions. However, authority over strategic decision-making regarding development plans for the company remains vested in the board of directors, which is almost always controlled exclusively by family members, in spite of the presence of influential Bumiputeras. This pattern of management indicates an attempt to incorporate managerial hierarchy to supplement entrepreneurial flair. These three businessmen also do not appear to have lost much control of their companies despite the restructuring required to accommodate Bumiputera equity participation.

In terms of company structure, all three companies have adopted the holding company approach as the size of their operations began to grow. This method has allowed such firms to decentralize management and move resources around for the benefit of the group as a whole. The corporate structure of all three groups also does not indicate that these men have implemented an intricate system of inter-company cross holdings to consolidate their corporate base in Malaysia.

In spite of the diversity of business style, the empirical evidence refutes the culturalist perspective brought to bear on the study of Chinese enterprise. All three case studies disprove the view that culture, shared identities and value systems have significantly shaped their pattern of growth or that these ethnic Chinese entrepreneurs have relied on co-ethnic business networks to reduce transaction costs or develop their corporate base. A historical review of Chinese enterprise in Malaysia does indicate that attempts by the Chinese to cooperate in business have not been effective, seen particularly in the failure of the corporatization movement, the loss of control of Maybank and the competition among Hokkiens in the banking sector. There is no evidence of interlocking stock ownership or interlocking directorates among any of these companies, or of a sharing of resources and information in an attempt to cooperate collectively as a means to bypass state control. Nor is there any evidence of mergers of Chinese (or Hokkien) enterprises to form an enlarged entity that can emerge as a major economic force in terms of asset base and expertise. None of these three Malaysian Chinese businessmen have shown a desire to develop business ties with other Chinese capitalists in East and Southeast Asia. The case studies do not indicate intra-ethnic business networking, but suggests much competition among Chinese businessmen. One reason for the inability of Chinese companies to maintain partnerships or implement mergers is attributable to their desire to retain control or dominance over the business empire created. This desire not to relinquish control has been another reason for leading Chinese businessmen not supporting the corporatization movement.

The significant point that emerges from this study is that in spite of limited state support and ethnic discrimination, the business deals effected by the Chinese have transcended the ethnic factor. A growing number of Chinese have begun to work with non-ethnic Chinese in business in order to develop their enterprises. Intra-ethnic business interaction does not appear important, nor are formal institutional channels being created by Chinese businesses to promote their corporate base or make representations to the government. Rather, Chinese businessmen are finding different routes to the state or in dealing with government policies. The networks that are being created are strategically based, between Chinese capital and the Malay political elite or with well-connected Bumiputera businessmen or between Chinese and foreign capital. These networks are proving more useful and important in the development of Chinese enterprise in Malaysia.

Notes

1 There had been an attempt in 1996 by the Pacific Bank to merge its activities with OCBC's banking operations in Malaysia. This has failed to materialize.
2 Of Malaysia's 22.33 m population in 1998, 57.8 percent were Bumiputeras, 25 percent were Chinese and 7 percent were Indians.
3 Oriental Assemblers was originally known as General Motors (M) Sdn Bhd. The company was incorporated on 1 May 1967 to assemble vehicles. Among the other current shareholders of Oriental Assemblers are Honda Motor Co. Ltd.
4 These manufacturing subsidiaries include Oriental Assemblers Sdn Bhd, Armstrong Auto Parts Sdn Bhd and Armstrong Cycle Parts Sdn Bhd. One of Oriental Holdings' largest subsidiaries is its plastic manufacturing concern, Teck See Plastics Sdn Bhd, which, in turn, is heavily diversified, owning a number of subsidiaries – Lipro Sdn Bhd, Lipro Electronics Sdn Bhd and Lipro Electrical Manufacturing Sdn Bhd.
5 Other major Chinese-owned banks, like Maybank and the United Malayan Banking Corporation Bhd (UMBC, now renamed the RHB Bank), were taken over by the government following a run on these banks, precipitated by allegations of mismanagement by their owners. Another Chinese bank, the Development & Commercial (D&C) Bank, eventually came under Bumiputera control after serious allegations of mismanagement were made against the controlling shareholders by the central bank, Bank Negara. D&C Bank is also under the RHB group now, controlled by Rashid Hussain. The Public Bank, however, has managed to maintain a record of being well-managed. See Gomez and Jomo (1997: 60–6) for a detailed discussion of how Bumiputera and state capital have secured significant control of the local banking sector from the Chinese.
6 Other major government construction projects that Yeoh Tiong Lay has been involved in include the Bukit Aman Police Headquarters in Kuala Lumpur and the Sri Iskandar sub-campus for Universiti Sains Malaysia (USM) (*Malaysian Business*, 1/16/1992).
7 Company records reveal that the shareholders and directors of Bara Aktif, an investment holding company incorporated on 26 April 1993, are Raja Wahid Raja Kamaralzaman and Mohd Zainal Abidin Haji Abdul Kadir. Both men are also directors of the Batu Tiga Quarry, a company incorporated on 26 October 1967 and owned by the Yeoh family.

Bibliography

Barth, F. (1967) *The Role of the Entrepreneur in Social Change in Northern Norway*, Bergen: Norwegian University Press.

Chandler, A. D. Jr. (1962) *Strategy and Structure: Chapters in the History of the American Industrial Enterprise*, Cambridge: MIT Press.

——(1977) *The Visible Hand: The Managerial Revolution in American Business*, Cambridge: Harvard University Press.

Cheong, S. (1992) *Chinese Controlled Companies in the KLSE: Industrial Counter*, Kuala Lumpur: Corporate Research Services Sdn Bhd.

Coase, R. H. (1937) "The Nature of the Firm," *Economica* 4.

East Asian Analytical Unit (1995) *Overseas Chinese Business Networks in Asia*, Parkes: Department of Foreign Affairs and Trade, Commonwealth of Australia.

Fukuyama, F. (1995) *Trust*, New York: Random House.

Gale, Bruce (1985) *Politics & Business: A Study of Multi-Purpose Holdings Berhad*, Petaling Jaya: Eastern Universities Press.

Gomez, E. T. (1994) *Political Business: Corporate Involvement of Malaysian Political Parties*, Cairns: Centre for Southeast Asian Studies, James Cook University of North Queensland.

——(1999) *Chinese Business in Malaysia: Accumulation, Ascendance, Accommodation*, London/Honolulu: Curzon/University of Hawaii Press.

Gomez, E. T. and Jomo K. S. (1997) *Malaysia's Political Economy: Politics, Patronage and Profits*, Cambridge: Cambridge University Press.

Heng P. K. (1988) *Chinese Politics in Malaysia: A History of the Malaysian Chinese Association*, Singapore: Oxford University Press.

Hong Liu (1998) Old Linkages, New Networks: The Globalization of Overseas Chinese Voluntary Associations and Its Implications, *The China Quarterly*, September (155).

Jesudason, J. V. (1989) *Ethnicity and the Economy: The State, Chinese Business, and the Multinationals in Malaysia*, Singapore: Oxford University Press.

——(1997) Chinese Business and Ethnic Equilibrium in Malaysia, *Development and Change*, 28(1).

Jomo K. S. (1994) *U-Turn? Malaysian Economic Development Policies After 1990*, Townsville: Centre for Southeast Asian Studies, James Cook University of North Queensland.

Kao, J. (1993) The Worldwide Web of Chinese Business, *Harvard Business Review*, March–April.

Kotkin, J. (1993) *Tribes*, New York: Random House.

Kuala Lumpur Stock Exchange (1996) *Annual Companies Handbook*, 21(1–4), Kuala Lumpur: Kuala Lumpur Stock Exchange.

Light, I. and Bonacich, E. (1988) *Immigrant Entrepreneurs: Koreans in Los Angeles, 1965–1982*, Berkeley: University of California Press.

Lim, L. Y. C. (1996) The Evolution of Southeast Asian Business Systems, *Journal of Asian Business*, 12(1).

Lim, L. Y. C. and Gosling, L. A. P. (1997) Strengths and Weaknesses of Minority Status for Southeast Asian Chinese at a Time of Economic Growth and Liberalization. In D. Chirot and A. Reid (eds), *Essential Outsiders: Chinese and Jews in the Modern Transformation of Southeast Asia and Central Europe*.

Malaysia (1996) *Seventh Malaysia Plan, 1996–2000*, Kuala Lumpur: Government Printers.

Penrose, E. T. (1980) *The Theory of the Growth of the Firm*, Oxford: Basil Blackwell.

Porter, M. (1980) *Competitive Strategy: Techniques for Analysing Industries and Competitors*, New York: Free Press.

——(1985) *Competitive Advantage: Creating and Sustaining Superior Performance*, New York: Free Press.

——(1990) *The Competitive Advantage of Nations*, New York: Free Press.

Portes, A. and Manning, R. D. (1986) The Immigrant Enclave: Theory and Empirical Examples. In Olzak, S. and Nagel, J. (eds), *Competitive Ethnic Relations*, Orlando, FL: Academic Press.

Putnam, R. D. (1993) *Making Democracy Work: Civic Traditions in Modern Italy*, Princeton: Princeton University Press.

Redding, S. G. (1990) *The Spirit of Chinese Capitalism*, Berlin: Walter de Gruyter.

Sabel, C. (1992) Studied Trust. In F. Pyke and W. Sengenberger (eds) *Industrial Districts and Local Economic Regeneration*, Geneva: ILO.

Schumpeter, J. A. (1943) *Capitalism, Socialism and Democracy*, London: George Allen & Unwin.

Weidenbaum, M. and Hughes, S. (1996), *The Bamboo Network*, New York: Free Press.

Williamson, O. E. (1975) *Markets and Hierarchies: Analysis and Anti-Trust Implications*, New York: Free Press.

Yeoh K. K. (1987) *A Study of the Malaysian Chinese Economic Self-Strengthening (Corporatisation) Movement – With Special Reference to MPHB, Other Communal Investment Companies and Cooperatives*, MEc Thesis, University of Malaya.

Yoshihara, K. (1988) *The Rise of Ersatz Capitalism in Southeast Asia*, Singapore: Oxford University Press.

Newspapers and magazines

Asiamoney, Asiaweek, Business Times, Far Eastern Economic Review, Investors' Digest, Malaysian Business, The Diplomat, The Edge, The Star, The Sun.

8

TRANSNATIONAL ENTREPRENEURSHIP AND CHINESE BUSINESS NETWORKS

The regionalization of Chinese business firms from Singapore

Henry W.-C. Yeung

Introduction

International business has become one of the most important fields of Chinese business activity in today's globalizing world economy. When Chinese business firms extend their operations across borders to become transnational corporations (TNCs), they are often entering into host business environments that are fundamentally different from their "home" countries[1] in terms of institutional and market structures, industrial organization, social relations and cultural practices. To overcome these barriers to globalization, the ethnic Chinese TNCs need actors who are creative, proactive, adaptive and resourceful in different countries; these are all aspects of transnational entrepreneurship. Sometimes, these actors are the owners or founding entrepreneurs themselves. They often participate actively in the establishment and management of foreign operations. More commonly, these actors in transnational operations are intrapreneurs or professional managers who are neither founders nor owners, but are given much autonomy to manage transnational operations. They may be as entrepreneurial in their approach to managing cross-border operations. An understanding of the nature, modus operandi and performance of these entrepreneurs/intrapreneurs is vital to the success of international operations by these Chinese business firms (see also Yeung 2002).

Despite decades of entrepreneurship research since Joseph Schumpeter and others (see recent collections in Casson 1990, 1995; Livesay 1995; Low and Tan 1996), however, we still know relatively little about the real actors and their behavior in transnational corporations. In the case of Chinese business literature, this lacuna is attributed to the fact that most studies of Chinese entrepreneurship tend to focus on the ethnic Chinese in their domestic setting (e.g. Lim and Gosling 1983; Redding 1990; Hamilton 1991a; Brown 1995; East Asia Analytical

Unit 1995; Hodder 1996; Lever-Tracy *et al.* 1996; Weidenbaum and Hughes 1996; Haley *et al.* 1998; Hefner 1998). It has been argued that strong entrepreneurship is one of the defining characteristics of Chinese businesses in the Asia Pacific region. These studies are concerned with the role of Chinese entrepreneurs in innovation, new business start-ups and economic development of their "home" countries in East and Southeast Asia. Moreover, Chinese entrepreneurship research has little interaction with mainstream research on international business and organizational behavior. The latter is preoccupied with the firm as their central unit of analysis. While Chinese entrepreneurship research tends to ignore entrepreneurs in international business, studies of international business and organizational behavior focus overtly on the nature and organization of TNCs at the expense of those actors and individuals who are managing the worldwide web of transnational corporations – the entrepreneurs and intrapreneurs themselves. There is thus a case for actor-specific studies of Chinese transnational entrepreneurship. This task is particularly important in an era of increasing global financial volatility and emerging crisis tendencies in global capitalism. To a large extent, the success and failure of Chinese business firms abroad are critically dependent on how entrepreneurial spirits in these firms are constituted and realized in different host countries and regions.

In this chapter, I take up this emerging issue in international business studies and Chinese business research by examining the role of transnational entrepreneurship in the regionalization of Chinese business firms from Singapore. I argue that transnational entrepreneurship plays an important role in the internationalization of Chinese business firms from Singapore, in particular those well embedded in regional, social and business networks. For these Singapore-based transnational corporations, transnational entrepreneurship can be analyzed in relation to two types of entrepreneurs: (1) owner entrepreneurs and (2) manager intrapreneurs. I argue that while owner entrepreneurs tend to exploit their social and business networks to take their businesses across national boundaries, manager intrapreneurs require substantial management control and autonomy bestowed on them by their headquarters in Singapore in order to put their entrepreneurial skills into best practice in the host countries. The data for this chapter originate from an ongoing research project in which personal interviews with top executives from fifty-four ethnic Chinese TNCs from Singapore and over fifty Singaporean entrepreneurs in Hong Kong and China were conducted.[2]

The chapter is organized into three sections. The next section starts with a reconceptualization of transnational entrepreneurship and its role in international business and the internationalization of Chinese businesses. The second section presents an analysis of data on the regionalization of Chinese business firms from Singapore. Case studies are also presented to illustrate the role of transnational entrepreneurship in this regionalization process. The choice of case studies is primarily driven by two motives. First, they must be relatively proactive and successful in weathering the Asian economic crisis, that is, satisfying construct validity. Second, they are selected on the basis of the completeness of their available information. All case studies are discussed here for illustration purposes. I have no intention nor belief that these case studies can provide universal generalization and invariant laws (Yin 1994; Yeung 1997a; Numagami 1998). In the context of the recent Asian economic crisis, the penultimate section of the chapter also draws some important implications for the future of Chinese business firms from Asia.

Transnational entrepreneurship: the missing link in international business and Chinese business studies?

This section aims to bridge entrepreneurship studies and international business studies through a reconceptualization of transnational entrepreneurship. It serves as an important theoretical point of departure for our understanding of the role and processes of transnational entrepreneurship in the internationalization of Chinese business firms. My argument is that many attributes of domestic entrepreneurship can be fruitfully exploited across borders to become transnational entrepreneurship. In the case of Chinese capitalism in Asia, this interconnection between domestic and transnational entrepreneurship is even more pronounced and important because of the extensive interpenetration of Chinese business networks throughout the Asian region. Successful Chinese businesses at the regional scale can be attributed to the transformation of the entrepreneurial skills of Chinese entrepreneurs from predominantly domestic foundations to increasingly regional and global orientations. In that sense, transnational entrepreneurs are capable of transferring their skills and goodwill from their "home" countries to the host countries.

Transnational entrepreneurship and international business studies

To date, a theoretical impasse clearly exists in entrepreneurship and international business studies. Entrepreneurship studies tend to assume that the entrepreneur will behave and act in the same manner irrespective of the geography of his/her business operations. In this literature, there seems to be no difference in the social, political and economic contexts of different countries in which an entrepreneur operates. Indeed, most entrepreneurship studies are primarily unilocational in their spatial unit of analysis. Only very limited studies have been done to offer a comparative analysis of entrepreneurship in different countries (e.g. DiConti 1992; Birley and MacMillan 1995, 1997). On the other hand, one needs to glance at most articles in recent issues of top international business studies journals[3] to realize that the unit of analysis is overwhelming the firm and the TNC, not the human actor and the entrepreneur. This heavy bias towards firm-level analysis reflects the methodological impoverishment of most international business studies in which predictive statistical tools are used to quantity international business activities. Human actors and entrepreneurs do not seem to have a place in this quantitative methodology, perhaps because their behavior and action cannot be consistently quantified and predicted. The net result is that the baby has been thrown out with the bath water altogether. We end up with highly "scientific" studies of global corporations without human actors and entrepreneurs.

Let me cite just one example in international business studies, which comes close to entrepreneurship studies – headquarters-subsidiary relationships. The relationships between the headquarters of TNCs and their foreign affiliates have received a good deal of attention in international business studies since the early 1970s (e.g. Alsegg 1971; Otterbeck 1981; Prahalad and Doz 1987; Martinez and Jarillo 1988, 1991; Bartlett and Ghoshal 1989; Roth and Morrison 1992; Birkinshaw and Morrison 1995; Birkinshaw 1996). One important missing link in this literature, however, is related to the role of social actors and their discursive construction of parent-subsidiary relationships (Yeung 2000a). It is perhaps useful to relate this critique to the emerging actor-network theory (Thrift 1996; Murdoch 1999; Olds and Yeung 1999). The idea here is that through networks, social actors are capable of exercising power and control "at a distance." While there may well be formal control and coordination mechanisms between parent TNCs and their subsidiaries, the realization of such mechanisms is often dependent on the discursive and entrepreneurial powers of those social actors involved, for example, CEOs, local managers and network partners. The relationships between parent TNCs and their subsidiaries are often socially constructed in the sense that they involve the participation and interaction of social actors, rather than merely formal rules. It is these elements of social construction that underscore the emergence of a new breed of organizing international business – the "network TNC" (see Yeung 1998a and d). As evident later in this chapter, Chinese business firms are often organized as network TNCs through the involvement of their entrepreneurs in extensive webs of cross-border social and business relationships.

To understand better the internationalization of business firms, we need to go beyond their corporate strategies and organizational characteristics; we need to examine the strategic intent of the real entrepreneurs behind these firms and their actions in different countries of their business operations. This brings us to the core concept of this chapter – transnational entrepreneurship that will be used to describe and explain the nature and processes of cross-border management by transnational entrepreneurs, both owner-entrepreneurs and manager intrapreneurs. In its essence, transnational entrepreneurship refers to an ongoing process of calculated risk-taking and foresight in foreign business venturing. It is a process because transnational entrepreneurship evolves from experience and learning gained through progressive involvement in foreign operations (see also Yeung 2002). Through these cross-border operations, transnational entrepreneurs not only learn how to deal with unexpected contingencies in the host countries, but also develop a deeper understanding of the realities of these host countries. Strong transnational entrepreneurship also requires the entrepreneur to take certain risks. Of course, not all risk-taking is good, at least from a firm's point of view. But transnational entrepreneurs must have certain inherent capabilities in absorbing calculated risks, that is, the kind of risks, that generate potential gain. This risk-taking behavior is particularly critical because operations in a foreign land are often filled with uncertainties and potential business dangers. In fact, the risk-taking capacity of an entrepreneur tends to increase with his/her experience with the host countries.

Another factor to enhance the risk-taking capacity of a transnational entrepreneur is the informal information and peer support he/she receives from the host country. The "network factor" becomes very important here because strong social and business networks can serve as the institutional foundations for transnational entrepreneurship. Social and political institutions significantly shape the attitudes and behavior of individual entrepreneurs and intrapreneurs. Transnational entrepreneurs are conceptualized as creative individuals embedded in wider cross-border business networks and social/political institutions. These networks and institutions provide the necessary strategic infrastructure to enable the success of these transnational entrepreneurs. On the other hand, intrapreneurs are professional managers who are empowered to manage transnational operations. This empowerment may come from the founding entrepreneurs themselves through a process of socialization. It may also be institutionalized within the organization itself when the top management from headquarters delegates power and control to professional managers abroad. This is known as "intra-firm" networks, which tend to facilitate headquarters' control and coordination of overseas subsidiaries through informal mechanism (see case studies below). Together, this institutional perspective goes beyond an analysis of the psychological and experiential attributes of individual entrepreneurs so commonly found in entrepreneurship studies. It also offers some understanding into the nature and processes of transnational management.

A final attribute in my definition of transnational entrepreneurship is foresight in foreign ventures. This aspect is important at least from the perspective of strategic management. It also distinguishes domestic entrepreneurship from transnational entrepreneurship because an entrepreneur is often well entrenched in his/her domestic market. There is a strong sense of inertia against venturing abroad, given his/her comfortable home market share. A transnational entrepreneur therefore needs to possess strong visions and foresight in order to position the future of his/her firm in an era of global competition. Though often assisted by professional analysts and strategists, he/she must be able to identify market opportunities abroad and tap into them. This relentless search for direct investments in foreign markets is important in today's global economy because market presence remains the fundamental drive for an entrepreneur to venture abroad, whether he/she runs a manufacturing or a service firm. If successful, this transnational entrepreneur will enjoy "first-mover" advantages unavailable to other firms and their actors. Every foreign venture, therefore, may appear as a new business start-up synonymous with the process of new firm formation so well documented in most entrepreneurship studies. The difference here, of course, is that once a foreign venture is established, a transnational entrepreneur must continue to resolve operational and management problems in a business context different from his/her home country. Taken together, transnational entrepreneurship is important in international business primarily for two reasons: (1) that foreign ventures are full of risks and uncertainties and (2) that strong visions and foresight can help diversify one's business portfolio beyond the domestic market. How then does this concept translate into practice in the case of Chinese businesses and how does it enhance the internationalization of Chinese business firms?

Spreading the "bamboo networks" abroad: the role of transnational entrepreneurship in the internationalization of Chinese businesses

Today, there is no doubt that the ethnic Chinese in East and Southeast Asia are well known to be exceptionally entrepreneurial in their domestic economies. In some Southeast Asian countries (e.g. Indonesia and Malaysia), the restrictive "home" institutional context explains the predominant focus of the ethnic Chinese on business activities. Many of these ethnic Chinese abroad have formed formidable "bamboo networks" embedded in "particularistic ties and multiplex relationships [which] are likely to figure prominently in situations of imperfect competition" (Wong 1988: 109). Redding (1990: 34) also cautions that "explaining networking in terms of purely ethnic reasons would be simplistic. There are reasons of hard economic and business expediency as well as ethnic loyalties behind much of this behavior." In other Asian economies dominated by the ethnic Chinese, these "bamboo networks" are constituted not only by fellow Chinese entrepreneurs, but sometimes also by political figures (e.g. in Taiwan and Thailand) and non-Chinese business people (e.g. in Hong Kong and Singapore). Early studies of Chinese capitalism in Asia were exclusively preoccupied with the domestic constitution of these "bamboo networks" and complex business practices embedded in these networks.

Since the 1970s, it has become clear that ethnic Chinese entrepreneurs are increasingly spreading their "bamboo networks" across countries and, sometimes regions. This process of the globalization of Chinese business firms is a significant development in the business history of the "Overseas Chinese" because their transnational operations require more than traditional skills and competitive advantages that ensure the success of these Chinese entrepreneurs in their "home" countries (see Yeung 1999a; Yeung and Olds 2000). Kao (1993: 32) may be right in arguing, "cross-border investments alone are responsible for turning the de facto network of loose family relationships into today's Chinese commonwealth." But he offers little to explain why and how such a transformation in the spatial organization of "bamboo networks" comes about. Here I would like to argue that transnational entrepreneurship plays a critical role not only in spreading these "bamboo networks" abroad, but also in transforming them into significant business opportunities. Three attributes of Chinese transnational entrepreneurship are particularly important in facilitating the transnational operations of Chinese business firms: (1) their greater possibility of internalizing overseas markets, (2) their trust and goodwill in host countries and (3) their reliance on transnational social and business networks.

First, transnational Chinese entrepreneurs tend to exhibit a greater tendency towards internalizing foreign markets through direct investments and other forms of equity investments. Within the Chinese psyche, there is a deep-seated and culturally embedded desire for self-ownership and autonomy in decision making (Bond 1986; Redding 1990). Although the family serves as a significant binding and centripetal force, Chinese entrepreneurs prefer to be their own boss. There is a famous Chinese proverb: "better be the beak of a cock than the rump of an ox" (cited in Wong 1988: 101). It is not surprising that the ethnic Chinese are well known for their entrepreneurial spirit. In the context of cross-border operations, this drive towards ownership and control implies that transnational Chinese entrepreneurs are more willing to venture into rather opaque business environments because once established, these foreign ventures tend to be less risky under the direct control and management of these entrepreneurs and their trusted lieutenants. These transnational Chinese entrepreneurs are also more likely to take a personal approach to these foreign ventures through direct participation in the negotiation stage and subsequently more frequent visits. These aspects of transnational entrepreneurship are particularly useful in host countries with opaque business environments and ineffective corporate governance systems (see case studies below). Direct ownership in highly competitive and open business environments (e.g. North America and Western Europe) requires both transnational entrepreneurship and significant competitive advantages (e.g. brand names, proprietary technology, management expertise and so on).

Second, there is no doubt that developing trust and goodwill form an integral part of Chinese business practice. For aspiring transnational Chinese entrepreneurs, having strong trust and goodwill in the host countries certainly helps to open doors and gain better acceptance by the host business and political communities. There is thus less necessity for complex and detailed contracts to be negotiated because verbal guarantees by a transnational Chinese entrepreneur, well known for his/her trustworthy behavior, are better than many contracts, which lay out all contingencies. This reliance on trust and goodwill rather than just formal contracts is much less common in Western business. Recent research has shown that formal contracts still play the most important role even in cooperative ventures among Western firms (see Lewis 1995; Willcocks and Choi 1995; Beamish and Killing 1997; Doz and Hamel 1998).[4] Trust and goodwill is important for transnational Chinese entrepreneurs not only to penetrate into difficult host countries in Asia, but also to establish themselves successfully in highly competitive business environments. On this latter point, some of today's transnational Chinese entrepreneurs are globalizing into North America and Western Europe. Trust and goodwill are significant sources of advantages to enable them to receive good support by bankers and financial analysts and therefore to gain access to global capital markets. This access to capital and finance also enables a widening of Chinese business networks to enrol strategically non-Chinese actors who function as bridges for transnational Chinese entrepreneurs to enter into these globally competitive markets (see Olds and Yeung 1999; Yeung 2000b and f).

While they may prefer to own and control foreign ventures, transnational Chinese entrepreneurs do not always take on an authoritarian approach to these ventures. They often delegate these responsibilities to trusted members of their inner circles. These members may be kin and relative from the families of these transnational Chinese entrepreneurs. Sometimes, they are non-family members who have been socialized into the entrepreneur's family through a process of "family-ization," defined as the gradual co-opting of non-family members through personal relationships and marriage alliances (see Chan and Chiang 1994: 297). There are at least two reasons for the necessity of "family-ization." One reason is that there is simply a shortage of capable family members to take over such key responsibilities as setting up foreign ventures. As Fukuyama (1995: 64) argues, "a single family, no matter how large, capable, or well educated, can only have so many competent sons, daughters, spouses, and siblings to oversee the different parts of a rapidly ramifying enterprise." An inevitable result of this succession problem is that most of the big Chinese family businesses today are stacked with professional managers. One fund manager, for example, has noted that "many of the people who actually run Robert Kuok's businesses are not linked to the family empire. Obviously, he has to trust these lieutenants, but he is prepared to delegate" (cited in *Financial Times*, 3/5/1998). Another reason for "family-ization" is that as a rule of thumb in Chinese entrepreneurship, a senior (sometimes a former employer) is obliged to help a junior to set up his/her own business if the latter is proven to be sufficiently entrepreneurial. Chen (1995: 53) notes that "when *guanxi* links two persons of unequal rank or social status, the weaker side usually expects more help than he or she can reciprocate in equal terms." This unwritten "cultural rule" is unthinkable in Western business because of culturally embedded individualism and competitive behavior (Hamilton 1991b, 1994, 1996). Foreign ventures are established to provide opportunities for both business expansion and internalizing enterprising employees. We begin to find more competent professional managers being socialized into Chinese family businesses such that over time, they become trusted "insiders" in these reshaped "Chinese" business networks.

Third, transnational Chinese entrepreneurs often rely on their social and business networks to facilitate foreign ventures, although as argued above, these networks are no longer exclusively Chinese in terms of their ethnic constituency. Studies of ethnic Chinese entrepreneurs from Hong Kong have revealed the importance of personal history and embedded interests in their transnational operations (e.g. Siu and Tseng 1992; Tseng 1992; Chan 1995; Yeung 1997b and c, 1998a). The contemporary Chinese people are experienced migrants and tend to form socially organized networks to provide emotional and personal support.

Sometimes, these social networks are constituted almost exclusively by family and clan members. As Kao (1993: 24) argues, "for many generations, emigrant Chinese entrepreneurs have been operating comfortably in a network of family and clan, laying the foundations for stronger links among businesses across national borders" (see case studies below). In other circumstances, transnational Chinese entrepreneurs may rely on their trusted friends and employees to develop business networks across borders. These strong personal relationships with key employees often result in the growth of transnational intrapreneurs who are empowered by their owners to develop foreign ventures. These transnational Chinese entrepreneurs therefore need to take significant risks and possess foresight in the selection and delegation of these transnational intrapreneurs. Having set up these analytical tools, I now turn to an empirical study of the role of transnational entrepreneurship in the regionalization of Chinese business firms from Singapore.

Transnational entrepreneurship and the regionalization of Chinese business firms from Singapore

Singapore is a city-state strategically located at the southern tip of the Malayan peninsula of Southeast Asia. It has grown from a British colonial entrepôt in the late nineteenth and early twentieth centuries to a modern economic center specializing in high value-added manufacturing activities and international financial and business services (Régnier 1991; Huff 1994; Perry *et al.* 1997; Low 1998; Mahizhnan and Lee 1998). Inward foreign investment has always been one of the cornerstones of the island economy (Hughes and Sing 1969; Yoshihara 1976; Mirza 1986; Rodan 1989; Low *et al.* 1993). Singapore is characterized by an export-led regime of accumulation in which domestic consumption is intertwined with production processes that are consistently shaped by the global strategies of foreign firms. In recent years, however, the state has explicitly called for a restructuring process in which Singaporean firms are encouraged to regionalize their operations (Kanai 1993; Régnier 1993; Yeung 1998b, 1999b, 2000c, 2002). Most existing studies of the internationalization of business firms from Singapore, however, have taken on a political-economy approach. The purpose of this section is to offer an analysis of the social organization of this regionalization process (see also Willis and Yeoh 1998; Yeung 1998c; Tan and Yeung 2000). My emphasis here is placed on the role of transnational entrepreneurship in the regionalization of Chinese business firms from Singapore. My empirical analysis is based on survey data from fifty-four Chinese family firms from Singapore, which have operations abroad, and qualitative data from personal interviews with over fifty top executives of subsidiaries of Singaporean TNCs in Hong Kong and China. After a brief introduction to the nature of Singapore's regionalization programme, I examine the role of transnational entrepreneurship in the regionalization efforts by the ethnic Chinese Singaporean entrepreneurs and intrapreneurs.

Going global: Singapore's regionalization program

Since its independence in 1965, the PAP-led (People's Action Party) state has planned and implemented several national development strategies to create and sustain Singapore's competitiveness in the face of accelerated global competition (Yeung and Olds 1998; Yeung 2000c). While the state was able to pursue a labor-intensive export-oriented manufacturing platform for industrialization in the 1960s and the 1970s, the strategy met its favorable global conditions when major American and European manufacturers were looking for alternative low-cost production sites to relocate their labor-intensive operations (an early process of economic globalization). By the late 1970s and early 1980s, Singapore was no longer competitive in attracting low-cost manufacturing assembly investment because cheaper production locations could be found throughout the world, notably in neighboring Asian developing countries. Singapore then faced a "competitiveness crunch" in the changing international division of labor. To regain its competitiveness in the global space of flows, the state revised its national strategies in favor of promoting high tech and high value-added manufacturing and business services (Rodan 1989; Ho 1993; Chiu *et al.* 1997; Brown 1998). This strategy worked well during the 1980s when Singapore was an attractive location for global corporations in computer and chemical industries. Since the mid-1980s, the state has introduced competitive packages of incentives to attract global corporations to locate their regional offices and/or regional headquarters in Singapore. The idea of promoting control and coordination functions of global corporations fits well into a world city formation when Singapore aims to be a major international business hub of the region.

By the early 1990s, Singapore had been transformed into a regional coordination center capable of significant R&D activities and management functions (Perry *et al.* 1998a and b; Perry and Tan 1998; Mathews 1999; Yeung *et al.* 2001). Although it had secured a niche in the competitive global economy, the Singapore economy was still very much dependent on global capital and its major markets in North America and Western Europe. To further consolidate its national competitiveness and to enable the expansion of domestic capital, the state has initiated a regionalization programme in 1993 through which Singaporean companies are encouraged to venture abroad. By building up its external wing, the state believes that Singapore can not only tap into the opportunities of the regional economy, but can also ride out of economic crisis in the domestic economy. The Department of Statistics (1991) estimates that at the end of 1976, foreign direct investment (FDI) from Singapore was slightly above S$1 bn. As shown in Table 8.1, this figure had grown to S$1.7 bn by 1981, S$13.6 bn by 1990 and S$55.7 bn by 1996 (Department of Statistics, 1998). I have examined elsewhere different aspects of the political economy of Singapore's regionalization program (Yeung 1998b, 2000c and d): (1) the regionalization of government-linked companies (GLCs) and companies set up by statutory boards and (2) "political entrepreneurship" through which the state opens up overseas business

Table 8.1 Outward direct investment from Singapore by country, 1981–96 (in S$ million)

Country	1981	1982	1983	1984	1985	1986	1987	1988	1989	1990	1991	1992	1993	1994	1995	1996
Asian countries	1289.9	1586.7	1662.4	1805.2	1721.4	1836.5	1908.5	1963.6	1968.4	7013.3	7401.5	9209.3	11480.0	17358.0	21511.0	32389.0
ASEAN	1078.5	1233.7	1241.7	1341.4	1133.3	1155.8	1180.5	1216.0	1138.4	3567.1	3995.6	4896.7	5933.8	9680.0	12467.0	18022.6
Brunei	3.7	6.0	9.0	49.1	52.9	50.0	54.2	57.4	56.6	66.2	69.4	88.5	91.2	77.0	37.0	88.8
Indonesia	39.5	39.7	44.4	56.3	65.0	67.7	58.6	59.8	53.3	224.8	267.3	328.1	517.3	1997.0	3448.0	3914.9
Malaysia	1006.9	1162.3	1162.6	1209.1	971.8	985.6	1008.4	1030.8	971.6	2790.1	3121.1	3916.5	4656.7	6500.0	7305.0	10753.0
Philippines	18.4	16.1	17.6	17.6	22.4	22.5	14.3	22.5	22.8	97.7	89.7	106.3	230.6	382.0	521.0	1073.4
Thailand	10.0	9.6	8.1	9.3	21.2	30.0	45.0	45.5	34.1	388.4	448.1	457.4	438.1	723.0	860.0	1558.7
Hong Kong	181.8	316.7	357.4	391.3	460.7	497.9	539.9	545.2	581.4	2266.2	2368.6	3051.1	4025.6	4940.0	5089.0	6326.5
Japan	0.3	0.4	0.6	0.7	5.0	6.0	16.1	16.7	33.9	51.8	73.5	75.8	109.4	171.0	382.0	482.7
China	—	—	—	—	57.6	93.8	101.4	79.1	47.4	239.7	220.0	282.6	444.1	1533.0	2445.0	5339.6
South Korea	—	—	—	—	—	—	—	14.8	15.9	—	—	—	—	—	—	—
Taiwan	12.9	14.8	24.9	27.1	32.9	37.8	26.0	54.3	86.0	494.8	287.0	349.5	354.5	496.0	530.0	594.5
Others	16.2	21.1	37.8	44.7	31.9	45.2	44.6	37.5	65.4	393.7	456.7	553.6	612.7	1034.0	1128.0	2257.5
European countries	50.7	58.0	57.7	71.5	89.3	167.2	358.2	303.4	203.4	1095.4	1397.6	1480.2	1549.7	2200.0	3844.0	6736.1
Australia	62.6	90.6	121.4	132.0	176.9	175.6	217.8	166.1	138.3	1889.0	1957.9	1969.1	1867.9	999.0	1116.0	4025.6
Canada	—	—	11.5	11.5	17.6	17.6	17.6	29.0	73.4	—	—	—	—	—	—	—
United States	31.8	44.3	47.5	54.4	66.1	65.4	69.3	107.7	160.0	689.7	1303.9	1589.5	1755.1	1681.0	2036.0	2851.1
Other countries	242.9	307.3	332.6	324.7	185.9	335.4	390.1	424.1	400.2	2934.3	3123.9	3493.1	4587.4	7527.0	8359.0	9710.6
Total	1677.7	2086.9	2233.1	2399.3	2257.2	2597.7	2961.5	2993.9	2943.7	13621.7	15183.8	17741.3	21240.2	29765.0	36866.0	55712.4

Sources: Department of Statistics (1991), *Singapore's Investment Abroad, 1976–1989*. Singapore: DOS. Department of Statistics (1996), *Singapore's Investment Abroad, 1990–1993*. Singapore: DOS. Department of Statistics (1997), *Yearbook of Statistics Singapore, 1996*. Singapore: DOS. Department of Statistics (1998), *Singapore's Investment Abroad, 1996*. Singapore: DOS.

Notes: Data from 1981–9 refer to direct investments abroad (D1), which are the amount of paid-up shares of overseas subsidiaries and associates held by companies in Singapore. Data from 1990–5 refer to direct equity investments (D2), which are direct investment (D1) plus the reserves of the overseas subsidiaries and associates attributable to these companies. For overseas branches, the net amount due to the local parent companies is taken as an approximation of the magnitude of direct investment. Data for 1996 refer to total direct investment abroad (D3), which are D2 plus loans granted to affiliates. Direct equity investment (D2) data for 1996 are not available in the Department of Statistics (1998).

opportunities for private capitalists and negotiates the institutional framework for such opportunities to be tapped by these Singaporean firms. Today, the public sector and GLCs account for about 60 percent of Singapore's GDP (Ministry of Finance 1993: 39; see also Singh and Ang 1998).

Having said that, I must emphasize that private capital from Singapore, a predominantly ethnic Chinese capital, has a much longer history of regionalization, particularly in Malaysia (see Yeung 1998c), Hong Kong and China. In 1996, these three destinations were the largest recipients of outward FDI from Singapore (see Table 8.1). For example, the earliest GLC investment in China took place in 1984 with the incorporation of the Chiwan Petroleum Supply Base Co. Ltd in Shekou, near Hong Kong. The Chiwan base was a joint venture between China's Nanshan Development Company and a consortium of Singapore's leading GLCs then, including Sembawang Maritime Ltd, Jurong Town Corporation, Jurong Shipyard, Intraco Ltd and Port Singapore Authority.[5] On the other hand, at least two of the fifty-four Chinese family firms from Singapore in my sample set up manufacturing operations in China during the 1970s.[6] Hock San Yuen Food Manufacturing invested in Qingdao as early as in 1975 to manufacture food and beverages. Upon the inauguration of China's "open door" policy in December 1978, Sunwa Construction and Interior Pte Ltd (formerly Siew Yong Garments) established a garment factory in Guangzhou in 1979 and subsequently moved it to Shenzhen in 1981. Another Chinese family firm, Eu Yan Sang Ltd, set up its first Chinese medicine shop in Hong Kong in 1910.[7]

Table 8.2 shows the historical geographies of these fifty-four Chinese family-owned TNCs from Singapore. It is clear that the internationalization of these

Table 8.2 The historical geography of fifty-four Chinese business firms from Singapore (percentage in parentheses)

Regions/countries	Mean year of establishment	Number of operating TNCs	Number of subsidiaries
Southeast Asia	na	na	91 (42.1)
Indonesia	1982	15 (27.8)	16 (7.4)
Malaysia	1983	32 (59.3)	55 (25.5)
Thailand	1988	7 (13.0)	7 (3.2)
Philippines	1994	6 (11.1)	6 (2.8)
Others	1994	7 (13.0)	7 (3.2)
East Asia	na	na	98 (45.4)
China	1991	40 (74.1)	77 (35.6)
Hong Kong	1981	14 (25.9)	17 (7.9)
Others	1993	4 (7.4)	4 (1.9)
Europe	1991	4 (7.4)	4 (1.9)
North America	1989	6 (11.1)	6 (2.8)
Other Regions	1985	6 (11.1)	17 (7.9)
Total	na	54 (100)	216 (100)

Source: Author's survey.

firms occurred well before the 1993 launch of Singapore's regionalization pro-
gram. In fact, their subsidiaries in Hong Kong, Indonesia, Malaysia and other
Regions (e.g. South America and Africa) were mostly established prior to 1985.
In terms of their geographical spread, these fifty-four Chinese family-owned
TNCs from Singapore are operating mainly in Asia, in particular China and
Malaysia, which have respectively attracted some 59 and 74 percent of them.
Very few of them are indeed global in their geographical scope of operations.
Of the four having operations in Europe, only two have operations in North
America and Asia. These two Chinese family-owned TNCs from Singapore are
therefore truly global in their operations. In terms of number of subsidiaries, the
same geographical pattern emerges where some 87.5 percent of all 216 subsidiaries are located in Asia, in particular Malaysia ($N = 55$) and China ($N = 77$).
On average, each Chinese family-owned TNC from Singapore in our sample
owns and controls at least four subsidiaries abroad. It is therefore imperative to
understand the nature and social organization of Singaporean investments in these
economies.

Exploiting networks at the regional/global scale: transnational entrepreneurs from Singapore

Given the long historical roots of ethnic Chinese investments from Singapore to
other Asian countries, I examine how transnational entrepreneurs in these
Chinese family firms from Singapore managed to extend their business operations across borders. The main focus here is on their capabilities in exploiting
social and business networks at regional and sometimes global scales. As shown
in Table 8.3, among the fifty-four Chinese family firms in my sample, some
thirty-seven key transnational entrepreneurs had some forms of connections/
network relationships with the host countries prior to the establishment of
transnational operations. These prior connections were particularly biased
towards business connections ($N = 37$), which imply that more transnational
entrepreneurs had conducted some businesses with host countries. Usually,
these prior business activities could be conducted at arm's-length level or through
introduction by other friends and business contacts. Once these transnational
entrepreneurs have gained more experience with the host country business environments, direct investments become much more attractive because of reduced
risks and uncertainties. High trust and goodwill relationships with host country
trading and business partners (mean score = 1.5) and personal contacts in host
countries (mean score = 1.9) were cited as most important in facilitating these
transnational operations. It is also interesting to note that while my sampled firms
had less prior family connections with host countries, the respondents still considered connections with relatives (mean score = 1.9) and close friends (mean
score = 1.9) as very important in facilitating their foreign ventures. Similarly,
prior political connections through personal contacts with host government officials (mean score = 1.8) and special access to government concessions (mean

Table 8.3 Types of connections between transnational entrepreneurs and host countries prior to overseas operations

Types of connections	Frequency	Percentage	Average importance[a]
1. Business connections	37	68.5	—
Personal contacts			1.9
Trading and business partners			1.5
Industrial and commercial associations			2.6
Customers, suppliers and subcontractors			2.3
2. Political connections	15	27.8	—
Personal contacts with government officials			1.8
Special access to government grants/concessions			1.8
Contracts from host governments			2.1
3. Family connections	15	27.8	—
Relatives			1.9
Close friends			1.9
Kinship and clan associations			2.4
4. Social connections	10	18.5	—
Ethnic groups			2.0
Religious groups			3.3
Total sample size	54	100.0	—

Source: Author's survey data.

Note

a The scale of importance ranges from Very Important [1] to Not Important At All [5].

score = 1.8) were very important in the transnational operations of these Chinese family firms from Singapore.

The transnational Chinese entrepreneurs in my sample firms are clearly capable of capitalizing on prior network relationships with host countries, particularly business connections, in order to venture into those countries. How then did these prior connections with host countries benefit their overseas operations? Three network advantages were voted most important by my respondents: (1) easier coordination with local headquarters (mean score = 1.4), (2) access to local information and knowledge (mean score = 1.9), and (3) access to new distribution channels and markets (mean score = 2.0). All these three advantages are related to better chances of penetrating into the host markets. In that sense, successful foreign ventures by transnational Chinese entrepreneurs from Singapore depend on their ability in exploiting network advantages, a defining characteristic of transnational entrepreneurship. It is important, however, to caution that these network advantages are not static. Instead, transnational entrepreneurs are expected to develop these ongoing connections when venturing abroad. My respondents identified five major ingredients in enhancing these ongoing

197

Table 8.4 Major problems faced and solutions by transnational entrepreneurs from Singapore by region (percentage in parentheses)

Problems/solutions	Southeast Asia	East Asia	Europe	North America	Other regions
Problems (mean score[a])					
1. High costs of operations	3.7	3.2	2.8	3.6	3.8
2. Lack of technological edge	4.1	3.9	4.0	4.7	3.8
3. Problems with local partners	3.3	3.4	5.0	5.0	4.0
4. Lack of market information	3.8	3.3	3.3	4.4	3.8
5. Lack of special connections with host countries	3.6	3.4	3.5	4.0	3.8
6. Lack of personal experience	3.4	3.1	2.0	3.8	3.5
7. Labor force problems	3.4	2.9	3.3	4.5	4.0
8. Government regulations	2.9	2.5	3.0	4.0	3.5
9. Lack of sufficient financial assets	3.8	3.3	3.3	2.8	3.8
10. Lack of home government support	1.9	1.9	2.0	—	2.0
Solutions (cases)					
1. Reliance on local partners/ connections	11 (18)	32 (44)	—	—	—
2. Sending trusted executives from Singapore to manage	2 (3)	—	—	—	—
3. Asking local government for help	—	9 (12)	1 (20)	—	—
4. Closing down the operations/downsizing	8 (13)	12 (16)	1 (20)	—	—
5. Personal involvement of top executives/entrepreneurs	9 (15)	6 (8)	—	1 (33)	3 (50)
6. Established procedures	12 (20)	2 (3)	—	—	2 (33)
7. Encourage higher worker productivity/training of local staff	4 (7)	3 (4)	—	—	—
8. Adopt local practices/ conform to local culture	11 (18)	4 (5)	1 (20)	2 (67)	—
9. Dismiss local staff/ change local partners	3 (5)	5 (7)	1 (20)	—	1 (17)
10. Compensate with better products and customer servicing	—	—	1 (20)	—	—
Total cases (multiple answers allowed)	60 (100)	73 (100)	5 (100)	3 (100)	6 (100)

Source: Author's survey data.

Note

a The scale of importance ranges from Very Important [1] to Not Important At All [5].

network relationships: (1) high trust (25.2 percent), (2) prior personal or family relationships (17.4 percent), (3) prior transactional relationships (14.8 percent), (4) involvement in established networks (12.2 percent) and (5) strong reputation and credit worthiness (10.4 percent). Together, these five ingredients accounted for 80 percent of all responses (see also the section titled "spreading the bamboo networks abroad"). These responses show that while prior relationships are important in extending emerging networks when venturing abroad, transnational entrepreneurs are expected to demonstrate their trust and credit worthiness through these cross-border operations. There is a dialectical and mutually reinforcing relationship between trust relationships and cross-border operations by transnational Chinese entrepreneurs. A Chinese entrepreneur with low trust relationships in the host countries tends to find it more difficult to venture abroad. The lack of success in foreign ventures by this entrepreneur also reduces further his/her trust and credit worthiness in the host countries.

Some of these mutually-reinforcing problems and their solutions are presented in Table 8.4. It is clear that the geographies of these problems and the solutions taken by transnational entrepreneurs are highly uneven across different regions. In terms of problems, the lack of home country government support is one major problem confronting all Chinese family firms in my sample, irrespective of their host regions of operations. For those operating in East and Southeast Asia, host government regulation is one particularly chronic problem. This is not surprising since most host countries in Asia have opaque rules and restrictive regulations on foreign investors. The implementation of these rules and regulations is also often unpredictable and subject to the likes of the host country government (see Backman 1999; also Yeung 2000d for a case on China). For host-developed countries in Europe and North America, the nature of problems is quite different from Asia. Here the main problems are the lack of personal experience (Europe) and the lack of sufficient financial assets (North America). The open competitive business environments in these regions indicate that to penetrate the market successfully, transnational Chinese entrepreneurs need to build up their experiential and financial capital bases. In order to resolve these problems in foreign ventures, transnational entrepreneurs in my sample seem to take different approaches in different host regions. For their Asian operations, these entrepreneurs are much more comfortable with: (1) reliance on local partners and connections and (2) adopting local practices in resolving operational problems, in particular in China. Their capabilities in exploiting network advantages tend to ensure the success of their foreign ventures in Asia. When asked for the key attributes of entrepreneurship in overcoming these problems of venturing abroad, most of my respondents chose one or more of the following interrelated attributes of transnational entrepreneurship: (1) personal experience and expertise (25 percent), (2) strong vision and accomplishment (17 percent), (3) risk taking (15 percent), (4) highly motivated and independent (12 percent) and (5) well connected and resourced (10 percent). These five attributes of transnational entrepreneurship constituted an overwhelming 80 percent of all responses.

Case study

I now examine a specific case study to illustrate how a transnational entrepreneur exhibits these attributes of transnational entrepreneurship and put them into practice. The story of Hong Leong Group's Kwek Leng Beng is well known (see Yeung 1998c, 1999a, 2000b, 2002; Backman 1999). In this section, I want to show how Kwek's transnational entrepreneurship, as manifested in his meticulous capitalization on family networks and linkages at a regional scale, has contributed to his successful international business operations in Hong Kong and China. The founder of the Hong Leong Group is the late Kwek Hong Png who came to Singapore from Fujian, China, in 1928. Over a period of half a decade, he managed to build up a vast business empire starting with trading, then expanding into property, finance and hotels. The Group's Malaysian branch started in 1963 when the late Kwek Hong Png sent his brother Kwek Hong Lye to Malaya (from which Singapore was soon to separate) to extend the family's operations there (East Asia Analytical Unit 1995: 332). Over time, the Malaysian family branch has grown substantially into one of the biggest conglomerates in Malaysia, with an annual turnover of US$1.3 bn. It had a strong foothold in Hong Kong's financial industry as its subsidiary, the Guoco Group, controlled the fifth largest local bank in Hong Kong – the Dao Heng Bank. When Kwek Hong Lye died in 1996, his son, Quek Leng Chan took over the Malaysian business. My focus here is on Singapore's Kwek Leng Beng, son of the late Kwek Hong Png and cousin of Quek Leng Chan in Malaysia. In 1994, Kwek Leng Beng took charge of the Hong Leong Group in Singapore after his father's death. Joining his father's business after finishing his law degree in 1963, Kwek initiated the take over of a loss-making listed company (City Developments) in the late 1960s and early 1970s and successfully turned it around to become a leading property developer in Singapore today. The Hong Leong Group is now one of the largest Chinese business groups in Singapore with a market capitalization value of US$16 bn, an employment strength of 30,000 worldwide and a stable of 300 companies, including eleven listed on various bourses in Singapore, Hong Kong, New Zealand, Manila, New York and London (*The Sunday Times*, 2/2/1997).

In many ways, Kwek is truly a transnational entrepreneur as defined by the interrelated attributes most cited in my survey. First, Kwek has tremendous personal experience and expertise in property development, finance and hotels. Through his public listed companies in Singapore (City Developments Ltd, Hong Leong Finance and Singapore Finance) and Hong Kong (CDL Hotels International Ltd), he has demonstrated an excellence in both business acumen and financial prudence. All three listed companies have shown healthy profits in 1998, despite the ongoing Asian economic crisis. Second, Kwek has a strong vision and accomplishment. Since he took over the helm of the Hong Leong Group from his father in 1994, he has expanded the Group to become a Chinese family conglomerate with truly global operations. His CDL Hotels International now has a hotel empire spanning twelve countries in Europe, the United States,

Australia, New Zealand, East and Southeast Asia. It is now the eighth largest hotel owner and operator in the world (Annual Report, 1997). Third, Kwek is a well-known calculated risk taker who fights against herd instinct to be the final captor (*The Straits Times*, 11/20/1998). Precisely because of his global hotel acquisition drive since the early 1990s, the Hong Leong Group suffers much less from the recent Asian economic crisis. He recalled that "when I went to London to buy hotels, everybody said, 'this guy is talking rot, talking rubbish,' but I did not listen. I smelled the market, I know" (cited in *The Straits Times*, 11/20/1998: 74). Fourth, Kwek is a highly motivated and independent businessman. Even before the departure of his late father, Kwek was able to freely implement his hotel acquisition strategy. As reported in *The Sunday Times* (2/2/1997: 3):

> Just as the "old man" [the late Kwek Hong Png] was famous for sniff-ing out good real estate deals, his son [Kwek Leng Beng] has been cred-ited with an astute eye for choice hotels at bargain prices, often picking them up at rock-bottom prices from receivers. In international hotel circles, Mr. Kwek is known as "a business-cycle bottom fisher" and is reputed to be a decisive and fast buyer.

Last but most importantly, Kwek is not only well connected and resourced, but also capable of capitalizing on these family and business networks to develop his foreign ventures. In the case of his businesses in Hong Kong and China, there is clearly a "triangular family network" for him to exercise his transnational entrepreneurship and to capitalize on its transnational business synergy. This "triangular family network" involves Kwek Leng Beng in Singapore and Quek Leng Chan, his cousin from Malaysia, as well as Gan Khai Choon, his brother-in-law stationed in Hong Kong. In 1985, Kwek's late father sent Gan, his son-in-law, to set up Hong Leong International (Hong Kong) Ltd and to be its Managing Director, with the intention to invest both in Hong Kong and China. The timing then was right because Hong Kong's property market was just recovering from a serious collapse in the period 1982–4. As Executive Director of the public listed CDL Hotels International in Hong Kong, Gan is also looking after Kwek's hotel businesses in Hong Kong and Taiwan. So how exactly does this "triangular fam-ily network" work in favor of Kwek's investments in Hong Kong and China? Let us examine just one specific transnational investment by Kwek – the Beijing Riviera residential property development project (see Figure 8.2).[8]

First identified by Gan in 1994, this project is a cooperative joint venture between a Singapore consortium led by Hong Leong Holdings Ltd and their Chinese partner (Beijing East Suburb Agriculture Industry Commerce United Corporation). The project has a good reputation from its beginning among investors in the United States, Europe, Japan and Taiwan for two reasons. First, these investors are impressed by the involvement of Kwek's Hong Leong Group, which has already achieved worldwide acclaim in its hotel businesses.

The participation of Temasek Holdings Pte Ltd, an investment arm of the Singapore government, has further boosted the image of the project as a clean and credit-worthy investment. Second, though required by the Chinese law, the local Chinese partner does not contribute any equity to the Beijing project. Instead, it guarantees the project's profitability. It also does not interfere in the decision-making of the project, contributing further to investors' confidence. By June 1998, 50 percent of the Beijing project had been completed and over 75 percent units had been sold. This is quite a remarkable achievement, given the serious downturn in property markets throughout Asia in the midst of its worst-ever crisis.

The division of labor in this "triangular family network" is rather straight-forward, an evidence of intra-family synergy and trust relationships. Kwek's Hong Leong Group in Singapore owns 51 percent of the project, split equally between Hong Leong Holdings and its 100 percent owned subsidiary in Hong Kong, Hong Leong International (HK). In Hong Kong, Kwek taps into his brother-in-law's expertise in and familiarity with property development in Hong Kong and China. Kwek also requests operational assistance from his Malaysian cousin, Quek Leng Chan, in two ways. First, financial transactions and insurance related to the Beijing project are handled by Quek Leng Chan's Dao Heng Bank in Hong Kong. Purchase loans and financing are also arranged by the Dao Heng Bank. Second, building materials for the Beijing project are acquired through Hong Leong Industries in Malaysia. Together, this "triangular family network" represents what Gan referred to as "group total effort" among members of the Kwek/Quek families and companies of the Hong Leong groups in Singapore, Malaysia and Hong Kong. Clearly, the Beijing project is not the first time Kwek Leng Beng has sought cooperation from his cousin in developing transnational operations. Kwek recently describes the relationship with his Malaysian cousin as "excellent" and reveals that they are looking for cooperative ventures into the global market:

> We played together, lived together when we were young. We now exchange views on matters we think our companies will have synergies ... It does not take a genius to realize that Singapore Hong Leong and Malaysia Hong Leong can be a real force to be reckoned with internationally.
>
> (cited in *The Sunday Times*, 2/2/1997: 3)

The case of Kwek Leng Beng and his Hong Leong Group, therefore, shows how a transnational entrepreneur can tap into his cross-border family and business networks to engage in successful foreign ventures.

Managing entrepreneurship in regionalization: Singapore's intrapreneurs abroad

Apart from such transnational Chinese entrepreneurs as Kwek and his family members who have been spearheading the internationalization of Chinese business firms from Singapore, we also witness an increasing professionalization of Chinese family business and the emergence of transnational intrapreneurs in these formerly ethnocentric organizations. Very often, transnational Chinese entrepreneurs are unable to manage all their operations abroad. They have to co-opt more professional and trusted managers who are then socialized into the corporate "family." This section considers the extent of transnational entrepreneurship among professional managers who are managing the foreign operations of Chinese family firms from Singapore. First, I examine the survey data to find out how many of the 54 respondents in my sample consider themselves as entrepreneurs. It turns out that 31 of them (57.4 percent) agreed that they could be considered entrepreneurs. Twenty-eight respondents were either Chairmen or CEO/Managing Directors of the Chinese family firms. Virtually all of them were the patriarchs or their family members. Seventeen of these 28 respondents (60.7 percent) claimed to be entrepreneurs. However, among the other 26 respondents who were not family members, only 14 (53.8 percent) considered themselves as entrepreneurs.

When I asked them what constitutes entrepreneurship in their views, there seems to be a major difference in the perceptions between family and non-family members. Those chairmen and CEO/Managing Directors who considered themselves as entrepreneurs cited "abilities to capitalize on opportunities" as the most important (18.4 percent) attribute of transnational entrepreneurship. Receiving equal percentage at 13.2 percent, other important attributes include: (1) risk taking, (2) strong vision and accomplishment and (3) highly motivated and independent. These three attributes are similar to those discussed in the earlier section. Together, they contribute to 57.9 percent of all responses from these twenty-eight family members. On the other hand, non-family members or intrapreneurs tended to cite "proactive adaptability to different environments" as the most important attribute (18.4 percent) of transnational entrepreneurship. Other important attributes are similar to those cited by family members. Based on their tentative empirical observations, it can be argued that transnational intrapreneurs are much more concerned with adaptability issues than owner entrepreneurs who are more opportunity-driven in their entrepreneurial behavior. This observation is not surprising because most trusted professional managers may be sent abroad to manage foreign operations. They have often been chosen because of their high adaptability to different business environments. Their performance is assessed on the basis of their success in managing and developing these foreign operations. Owner entrepreneurs, however, are less concerned with management issues since they can entrust their transnational intrapreneurs with management responsibilities. Rather, owner entrepreneurs are keen in expanding the overall business activities of the group through capitalizing on business opportunities, which may arise in different countries and/or regions. I now consider a case study of how a transnational intrapreneur has been entrusted by the second-generation patriarch of a Chinese family firm to manage and develop the family's business interests in China.

Case study

Founded in 1968 by its current Chairman Mr Chua Seng Teck, Teck Wah Paper Products Pte Ltd is a modern Chinese family firm from Singapore, which specializes in creative printing and packaging. From its humble beginnings as a manufacturer of cardboard boxes, Teck Wah Seng Kee Company (later to be known as Teck Wah Paper Products Pte Ltd) was born out of a need to pursue a personal vision and a desire to fulfil an entrepreneurial calling. The Group has come a long way in this respect, with fourteen subsidiary companies, over 500 dedicated staff serving in an overseas business network that encompasses Singapore, Malaysia, China, Indonesia and the United States (corporate web site: www.teckwah.com.sg). Today, the management of Teck Wah falls under the second-generation family members, namely Mr Chua's two sons. Whereas his elder son (Thomas Chua) serves as the Group Managing Director, the younger brother (James Chua) is the head of the sales and marketing division. However, the management of Teck Wah's overseas subsidiaries is entrusted in the hands of professional managers. As Mr Chua Seng Teck said, "capital is important, but people are our most important asset." This is a typical transformation in an entrepreneurial Chinese family firm during its internationalization processes. Key family members are kept within the home country so that they can be groomed to take over from the founder and/or patriarch when the time is ripe. Though these family members may be involved directly in the establishment and management of overseas subsidiaries, they are often required to take over more important group strategic management functions.

Here I want to consider specifically Teck Wah's joint venture in China and to show how an entrepreneurial decision to invest in China had turned into a management nightmare, which could only be salvaged by sending an entrusted intrapreneur.[9] In 1994, Teck Wah Paper entered into a majority joint venture (51 percent) with a local town and village enterprise (TVE) in Wuxi, China, to set up Wuxi Teckwah Paper Products Co. Ltd (Wuxi Paper), a modern printing factory with sixty-three staff in July 1998. While Wuxi Paper represents Teck Wah's long-term strategic vision to tap into the enormous market potential in China, the choice of Wuxi and the local partner was made on the basis of an introduction by a Mainland Chinese staff employed in Teck Wah Paper in Singapore. The Wuxi relative of this Chinese staff actually knew of one new TVE project in Wuxi, which had just built a new factory and brought in new printing machines. Though almost confirming a factory site in Shanghai at that time, Teck Wah Singapore decided to inject its 51 percent equivalent of equity to enter into a joint venture with this Wuxi TVE, thinking that Wuxi Paper is a ready-made printing factory with an existing customer base. The investment was therefore more opportunistic and entrepreneurial, reflecting the transnational entrepreneurship of second-generation family members.

What the Chua brothers in Singapore did not realize, however, is that Wuxi Paper then was strapped with cash flow problems, which in turn led to significant management problems in view of obstacles from the local partner. My interviewee said that the initial cash flow problem was due to China's massive decentralization of decision-making to local and village governments and the availability of easy credits from state banks to aid the growth of these TVEs during the early 1990s (see also Yeung 2000d, 2002). In fact, before the formation of the joint venture the Chinese factory manager of Wuxi Paper knew nothing about printing at all and they had one state-owned enterprise in Wuxi as their only customer! The decision to construct the printing factory and to purchase the new machinery and equipment was linked to potential personal gain by the factory manager and his cronies in the TVE. According to the joint venture agreement, Teck Wah Singapore would send one general manager and the local TVE would send three deputy general managers. Significant management problems emerged soon after the joint venture was in operation. One deputy general manager was the former factory manager who benefited personally from kickbacks during the establishment of the factory and acquisition of machinery. Once the joint venture was in operation, he clearly had neither intention nor incentive to make the joint venture work because he now had no control over the financial matters of Wuxi Paper and had to work with a "foreign" general manager. He therefore put up formidable labor problems to confront the first general manager who was sent from Singapore. As recalled by my interviewee who is the second general manager,

> He [first general manager] would just give any instructions and people would follow. But now he got no power at all. Everything he has to listen to the GM. So he does not like it. Then he would try to push the GM out and create problems for him. And after that, all subordinates boycotted all the GM's instructions.

This Singaporean general manager was a bad choice as far as Teck Wah Singapore is concerned. He only managed to survive as the general manager of Wuxi Paper for three months after the commencement of operations. As a result of mounting management pressures and lack of cooperation from his Chinese deputy general managers, he resigned and left the Teck Wah Group.

Faced with serious management problems in Wuxi Paper, the Chua brothers now had to do something to get the factory into operation. Since they were both very busy with Teck Wah Group's business activities, they had to entrust this difficult task to a faithful manager who could act as a transnational intrapreneur with strong adaptability and management mandates. This is how my interviewee, Mr Mah Kok Hui, was called upon to take over as the second general manager of Wuxi Paper. To start with, Mr Mah is a truly transnational intrapreneur. He first joined the Teck Wah Group in 1991, as the Production Director of Teck Wah Manufacturers Sdn Bhd in Malacca, Malaysia. Mah was offered the position and some shares of Teck Wah Malacca because of his trust relationships with Mr Thomas Chua (Group Managing Director) and Mr Mok (then Executive Director). In fact, Mah was the classmate of both Thomas and Mok during their pre-university education. After joining Teck Wah Malacca, Mah demonstrated to both Thomas and Mok that he could be a truly transnational intrapreneur. Before Teck Wah, Mah was working for a Japanese oil company in Malaysia. In Teck Wah Malacca, Mah was able to contribute to the company's growth at least in two ways. First, he engineered some acquisitions of old machinery from his former Japanese oil company, which had since been closed down. Second, he developed a total packaging concept and advised that Teck Wah Malacca should not just specialize in printing, but should also develop capabilities to print, assemble and pack products manufactured by leading foreign TNCs in Malaysia. His business strategy was subsequently proven successful and the factory was well integrated with two existing Teck Wah manufacturing operations in Malacca. Mah was given virtually full autonomy by Thomas and Mok to run the Malacca operation.

Once Mah had demonstrated his transnational entrepreneurship and been socialized into the "Teck Wah family," he was deemed an insider in the top executive elite group. After the general manager in Wuxi Paper had resigned, Teck Wah was looking for a replacement urgently. Several general managers of Teck Wah's other factories in Singapore and Malaysia turned down the offer because they lacked experience in China. Thomas Chua then asked his trusted lieutenant, Mah, to take over the troubled Wuxi Paper in 1994. Mah recalled:

> Because China project to them [Teck Wah] is very important. Then, they were in such a hurry at that time because the GM had resigned. Then they needed to get a person to replace. They actually asked all the subsidiary GMs: "who wants to come?". And then finally, I think when they talked to me at that time, those people requested to come didn't want to come ... Actually, at that time, I could see that China was a good place and time to come because they were just starting. Then, I think we did know what was the problem here.

Mah has strong adaptability to different business environments and is proactive and pragmatic in his approach to problems in transnational operations. These are key attributes of transnational entrepreneurship as defined earlier. His positive attitude towards problem solving is important in addressing thorny labor and marketing problems in Wuxi Paper. When asked whether he had considered leaving Wuxi Paper, Mah said:

> No, I don't think that. Because I have faced all kinds of people even in Singapore. There are always good and bad people. Everywhere you go is the same, even in Thailand and Malaysia. You will face the same kind of problem ... So, at that time we were facing a lot problems and we had to think of solving some of the main problems. So, we selected some of the main problems we faced because the first problem that we faced was marketing. We needed to survive. All these [other] problems we can leave it one side first.

Mah's approach to marketing and sales problems in Wuxi Paper was interesting. He did not believe in just forcing his Chinese salesmen to marketing Wuxi Paper's products without giving them sufficient training. His view was that employees must feel a sense of belonging to the company, which must provide good training and support to encourage the staff to perform:

> Control means the people first. We had to push them to run business because all the salesmen didn't want to go out. But the other way is that as a GM, we should teach them how to do the marketing. If we just push them without teaching them and then just push them out to sell, they also will not know how to do. Because they have no experience. So after three months we got one Singapore marketing manager to come here and support for nine months and to help out and train the people here.

Mah reshuffled the original management team in Wuxi Paper. He was given substantial autonomy and trust in transforming the management team. In a period of four years, he has changed up to 70 percent of top management positions in Wuxi Paper. There is now only one deputy general manager from the TVE partner who is put in charge of factory welfare and plays no effective role in shaping management decisions.

Mah's training and restructuring program proved to be effective. Within the first year of his arrival, Wuxi Paper managed to attract some customers, compared to only one customer at the time of its establishment. Today, all customers of Wuxi Paper are 100 percent foreign companies or joint ventures from Japan, Guangzhou and local governments. It is the only printing company in China that supplies to all three top bubble gum manufactures in China. The company is also profitable if machine depreciation is excluded. These results are good in view of strong competition from state-owned enterprises in Shanghai, which are endowed with strong local connections and good imported machines. Since the Chua family has strong faith in Mah's entrepreneurial performance, Teck Wah Singapore's stake in Wuxi Paper increased from 51 percent in 1994 to 90 percent by June 1998. To sum up, Mah's transnational entrepreneurship plays a critical role in turning Wuxi Paper around from a typical foreign investor's nightmare to a relatively profitable venture.

Conclusion: transnational entrepreneurship beyond the Asian economic crisis

Transnational entrepreneurship should be viewed as an ongoing process, implying that it can be learnt through accumulated experience and knowledge in foreign ventures. It is different from our traditional conception of entrepreneurship in the domestic economy because foreign ventures involve significantly higher risks and uncertainties. These difficult elements of foreign ventures tend to accentuate the greater need for transnational entrepreneurs to be highly proactive and adaptable to different business environments. Based on both survey data and personal interviews, this paper has shown that transnational entrepreneurship plays a very important role in explaining the success of the internationalization of Chinese family firms from Singapore, irrespective of whether the process is spearheaded by transnational Chinese entrepreneurs or their trusted intrapreneurs. It is clear that many transnational Chinese entrepreneurs from Singapore tend to capitalize on their cross-border social and business networks to facilitate their foreign operations. Not all Chinese entrepreneurs, however, are always available to manage their foreign operations. In some cases, this unavailability is attributed to the involvement of the transnational entrepreneur in many other foreign businesses. In other cases, an entrepreneur is simply incapable of managing his/her foreign ventures directly. This calls into question the role of transnational intrapreneurs who are the trusted members of the inner circle of Chinese entrepreneurs. Through a process of "family-ization," these transnational intrapreneurs are socialized into the corporate "family" and entrusted to manage foreign ventures. Because of their specific strengths and experience, these transnational intrapreneurs are often capable of both resolving operational problems and ensuring success in foreign ventures of Chinese family firms from Singapore.

What then are the implications of these transnational entrepreneurial tendencies for our understanding of the recent Asian economic crisis and the strategies of crisis management by Chinese family firms? I believe there are two specific issues: (1) networks and risk management and (2) transnational entrepreneurship and family control. First, it is clear that many Chinese family firms in Asia have not only invested a lot in "network capital," but also become dependent on these networks and connections. For example, intra-corporate financial transactions and insider trading are often cited as the "dark side" of Chinese businesses in Asia (see Backman 1999). Many patriarchs in Chinese family firms have pursued aggressive expansionary programs at the expense of minority shareholders in their public listed companies. Before the outbreak of the Asian economic crisis, this heavy dependence on networks and connections did not seem to matter much because everything remained rather rosy and investors, including fund managers, in these Chinese family firms did not quite bother with these irregular business practices. If these Chinese entrepreneurs tapped into cross-border business networks and connections, it became even more difficult for minority investors to notice these irregularities. Many leading Chinese business conglomerates from Southeast Asia, for example, managed to expand rapidly within two decades to become major regional competitors just before the Asian economic crisis. Their internationalization processes were largely embedded in wider social and business networks at a regional scale (see Yeung 1999a). Sound corporate governance across borders was not an issue. Rather, these transnational Chinese entrepreneurs were concerned with building up their transnational "network capital" and expanding their operations in almost every industry in every other Asian country.

By today, we have seen the powerful unfolding of the 1997/1998 Asian economic crisis and its negative impact on the social organization of Chinese capitalism in East and Southeast Asia (see Yeung 1999c, 2000g). While it is true that Asian economies with a predominantly Chinese population were less scathed by the crisis, it is also true that many Chinese family firms investing heavily in Asian economies with least corporate governance and business regulation standards tended to suffer most. This is primarily because many of these Chinese firms relied on personal connections and political alliances with the ruling elites to make their investment decisions. They often invested in host country companies on the basis of a potential windfall gain because of a license or monopoly right granted by their political "allies." This phenomenon is best seen in the case of the collapse of Peregrine Investment Holdings from Hong Kong in January 1998 because of a controversial unsecured "bridge loan" granted to PT Steady Safe taxicab company in Indonesia, which had the personal blessings of ex-President Suharto's daughter.

Although I agree with Backman's (1999: 365) assessment that "old habits are hard to break" particularly in the context of opaque and corruptive business environments in some Asian countries, I believe that many enlightened transnational Chinese entrepreneurs would learn from the crisis and pursue at least two key strategies to ensure the future success of their business empires (see also Yeung 2000b). The first strategy is globalization, which is a better alternative to specialization in regional markets as currently practiced. The globalization of Chinese business firms beyond Asia will be a significant form of insurance to hedge against major regional downturns. In a related sense, the second strategy for Chinese family firms is to seek access to global capital markets for funds. To date, very few Chinese family firms have tapped into global capital markets and gained the trust and favor of major investment houses based in global financial centers outside Asia (see Yeung and Soh 2000). This access requires significant improvement in corporate governance and accounting transparency of Chinese family firms, implying that they need to drop their "old habits" and develop a modern management system, which brings us to the next implication of this paper.

Second, while transnational entrepreneurship seems to be a highly positive and desirable attribute for business success, it should not be forgotten that a highly entrepreneurial individual tends to assume too much control and risks without due diligence. If the bottom line turns out to be fine, the transnational entrepreneur's judgement will not be questioned. This is particularly so if he/she owns much of the company. As the recent Asian economic crisis has demonstrated, rogue decisions could lead to significant corporate disasters that culminated in serious losses by minority shareholders. Poor bankruptcy laws in some Asian countries meant that the majority shareholders might get away with their wrong decisions. These sad events happened not because minority shareholders and/or professional managers did not object to the majority shareholder's "entrepreneurial" decisions, but rather because there was simply no room for them to stop the irrational and stubborn behavior of the patriarch. One single lesson we should learn from the crisis is that many Chinese family firms need to professionalize their management systems and corporate governance. This is easier said than done because one may argue that the very existence of Chinese family firms is to provide for the family. But surely there is a big difference between providing for the family and managing a huge conglomerate with diverse business interests in different regions and countries. While simple ownership of shares would satisfy the former requirement, it takes a long time to professionalize the management of a sound conglomerate.

Although I do not quite advocate the separation of ownership and management as in the case of the emergence of American corporations and managerial capitalism (Chandler 1977, 1990), I believe that any Chinese family firm today must have an explicit strategy for succession. By succession, I mean a clear system of promotion to senior executive positions on the basis of some rational criteria, even though kinship relations may be one key criterion. The options are two-fold, either grooming family members (typically sons and nephews) to become successful transnational entrepreneurs or socializing capable professional intrapreneurs into the "family" and becoming the future heir to top management. For the first option, many Chinese patriarchs are sending their children to be educated in top universities and business schools. They also get their children involved as interns in many leading global corporations before returning to manage family businesses (see Yeung 2000e).[10] These new generation successors of Chinese family business tend to gain better recognition among bankers, financiers and analysts based in major global financial centers. In this chapter, I have already shown how Hong Leong Group's late founder groomed his son, Kwek Leng Beng, to become a transnational entrepreneur in his own right.

On the other hand, it is true that as the family business empire expands across regions and countries, a Chinese family firm will eventually run out of family members. There is thus a strong need to develop a modern management system in order to unravel significant entrepreneurial managers who can be delegated important management functions. An intrapreneur program is required in these Chinese family firms so that they can survive beyond Wong's (1985) dilemma of three generations of Chinese family business. In this chapter, I have shown how in the case of Teck Wah Paper, a trusted classmate can be a very useful transnational intrapreneur to assist the internationalization of the family business. Taken together, the successful professionalization of management in Chinese family firms not only enables them to gain better recognition from worldwide business communities, but also reduces the necessity for too much personal control by founders and patriarchs. In today's era of accelerated global competition, the Asian economic crisis may be the last wake-up call for Chinese family firms to reform themselves. Whether such reforms and transformations in Chinese capitalism will enable it to survive the new millennium is quite another story.

Notes

1 I use "home" here because many Southeast Asian countries might not be the birthplace for the first and, sometimes, second generations of many of these transnational Chinese entrepreneurs.

2 Empirical data in this paper are derived from a larger set of very detailed firm-level database on the globalization of 204 Singapore-based transnational corporations (SINTNCs). This database is developed on the basis of a large-scale research project conducted between November 1997 and January 1999. At the initial stage of this project, we compiled basic corporate information of some 1,246 Singapore TNCs into the database. This information was gathered from various business directories and company reports between November 1997 and January 1998. Of these 1,246 companies, 340 companies had only correspondence information in China. As such, they could not be used for our survey in Singapore. Moreover, the database included 84 foreign TNCs in Singapore, which were subsequently discarded in accordance with the requirements of the research project. Together, only 822 companies in our database fulfilled the preliminary requirements of being Singapore-incorporated TNCs. At the end of the survey in Singapore in January 1999, another 34 companies were disqualified because either they had been closed down ($n = 11$) or had no foreign subsidiaries and investments ($n = 23$). This means an *effective* population of 788 Singapore TNCs for our corporate survey in Singapore through which we have successfully interviewed 204 parent companies, representing a 25.9% response rate. Some 54 of these 204 parent companies (26.5%) are owned and managed by ethnic Chinese families.

The second stage of the research involved personal interviews with subsidiaries and affiliates of Singapore TNCs in Hong Kong and China during May–June 1998. In contrast to the corporate survey in Singapore, I did not use any questionnaire during all interviews. Instead, these interviews were completely unstructured and virtually all taped (Yeung 1995). Their duration ranged from one to several hours. I managed to interview the top executives of 29 Singaporean firms in Hong Kong SAR and 13 in Guangdong province and 14 in Jiangsu province, China. Of these 56 personal interviews, 50 were taped and transcribed to provide qualitative information for this paper.

3 These journals include *Journal of International Business Studies, Management International Review, International Business Review* and related journals such as *Academy of Management Review* and *Strategic Management Journal.*

4 Having said that, it can also be argued that in a well-functioning market system, formal contracts enable businesses to be conducted among complete strangers, thereby contributing to greater transparency and economic efficiency.

5 Based on information from interviews with Mr Billy Lee, President of Sembawang Marine & Logistics, in Singapore, 18 May 1998 and Mr Ronnie Yuen, Deputy General Manager of Chiwan Petroleum Supply Base Co. Ltd, in Shekou, 12 June 1998.

6 Based on information from interviews with Mr Jack Teo, Managing Director of Hock San Yuen Food Manufacturing, in Singapore, 2 October 1998 and Ms Pamela Heng, Operation Manager of Sunwa Construction & Interior (Pte.) Ltd, in Singapore, 2 November 1998.

7 Based on information from an interview with Mr Richard Eu, Managing Director of Eu Yan Sang Holdings International, in Singapore, 24 November 1998.

8 All information reported here is based on an interview with Mr Gan Khai Choon, Managing Director of Hong Leong International (HK) Ltd and Executive Director of CDL Hotels International Ltd, in Hong Kong, 11 June 1998. Other information comes from printed publicity materials and company annual reports kindly supplied by Mr Gan.

9 All information reported here is based on an interview with Mr Mah Kok Hui, General Manager of Wuxi Teck Wah Paper Products Co. Ltd, in Wuxi, 6 July 1998. Other information comes from printed publicity materials and company annual reports.
10 See Magretta (1998) for the case of Victor Fung of Li & Fung and Olds (1998; 2000) for the case of Victor Li of Cheung Kong Holdings.

Bibliography

Alsegg, R. J. (1971) *Control Relationships Between American Corporations and Their European Subsidiaries*, New York: AMA.

Backman, M. (1999) *Asian Eclipse: Exposing the Dark Side of Business in Asia*, Singapore: John Wiley.

Bartlett, C. A. and Ghoshal, S. (1989) *Managing Across Borders: The Transnational Solution*, London: Century Business.

Beamish, P. W. and Killing, J. P. (eds) (1997) *Cooperative Strategies*, 3 Vols, San Francisco, CA: The New Lexington Press.

Birley, S. and MacMillan, I. C. (eds) (1995) *International Entrepreneurship*, London: Routledge.

——(eds) (1997) *Entrepreneurship in a Global Context*, London: Routledge.

Birkinshaw, J. M. (1996) How Multinational Subsidiary Mandates are Gained and Lost, *Journal of International Business Studies*, 27(3), 467–95.

Birkinshaw, J. M. and Morrison, A. J. (1995) Configurations of Strategy and Structure in Subsidiaries of Multinational Corporations, *Journal of International Business Studies*, 26(4), 729–53.

Bond, M. H. (ed.) (1986) *The Psychology of the Chinese People*, Hong Kong: Oxford University Press.

Brown, R. A. (ed.) (1995) *Chinese Business Enterprise in Asia*, London: Routledge.

Brown, R. (1998) Electronics Foreign Direct Investment in Singapore: A Study of Local Linkages in "Winchester City," *European Business Review*, 98(4), 196–210.

Casson, M. (ed.) (1990) *Entrepreneurship*, Aldershot: Edward Elgar.

——(1995) *Entrepreneurship and Business Culture: Studies in the Economics of Trust*, Aldershot: Edward Elgar.

Chan, K. B. and Chiang, C. Claire (1994) *Stepping Out: The Making of Chinese Entrepreneurs*, Singapore: Simon and Schuster.

Chan, W. K. K. (1995) The Origins and Early Years of the Wing On Company Group in Australia, Fiji, Hong Kong and Shanghai: Organisation and Strategy of a New Enterprise. In R. A. Brown (ed.), *Chinese Business Enterprise in Asia*, London: Routledge, pp. 80–95.

Chandler, A. D. Jr. (1977) *The Visible Hand: The Managerial Revolution in American Business*, Cambridge, MA: Harvard University Press.

——(1990) *Scale and Scope: The Dynamics of Industrial Capitalism*, Cambridge, MA: Harvard University Press.

Chen, M. (1995) *Asian Management Systems: Chinese, Japanese and Korean Styles of Business*, London: Routledge.

Chiu, S. W. K., Ho, K. C. and Lui, T.-L. (1997) *City-States in the Global Economy: Industrial Restructuring in Hong Kong and Singapore*, Boulder, CO: Westview.

Department of Statistics (1991) *Singapore's Investment Abroad, 1976–1989*, Singapore: DOS.

Department of Statistics (1996) *Singapore's Investment Abroad, 1990–1993*, Singapore: DOS.

Department of Statistics (1997) *Yearbook of Statistics Singapore, 1996*, Singapore: DOS.

Department of Statistics (1998) *Singapore's Investment Abroad, 1996*, Singapore: DOS.

DiConti, M. A. (1992) *Entrepreneurship in Training: The Multinational Corporation in Mexico and Canada*, Columbia: University of South Carolina Press.

Doz, Y. L. and Hamel, G. (1998) *Alliance Advantage: The Art of Creating Value through Partnering*, Boston: Harvard Business School Press.

East Asia Analytical Unit (1995) *Overseas Chinese Business Networks in Asia*, Parkes, Australia: Department of Foreign Affairs and Trade.

Financial Times, 3/5/1998.

Fukuyama, F. (1995) *Trust: The Social Virtues and the Creation of Prosperity*, London: Hamish Hamilton.

Haley, G. T., Tan, C.-T. and Haley, U. C. V. (1998) *The New Asian Emperors: The Overseas Chinese, Their Strategies and Competitive Advantages*, Oxford: Butterworth-Heinemann.

Hamilton, G. G. (ed.) (1991a) *Business Networks and Economic Development in East and South East Asia*, Hong Kong: Center of Asian Studies, University of Hong Kong.

——(1991b) The Organizational Foundation of Western and Chinese Commerce: A Historical and Comparative Analysis. In G. G. Hamilton (ed.), *Business Networks and Economic Development in East and South East Asia*, Hong Kong: Center of Asian Studies, University of Hong Kong, pp. 48–65.

——(1994) Civilizations and the Organization of Economies. In N. J. Smelser and R. Swedberg (eds), *The Handbook of Economic Sociology*, Princeton: Princeton University Press, pp. 183–205.

——(1996) Overseas Chinese capitalism. In W.-M. Tu (ed.), *Confucian Traditions in East Asian Modernity: Moral Education and Economic Culture in Japan and the Four Mini-Dragons*, Cambridge, MA: Harvard University Press, pp. 328–42.

Hefner, R. W. (ed.) (1998) *Market Cultures: Society and Values in the New Asian Capitalisms*, Singapore: Institute of Southeast Asian Studies.

Ho, K. C. (1993) Industrial Restructuring and the Dynamics of City-State Adjustments, *Environment and Planning A*, 25(1), 47–62.

Hodder, R. (1996) *Merchant Princes of the East: Cultural Delusions, Economic Success and the Overseas Chinese in Southeast Asia*, Chichester: John Wiley.

Huff, W. G. (1994) *The Economic Growth of Singapore: Trade and Development in the Twentieth Century*, Cambridge: Cambridge University Press.

Hughes, H. and Sing, Y.-P. (eds) (1969) *Foreign Investment and Industrialization in Singapore*, Madison: University of Wisconsin.

Kanai, T. (1993) Singapore's New Focus on Regional Business Expansion, *Nomura Research Institute Quarterly*, 2(3), 18–41.

Kao, J. (1993) The Worldwide Web of Chinese Business, *Harvard Business Review*, March–April, 24–36.

Lever-Tracy, C., Ip, D. and Tracy, N. (1996) *The Chinese Diaspora and Mainland China: An Emerging Economic Synergy*, London: Macmillan.

Lewis, J. D. (1995) *The Connected Corporation: How Leading Companies Win Through Customer-Supplier Alliances*, New York: The Free Press.

Lim, L. Y. C. and Gosling, L. A. P. (eds) (1983) *The Chinese in Southeast Asia*, Singapore: Maruzen Asia.

Livesay, H. C. (ed.) (1995) *Entrepreneurship and the Growth of Firms*, Aldershot: Edward Elgar.

Low, L. (1998) *The Political Economy of a City-State: Government-Made Singapore*, Singapore: Oxford University Press.

Low, A. M. and Tan, W. L. (eds) (1996) *Entrepreneurs, Entrepreneurship and Enterprising Culture*, Singapore: Addison-Wesley.

Low, L., Toh, M. H., Soon, T. W., Tan, K. Y. and Hughes, H. (1993) *Challenge and Response: Thirty Years of the Economic Development Board*, Singapore: Times Academic Press.

Magretta, J. (1998) Fast, Global, and Entrepreneurial: Supply Chain Management, Hong Kong Style: An Interview with Victor Fung, *Harvard Business Review*, 76(5), 103–14.

Mahizhnan, A. and Lee, T. Y. (eds) (1998) *Singapore: Re-Engineering Success*, Singapore: Oxford University Press.

Martinez, J. I. and Jarillo, J. C. (1988) The Evolution of Research on Coordination Mechanisms in Multinational Corporations, *Journal of International Business Studies*, 20, 489–514.

—— (1991) Co-ordination Demands of International Strategies, *Journal of International Business Studies*, 22(3), 429–44.

Mathews, J. A. (1999) A Silicon Island of the East: Creating a Semiconductor Industry in Singapore, *California Management Review*, 41(2), 55–78.

Ministry of Finance (May 1993) *Interim Report of the Committee to Promote Enterprise Overseas*, Singapore: MOF.

Mirza, H. (1986) *Multinationals and the Growth of the Singapore Economy*, London: Croom Helm.

Murdoch, J. (1999) The Spaces of Actor-Network Theory, *Geoforum*, 29(4), 357–74.

Numagami, T. (1998) The Infeasibility of Invariant Laws in Management Studies: A Reflective Dialogue in Defense of Case Studies, *Organization Science*, 9(1), 2–15.

Olds, K. (1998) Globalization and Urban Change: Tales from Vancouver via Hong Kong, *Urban Geography*, 19(4), 360–85.

—— (2000) *Globalization and Urban Change: Capital, Culture and Pacific Rim Mega Projects*, New York: Oxford University Press.

Olds, K. and Yeung, H. W.-C. (1999) (Re)shaping "Chinese" Business Networks in a Globalising Era, *Environment and Planning D: Society and Space*, 17, 535–55.

Otterbeck, L. (ed.) (1981) *The Management of Headquarters-Subsidiary Relationships in Multinational Corporations*, Aldershot: Gower.

Perry, M., Kong, L. and Yeoh, B. (1997) *Singapore: A Developmental City State*, London: John Wiley.

Perry, M., Poon, J. and Yeung, H. (1998a) Regional Offices in Singapore: Spatial and Strategic Influences in the Location of Corporate Control, *Review of Urban and Regional Development Studies*, 10(1), 42–59.

Perry, M., Yeung, H. and Poon, J. (1998b) Regional Office Mobility: The Case of Corporate Control in Singapore and Hong Kong, *Geoforum*, 29(3), 237–55.

Perry, M. and Tan, B. H. (1998) Global Manufacturing and Local Linkage in Singapore, *Environment and Planning A*, 30, 1603–24.

Prahalad, C. K. and Doz, Y. (1987) *The Multinational Mission: Balancing Local Demands and Global Vision*, New York: The Free Press.

Redding, S. G. (1990) *The Spirit of Chinese Capitalism*, Berlin: De Gruyter.

Régnier, P. (1991) *Singapore: City-State in South-East Asia*, Hawaii: University of Hawaii Press.

—— (1993), Spreading Singapore's Wings Worldwide: a Review of Traditional and New Investment Strategies, *The Pacific Review*, 6(4), 305–12.

Rodan, G. (1989) *The Political Economy of Singapore's Industralization: National State and International Capital*, London: Macmillan.

Roth, K. and Morrison, A. J. (1992) Implementing Global Strategy: Characteristics of Global Subsidiary Mandates, *Journal of International Business Studies*, 23(4), 715–35.

Singh, K. and Ang, S. H. (1998) *The Strategies and Success of Government Linked Corporations in Singapore*, Research Paper Series #98-06, Faculty of Business Administration, National University of Singapore, Singapore.

Siu, W.-S. and Tseng, C.-S. (1992) Internationalization of Small Business in Hong Kong: A Case Study Approach, *Proceedings of the ENDEC World Conference on Entrepreneurship*, August 11–14, 1992, Marina Mandarin, Singapore, pp. 55–8.

Tan, C. Z. and Yeung, H. W.-C. (2000) The Regionalization of Chinese Business Networks: A Study of Singaporean Firms in Hainan Province, China, *The Professional Geographer*, 52(3), 437–54.

The Straits Times, Singapore, 11/20/1998.

The Sunday Times, Singapore, 2/2/1997.

Thrift, N. (1996) *Spatial Formations*, London: Sage.

Tseng, C. S. (1992) Entrepreneurship and Outward Foreign Direct Investment by PRC Multinationals, *Proceedings of the ENDEC World Conference on Entrepreneurship*, August 11–14, 1992, Marina Mandarin, Singapore, pp. 447–58.

Weidenbaum, M. and Hughes, S. (1996) *The Bamboo Network: How Expatriate Chinese Entrepreneurs Are Creating a New Economic Superpower in Asia*, New York: The Free Press.

Willcocks, L. and Choi, C. J. (1995) Co-operative Partnership and "Total" IT Outsourcing: From Contractual Obligation to Strategic Alliance? *European Management Journal*, 13(1), 67–78.

Willis, K. D. and Yeoh, B. (1998) The Social Sustainability of Singapore's Regionalisation Drive, *Third World Planning Review*, 20(2), 203–21.

Wong, S.-L. (1985) The Chinese Family Firm: A Model, *British Journal of Sociology*, 36, 58–72.

—— (1988) *Emigrant Entrepreneurs: Shanghai Industrialists in Hong Kong*, Hong Kong: Oxford University Press.

Yeung, H. W.-C. (1995) Qualitative Personal Interviews in International Business Research, *International Business Review*, 4(3), 313–39.

—— (1997a) Critical Realism and Realist Research in Human Geography: A Method or a Philosophy in Search of a Method? *Progress in Human Geography*, 21(1), 51–74.

—— (1997b) Business Networks and Transnational Corporations: A Study of Hong Kong Firms in the ASEAN Region, *Economic Geography*, 73(1), 1–25.

—— (1997c) Cooperative Strategies and Chinese Business Networks: A Study of Hong Kong Transnational Corporations in the ASEAN Region. In P. W. Beamish and J. Peter Killing (eds), *Cooperative Strategies: Asia-Pacific Perspectives*, San Francisco, CA: The New Lexington Press, pp. 22–56.

—— (1998a) *Transnational Corporations and Business Networks: Hong Kong Firms in the ASEAN Region*, London: Routledge.

—— (1998b) The Political Economy of Transnational Corporations: A Study of the Regionalisation of Singaporean Firms, *Political Geography*, 17(4), 389–416.

—— (1998c) Transnational Economic Synergy and Business Networks: The Case of Two-Way Investment between Malaysia and Singapore, *Regional Studies*, 32(8), 687–706.

—— (1998d) The Social-Spatial Constitution of Business Organisations: A Geographical Perspective, *Organization*, 5(1), 101–28.

Yeung, H. W.-C. (1999a) The Internationalization of Ethnic Chinese Business Firms from Southeast Asia: Strategies, Processes and Competitive Advantage, *International Journal of Urban and Regional Research*, 23(1), 103–27.

—— (1999b) Regulating Investment Abroad? The Political Economy of the Regionalisation of Singaporean Firms, *Antipode*, 31(3), 245–73.

—— (1999c) Under Siege? Economic Globalisation and Chinese Business in Southeast Asia, *Economy and Society*, 28(1), 1–29.

—— (1999d) *The Political Economy of Singaporean Investments in China*, Paper Presented at the East Asia Institute seminar, National University of Singapore, 19 March 1999.

—— (2000a) Embedding Foreign Affiliates in Transnational Business Networks: The Case of Hong Kong Firms in Southeast Asia, *Environment and Planning A*, 32(2), 201–22.

—— (2000b) Managing Crisis in a Globalising Era: The Case of Chinese Business Firms from Singapore. In David Ip, Constance Lever-Tracy and Noel Tracy (eds), *Chinese Businesses and the Asian Crisis*, Aldershot: Gower, pp. 87–113.

—— (2000c) State Intervention and Neoliberalism in the Globalising World Economy: Lessons from Singapore's Regionalisation Programme, *The Pacific Review*, 13(1), 133–62.

—— (2000d) Local Politics and Foreign Ventures in China's Transitional Economy: The Political Economy of Singaporean Investments in China, *Political Geography*, 19(7), 809–40.

—— (2000e) Limits to the Growth of Family-Owned Business? The Case of Chinese Transnational Corporations from Hong Kong, *Family Business Review*, 13(1), 55–70.

—— (2000f) The Dynamics of Asian Business Systems in a Globalising Era, *Review of International Political Economy*, 7(3), 399–433.

—— (2000g) Economic Globalisation, Crisis, and the Emergence of Chinese Business Communities in Southeast Asia, *International Sociology*, 15(2), 269–90.

—— (2002) *Entrepreneurship and the Internationalisation of Asian Firms: An Institutional Perspective*, Cheltenham: Edward Elgar.

Yeung, H. W.-C. and Olds, K. (1998) Singapore's Global Reach: Situating the City-State in the Global Economy, *International Journal of Urban Sciences*, 2(1), 24–47.

—— (eds) (2000) *The Globalisation of Chinese Business Firms*, London: Macmillan.

Yeung, H. W.-C., Poon, J. and Perry, M. (2001) Towards a Regional Strategy: The Role of Regional Headquarters and Regional Offices in the Asia Pacific, *Urban Studies*, 38(1), 157–83.

Yeung, H. W.-C. and Soh, T. M. (2000) Corporate Governance and the Global Reach of Chinese Family Firms in Singapore, *Seoul Journal of Economics*, 13(3), 301–34.

Yin, R. K. (1994) *Case Study Research: Design and Methods*, 2nd Ed., Thousand Oaks: Sage.

Yoshihara, K. (1976) *Foreign Investment and Domestic Response: A Study of Singapore's Industrialization*, Singapore: Eastern University Press.

9

PERSONALISM AND PATERNALISM IN CHINESE BUSINESSES

Tong Chee Kiong and Yong Pit Kee

Understanding Chinese business organizations – an institutional perspective

Most studies on business organizations have tended to adopt either a "market" or "cultural" perspective. The main concern of the "market" perspective is to understand how economic interests shape organizational structure and behavior. Chandler (1984) and Williamson (1985), for example, place emphasis on the efficient adaptation of organizations to market pressures. These approaches presuppose that entrepreneurial responses to environmental pressures are economically rational and geared towards producing maximum profits. Blau *et al.* (1976), in particular, has shown how size, technology and differentiation of the task environment shape organizational structures (see also Pugh and Hickson 1976). Contingency theorists such as Donaldson (1987), though advocating that there are various "ideal" organizational types contingent upon the environment, still emphasize the concern for economic efficiency to be a congruence between environmental factors, and organizational structures and processes. Though important, the above perspectives reflect an "undersocialised" concept of human action (Granovetter 1985).

The "market" perspective generally predicts a convergence with regard to organization forms. It is anticipated that the pressure on efficiency will result in more organizations, globally, becoming less different from each other (Clegg 1990: 151). However, they cannot explain the diversity of economic structures demonstrating economic success, even when different market conditions are taken into account. The "cultural" perspective, in contrast, provides explanations for such diversities. It emphasizes the impact of cultural factors on economic structures and behavior. These cultural studies question the assumption of a universal administrative rationality, which the previous approaches take for granted. They provide insight into the non-rational, subjective aspects of organizational life. Scholars using this approach generally attempt to link organizational patterns with the cultural practices of the larger society. Marsh and Mannari (1981) and Horvath *et al.* (1981), for example, show how management systems differ under contrasting value systems. Ouchi (1984) links cultural factors to economic tradition, looking at how cultural values such as "trust" influence whether individuals utilize contracts or other devices of control to mediate transactions (see also Maitland *et al.* 1985; Gambetta 1988).

In East Asia, the cultural perspective is becoming increasingly popular. Kahn, for example, proposed that the success of organizations in Hong Kong, Taiwan, South Korea, Japan and Singapore was due mainly to certain salient features shared by the majority of organization members. Silin's (1976) study in Taiwan focuses on traits, which he asserts, are common to all economic organizations. He looks into aspects of the Confucian tradition to make sense of organizational forms and behavior. Similarly, Redding (1980) underscores the cognitive aspect to explain the differences between Chinese and Western managerial behavior and organizational forms. Bond and Hwang (1986), and Redding and Wong (1986) pay particular attention to the psychology of the Chinese to explicate their organizational behavior.

Despite acknowledging the factors that the market approach has ignored, Roberts criticized that, too often, culture was used "as a kind of residual variable which was taken to influence every individual actor's perceptions and actions, by-passing 'macro' explanatory variables, specifically those of the environment relevant to an organization, and variables at the total organizational and sub-units level" (in Sorge 1977: 68). Hamilton and Woolsey Biggart (1986: 20) assert that most cultural explanations concentrate too much on secondary causes: "…the cultural explanation works poorly when attempting to examine a changing organizational environment to analyze differences among organizations in the same cultural area."

The cultural approach is in essence, in Granovetter's (1985) term, an "over-socialised" view of economic action. Though the cultural perspective is the direct anti-thesis of the "undersocialized" view, it is equally as deterministic in its explanation of organizational forms. It assumes too much strength in cultural transmission (Clegg 1990), which implies that, for example, Chinese businesses are family-based because of Confucian traditions thus leaving little room for economic structures or political restrictions.

It is perhaps pertinent to qualify that neither culture nor economics is irrelevant. On the contrary, both are equally important factors to understand business behavior. This paper is based on an "institutional" perspective, which ties both market and cultural forces together. This approach underscores that organizational form is often not necessarily the result of task requirements or the need for efficiency. Rather, it is an elaboration of institutional belief systems. Furthermore, it makes reference to culture but strives to establish it in its institutional specificity. Culture does not determine organizational form but provides a framework, which enables as well as constricts action (Clegg 1990: 150–1).

The institutional approach also recognizes that economic actions and relations are not only embedded in spatial terms but also in temporal terms (Clegg and Redding 1990: 24). The importance of history, to a large extent dismissed by market and even cultural approaches, is emphasized here.

We will now proceed with a detailed case study of the Lee Rubber Group; after which the principles of Chinese business organization, such as ownership patterns, authority structures and developmental patterns will be analyzed.

Case study: the Lee Rubber Group

Lee Kong Chian (henceforth, LKC) was the founder of the Lee Rubber Group. Born in Fujian in 1894, he came to Singapore in 1904 to join his father. Around 1916, Tan Kah Kee (henceforth, TKK), required an assistant fluent in English since he had wanted to export his rubber directly to England. He knew of LKC as he was working for TKK's friend. TKK requested his friend to release LKC and offered him a job in his rubber department. LKC proved to be so efficient that in 1920, as one informant said, "Kah Kee quickly married his daughter to him because [he] was afraid Kong Chian would leave."

In 1927, LKC ventured out on his own and started a smoke house in Muar (near Malacca) with a friend. This friend, together with LKC's distant cousin (also a Lee) looked after most of the operations, as LKC could only go up to Muar on weekends, as he was still managing TKK's business. Although many informants told us that normally, an employee could only establish his own business if it did not compete with the interests of his employer, LKC apparently had managed to secure the approval of his father-in-law because TKK had already ventured into the manufacturing of rubber goods and was losing interest in rubber processing. Both men agreed that LKC would stay clear of manufacturing (which he did, completely).

The 1930s depression caused the foreclosure of many of the bigger rubber companies. Lim Nee Soon, a friend of LKC who owned a very big factory in Seletar, Singapore, ran into debts. LKC helped settle part of the debt for Lim who then leased this factory to LKC. A new company, Lam Aik (Lee Rubber Co.), was set up to manage this factory. This company began as a partnership between LKC, Lee Phie Soe (who was from the same village as LKC in China, and was then a successful businessman in Medan) and Yap Twee, a good friend of LKC. They chipped in "as friends to help [LKC] establish the business ... [it] was a very big factory (mill), and required a lot more capital [than the Muar smokehouse], so as friends, they came in to support. But LKC ran the business." Lim Nee Soon's son who had a small share in Lee Rubber also worked there. This arrangement was Lim's request to LKC. Here, we note the important role of non-kin relationships (*guanxi*) in setting up businesses.

Though it started off as a partnership, Lee Rubber was quickly converted into a private limited company to protect the other shareholders, especially Lee Phie Soe and Yap Twee, who were "richer than LKC and would be in great danger of having to bear the main burden." Nonetheless, this did not change the way the business was run. As other rubber factories closed down, Lee Rubber was able to lease them and expand the volume of production. LKC began to set up other companies in Malaya such as the Lian Hin Group. By 1939, he had also established separate companies in Indonesia (Hok Tong Group), and Thailand (Siam Pakthai, 1934). The South Asia Corporation was established in New York in 1938 to handle the export of rubber to the USA. LKC had also started accumulating rubber estates in Malaya. In each of these companies, a relative or clansman was put in charge. For example, the persons heading three of the subgroups in Malaysia were: Lee Seng P'ng, a cousin of LKC (Lian Hin); Lee Boon Chim, a clansmen (Lee Rubber Selangor); and Lee In Tong, a distant cousin (Teck Bee Hang, Thailand). The Managing Director of Kota Trading is also another Lee: Lee Kai Tong. One informant, a Lee himself, said:

> Although he knew little about managing estates, my grandfather looked after the rubber estates of LKC in Malaya. Because he is a relative (my father is LKC's distant cousin), LKC felt he would not cheat... and around 1937, my father was made manager of the Lee Rubber company in Telok Anson, Perak, and my older brother was sent up to Thailand.

This informant added that all these various companies were subsidiaries of Lee Rubber in Singapore. LKC, however, ensured that the whole corporate structure was compartmentalized (at least from the legal perspective), so that if one part of the group met with problems, the rest would not be affected. To give his Thai operations some autonomy from his corporate group without losing control, LKC had decided that the best way was to create an appearance of independence. He disclaimed all formal interests in the new company, but retained control through his kin. He relied on the *xinyong* of this relative to protect his family interests: "Everything was entrusted to my father. LKC put everything in my father's name. My father was to hold the shares in trust, you see."

Through the employment of personal relations trusted to act in his interest, LKC was able to retain control even as the business continued to expand. In Malaya, before the war, LKC had already accumulated twenty branches with factories and offices. In Indonesia, Hok Tong had about four or five factories. These were all managed by his relatives and clansmen. *Guanxi* relations beyond the immediate family are very important for the maintenance of personal control, especially when immediate family members are limited.

Besides rubber, LKC also ventured into other businesses. Before the war, he had expanded into planting pineapples and biscuit manufacturing. These businesses were operated under subsidiary companies of Lee Rubber: for example, Lee Pineapple and Lee Biscuit. After the war, the group ventured into sawmills, refining of coconut oil and so on. The sawmill business was an offshoot of the pineapple plantations business. When the forest was cleared to grow the pineapples, the company had to dispose off the trees. Rather than burning the trees, a department was set up within Lee Pineapple to handle the timber business. When the timber division expanded, Lee Sawmills was established.

As the community of workers grew, the company also ventured into the grocery business, setting up sundry-goods shops to provide for the household needs of the workers and their families. The company also expanded into the business of leasing tractors, which were needed to clear the fields. And since the company consumed petroleum for its clearing and transportation operations, it also became an agent for "Esso," and later started setting up its own petrol stations.

However, LKC and his family found that the rapid expansion soon created a number of problems. First, they were not properly equipped to deal with so many types of businesses. This was, perhaps, largely due to the fact that there was no proper managerial control. There was a lack of trusted personnel to manage the different sectors, and to manage them well. Gradually, these "fringe" activities were shut down and the group focused its energies on rubber, pineapples and biscuit manufacturing.

Apart from these businesses, LKC was also involved in banking. During the 1930s depression, Yap Twee, who was then the managing director of the Chinese Commercial Bank, invited LKC to be a director. When the bank later amalgamated with the Ho Hong Bank and Overseas Chinese Bank to form the Overseas Chinese Banking Corporation (OCBC), LKC took an active part in the merger negotiations. He was appointed as Chairman in 1932 despite his small share of the bank's equity, as he had influential backing among the major shareholders. After the war, he increased his equity to become the largest shareholder. Presently, the Lee family holds about 20 percent stake in OCBC via various companies. Lee Rubber Co. itself holds about 5 percent.

One point to note about the development of ownership of the businesses outlined above is the fact that the various partnerships LKC had with his friends and clansmen were eventually absorbed by LKC's family. LKC's family later became the sole owners of the Lee Rubber empire. Yap Twee's and Lee Phie Soe's shares had been given to their sons who had, over the years, sold theirs to LKC's family. Some managers who sit on the board of directors do own some token shares, amounting to less than 0.2 percent each. Other than that, the majority of shareholders are family members who own the whole business either directly or through "double-back" ownership.

Though the Lee Foundations of Singapore and Malaysia also own a substantial proportion of various companies, to prevent any intrusion by outsiders and the possible subsequent loss of control by the family, management shares (which have no monetary value, only voting rights) were issued to family members to further consolidate the family's control. This control is further tightened through intense interlocking of directorships within the business group.

LKC had planned for a smooth transition of leadership. When he felt his sons were old enough, they were deployed at the factories to assist and learn the business "from scratch." When they had gained sufficient experience, LKC gave his sons executive responsibilities and appointed them to the management boards of his key companies. Before LKC's death, his three sons had already taken over the reigns of managing the businesses, and they continue to do so till today (although Lee Seng Gee and Seng Tee retired recently).

Ownership patterns

Our informants often referred to Chinese businesses as "all family business, especially in rubber." Redding and Wong (1986: 275) also wrote "Overseas Chinese organizations are virtually all family businesses." We found this to be generally true. Our analysis of ROCB (Registry of Companies and Businesses) documents of 98 sampled rubber firms included four sole proprietorships and four partnerships. Of the four partnerships, one is between a father and son, another is a partnership comprising other types of relatives; and the other two are owned by partners who were friends. The rest of the 90 firms are private limited companies. Individuals (holding more than 50 percent of the stocks) who are related to one another own 61 percent (55) of these. Of the 55 companies studied, 85 percent (47) are owned by families who possess more than 80 percent of the shares. Whole families holding between 50–79 percent of the shares own 15 percent (8) of the companies.

However, companies with shareholders who do not share a kinship base make up 36 percent (32) of the total (90). This suggests that the significance of firms owned by non-kin could have been undervalued. We realized that it is also necessary to look at the firms at varying stages of their maturity. The average age of family-owned firms is 24.5 years, and that of non-family, 15.5 years, with an average difference of 9 years. If we look at the outset of each, a slightly different picture evolves. It is interesting to note that for about 20 percent (11) of the present family-owned companies the family ownership is less than 50 percent. In other words, 46 percent (45) of the firms had begun without any one family or person owning more than 50 percent of the business. This is similar to the history of Lee Rubber Company and reveals a relatively high reliance on non-kin for initial capital outlays. Commenting on the model of Chinese family business, S. L. Wong (1985: 62) notes that:

> ... we should not too hastily deduce ... that "most Chinese firms [start] as a family concern" because it is unlikely that the funds mustered by an individual and his *jia* alone are sufficient to set up an enterprise other than a very modest one. The common format for a new business to assume ... is that of partnership in which financial resources are pooled by persons largely unrelated by ties of descent or marriage.

From our interviews, we found that family ownership is regarded as an ideal by the informants. The ROCB records show that in the initial years, other *guanxi* bases besides kinship are important in providing business partners (preferably "silent" or otherwise). Over the years, one person and his family (like Lee Kong Chian) may gradually attain the majority ownership of the company by buying out the other non-family shareholders. As one informant related: "My father started this company with some friends. Later on, he bought over most of their shares, becoming the major shareholder."

Many of the presently family-owned companies were actually built up with the capital gained through earlier partnerships. The capital of non-family members is an important source of start-up finance for establishing a business. Non-family members do have important roles to play in the development of the Chinese family business. Although many firms do not begin as a family-owned business because of insufficient funds, efforts would be made to secure a controlling interest in the firm eventually.

Authority structures

There is a strong overlapping of ownership and management in Chinese businesses, which facilitates the paternalistic style of controlling of the firm. This characteristic style of authority in Chinese management has been observed by several researchers. Hofstede's (1980) study of Chinese organizations in Hong Kong, Singapore and Taiwan found managers to be authoritative. K. K. Hwang (1983) and Redding (1980) also described such leadership patterns in which the leader could implement ideas as he pleased. Silin (1976) described Chinese leadership style as "didactic," implying that the leader's role is similar to that of a teacher. Redding and Wong (1986: 278) further explain that such a leader "holds information, and thus power, and doles it out in small pieces to subordinates, who thus remain more or less dependent." As outlined above, the leader also "does not normally commit himself openly to a line of action, but rather keeps his options open, leaving the direction of his organization or department to follow the lines detected by a somewhat nebulous but nevertheless powerful set of personal intuitions. The latter are the responsibility of the leader ... ."

Chin (in Tan, 1976) writes of managerial styles in Hong Kong where subordinates, deprived of information, keep going back to supervisors for even minor decisions. As one interviewed company director remarked: "But whatever the responsibility delegated, we have to go back to the boss. He wants to make all the decisions. Most Chinese companies need you to refer back [to him]." Similarly, another informant added, "Sometimes, even the approval of $200 to buy something has to go all the way up to the Chairman!"

This lack of delegation of authority has also been observed by researchers of Chinese firms in Singapore (e.g. Tong 1989). Other evidence derived from the interviews also support observations of highly centralized power. The secretary of one rubber association told us: "Chinese rubber firms tend to be very much controlled by one man. If the *thau-ke* (boss or founder-owner) goes, the company goes." A retired trader remarked:

> Even though my uncle owned the largest rubber miller, and was the largest trader in Singapore, he continued to run [the business] the way he wanted. I was made Managing Director, but the business continued to be managed by him. It was in effect a one-man show.

A retired manager, echoing the opinions of many other informants, explained the logic for such a leadership style, which characterized even large firms he had worked in previously:

> In the rubber trade, there can never be two heads ... because you are going to lose money. There must only be one leader. He decides. But you must have all the information available for him. So, he must have good assistants. Go out and mix, ferret out the information. Give it to him. Sit down and consult with each other. But the final say must rest with the top man. He must decide. Whether to go long or short. Must! I have seen companies with two heads, always [fail]. Because you come to a stage when the market is difficult, one guy will say, "let's sell," and the other guy may say, "let's buy." When they both cannot agree, they say: "Alright, we don't take any active position." They lose money. Always the case. You notice, the big powerful companies: only one man. He makes the final decision, either good or bad.

The legitimacy of the authority of the boss largely hinges on the fact that he is the owner of the firm. This strong overlapping of ownership and management in turn facilitates the authoritative style of management and in particular propagates personalism. As one director remarked of the Chairman:

> After all, the company is his. So there is no need for board meetings. No such thing as voting. Vote what? He and his family own more than 70–80 percent! He alone is the majority. If he wants to promote his son, he can. No need to ask the board. We only meet when he wants to tell us things, or to get information from us.

The effective management of his business is also partially facilitated by the boss employing persons whom he could personally trust, or who are tied to him personally via *guanxi* ties, or, at least, share a common *guanxi* base from which a personal *guanxi* and *xinyong* can be established. Chinese businessmen hold a discriminatory system in ranking the trustworthiness of people with varying social distance from them. The nearer the social distance, the more likely the presumption of trust:

> Rubber has many undefined and intangible factors, unlike the usual retail trade. In the retail trade, there is a fixed price. In rubber, there are many ways of processing each type of raw material. As a result, the quality varies. There no fixed costs and many gray areas ... Very easy to cheat the company without the boss knowing. The opportunities are too many and too tempting. Therefore, we always like to employ our own people.

Nevertheless, while one's own people warrant the presumption of trust when no other criteria exist for determining *xinyong*, the social obligations towards them may also prove to be crippling. Thus, Wong (1988) distinguished between active and passive nepotism. His study of spinners in Hong Kong revealed that 51 percent of his respondents felt an obligation to appoint relatives against their better business judgement – passive nepotism – rather than positively preferring their employment – active nepotism – because they are more worthy of trust.

Our fieldwork data suggest that nepotism can be both active and passive at the same time. For example, though one owner manager talked about trusting one's own people more, he also lamented about having to keep a kin in employment, "… even though he (the kin) had made a mistake that cost us $700,000. What did we do? Nothing. We still employ him. I quote this as our management attitude."

Another informant pointed out the burden of social obligations:

> Of course, you trust your own people more … [But] it is difficult to correct your own people when they don't perform well. You can tell them once or twice. But too many times, it is not so nice. They don't like it. It makes you feel difficult. You may want them to leave, but it is hard to fire your own people.

Hence, there is a great deal of ambivalence towards kin. Concern for reducing the burden of social obligations prompts entrepreneurs to restrict nepotistic tendencies. We found that, on the whole, nepotism only extended to family members. Only the Lee Rubber case and two other older, larger enterprises reflected a higher utilization of clansmen and fellow-villagers. Even so, the number of kinsmen, clansmen or fellow-villagers makes up only a small fraction of the personnel employed. The remaining cases studied are presently not nepotistic beyond the family. This is in line with what Wong (1988) discovered of the spinners in Hong Kong. He noted that the overwhelming majority of kinsmen employed were family members, with a few examples of relatives. Distant relatives and clansmen were not found. Therefore, it can be concluded that Chinese entrepreneurs tend to be nepotistic towards their own family members and much less so with the outer kin network and clan members. In addition, our fieldwork confirmed that such nepotism is most consistently practiced where key positions are concerned.

We also found that family members do not always occupy the top positions. In many of the companies visited, only one (or two) representative of the family was present (usually the father). Despite the absence of family members in the daily operations of the business, our informants still regarded their business as a family-based one because of its orientation. That is, while family members may not be occupying strategic positions in the firm, these positions are ultimately reserved for them. Hence, Chinese businesses are family-oriented: entrepreneurs work towards establishing family ownership of the business eventually, keeping succession for family members only, retaining ultimate control of the business within the family. This family-orientedness characterizes the fabric of development of Chinese enterprises and also implies certain problems, as the next section will show.

Development patterns – the "Centrifugal" tendency

It is often difficult to decide at what point a business originated. For example, we found that all founders of a firm seem to have started out in the business, in a similar fashion, as employees. It seems that it is through working as an employee that skills and experience are picked up and *guanxi* is established. This makes the workplace an important *guanxi* base. Many businesses began like Lee Rubber, using another company as a springboard to set up partnerships between non-kin. Thus, TKK's company had not only been a springboard for LKC; it was also a foundation from which numerous rubber firms started. Several informants mentioned that their fathers, and in some cases, uncles, had first worked for TKK before they set up their own firms:

> My father and two uncles worked for Tan Kah Kee. They learnt everything about the rubber trade whilst working for him. Then later, of course, they decided they should set up their own rubber business.

These firms, in turn, acted as springboards for others:

> My father was a junior clerk in Lee Kong Chian's firm before he branched out on his own. In fact, my uncle is still working for Lee Rubber.

Tam (1990) has described this pattern of business development as "fissioning." The roots of fission may be located in the family-orientedness of a business. Since the top positions are reserved for family members, the career path for non-kin employees will always be blocked. One owner-manager, reflecting the views of other traders, remarked:

> If you are a non-family member, the highest you can go is the second man, never the top.

Therefore, capable and ambitious employees find it more attractive to set up their own business. However, one informant pointed out a problem arising from fissioning:

> People who work in a Chinese company, the purpose is to learn. Once they have learnt, they can leave and set up their own companies, become *thau-ke* himself. So, there is a problem. The employee becomes a competitor.

This informant suggested that one way to deal with new competition arising from the newly fissioned company is for the trader to enter into some kind of business co-operation with his ex-employee. Tam (1990) made similar observations in Hong Kong where established firms tend to promote the formation of newer firms, which depend on them to build up own networks, and surround themselves with a ring of

226

dependable units. Silin (1976: 78) in contrast noted that some bosses clearly interpret departure as personal betrayal and react strongly. But if the new company can
be integrated into the orbit of the older firm, many bosses will attempt to either
make direct investments or establish business relations of some kind. The extent to
which pain is inflicted on the firm by the "breakaways" is partially dependent on its
ability to integrate them into its orbit. One reason why Lee Rubber was able to
remain strong despite the numerous fissions was due to its success in encouraging
the dependence of the new firms. One retired trader said:

> After setting up on my own, I still continued to do work for Lee Kong
> Chian. My company acted as a commission agent for his factories in
> Indonesia.

Data from the ROCB also revealed that Lee Kong Chian had invested in
the above fissioned firm. The investment gradually grew and the company was
"fusioned" back into Lee Rubber.

The above centrifugal tendencies form but part of the total picture. The fieldwork revealed that new partnerships also tend to fission. They take either one of
two developmental paths: (a) one shareholder (and his family) makes a bid to buy
out the other shareholders (who in turn set up their own individual company),
such that the original firm becomes (single) family-owned (as in Lee Rubber): or
(b) the old company is liquidated and the individual partners each set up their
respective firm. A variant of (b) is where the original firm is not liquidated, and
investors remain as partners in it but each proceeds to set up their own enterprise.
This centrifugal tendency in Chinese firms is in line with the family-orientation
of non-kin partners.

The principle of family-orientation confronts rubber traders with one major
problem. In the words of one informant: "No children to carry on the business!"
Many rubber businesses had folded up because of succession problems. Owners
preferred to close their business rather than sell it. One informant, who worked
together with his father, said:

> Many Chinese businessmen, like my father, are self-made, came up from
> nothing. When the children are not interested, as it is a family business,
> they will not bring in other people to run the business. They might try to
> sell the company, but [I doubt] ... They will not take in other people to
> run the business for him. They would rather close the business.

One young dealer, working with his father, commented on the general attitude
of the "younger generation":

> If the rubber business is viable, people from my generation will come in
> and continue. But many are already professionals in other fields. For
> example, doctors, engineers, teachers, journalists ... they are not likely
> to be interested.

An elderly manager lamented:

> The younger generations have their own thinking. With further educa-
> tion, there is even less chance of them coming back into the family's
> business. This is the problem with the Chinese companies now. The
> children, after studying abroad, their way of thinking is different.

Some struggle with the problem of succession by trying to groom younger
brothers or nephews (brothers' sons) to take over. But there is little evidence of
moving beyond this "near kinsmen from family *guanxi* base" (Landa 1983).
Marrying daughters off to capable employees is another alternative, although it
is not widely practiced nowadays. A third option is to groom capable employees
who have proven their loyalty to act as regent. But if, and when, sons are ready
to take over the reins of the company, they are expected to step down. In the
course of the fieldwork, three such cases were encountered. However, the loyalty
and *xinyong* of such a person is frequently held in suspect. For example, in one
case, the son of an old friend of the dominant shareholders was appointed as
Managing Director. He was given a free hand in the running of the business and
his co-directors (owners) were only involved in major strategic decisions involving large capital outlays. Even so, one significant shareholder was present to
"assist" him, together with the son of another shareholder, who was present "to
help out," but this informant said, "he's actually here to watch over his father's
interests."

This shows that even though a close *guanxi* may be trusted sufficiently to be
given an important position of responsibility, there is still quite a high degree of
distrust and insecurity as far as one's own (or family's) interests are concerned.
The degree of trust in a non-kin over his fiduciary responsibility towards the
owners is always considerably lower than in a family member. Our informants
mentioned the many "dangers of trusting outsiders." Since Chinese businessmen
place family first, they believe that their employees will also give priority to the
interests of their own respective families. There is, thus, a perpetual fear of fission. One specific fear is that of employees "stealing" the contacts for their own
business. This fear prompted one informant to remark:

> To survive, a Chinese company must handle many items. If staff
> takes away business, it is only part of your business – I mean, he
> may handle pepper, or coffee, rubber, but not all items. So, this is a safer
> hedge ... so you see many rubber companies also doing other businesses.

Informants told of another way, which they thought would best circumvent the
problem of fission. A long-serving employee of a firm said:

> Therefore, I say, if [you] treat people well, give them incentives, [stan-
> dard] of living is sufficient, people won't jump ... [give them] good
> bonus. That is how to keep the staff working.

The solution offered once more reflects the assumption that employees will always put self-interest first, and act to pursue individual gain. They are perceived as less likely to fulfill their fiduciary responsibilities without attractive extrinsic rewards. Thus, to harness their cooperation and loyalty, monetary incentives must be provided to satisfy them. Therefore, one must not be over reliant on this form of loyalty.

The problem of trust in rubber trading makes the succession problem all the more crucial because grooming a successor in rubber trading involves the nurture as well as transfer of *guanxi* and *xinyong*. One dealer explained how a smooth transition of leadership takes place:

> For a smooth transition, let the next man take over while you are still behind the scene. When people deal with the new man, they will slowly get to know him and know whether they can trust him or not. So when the other person goes, they will continue to deal with the new man ... This was how my father facilitated the transition.

The "new man" is inevitably not just an employee on the payroll because of the fear of fission. Owners are always afraid that in nurturing an employee, transferring *guanxi* and *xinyong* to him would enable him to use such resources to venture out on his own. As one informant elaborated:

> Nowadays, it is difficult to get people [to take over]. Children may go to the university and don't want to do the business. The Chinese is also scared that the new guy will "kill" him if he learns too much in the business, especially if the business depends on a lot of contacts (*guanxi*), credibility (*xinyong*), like in trading. If he learns too much, he will branch out. When he branches out he will take away contacts. If the business is very big, and is capital intensive, then not so scared because it will be difficult for him to branch out. But most Chinese companies cannot afford this because of [their] low capital base.

The importance of *guanxi* in the establishment and transaction of Chinese businesses, coupled with the question of the reliability (or the lack of it) of various *guanxi* bases, steer the majority of entrepreneurs to shut down their businesses when children or near relatives are not available to carry on. The option of having an employee carry on the business is not always desirable because of the fear of "betrayal." This makes the entrepreneur reluctant to share secrets, to nurture *guanxi* and *xinyong* of non-family members. Centralization in decision-making and intensity of supervision is thus frequently increased to prevent such "betrayal." This in turn increases the likelihood of fissioning of the firms.

Conclusion

The analysis of the Lee Rubber Group of Companies has exemplified that the management of Chinese family firms is highly personalistic. This is partially facilitated by employing persons whom the boss can personally trust. Personal control of the business is also executed through family ownership. Although other *guanxi* bases other than the family are important in the initial stages of establishing an enterprise, entrepreneurs work towards establishing eventual family ownership. A feature of this pattern of development is that business partnerships between friends tend to fission into smaller, family-owned firms. And as these newly fissioned firms will provide competition to the original company, such a threat often results in the preferred reliance on kinship *guanxi* (despite its cumbersome obligations).

Together, the desire to control and the nature of trust result in a centrifugal tendency for Chinese firms. While this may be harmful to the individual firm, the business community gains "a new lease of life because of fission and refusion." Hence, despite the fears expressed by our informants that the trade will eventually die out, or at least, be phased out due to problems of succession, the constant disintegration of firms into smaller units sponsors renewal.

Bibliography

Blau, P. M., Falbe, C. M., McKinley, W. and Tracy, P. K. (1976) Technology and Organisation in Manufacturing, *Administrative Science Quarterly*, 21, 20–40.

Bond, M. H. and Hwang, K. K. (1986) The Social Psychology of Chinese People. In M. H. Bond (ed.), *The Psychology of Chinese People*, Hong Kong: Oxford University Press, pp. 213–66.

Chandler, A. D., Jr. (1984) The Emergence of Managerial Capitalism, *Business History Review*, 58, 473–502.

Child, J. (1981) Culture, Contingency and Capitalism in Cross-National Study of Organisations, *Research in Organisational Behaviour*, 3, 303–56.

Clegg, S. R. (1990) *Modern Organisations: Organisation Studies in the Postmodern World*, London: Sage Publications.

Clegg, S. R. and Redding, S. G. (eds) assisted by Monica Cartner (1990) *Capitalism in Contrasting Cultures*, Berlin, New York: de Gruyter.

Donaldson, L. (1987) Strategy, Structural Adjustment to Regain Fit and Performance: In Defence of Contingency Theory, *Journal of Management Studies*, 24(2), 1–24.

Gambetta, D. (ed.) (1988) *Trust: Making and Breaking Cooperative Relations*, New York: Basil Blackwell.

Granovetter, M. (1985) Economic Action and Social Structure: The Problem of Embeddedness, *American Journal of Sociology*, 91(3), 481–510.

Hamilton, G. G. and Woolsey Biggart, N. (1986) *Market, Culture and Authority: A Comparative Analysis of Management and Organization in the Far East*, Program in East Asian Culture and Development Working Paper Series, No. 1, University of California, Davis: Institute of Government Affairs.

Hofstede, G. (1980) *Culture's Consequences: International Difference in Work-related Values*, London and Beverly Hills: Sage.

Horvath, D., Azumi, K., Hickson, D. J. and McMillan, C. H. (1981) Bureaucratic Structures in Cross-National Perspective: A Study of British, Japanese and Swedish Firms. In G. Dlugos and K. Weiermair (eds), *Management under Differing Value Systems: Political, Social and Economical Perspectives in a Changing World*, New York: Walter de Gruyter, pp. 537–63.

Hwang, Kwang-kuo (1983) Business Organisational Patterns and Employee's Working Morale in Taiwan, *Bulletin of the Institute of Ethnology*, Academica Sinica, 56, 85–133.

Landa, J. T. (1983) The Political Economy of the Ethnically Homogeneous Chinese Middleman Group in Southeast Asia: Ethnicity and Entrepreneurship in a Plural Society. In L. Y. C. Lim and P. Gosling (eds), *The Chinese in Southeast Asia*, Vol. 1, Singapore: Maruzen Asia, pp. 86–116.

Maitland, I., Bryson, J. and Van de Ven, A. (1985) Sociologists, Economists and Opportunism, *Academy of Management Review*, 10, 59–65.

Marsh, R. M. and Hiroshi Mannari (1981) Divergence and Convergence in Industrial Organisations: The Japanese Case. In G. Dlugos and K. Weiermair (eds), *Management Under Differing Value Systems: Political, Social and Economical Perspectives in a Changing World*, New York: Walter de Gruyter, pp. 447–60.

Ouchi, W. (1984) *The M-form Society*, Reading, MA: Addison-Wesley.

Pugh, D. S. and Hickson, D. J. (1976) *Organisational Structure in its Context: the Aston Programme I*, London: Saxon House.

Redding, S. G. (1980) Cognition as an Aspect of Culture and its Relation to Management Processes: An Exploratory View of the Chinese Case, *Journal of Management Studies*, 17, 127–48.

Redding, S. G. and Wong, G. (1986) The Psychology of Chinese Organisational Behaviour. In M. H. Bond (ed.), *The Psychology of Chinese People*, Hong Kong: Oxford University Press, pp. 267–95.

Silin, R. H. (1976) *Leadership and Values: The Organisation of Large-Scale Taiwanese Enterprises*, Cambridge, MA: Harvard University Press.

Sorge, A. (1977) The Cultural Context of Organisation Structure: Administrative Rationality, Constraints and Choice. In M. Warner (ed.), *Organisational Choice and Constraint: Approaches to the Sociology of Enterprise Behaviour*, United Kingdom: Saxon House, pp. 57–78.

Tam, S. (1990) Centrifugal Versus Centripetal Growth Processes: Contrasting the Ideal Types for Conceptualizing the Development Patterns of Chinese and Japanese Firms. In S. R. Clegg and S. G. Redding (eds), assisted by Monica Cartner, *Capitalism in Contrasting Cultures*, Berlin, New York: de Gruyter, pp. 153–83.

Tan, S. Y. (1976) *Management Practices in Industrial Organizations: A Cultural Profile*. Unpublished Academic Exercise, Department of Sociology, National University of Singapore. Singapore.

Tong, C. K. (1989) Centripetal Authority, Differentiated Networks: The Social Organization of Chinese Firms in Singapore. In G. Hamilton (ed.), *Business Networks and Economic Development in East and Southeast Asia*, Hong Kong: Centre for Asian Studies.

Williamson, O. E. (1985) *The Economic Institutions of Capitalism*, New York: The Free Press.

Wong, S.-L. (1985) The Chinese Family Firm: A Model, *British Journal of Sociology*, 36, 58–72.

——(1988) *Emigrant Entrepreneurs: Shanghai Industrialists in Hong Kong*, Hong Kong: Oxford University Press.

10

*GUANXI**

Sentiment, performance and the trading of words[1]

Yao Souchou

Introduction

In an age when 'Chinese triumphalism' has become a part of the post-Cold War discourse of global capitalism, it is increasingly tempting to write about the Chinese and their cultural behaviour with a quick rhetorical ease (Dirlik 1997). 'No one who has had first hand experience with Chinese society could fail to note that Chinese people are extremely sensitive to *mien-tsu* (face) and *jen-ch'ing* (human obligation) in their interpersonal relationships', opines Amrose Yeo-chi King (1991: 63). And he continues with the same flourish:

> Likewise, no one who has lived in Mainland China, Taiwan, Hong Kong, or any other overseas Chinese society could be totally unaware of a social phenomenon called *kuan-shi* (personal relationship). It is no exaggeration to say that *kuan-shi, jen-ching*, and *mien-tsu* are key socio-cultural concepts to the understanding of Chinese social structure. Indeed, these are sociocultural concepts are part of the essential 'stock knowledge' ... of Chinese adults in their management of everyday life.

A common sense quality prevails in these assertions. That *kuan-shi (guanxi), jen-ching (renqing)*, and *mien-tsu (mianxi)* are the operating concepts for the Chinese in their daily dealings is only too apparent to anyone who knows anything about China and its people. The reverse of this is also true: if you do not recognize these 'quin-tessential Chinese traits' then you obviously have no 'first hand experience with Chinese society'. The doubling of appeal to 'those in the know' embraces readers and the author in a cosy agreement of what constitutes the 'Chinese social structure' and its operating 'stock knowledge'. But what exactly is the notion of *kuan-shi (guanxi)* – and its associated ideas – in Chinese society? And how do they operate socially, and why do they seem so remarkably effective in shaping Chinese behaviour in daily life? King's approach to these questions is perhaps typical of that which has come to dominate the literature: by returning to 'Confucian social theory'.

233

There is no sense of contested readings here; Confucianism is seen unambiguously in conservative terms 'concerned with the question of how to establish a harmonious secular order in the man-centre world' (King 1991: 65). In the culturalist explanation of King and others, Confucianism is the foundational text. Since Confucianism has said that 'man is a relational being', the contemporary Chinese approach to social relatedness, taking a leap of a thousand years or so, across Western imperialism, two major revolutions, tens of bloody rebellions, nationalism and globalization, must be *ipso facto*, in some tortuous way, still explainable by such philosophic pronouncement. I have elsewhere posed a critique of the ahistoricism and essentialism of such an approach (Yao 1997, 1998). My point in these discussions, however, is not to show categorically that the Chinese indeed do or do not operate with notions of social relatedness like *guanxi* and *renqing*. This is a question that can only be settled empirically in contexts. The problem with the culturalist explanation is precisely because it does its job too well; it too quickly establishes a singular truth about 'Chinese culture' and its determining effects by appealing some primordial notion of culture and its values. On the contrary, where such a notion is talked about, as they help to negotiate the meanings and practicalities of daily life, it is not Confucianism as such but more crucial issues of power and performance that command our analytical attention. The social relevance of *guanxi* is less a matter of 'Confucian heritage' than the fact that deployment of such a term makes a certain sense, in 'inciting' a certain social/ethical response, and thus helping to shape – but never determine – desired transactional outcome.

This chapter is a general analysis of the Chinese cultural model of *guanxi*. The abstract argument is grounded in three major assertions. First, we have to move beyond the feitishized notion of culture if we are to explain why *guanxi* works in a specific situation. Second, culturally inscribed *guanxi* transaction is subject to the risk of failure, so that the 'art of *guanxi*' (Yang 1989) is concerned as much with making new and useful connections as with managing the danger of collapse of existing ones. Finally, since *guanxi* transactions do not always deliver the goods, Chinese actors are often ambivalent towards this mode of exchange as they attempt to strike a delicate balance between individual interest and social consideration.

These three assertions ally themselves to a major point. This is that *guanxi* can be – for analytically and empirical reasons – regarded as a cultural model with which Chinese actors strategically and selectively operate in order to manage certain social meaning and economic benefit. Avoiding the pitfall of essentialism, the cultural model of *guanxi* has to be seen as always already 'ill' or 'diseased'. The model is cultural in the sense that the Chinese often have genuine satisfaction in doing things the '*guanxi* way'; however, this pleasure is not always realized, neither is the pragmatic rewards invariably assured. To borrow the insight of English philosopher J. L. Austin (1962), the idea of *guanxi* may get sick,[2] so to speak, circulates two points of emphasis. First, Chinese transactional relationship as an exchange of goods and meaning carries an imperfection that casts a shadow over its (imagined) cultural perfection and practical significance. Second, there cannot be a perfect fit between the cultural model and actual behaviour, between what the model says and what it actually delivers.

My analysis therefore enlists the idea that *guanxi* is a culturally inscribed set of ideas and practices among the Chinese. I do this, however, heuristically and in the provisional sense I have outlined. Rather than as a part of a historical 'stock of knowledge', the social relevance and moral force of *guanxi* has to be seen in the context of strategic needs and individual performance. In so far that the idea of *guanxi* is culturally inscribed, such inscription is not about a perfect merging of altruism and individual gain in a consensual 'win–win' exchange, as is often described in the literature. Such an outcome, I suggest, is one in a repertoire of transactional possibilities. What is more primarily 'cultural' is an imagining say in the Chinese business world, of the value and feasibility of recruiting simulta-neously social pleasure and mutual benefits in a *guanxi* exchange. Against this imagining, however, Chinese actors are often caught by the practical difficulties in the realization of the twin goals. Consequently, complex manoeuvres and social performance, and not just the harvesting of rewards, become a critical aspect of the 'art of *guanxi*'. My point of departure, therefore, draws attention to the structural incongruity in the Chinese transactional game. In the context of such incongruity, the transaction is neither primarily about ethical binding senti-ment, nor only concerned with bloodless pragmatic calculations; but is tracked by a constant movement between the two. It is the negotiation and management of this mobility, I suggest, which goes to the heart of *guanxi*.

Guanxi and its surpluses

The singular theme that dominates the discussion of the Chinese practice of *guanxi* emphasizes the use of existing social relationship for economic and polit-ical ends.[3] *Guanxi* is thus a distinctive mode of relationship, something 'particular' in the universe of relationships in which a person operates (Jacob 1979). As a cultural discourse, *guanxi* is marked by a pre-assumption. The talk of *guanxi* invites a certain prompting 'before the fact', as Chinese actors are given to believe that the associated social and economic goals are both desirable and possible, and where difficulties arise, they can be remedied by the social skill or 'art of *guanxi*'. There is a critical slippage here, as we have seen in the assertions of King (1991). For clearly what is desirable is not always feasible; but the collapse of the desir-able with practical outcome is precisely the emphasis for those who (over-) subscribe to the cultural model. Inevitably, this emphasis is to involve significant erasure and silences with regard to the success and failure of *guanxi*.

Before turning to the actual operation of *guanxi*, it is useful to examine its 'cultural depth', which makes the rewards from this mode of exchange so natural and even common sense among the Chinese. When Chinese informants assert that *guanxi* is indeed 'the Chinese way' that unlike Western market culture gives considerable leeway to sentiment and social continuance, this should not be seen purely as an ideological illusion, as a way of concealing the self-interest of exchange partners. In what may be called the 'ideological school' of Chinese economic behaviour, Susan Greenhalgh (1994), for instance, highlights the specific use of Confucian values by family firms in Taiwan as a means of exploitation of those most vulnerable in the Chinese family system: women and younger sons. Similarly, Arif Dirlik (1997) sees the discourse of 'Confucian capitalism' as a part of the processes of global capitalism in which the Chinese diaspora in East and Southeast Asia play a crucial role. While the ideological deployment of 'Chinese culture' is undoubtedly true in these cases, ideological delusion and political power cannot tell the whole story about what is taking place. The question we still need to ask is: what makes notions like the family and *guanxi* such potent tools of mystification and discursive construction? As I have illustrated elsewhere, and following Bourdieu (1977), the social relevance of these reified notions has to be explained in the context of their 'cultural reproduction': the banal and day-to-day realities where the key ideas and practices associated with the family, for example, are brought to bear in practice (Yao 1998).

Building on this argument, it can be suggested that cultural reproduction is aided by a crucial process: a linguistic practice that normalizes the centrality of social relatedness in all transactions. Without returning to 'Confucian heritage', what I have in mind here is the elementary fact that in Chinese, the term *guanxi* refers to any form of 'relatedness'; it does not have a specific relevance in the commercial and political arena. *Guanxi* is in fact a generic term with which phrases (*cizu*) denoting more specific forms of 'relatedness' are built. Thus, we have *guoji guanxi* or international relations, *routi guanxi* or carnal relationship, *fuji guanxi* or marital relationship and so on. All these kinds of *guanxi* vary in terms of their respective emotional depth, social proximity and ethical bond. The 'social connectedness' in the commercial world represents just one type of *guanxi* among many; and we should strictly call it *shangye guanxi* or 'commercial *guanxi*', which is our major concern in this discussion.

From the view of discursive analysis, the denotative 'malfunction' of the term *guanxi* raises a number of interesting issues. On a practical level, it means that Chinese speakers are able to place a specific form of relatedness – *sayshangye guanxi* – at the same platform as the other quite different forms of *guanxi*. To speak of *fuji guanxi, guoji guanxi* and *shangye guanxi* in the same breath is to flood into each term meanings and connotative significance from other realms. The process is a classic example of what the French critic Jacques Derrida has called as the 'supplementary operation of meaning' (Derrida 1986: 161). Following Derrida then, we may say that any meaning of *guanxi* cannot confine itself to the discursive boundary of its specific realm, being marital, carnal, international, commercial or whatever. Since each mode of *guanxi* is defined by its specific sphere and yet surreptitiously draws meanings from other realms, significance in one offer, theoretically at least, a potential to inscribe the connotative range of other forms of *guanxi*. Thus, when an informant describes his relationship with his business partner as akin to *pengyou guanxi* (friendship) or even *jiating guanxi* (familial relationship), he imperceptibly registers his commercial dealings with ethical norms of these spheres of social relationship. I suggest that it is this slippage, aided by the Chinese language, which helps to explain what many researchers have observed: the apparent freedom with which Chinese actors move between the language of competitive gain – even violence – and that of ethical/social responsibility. The practice and cultural discourse of *guanxi*, as I shall illustrate, are highly mobile, as they underwrite the realization of the twin goals of exchange. And in the mobility, words and ideas – along with goods themselves – have to be traded between exchange partners in order to give their relationship specific cultural meaning and practical significance.

Thus, there is a sense that the Chinese culture does indeed legitimize *guanxi* as both an economic and a social-cultural project. What the discourse of 'Chinese family business', or 'Confucian capitalism' signifies is precisely its uncritical adoption of this powerful yet problematic cultural imagining. For if *guanxi* valorizes the feasibility and enjoyment of harnessing of extra-economic agendas onto a commercial enterprise, the practical result is highly ambiguous.

On the one hand, among Chinese actors, it becomes relatively simple to invest an existential aura into a business enterprise, particularly that which is owned and managed by family. In the remote township of Belaga, for example, 'doing business' or *zao sheng yi* reclaims its literal meaning, as making a livelihood becomes refashioning of life itself (Yao 1997). The parallel can be found in what I call the 'immigrant enterprise syndrome' among newly arrived immigrants, for whom opening a shop in Sydney, Los Angeles or New York is as much about making a living as envisioning a better future for themselves and their families in the new environment (cf. Waldinger 1990; Yao 2002).

At the same time, the grafting of social and existential meaning on commercial enterprise tends to excessively socialize the latter and its operating relationships. As in the classic pre-capitalist *Gemeinschaft* community, or in the context of what Hans-Dieter Evers has described as the 'moral dilemma of market traders', every exchange of material significance must take on a social and moral significance (Evers and Schrader 1994). In these situations, the (over-)personalization of the exchange process becomes a cultural ideal that people are often committed to realize in practice. In the *guanxi* environment, the wavering movements of words and deeds articulated in such notions as trust (*xing yong*), sentiment (*gang qing*) and networking (*lai wang*) give Chinese businesses much of its 'romance' especially to those in the business school circle. It is against this 'romance' – of Confucian capitalism – that the 'ideological school' has located its critique. Nonetheless, the point is worth remaking. The personalization of Chinese businesses is no mere cultural delusion or ideological tools, nor are Chinese merchants sentimental rationalists forever preoccupied with personal relationships, networks and whatnot. When a person is drawn into a *guanxi* transaction, he/she enters a relationship in which both pragmatism and sociality rule, contradictory as it may sound. The practical logic of *guanxi* is primarily about the harvesting of exchange rewards just as it is concerned with the management of such a contradiction.

Guanxi in motion: a cultural model

From our discussion so far, a heuristic cultural model of Chinese transactional behaviour can be formulated this way:

> *Guanxi* exchange is a highly mobile and contradictory mode of transaction in which (Chinese) actors attempt to recruit pleasure of sociality from an exchange of pragmatic significance, just as they, in reverse, insist on extracting competitive rewards from an ethical framework of social relationship.

Guanxi transaction, putting it simply, is one that recognizes both the ethics of sociality and individual gain as its primary objectives, however contradictory it may be.

The model is thus built upon three fundamental premises. First, that the discourse of *guanxi* admits both social continuance and individual gain as feasible and desired goals of exchange. What is characteristic of this form of transaction is not, as is often stated, the building of an economic relationship upon existing social connectedness. Instead, the dominating feature rests on the 'wish' by transacting partners to ride on the knife-edge between friendship and profit, altruism and rivalry, social harmony and competitive gain. The second premise concerns the idea that there is often an implicit understanding among Chinese actors of the fundamental difference – and even incompatibility – between these two transactional goals. In a *guanxi* relationship, such an understanding puts any transaction under considerable strain. At risk are not only the uncertainty of outcome, but also the rupture of a relationship as transacting partners constantly reevaluate its costs and gains. All this leads to my final point: making *guanxi* work requires socially appropriate performance. Such a performance takes the form of public and interpersonal ritual, which attempts to manage the structural difficulties and social meaning of the exchange.

These three points orchestrate much of the discussion below, which requires some immediate clarifications.

One issue that comes to mind is that *guanxi* transaction represents only one of the exchange behaviours in the Chinese society. This takes us away from the determinism typical of the 'culturalist explanation'. In other words, we no longer have to operate with the fallacious assumption that since *guanxi* is culturally inscribed as the 'Chinese way', Chinese actors must be *ipso facto* compelled to privilege this over other forms of exchange. This is a plain but significant point. For example, Chinese actors may find themselves in a situation where valorization of social relatedness and long-term networking (*lai wang*) is socially irrelevant and strategically counter-productive – however culturally and personally attractive these may be. Subject to variable meanings in contexts, *guanxi* exchange often has to incorporate an 'escape route' for a partner to move out when it is no longer the best transactional choice. In any case, what all this suggests is that *guanxi* relationships become highly mobile. They are subject to revision as a Chinese attempts to consolidate those connections that are socially and materially rewarding, while abandoning others that fail to deliver. In practice, it is this revision of a portfolio of meaningful – and useful – relationships, rather than simply building 'particularistic ties' (Jacob 1979), which typifies *guanxi* transactions.

The cultural model I have formulated has the virtue of being closer to what empirically takes place in diverse situations. It acknowledges the cultural aspiration of Chinese actors in seeking a perfect blending of sociality and individual reward, while it highlights the structural incongruity of these goals and the practical difficulties in their realization. This kind of theoretical realism, I suggest, is crucial in handling a subject so frequently mystifying. To do business with friends and relatives, as Chinese informants are quick to point out, is a double pleasure or a twin advantage over dealing with strangers. If 'making money with friends' represents the final ideal of *guanxi*, what the model hopes to 'dramatize' is precisely the costs and rewards involved, and the tortuous routes in which an exchange partner has to travel. What I shall describe as the 'mobility' of *guanxi* refers to the oscillating movement in the trading of words and signs as each partner attempts to harvest one transactional goal without losing sight of the other. In this sense, the exchange relationship as culturally inscribed always embraces a dialectic. Any singular movement towards pure altruism, or in reverse, competitive violence, would make the relationship more than what the cultural ideal of *guanxi* signifies. It is only the unique exchange game where making friends and making money are simultaneously feasible that constitutes proper *guanxi*.

Profit and social pleasure: the twin goals of *guanxi*

Leaving more detailed ethnography elsewhere,[4] it may be useful to ground the abstract discussion so far with a relatively simple case from my fieldwork:

> It is Qing Ming, the Chinese festival of ancestral remembrance, and we – Lao Chong, his wife and the anthropologist – are travelling on the ferry to Mrs Chong's family home in Kapit, to give ritual offerings to her ancestors, and to discuss a 'small matter of business' with the father-in-law. Lao Chong's father-in-law Wong Kam Fook has made his fortune from the marine engine business in Kapit – first in distributing, and latter on, in repairs and wholesales of motor grease and petrol. When Lao Chong founded Shun Fatt Provision Shop in Karjan in 1976, it seemed at first to present a means of expanding Wong's business further up the Rejang where petroleum products are almost twice the price in Kapit due to transport cost and higher marginal profit. If Lao Chong

were to take on the agency right, the cooperation would have become a classic one of *guanxi*, unifying economic interests and kinship.

However, pleading lack of experience in the petroleum trade, Lao Chong turned down the offer. As he explains, 'The deal would be too complicated (for our relationship). I don't know anything about engines, and it is not good to be over ambitious by getting into debt. Shun Fatt is a small business, at least it is my own and I sleep well at night (for the lack of worries)'. Nonetheless, the two men do build an economic relationship in other way. Half compelled by his wife who counsels that it is pure foolhardy not to 'accept offers from one of the family', Lao Chong sometimes turns to her father for what he needs most for his small business – occasional small loans to tie over cash flow problems. These loans are of the amount of $3,000–10,000, over a period of a week to a month, with an interest of 10–13 percent a month – rates normally charged for non-bank loans by Chinese shops. Since it is Qing Ming, and there will be annual dinner of the Hakka Association to attend, it seems the perfect occasion to travel downriver for a social visit and to sort out the loan with the father-in-law.

The ferry arrives at about three o'clock in the afternoon. We unload the presents and offerings to Mrs Chong house. The old man is genuinely happy to see us. In the late evening, about nine-thirty, and after taking a half-bottle of Remy Martin from the office desk, he declares that we are going out for *xiao ye* (late night supper). (The anthropologist is invited because he is to be treated with a delicacy he cannot have in Australia – fresh mud-crabs air-flown from Pakistan.) We arrive at Wong's favourite Loong Kee Restaurant overlooking the river. Over glasses of cognac and tea, we pick over boiled shrimps, chilli crabs and broccoli with oyster sauce, and listen to the old man's loquacious monologue about the way of Chinese business, and the financial successes and investment follies of friends and competitors. Half-dazed by the enjoyment of food and conversation, not to mention cognac served in beer glasses, the two men move in and out of these exchanges in which the issue of money – a loan of $8,000 – is subtly inserted.

Two days later, we are on the way home. Burdened with gifts and food – offerings to the ancestors – we board the ferry. Lao Chong pats his bulging trousers pocket where the fruits of his *guanxi* is securely put, and says to me, half-jokingly, 'I have to be careful [with this money]; it would fly back to Kapit [to its owner] if I am not careful'. I congratulate him, and tease him about worrying too much that he may not get the loan. He sighs, and says, 'It is the fate of running a small business. The banks won't give you an overdraft, or if they do, we can't afford the interest. So we turn to our relatives; but then you know that is not easy either. You become dependent on other people; when they lend you money it is like they are doing charity (*haoshi*)'.

I have described the encounter at length in order to give a sense of its background and the ambivalent responses of those involved. It might be said that the socially absorbing conversation and enjoyable dinner are but a 'pretext' that softens the ground for the ensuing matter of money to take place. Explained thus, the sociality in the relationship is but a mere backdrop, a functional platform from which to launch what is really the issue – the successful cementing of a financial deal. Against this kind of crude economic reductionism, it is sufficient to quote just one major critique, that of economist Amartya Sen. In his by now classic article *Rational Fools: A critique of the behavioural foundations of economic theory* (1996), Sen undercuts the instrumentalist, individualist assumptions of economic theory. People are not only driven by self-interest, Sen argues; they are able to make choices against their immediate benefits out of sympathy with others, or commitment with an ideological cause. Putting it in transactional terms, such altruistic sentiments are from a social point of view, highly rational. When people find themselves in a situation in which moral and social considerations appear in conflict with immediate personal gain, we cannot assume a priori that the former would be sacrificed to make way for the latter. Indeed, altruism has to be seen as having its own social-cultural logic and thus desirable 'in itself'. And in our case, the pleasure and meaning of social intercourse in a '*guanxi* game' cannot be seen merely in terms of their possible role in facilitating present and future exchanges, much less in the actual extraction of profit.

By the same token, returning to our case study, what we have witnessed in the relationship of Lao Chong and his father-in-law is a dynamic mixture of genuine social enjoyment and individual interests. They attempt to 'realize' both these goals without compromising one or the other. Even given their disparity in the kinship order and financial resources, the loan unifies them, reminding them of the conventional wisdom that it would be foolish not to make use of their special *guanxi* for mutual benefit. And in that act, the exchange so exquisitely demonstrates the Chinese way of doing business, as they know it. 'You open your hand, but you can't help but folding the fingers back', Wong has explained, 'In the same way, when you do business, you think of your kinsmen first because they are your own people'. Past difficulties are pushed aside and forgotten. When Chinese merchants like Lao Chong and Wong talk about *guanxi*, there is always a sense of amnesia or selective remembering, with regard to their understanding of how the transaction operates, and its special significance in the context of the riverine trade in the Sarawak interior (Yao 2002).

Nonetheless, for Lao Chong at least, there is always a moment when the 'reality' of the transaction comes back to haunt him. Equally giving to fond monologue about 'the Chinese business ways', he is not without occasional insight to his predicament. 'A secured loan which may fly back to its original owner' is his own brand of sardonic humour, a bittersweet response to a relationship in which, when he looks back, he is not always sure that he is a winner like his father-in-law. Yet, without access to a bank overdraft, the loan from the older man even at 12 per cent a month may perhaps still be considered as favour. Is the loan illustrative of the ethics of mutual benefit in accordance of the discourse of *guanxi* or it is a specific form of exploitation taking place within the norm of kinship? In discussions with Lao Chong, his responses to these questions are ambiguous as they are evasive. This is perhaps the major problem with his *guanxi* relationship as he sees it: the difficulties in discovering in any absolute sense the economic win or loss in the exchange. Even if Lao Chong may have preferred to deal with the bank if he could, he nonetheless feels the need – if partly under pressure by his wife – to keep in good terms with the older man, a man whom he appears to genuinely like and whose business experiences and commercial connections, not to mention capital resources, he does not regard lightly. From his point of view, the *guanxi* relationship is endowed with a specific social meaning – and cultural logic – that cannot be reduced to mere economic utility.

To grant specificity to what Lao Chong says and believes in is, however, not to fetishize the 'native's point of view' that he represents; this has been the classic lesson of anthropological interpretation.[5] Rather, a methodological entry has to be found in order to illuminate the cultural investment and social significance that Chinese actors like Lao Chong and Wong give to their social and economic dealings. The opposite would be economic reductionism that, in imposing a significance outside their understanding and subjective positions, have the consequence of calling them 'liars'.

Guanxi in motion: the gift and commodity relationship

If we are to take seriously a Chinese actor's subjective position as an issue worthy of analytical attention, then social and ethical consideration, and even enjoyment itself, has to be placed at the centre of the Chinese cultural model of *guanxi*. This is indeed what I have attempted. For Lao Chong and Wong, the pleasant sociality comes as much from the gift exchange and culinary feasts, as from the knowledge that they are 'doing things properly', according to the culturally recognized way of 'Chinese business'. Yet, 'doing business' (*zao sheng yi*) cannot be purely about altruism or social enjoyment; just as it cannot be solely concerned with the bloodless calculation of profit in a context of competitive violence; but implicates both. A cultural model of *guanxi* has to embrace the dialectics of these objectives. For a transactional relationship that steers towards one, or the other, immediately takes itself away from what is socially recognized as such; and Chinese traders in Belaga have a rich array of terms that describe examples of such deviation. Consider the following discussion with Lao Chong:

ANTHROPOLOGIST: Isn't *guanxi* about feelings (*gang qing*) and social dealings (*lai wang*)?

LAO CHONG: Yes, but we must always look at the wider picture. A person who acts from feelings (*gang qing*) acts like a woman, always from emotions, and cannot be practical (*shiji*). He is blinded by small matters, and has forgotten the bigger matter befitting of manly ambitions.

ANTHROPOLOGIST: So men are more practical, less emotional...

LAO CHONG: All this [about the emotionality of women] is just the way we explain things. We Chinese say the world of commerce is like a battle-field (*shang chang ru zhang chang*); and in business you may find your brother on the other side of the battle. That is why sometimes, doing business with 'strangers' (non-kinsmen) is more straightforward. You make your profit, and if the other side gets hurt, that is the end of the story. But hurting your brother or a cousin, you have the 'Old Woman' (*lao ma zi*, i.e. the mother) to contend with [laughter].

ANTHROPOLOGIST: So what, in your view, makes 'good business'?

LAO CHONG: The best business is where everyone has a share [of the profit]; and you share with you business partner because you made a profit with him. You keep your connection, and you make your profit. Well, we cannot always achieve this, but if you have to say it, then that is what people mean by doing things the *guanxi* way.

In the discussion, Old Chong clearly admits that, under some circumstances, dealing with 'strangers' is preferable precisely because the absence of strong emotional ties and established relationships makes any possible conflict or failure easier to manage. The relatively impersonal, one-shot transaction thus offers a sharp contrast with the cultural ideal of *guanxi*, socially desired but not always achievable. Indeed, Lao Chong's references to women's excessive emotionality and men's cold pragmatism have a significance beyond the expression of gender prejudice. More generally, such references mark a distinction in the Chinese informants' mind, between two modes of exchange that they have to contend with in their day-to-day activities. And these modes of exchange have a clear echo in what has been long debated in sociology and anthropology: the differences between commodity and gift, and the types of relationship they constitute.

In Marx's critique of a capitalist political economy, commodity is seen as a product of alienated labour, a 'thing' detached from the social subjectivity of its producer. In the hands of neo-classical economists, Marx's conceptual emphasis has become hardened, transforming commodity into a pure product of capitalism dominated by its specific culture of market profitability (Appadurai 1986: 9). Whether or not Marx is responsible for this conceptual tendency, what is clear is that critics of this approach invariably turn to sociologizing commodity, by highlighting its social uses and meanings, its power to make and redraw social life and institutions, particularly in traditional – non-capitalist – societies. The classic text that aids this argument is *The Gift* (1969) by Marcel Mauss. Its major thesis is that 'things', especially those in circulation between social groups, are located in a social totality from which they cannot be extracted to become pure commodities. Since sociality is always imbedded, 'things' in social circulation give people the power to act, to communicate ideas and feelings: they are in fact gifts. Gifts, unlike commodities, are socially and culturally inscribed 'things'; they recruit their values not from market exchange, but by being attached to a giver, and thus his/her relationship with others. Mauss bases his study on examples of archaic (non-capitalist) societies where meanings of gifts and gift exchanges were highly ritualized; questions about what and how to give, who could receives and the rules of reciprocity were formalized and regulated. The blurring of boundary between persons and things, that 'the thing has a soul', and 'things create bonds between souls', are the major legacy of Mauss (Godelier 1999).

The sociological conception of the differences of gift and commodity has a special relevance in our discussion. Not only are gift exchanges a part of the comings and goings (*laiwang*) in the business world, the social qualities of *guanxi* are remarkably analogous to those of the gift relationship in Mauss' formulation. With his implicit socialist critique of capitalist modernity, Mauss has raised the question as to why in traditional societies, the principle of sociality prevails charted by an economy and a moral code dominated by gift exchange. There is an almost Confucian flavour in his answer. Such societies emerge, Mauss concludes, when a major condition prevails: when 'personal relations must play an important or even dominant role in producing the social relations which constitute the framework of a society' (Godelier 1999: 14). To give in to an even more substantive Confucian reading, one may say that a gift relationship is a perfect metaphor of a society dominated by social ethics and responsibility; it is a Confucian relationship par excellence. Under Confucian cosmology, all things exchanged are gifts rather than commodities. When transactions take place among social actors already bound in a web of personalistic ties and social ethics, commodity and commodity relationship are a cultural anachronism. All this can be pushed towards its final totalizing logic: social actors in a Confucian-based society are culturally immune from, and unable to operate in, market relationships constituted by commodity exchange.[6]

Gifts, commodity and bribe

The absurd extremity of such a position is inevitable when we begin to unpack the powerful ideological discourse of 'Chinese/Confucian capitalism'. Yet, ironically, Confucian capitalism constituted by *guanxi* or gift relationships operates precisely by carving a preserve of market relationships, which are then tamed and socialized by the moral force of Confucian ethics. We may begin to examine the problem of such a conception by recruiting the insight of anthropology, which long criticized the over-exaggerated differences between gift and commodity in both tribal and modern societies. Echoing Sen, Godelier (1999), for example, has argued that competitive violence is not the unique purview of a commodity relationship; just as altruism and social considerations are not the exclusive features of transaction where things exchanged are socially recognized as gifts. Godelier is undoubtedly correct. However, if we take him to mean that all exchanges are reductively social, including those with negative consequences, as those taking place among warring enemies, then there is a danger in erasing the contrasting and conflicting types of sociality in transactions. To return to some notion of differences of gift and commodity is, however, not to resurrect the fetishized distinction arguably traceable to the legacies of Marx and Mauss, but to give fidelity to what the Chinese informants believe and do on the ground. Even if one-go, the competitive market relationship involves 'social considerations' of a kind – for there is honour among thieves, as the saying goes – this contrasts dramatically with the situation in which dialectics of social continuance and economic utility dominates. In a *guanxi* exchange, the material promises of commodity relationship however we may define it, remain a major – though not the sole – transactional goal the realization of which requires intricate, culturally-specific, strategic management.

What all this leads up to is perhaps this: that a return to the gift-commodity binary may be a necessary 'methodological fetishism' (Appadurai 1986: 5). For Appadurai, the return is in part a 'corrective to the tendency to excessively sociologize transactions in things', as he writes powerfully:

> ... the anthropological problem is that (the) formal truth (that things have no meaning apart from those that human transactions ... endow them with) does not illuminate the concrete, historical circulation of things. For that we have to follow the things themselves, for their meanings are inscribed in their forms, their uses, their trajectories. It is only through the analysis of these trajectories that we can interpret the transactions and calculations that enliven things.

> (Appadurai 1986: 5)

What Appadurai offers is a crucial resolution of the contrasting differences of gift and commodity by looking at their respective 'social lives': how and under what circumstances an object becomes one or the other. Once we see it in a specific social context, a commodity is longer simply an impersonal product of market relationship, but subject to 'a shifting compromise between socially regulated paths and competitively inspired diversions' (Appadurai 1986: 17). To borrow Appadurai's brilliant insight, we can similarly speak of *guanxi* relationship – and the gift exchange that greases it – as charted by a crucial mobility. *Guanxi* transaction – with its social and material goals – too travels temporally and spatially on a socially defined route, just as it is always in danger of breaking out into other more utilitarian diversions. This rupture suggests several possibilities.

In the first place, a *guanxi* exchange, as it moves along a path of continuous evaluation by the partners, may shift to a 'pure' gift or commodity mode. The divergent results, we recall, precisely inform Lao Chong's discrimination of 'women's affair' and 'men's business'. Timing and assessments are all important. What this means is that a transaction that begins with a perfect matching of 'making friends' with 'making money' may turn out to be something else, a socially recognized 'commodity relationship' (in a men's world, as Lao Chong would say). The other way is also true. A relationship based on gift exchange can be taken along a trail where social and emotional considerations are all important and befitting of a 'women's business'.

However, there is another more crucial uncertainty, one which infects all *guanxi* transactions. If *guanxi* indeed operates on dialectics of social and economic significance, then the central strategic problem facing Chinese actors is how to prevent the exchange from falling into the abyss on one side or the other. Against this problem, the all important 'art of *guanxi*' has to be simultaneously creative and preventive. For a *guanxi* relationship falling on the wayside is no longer what it is: it becomes a gift relationship in which social ethics blunts the efficient extraction of material profit, or it may transform itself into a commodity relationship in which social rupture is not considered as a serious risk. Even in socialist China, where 'right connections' are important, *guanxi* is not simply a matter of that classic commodity exchange: bribe. For this point we can draw on the analysis of Mayfair Yang who has described the 'art of *guanxi*' in the People's Republic as aiming at 'building up symbolic capital because it is the key to conversion into usable gift capital' (1989: 47). What Yang's analysis addresses is the conditions in China where the failure of the state redistributive system has compelled the emergence of a gift economy, which people have to negotiate in daily life. However, when one gives something of value to an official in order to change jobs, to get an apartment, or to buy a railway ticket, the present is not a bribe as such. It is still a gift because it is never given blind, so to speak. As Yang emphatically writes,

> Instead of the impersonal relationship of bribery linked by mutual mate-rialistic utility, the gift economy integrates utility into non-state person-alistic relationships of friendship and kinship, such as classmate, neighbor, native-place, co-workers, and superior-subordinate relationships.
>
> (Yang 1989: 411)

The question that can be raised here is, if a relationship that 'integrates utility into personalistic ties' represents just one type in addition to those marked by gift or commodity, then a gift which smoothens the path of *guanxi* is surely a special kind of gift. The unique feature of such a gift lies in it's breaking the divide of gift and commodity as conventionally perceived in sociology: we may call it '*guanxi* gifts'. A *guanxi* gift is thus both a gift and commodity. Put in Appadurai's terms, '*guanxi* gifts' arrive at their 'tournament of value' by navigating along the slim line between the divergent paths of practicality and the ethics of sociality (Appadurai 1986: 21). We are back to our familiar territory.

Guanxi, culture, performance

To emphasize the difficult, dialectic duality of Chinese transactional goals is to highlight the 'illness' of the cultural model of *guanxi*. *Guanxi* fallen 'sick' reveals the basic incongruity of the twin – social and economic – goals of *guanxi* transaction. Following Appadurai, the restoration of the gift-commodity distinction allows us to see the types of relationship they, respectively, imply, and the need for actors to negotiate such differences. If practical utility remains at the centre of all *guanxi* relationships, despite the attempt to sociologize it, to tame it within the heart-warming ethics of *reng qing* ('human considerations'), *lai wang* ('social dealings'), or whatever; then the problem of its realization has to be seen within the total logic in which both utility and sociality have a place. Neither is easily erased in the desire of the Chinese actors caught with the seductive promises of *guanxi*. And the analytical lesson is surely this: since neither social pleasure nor calculative gain can be in itself the dominant ethos, *guanxi* in operation must be characterized by a subtle movement between the two. Each transactional aim must always deny itself, yet it insists on its presence. For the main cause of *guanxi* 'fallen sick' is precisely when either altruism or commodity relationship has come to settle as the dominant organizing principle and social meaning. The result in either way will be unsatisfactory. To prevent a *guanxi* from falling ill requires, therefore, considerable mobility in the management of the associated social rituals and cultural signs. In practical terms, what all this means is that each time a transaction seems to be moving to a direction suggestive of pure sociality, each partner must urgently bring to the fore the feasible goal of (mutual) profitability. The reverse is also true. When the exchange appears to lean towards calculative rewards, each actor must subtly signal that the relationship is more than that, encompassing certain ethics and sentiment. If both partners have a mutual interest in maintaining their relationship in a *guanxi* state, then they must be vigilant with regard to the rupture of 'common interests' as well as the direction in which the exchange may be developing.

More concisely, each partner must strive to prevent the transaction from being settled in a single mode; just as he/she would assure the other – if only by words – that the nature of their dealings is more that what is defined by the dominant ethos at the moment. This fluid situation can be illustrated with a simple diagram (Figure 10.1).

One is tempted to call this, for want of a better phrase, a ping-pong model of Chinese exchange. The sense of mobility, the nervous 'constantly-looks-over-the-shoulder' quality, are inevitable in a situation in which the twin transactional goals are always in danger of failing to stay within the singular dialectical path. The attempt to make the contrasting objectives compatible gives *guanxi* a distinct 'have-the-cake-and-eat-it-too' feature, culturally exact, materially rewarding and

	Settled modality		Modality signified
A.	Materialistic utility	---------->	Personalistic considerations
	Modality signified		Settled modality
B.	Materialistic utility	<----------	Personalistic considerations

Figure 10.1 A ping-pong model of Chinese exchange.

practically uncertain. If the surpluses of meaning in the very word already make such a feature possible, as I have suggested, then *guanxi* is always burdened with a restless incompletion. This tension is not so much the 'darker side' of *guanxi*, as something lying at the heart of all culturally inscribed Chinese transactional behaviours. The social comfort of 'doing business with friends', the ruling ethics of mutual benefits, turn out to be something that requires considerable strategic management, if not cynical manipulation and cultural performance.

Orchestrating *guanxi*

The idea of performance is critical in the examination of the concept and practice of *guanxi*. It has to be seen in this context as a remedial gesture, the need for which arises precisely because of *guanxi*'s inherent instability and potential failure to juggle its delicate balancing act. By the term, I refer to two senses: first, as a socially effective transformative act – it changes things; and second, as a staging of socially and culturally appropriate behaviour in an arena of interpersonal relationships or wider social sphere. Performance does not have to be a highly theatrical or dramatic interpersonal or public event; it certainly encompasses 'citational processes' in the speaking – and writing – of words and their embodied concepts (cf. Derrida 1982). In the poststructuralist usage I have adopted, performance does not so much imply the creating of an illusion, as emphasizing the strategic 'staging' of an act by words or by deeds, according to a socially recognized 'script' in the attempt to affect a change of a certain state of affair (cf. Parker and Sedgwick 1995).

From the view of anthropology, what facilitates such a process, what makes one performance more socially significant than the other, is a person's cultural capital. The term is taken from Bourdieu (1984); transposed to the Chinese context, it would refer to a person's social-political status in the community, or face (*mianzi*), as well as knowledge and skill in social rituals and ceremonies.[7] Appropriate performance in this context draws on such capital, which is further enhanced by the display of competence in 'doing things properly' as recognized socially. There is no comfort of determinism in this formulation. Just as a person will muster all the skill and resources in the staging of a performing act, the audience nonetheless can exercise a certain choice in giving in to the magic or resist the power of such a staging. Before I return to my ethnographic case, it is useful to illustrate the above with an example. Yunxiang Yan's *The Flow of Gifts* (1996) is an anthropological study of network building and gift exchange in a village in Socialist China. In an interesting discussion of cigarette sharing among villagers, Yan details the performative strategies that afford different kinds of sharing, as well as resistance against the obligations for reciprocity:

> I was told that one must take a quick decision when facing a group about whether to share one's cigarettes with the group. As the obligatory distribution of cigarettes may cost too much for low-income Chinese,

some people may choose not to smoke in public in order to save both money and face. If one is offered a cigarette by someone, one also needs to decide whether to accept the offer, because accepting a cigarette initiates an obligation to return the gift, thus entailing a cost. A decision not to accept requires good excuse. Often, if one's cigarettes are of inferior quality, that person may decide not to smoke in public. A cigarette brand symbolizes one's social and economic status, so smoking cheap cigarettes can be embarrassing.

(Yan 1996: 132)

In the smoked-filled scenario, villagers enact and move freely between a range of performative alternatives: from sharing, refusal of an offer, to the decision not to smoke in public. (One can think of an additional, more straightforward move: accepting an offer and then 'forgetting' to reciprocate.) Most of these tactics, one should think, represent subtle resistance if not subversion of the ethics of reciprocity supposedly driven by the idea of *ganqing* or *guanxi*. Faced with these behaviour choices among the villagers, Yan is quick to acknowledge the problematic nature of the rules of reciprocity that often 'appear to conflict with each other', and the 'realization [of which] varies depending on many dynamic factors' (Yan 1996: 127). These dynamic factors would have opened up the performative strategies, which valorize just as they work against 'culture'. However, Yan's approach bypasses such an investigation. And the return to some foundation of Chinese cultural behaviour is predictable as it is analytically precarious; as Yan writes:

Gift exchange, while existing in all societies, appears to be central to Chinese culture throughout its long history. ... In contrast to many other societies, the structure of social relations in China rests largely on fluid person-centered social network, rather on institutions. ... It is axiomatic, therefore, that by studying gift exchange one should begin to understand *the core features of Chinese culture*.

(Yan 1996: 16, emphasis added)

For what takes place among the village smokers is precisely that which occurs in all *guanxi* situations: the manoeuvre between different relationships underpinned by gift and commodity. Cigarettes can take the status of one or the other; the various modes of sharing (and non-sharing) in fact chart the 'different points in their social life', to borrow a phrase of Appadurai (1986: 13). If this is a viable analytical vision, clearly its richness can only be discovered if one resists the temptation of 'culturalism'. There is a similar lesson to be reaped from the *guanxi* – the engagement between Lao Chong and his father-in-law in our case study. What is their common anxiety except the fear of being 'trapped' by the singularity of 'culture'. For being too good as kinsmen would deny them the moral freedom of competition, just a moving in 'a men's world' of hard calculations would alienate those whose well-being and judgements still matter. When Wong hints at the younger man's lack of ambition in not eagerly taking up his offer of a motor grease dealership in Belaga, he cannot but express a sense of impatience. 'Chong is a good son-in-law; but I also want to help him to be a good business-man', Wong has said. In a proper *guanxi* relationship, being too good to one or the other is obviously not desirable. For Lao Chong, it is enough that they remain a 'good relative' in his own way. By keeping the loan small, he nonetheless signals that he too has an economic interest in mind, but it has to be one that does not strain the delicate balance between their relationship continuing and economic dealings.

In the restaurant by the Rejang River in Kapit, over Pakistani mud-crabs, cognac and tea, transactions are not only financial loans, but also words and signs beaconing these common and yet contrasting wishes. There are surely more banal questions to be raised: Would it matter if the business about money was con-ducted elsewhere, say in Wong's air-conditioned office, during the calm of the afternoon before dinner? More rational still, could not Lao Chong have rung the old man and asked his wife to pick up the cash without having to make the long trip away from his busy shop? If social etiquette means anything, it is surely the almost instinctive sense of knowing the 'cultural thing to do' in a specific situa-tion. There is no question that Lao Chong could approach the loan in a more 'rational' and less time-consuming way. Putt in a more analytical term, the deli-cious dinner is a culturally appropriate performance, which stages the promises of social enjoyment and economic reward, the fruits of *guanxi*. The culinary enjoyment is an appropriate context in which their respective wishes can be reg-istered, just as it is a perfect platform across which travel words of assurance that none is interested in only being 'good relatives' nor solely being 'good business-men'. Context and timing are the keys. Words must be spoken just when the inten-tions they signify seem to be on the verge of being forgotten, just as when the interaction seems to steer towards 'the other way'. Anxious as he is, Lao Chong waits. Drinks are poured, dishes come and go; and in the midst of all this, when Lao Chong opens his mouth, it is also to spit out words:

> The crabs is good, but perhaps a bit too much chilly. Is Ah Lee [the cook] still working in the kitchen? [Licking his fingers, he continues]. The cheque went through [the bank] all right? I am thinking of asking you for another $8,000 for the next month...

Conclusion: *guanxi* and its uncertain fate

I began the discussion, unfairly perhaps, with assertions of King (1991). But they are useful starting points because King's discursive return to the notion of 'real Chinese way' typifies the kind of cultural foundationalism one is to find, for example, in the works of Yan (1996) and even more dramatically, Redding (1990), whose formulation of 'Chinese capitalism' is as nostalgic as it is analytical and hollow. In a way, these have been easy targets of critique for anyone with an elementary awareness – if I may mimic King – of the complex historical and ideological trajectories that Chinese societies both in and outside China had gone through over the decades or centuries, whichever one may pick. But the overemphasis on harmony and consensus in a supposed Confucian social order is not the only issue facing any critique. On the opposite ideological spectrum, what I have called 'the ideological approach' operates with such a virulent scepticism with the notion of culture that it turns Chinese transactional actors into super-rational 'homo-materialis', hapless victims of political–cultural manipulation. People without culture, or at least, culture as nothing more than mystification or delusions, become the dominant analytical tenor (cf. Hodder 1996).

In spite of their different ideological positions, both approaches rely centrally on functionalism. It is what culture can do – in shaping *guanxi* behaviour, in the delivery of transaction rewards, and in making ideological delusions and thus the conditions of political repression – that counts. In these uncertain and yet invigorating times of post-marxism and post-coloniality, it is fitting that these conflictual approaches should be taken to task. This has been the aim of this chapter. With the wisdom of theoretical hindsight, one can longer simply go back to the (neo-marxist) political–economy explanation in order to interrogate the ideological fetish of 'culturalism' dominating the current discussion of Chinese economic behaviour. For those who choose to remember, there is a certain déjà vu in the celebration of Confucianism by such diverse people as Lee Kuan Yew, Gordon Redding and those engaging in the Confucian revival in East Asia. It always strikes one as remarkable that their undertaking can so easily ignore the massive revolt against Confucian discourse and its devastating effect on China in the past, as if the Late Qing Reform of Kang Youwei and Lian Qichao, and the May Fourth Movement of 1919 did not happen. Historical memory is indeed short; however, what makes the culturalist project possible, I suggest, is the fatal attraction of functionalism. For to ask once again, those perennial questions: what is Chinese culture, and how does this culture 'make the Chinese tick', is to lead one to question the all embracing culture in which anything about the Chinese – from business transaction, gift giving, to sharing of cigarettes – magically makes sense. This is where the insight of Appadurai is so critical. To rework his analysis of the way 'things' take on values, we can rephrase the conventional question about Chinese culture by asking: How have certain values and social behaviour come to take on – or have the tendency to do so – the aura of 'Chinese culture proper'?

In the light of this question, the discourse of *guanxi* should always be approached with the right amount of critical suspicion. Rather than as the core values at the heart of pensee chinoise, the complex and varied words and ideas of *guanxi* represent 'a certain kind of Chinese culture'. It is 'a kind of Chinese culture' that is constructed in context, and is strategically contingent, even though it has all the aura of timeless, historical generality. And my analysis has been devoted to examining how this has come about. I suggest that what gives *guanxi*-culture its specificity, its innovative quality, is the reworking of 'words' of substantial cultural capital, as well as the 'performance' of their meanings in a given social situation. The social performativity of cultural meaning becomes crucial when we begin to see that Chinese actors themselves often recognize the very problem of culture: the experienced truth that ones' observance of cultural rules does not always produce the right responses from others, just as practicing the wondrous idea about *guanxi* and *renqing* cannot guarantee a profitable exchange outcome. Performance in this context is extra-cultural, even though it is – in an innovative and even a subversive sense – choreographed by certain cultural ideas. Given the illness of culture, so to speak, the performative in *guanxi* exchange is an attempt to guide the transaction to its proper dialectical path where social continuance and economic utility have to be imagined as both desirable and practicable, whatever the difficulties in realization.

Notes

* A *related version* of this chapter appears in Souchou Yao (2002) *Confucian. Capitalism: Discourse, Practice and the Myth of Chinese Enterprise*, London: RoutledgeCurzon.

1 The study is based on several stretches of fieldwork in the town of Belaga, Sarawak, East Malaysia, between February 1992 and August 1998. The names of the informants have been changed to protect their anonymity. Thanks to Solvay Gerke and Thomas Menkhoff for inviting me to the Conference on Crisis Management, Chinese Entrepreneurs and Business Networks in Southeast Asia, at the University of Bonn, 28–30 May, 1999, where this chapter was presented. The revision of the chapter has greatly benefited by the insightful comments of Hans Dieter Evers, Terence Gomez, Tong Chee Kiong, Mayfair Yang and other participants of the conference.

All values are in Malaysian dollar or Ringgit. At the time of writing – June 1999 – the exchange rate of Ringgit to US dollar was M3.76 to US$1.

2 Austin is concerned with the likelihood that verbal utterance may not always achieve its performative social effect; with such failure, the utterance becomes 'in general unhappy' or 'ill' (1962: 14, 18).

3 The major tenent of this highly mystified approach can be gleamed from much of the literature in business management and social sciences. See, for example, Chen (1995), Pyle (1992), Hofstede and Bond (1988), Jacob (1979), and many others. Yang (1989, 1994) and Smart (1993) remain the few rare instances where *guanxi* is seen as located in a nexus of power relations and the problematic of politics and inequality.

4 Space does not permit me to produce the ethnography and geographical location of Belaga here, which can be found in Yao (1997).

5 In economic anthropology, this is articulated in the debate between the 'substantivist' and 'relativist' schools, essentially over the applicability of concepts of economics as developed in the West – profit maximization, efficiency, etc. – across cultures and societies.

6 It is precisely the 'Asian values' discourse as offered by the Singapore state that turns this logic by arguing the opposite: that Confucian relationship can form the basis of capitalist development as well as a Thatcherite social welfare policy. For a most succinct justification of the approach, see an article by Tommy Koh, Singapore

Ambassador-at-Large, *10 Asian Values That Help East Asia's Economic Progress, Prosperity* (*The Straits Times*, 12/14/1993, p. 29).

7 For a brilliant recasting of Bourdieu's framework in the Chinese transactional context, see Smart (1993).

Bibliography

Appadurai, A. (1986) *The Social Life of Things: Commodities in Cultural Perspectives*, Cambridge and New York: Cambridge University Press.

Austin, J. L. (1962) How to Do Things with Words. In J. O. Urmson (ed.) *The William James Lectures Delivered at Harvard University in 1955*, Oxford: Clarendon Press.

Bourdieu, P. (1977) *Outline of a Theory of Practice*, Cambridge: Cambridge University Press.

——(1984) *Distinction*, Cambridge, MA: Harvard University Press.

Chen, M. (1995) *Asian Management Systems: Chinese, Japanese, and Korean Styles of Business*, London and New York: Routledge.

Derrida, J. (1982) *Margins of Philosophy*, A. Bass (trans.), Chicago: Chicago University Press.

——(1986) *Glas*, J. P. Leavey Jr. and R. Rand (trans.), Lincoln: University of Nebraska Press.

Dirlik, A. (1997) Critical Reflections on 'Chinese Capitalism' as Paradigm, *Identities: Global Studies in Culture and Power*, 3(3), 303–30.

Evers, H. D. and Schrader, H. (1994) *The Moral Economy of Trade: Ethnicity and Developing Markets*, London: Routledge.

Godelier, M. (1999) *The Enigma of the Gift*, N. Scott (trans.), Cambridge, UK: Polity Press.

Greenhalgh, S. (1994) De-Orientalizing the Chinese Family Firm, *American Ethnologist*, 21(6), 746–75.

Hodder, R. (1996) *Merchant Princes of the East: Cultural Delusions, Economic Success and the Overseas Chinese in Southeast Asia*, Chichester: John Wiley.

Hofstede, G. and Bond, M. H. (1988) Confucian Connection: From Cultural Roots to Economic Growth, *Organizational Dynamics*, 16(4), 5–21.

Jacob, B. (1979) A Preliminary Model of Particularistic Ties in Chinese Political Alliance: Kan-ch'lng and Kuan-hsi in a Rural Taiwanese Township, *China Quarterly*, 78, 237–73.

King, A. Yeo-chi (1991) Kuan-hsi and Network Building: A Sociological Interpretation, *Daedalus*, Spring, 63–84.

Marx, K. (1972) *Economic and Philosophic Manuscripts of 1844*, Dirk Jan Struik (ed.), New York: International Publishers.

Mauss, M. (1969) *The Gift: Forms and Functions of Exchange in Archaic Societies*, I. Cunnison (trans.); with an Introduction by E. E. Evans-Pritchard, London: Cohen & West.

Parker, A. and Sedgwick, E. K. (1995) (eds) *Performativity and Performance*, New York and London: Routledge.

Pyle, L. (1992) *Chinese Commercial Negotiating Style*, New York: Quorum Books.

Redding, S. G. (1990) *The Spirit of Chinese Capitalism*, Berlin and New York: Walter de Gruyter.

Sen, A. K. (1996) Rational Fools: A Critique of Behavioral Foundation of Economy Theory. In A. E. Komter (ed.), *The Gift: An Interdisciplinary Perspective*, Amsterdam: Amsterdam University Press.

Smart, A. (1993) Gifts, Bribes, and *Guanxi*: A Reconsideration of Bourdieu's Social Capital, *Cultural Anthropology*, 8(3), 388–409.

Waldinger, R. (1990) Immigrant Enterprise in the United States. In S. Zukin and P. DiMaggio (eds), *Structures of Capital*, Cambridge: Cambridge University Press.

Yang, M. (1989) The Gift Economy and State Power in China, *Comparative Studies and History*, 31, 25–54.

——(1994) *Gifts, Favors, and Banquets: The Art of Social Relationships in China*, Ithaca, NY: Cornell University Press.

Yao, S. (1997) The Romance of Asian Capitalism: Geography, Desire and Chinese Business. In M. T. Berger and D. A. Borer (eds), *The Rise of Asia: Critical Visions of the Pacific Century*, London: Routledge.

——(1998) *The Cultural Limits of 'Confucian capitalism': Power and the Invention of the Family among the Chinese Traders in Sarawak*, Unpublished Manuscript, Department of Anthropology, The University of Sydney.

——(2002) *Confucian Capitalism: Discourse, Practice and the Myth of Chinese Enterprise*, London: Curzon/Routledge.

Yan, Y. (1996) *The Flow of Gifts: Reciprocity and Social Networks in a Chinese Village*, Stanford: Stanford University Press.

11

THE GLOBALIZATION OF SOUTHEAST ASIA AND ROOTED CAPITALISM

Sino-*Nusantara* symbiosis

Wazir Jahan Karim

Introduction

The expansion of indigenous capitalist enterprise has been the Asian mode of establishing business networks for centuries. Although most of these businesses have been founded in family-based institutions – nuclear, extended, lineages, clan, bilateral, consanguinal or cognatic, these enterprises have always traditionally leaned towards global trade markets, by virtue of the origins of the traders and businessmen from China, India, Yemen, Kuwait, Saudi and other regions of Asia and the *Nusantara*. Chinese businesses have been similar to Indian in the way products from these two countries have been traded for local commodities like spices, tin, gold, textiles, resin and other forest products.

In most of these enterprises, structures of familism are combined with globalization and a strong commitment to labor and personal capital. Some of the common features of these enterprises based in familism were as follows:

- Family systems were redesigned to work as business enterprises (the firm family) with the most capable and interested children required to take on positions of responsibility and management.
- Systems of leadership and management were gendered and male-centered but there remained an overall commitment to train, educate and assume responsibility over housing, health, welfare and security of other members of the family or kinsmen.
- Commitment to labor is significantly carried to the extreme in the absence of lay-offs or retrenchments but promoted the practice of underemployment. Any loss from earnings in the recruitment of kinsmen is compensated by low wages and shared household resources.

- Farm-based households often used communal labor systems, which did not involve direct cash payments but generalized labor reciprocity, which ensured efficiency and expediency.

For Chinese family businesses, the management style remains conservative and undemocratic with the elder son assuming the role of a benevolent yet uncompromising patron. Chan and Chiang (1994: 350) have this to say about Chinese management styles:

> Authority was centralized – also paternalistic and benevolent at the same time. He had to realistically balance several tasks: how to enforce leadership yet also listening to his employees, how to set himself up as role model yet not becoming overly autocratic; how to delegate his power but not abusing it; how to say "no" and when to say "yes" to his subordinates, without fearing his authority being undermined; how to adopt a modern organizational structure without foregoing the traditional modes of interpersonal communication. The mutuality of trust, reciprocity and decision-making set by boundaries of the family, close personal relationships or affinity group membership between employer and employees formed on the one hand a powerful ethnic resource that explained the preponderance and success of family business in an ambiguous and disordered environment: on the other hand, they also explained their stultification and stagnation due to over-centralized management styles and ineffective nepotism.
>
> At the entrepreneurial level, he had to modernize and to expand, sourcing out new opportunities, taking risks and overcoming business failures. He had to cope with his growing firm, new technologies, volatile consumer demands, increased product complexity as well as economic competition. He either diversified his economic niches or reaped economies of scale by growing bigger. The progression was not easy but it was compelling; work life and family life became blurred, private and public time was indistinct – work and leisure no longer located themselves within clear domains. "Work is passion, life is work" became a driving dictum. In the final analysis, every entrepreneur believed: "I am the business." As Sartre would put it, "What happens to me happens *through* me .... Moreover everything which happens to me is *mine*." He was the helmsman at the head of the organization; he was always the patriarch at the top of the work hierarchy. There were no two ways about it because he was either in control or he withdrew.

An important dimension of these family-based businesses is their resilience to global crises such as contagion effects of finance capitalism, since they are not inclined to behave in the same way as foreign global investors in the Asian or Southeast Asian region. Businesses founded in Southeast Asia by the migrant Chinese are not relocated so easily first just because the region has been destabilized through finance speculation, money trading or civil unrest. The tendency is to stay unless personal security becomes a threat as in Indonesia. In this chapter I explain the trend towards the consolidation of Sino business interests with Bumiputera and critically examine Sino-Bumiputera strategies of evaluating and monitoring market changes to ensure optimal gains in a worsening economic situation and techniques of recognizing winning streaks in a destabilized economic sociopolitical environment.

Confidence, contagion, crises

A "culture of confidence" in economics describes a prevailing sentiment of trust in the governance of finance and business, leading to a continued or upward swing of investment, in the form of foreign direct investment in industries, financing of capital in stocks and securities or direct savings through unit trusts or fixed deposits. The general scenario in Southeast and Northeast Asia between 1997 and 1999 has been a downsizing in confidence and a poor investors' climate, necessitating Asian governments to rebuild a climate of confidence to allow for economic growth and to prevent a recession: generally explained as two or more quarters of negative economic growth in a country. Economic factors have generally been linked to "confidence," through economic fundamentals relating to a strong banking system, good loan repayment capacity, low foreign debt, transparency and accountability. However, with the increasing globalization of the Malaysian and Asian economy, it has become apparent that economic fundamentals alone cannot explain "confidence."

A "culture of confidence" is generated by complex geo-political and sociopsychological factors that have yet to be studied – how they influence one another; which are the precipitating factors and which are consequential; how foreign capital flight influences decisions of domestic investors and so on. One of the objectives of the National Economic Action Council in Malaysia is to "restore public and investor's confidence" and to ensure a speedy economic recovery. The so-called "contagion effect" of massive capital flight in one country, leading to withdrawal from another within a geo-political region, has been described as "new" by the Malaysian government (Daim 1998). Yet, earlier European scholars of finance capital such as Hilferding (1970) writing from observations of capital build-up at the turn of the twentieth century in Europe and the United States had discussed that a fundamental principle of finance capitalism is the sociopsychological motive to accumulate profits for the sake of profits, promoting a mass psychology of nomadism, a preying phenomena (to go for the quick kill; first in, first out), which can develop into a herding instinct with capital flight (Brewer 1980). Capitalism itself operates from this nomadic, tribalistic function and so-called long-term gains in familiarity with a country or region has never been a major factor of consideration. In an exclusive interview with Anthony Giddens, George Soros stated that once globalization was indeed global, no country or region could be spared and only global intervention through international monetary bodies could stop region-wide bankruptcy (*LSE Magazine*, No. 1, 1998).

Others have viewed the complexities of confidence, through the political economy perspective mostly recently (Preston 1998), suggesting that the so-called internal weaknesses of a developing economy like Malaysia increasingly attributed to "second-order" fundamentals (Rajah Rahsiah 1998) such as chronic economic imbalances, worsening saving, investment gaps and soaring credit is a manifestation of developing economies caught in a double-bind of succumbing to pressure to liberalize and draw in foreign investment, while simultaneously not being prepared for a "worst case scenario" when devestment occurs. In this sense, developing economies can never really compete equally with powerful world-class economies since the rules of liberalization in itself create opportunities for the Euro–American to practice monopoly capitalism through finance capitalism, ultimately resulting in take-overs, mergers, downsizing, retrenchments, slave salaries and massive destitution (Mander 1996). This creates a vicious circle of declining confidence in developing economies causing others to practice over-caution. The phenomena of "declining confidence" then is applied retrospectively and the economy moves in a recession with a further decline in sentiment. "Confidence-building" may be successful only when the same sociopsychological sentiments are now reversed in favor of bargain-hunters and availability of greater dependency on foreign loans and external rules of finance, auditing and trade. Confidence can be restored through the language of global players and hunters.

What was earlier mistaken as foreign confidence in a developing economy is more closely linked to a Eurocentric or American perspective of "Asia" as a "land of opportunity" for "bargain-hunting," evoking its image as a region to be occupied for profit. According to Frank Gunnar (1998), this image of "Asia" and "Southeast Asia" has been crystallized in the European and American imagination through history, making it the most vulnerable region to observe in the twenty-first century as the global economy verifies the continued strength of Western civilization over contemporary Asia. Hence, if Asia is what and how the West would like it to be, "confidence" and "confidence-building" would be to firmly locate the geo-politics of dependency economies in the global economy; to renew strategies of foreign investment for long-term sustainability, without targeting fixed economic growth rates; to attempt to change the image of Southeast Asia as "easy game" or back-street casino, and to remove all targets of accusation now and in the future that East and Southeast Asia is practicing its own form of "rooted capitalism" (Karim 1998) through familism, cronyism and Bumiputeraism.

Sino-Malay systems of patronage

But should rooted capitalist enterprises based in familism be always linked to cronyism through patronage of politicians and other influential individuals in society? As explained by Suryadinata (1992), Chinese businesses in Southeast Asia in particular Indonesia, have always been based on political patronage and are always defensive of the sociopolitical status quo since its destabilization would be destructive to its expansionism. Malay businesses follow the same logic of patronage with one extra proviso which is that it attempts to challenge the status quo of the political basis of allocating economic resources when it is seen to be undemocratic or favoring a selected few. Chinese businessmen will strive to be one of the selected few and those who cannot get near the preferred system of patronage will attach themselves to the next in line. Malays, however, will try and set up new patrons; creating other horses with winning streaks. Hence, Chinese systems of patronage may be more conventional and suitable for long-serving patrons, encouraging them in turn to assist the patron to be long serving by supporting their political platform. The Malay system of patronage may be more volatile and inventive, suitable for moderate-serving patrons who will be encouraged to challenge the politics of the long serving. In a sense, the Chinese management styles may contradict the Malay who is concerned with changing the patrons if his politics is not right. The Chinese will accommodate to the politics and keep the patron; the Malay will generate new political interests and find another. In the long run, the Malays and Chinese will eventually find one another through the politics of patronage and on this level express some degree of business symbiosis. In this sense, Sino-Malay business networks express the extension of a productive pluralistic consciousness – that both ethnic communities are interdependent on one another, but that the construction of the politics of business in determining the patronage and the politics is best left to be decided by the Malay partner.

An interview by The Star with the timber King of Sarawak, Datuk Lau Hui Kang, would invariably arouse concern among local native Sarawakians that the most lucrative industry in tropical timber is controlled by the Chinese. Yet, it demonstrates the importance of political patronage accentuating conflict between rules of granting concessions to logging and ancestral rights over trees, which no longer apply. The persons who chop down trees own them, ancestral rights have no economic value and modernity only recognizes those who work hard for a profit (*The Star*, Thursday, September, 1991: 11).

> The timber business in Sarawak is synonymous with the Chows, who are mainly responsible for the development of the industry.
>
> They owned most, if not all the major wood based companies and are also reputed to enjoy controlling interests over the entire logging industry.
>
> A famous son of this clan is Datuk Lau Hui Kang, who is the chairman of the Malaysian Timber Association and of course, the United Chinese Association in Sibu.
>
> In a telephone interview with Star Business in Sibu, Datuk Lau recalled the early years of the Foo Chows landing in Sibu, and how the clan gained control of the industry.
>
> This is Datuk Lau's story:
>
> At the turn of this century, there was a large outflow of Chinese immigrants from China to other parts of Southeast Asia in search of greener pastures.

Among them were the Foo Chows from the Hokkien province, braving the rough sea in their junks. Many landed in Borneo.

Most were lured to Sibu, a place where they were promised fortune and wealth by another clansman, Wong Nai Siang.

The enterprising Mr. Wong used his influence to secure a contract from the ruler then, the White Raja of the Brooke family, to supply labourers to Sibu, which had been earmarked for development.

Being a Foo Chow, Mr. Wong sailed back to his village and spread the good news among his fellow clansmen, thus paving the way for the entry of more Chows into Sibu 90 years ago.

The rolling hilly terrain in Sibu awaited the immigrants who easily acclimatised themselves to the local environment, as their province back home was geographically similar.

They became labourers, farmers, rubber tappers, and whatever field jobs they could lay their hands on.

Timber business meant hard money those days – long periods of time in the thick steamy jungle with little or no infrastructure facilities and poor medical services.

Others such as the Hakkas soon abandoned the trade because of the harsh conditions, leaving the more robust Foo Chows to carry on.

Timber felling then was very primitive and also highly dangerous.

The loggers had to use handsaws to fell the huge trees. Work was tedious, slow and back breaking.

Nowadays, skidders trucks make the job easier and more efficient.

Gradually, a handful of Foo Chows pooled together some capital and formed the first two sawmills, Lee Hua and Hua Seng, between 1925 and 1930.

By this time, more Foo Chows had landed in Sibu from China and were recruited into the trade.

Bosses and workers slogged together in the timber operations and they worked doubly hard in meeting the increased global demand for tropical hardwood after World War Two.

Log vessels from Europe and the United States were berthing at the ports in Sarawak, and soon a whole network of supporting facilities like transportation, banking and trading houses were set up.

Prices for timber began to increase. The industrial Foo Chows seized the opportunities and migrated to places such as Kuching, Simanggang, and even to Indonesia to work the forests. To date, the Foo Chows can be said to control 90 percent of the forestry sector in Sarawak.

From the time of the Foo Chows to the contemporary scene in Southeast Asia, Chinese businesses have been rapidly expanding through networks, which are both politically strategic and inventive. Although political patronage is very much favored by both the Chinese and Bumiputera businessman, recent listings in the

Kuala Lumpur Stock Exchange (KLSE) shows significant structural shifts in partnerships or changes, from traditional Chinese family-based organizations to Sino-Bumiputera alliances. There was a time when many of these alliances were linked to Ali Baba enterprises, or sleeping partnerships' but it appears that the combination of sociopolitical patronage, business acumen and access to finance capital is not necessarily dichotomized in terms of what "Malays are best at" or "what the Chinese can do better." A subtle combination of factors, like access to foreign capital, negotiation for contracts or tenders, knowledge on strategic personal contacts and smart partnerships transcend ethnicity. Malay entrepreneurs have proven their prowess at this game just as purely Chinese business acumen in family-based companies appear limiting in the wake of global competitiveness.

If Chinese businesses are still seen as free-floating opportunistic enterprises in untapped and underdeveloped markets, the emerging trends towards Sino-Bumiputera partnership will serve to "root" the Chinese more firmly in the *Nusantara* region. As argued by Wu and Wu (1980: 46), a long serving argument against Chinese businesses in the *Nusantara* has been their indifference to develop or assist in the development of indigenous entrepreneurship. They argue that while it is partly true that Chinese enterprises have been monopolistic "and that such practices have been responsible for the lagging performance of indigenous entrepreneurs," the removal of Chinese competition would not resolve the problem since indigenous enterprises will have to be more competitive and productive. Wu and Wu (1980: 45) also discuss the trend towards patronage as the starting or entry point of Sino-Bumiputera business:

> Ethnic Chinese enterprises have also been converted nominally into joint ventures through the participation of socially, and often politically prominent indigenous figures as directors, partners, or principal officers. Politicians and military men often play this role, at varying levels.

In an article by Goad (*Asian Wall Street Journal*, 3/12–13/1999: 3), an argument was put forward that one of the consistent features of Asia's crumbling businesses was a high degree of family ownership and control of listed companies, but this may not be a significant factor in the analysis of "what made the cookie crumble" since "dominant shareholders are the norm in emerging markets world wide, and the figures for Asia are not out of line." What is more interesting in the case of Malaysia is the trend towards two dominant shareholders, the family and individual or two individuals of Chinese and Bumiputera descent. This indeed may be a strengthening rather than a weakening factor. *Malaysian Business* (3/1/1999: 32–46) recently named twenty-eight new companies listed on the Main Board of the KLSE. Of these twenty-eight companies, twelve were Sino-Bumiputera partnerships in which two were solely Bumiputera-based companies. The numbers of Bumiputera entrepreneurs teaming with Bumiputera was insignificant but the number of Chinese-based companies standing alone or teaming with other Chinese companies was still high and equivalent to these new smart Sino-Bumiputera partnerships.

Only one Bumiputera company (Habib Corporation) stood alone without forming partnerships with other Bumiputera or Chinese businesses. Hence, in the
period of business expansionism and mergers to gain access to public capital, the
traditional structures of familism continue to govern strongly with an additional
feature of preference towards Sino-Bumiputera partnerships, family or individual.
Although mergers with transnationals from Asia or outside Asia were insignificant, it seems that new lines of trust and confidence in business management
and ownership are moving towards local rather than global mergers with a push
towards capturing the larger share of the local and regional markets in Asia.
In the case of P&B Engineering Bhd it seems that Leading Builders, as 51 percent owner, controls the bulk of the potentially tendered projects worth
RM643 m and that the individual Bumiputera major shareholder with 9.5 percent
of the share market represents the local business partner of this major construction group (Goad 1999: 3).

Technology and technology transfer

An area of concern in these new trends towards smart partnerships is the control
of technology and technology transfer. In the earlier spread of business networks
of SMEs and SMIs in Asia, the kinds of technologies associated with technical
services, retailing and construction and manufacturing were either acquired over
years of training and appropriating or developed through larger government sub-
sidized research and development centers. These mainly pertained to products
generated from agriculture and forestry and in the case of Malaysia, reflected the
high emphasis on Research and Development in large-scale industries like palm
oil, rubber, pineapple and cocoa. Over the last five years or so, with increasing
globalization and monopolistic development of technologies in large research and
development centers in the United States and Europe, companies moving in similar areas had to work within the scenario of producing components for large
global companies like INTEL or Motorola, and this is now legitimately supported
by state governments as the next move in the "global swing of SMEs and SMIs."
Contractual jobs are created by global companies and when the scene in another
Asian country is more competitive, in terms of labor and quality, the tendency is
for these companies to go where components can be produced more cheaply.
Since these local enterprises are not local sources of knowledge production, the
fact remains that these technologies can never ever be transferred or appropriated
in the future. Yet, from statements made by local Heads of State like Penang's
Chief Minister Tan Sri Koh Tsu Koon, one of the underlying objectives behind the
global swing of SMEs and SMIs is that they will in this way become the big
global players in the manufacturing of electrical–electronic components. I refer to
the article by Noor Adzman Baharuddin on the proposed Asia Interprise, Penang-
Malaysia, 1999, launched in the month of May, 1999:

> Confident in their potential to become "world players," the Penang
> State Government will continue to put emphasis on the development of

small and medium enterprises involved in the electronics and electrical, automotive and tool as well as mould and die-making activities, Chief Minister Tan Sri Dr. Koh Tsu Koon said yesterday.

He said many local SMEs have "graduated" into world-class players in the various industries although they started as a family business operating from their homes.

Take Eng Teknologi, for instance. It started off as a small-time business concern and is now one of Malaysia's top precision mechanical parts manufacturers.

It is just like the US-based Hewlett-Packard.

"The two partners started in a garage and today, the multinational is enjoying revenues exceeding US$47 bn (RM178.6 bn) annually," he said when announcing the appointment of Hewlett-Packard as the official IT sponsor for Asia Interprise Penang 1999.

AIP '99 is a business-matching event, to be held at Hotel Equatorial, Penang for two days from April 26.

The event, being held in Asia for the first time, allows SMEs from Asia to meet and network with their counterparts from the European Union.

Also present was AIP '99 organising chairman Datuk Dr. Sak Cheng Lum and Hewlett-Packard Sales Malaysia Sdn. Bhd. Managing director Badlisham Ghazali.

Koh was asked if the State Government was also considering developing SMEs involved in other high technology sectors, including bio-technology.

He said, "No, we are not neglecting any other sectors."

"However, we feel we have strength in certain areas and we want to further strengthen them."

"Also, it is not just electronics and electrical sectors that we are giving greater emphasis to, we are also encouraging greater development in the automotive and tool as well as mould and die-making," he added.

Koh stressed that the emphasis given on the three activities was in line with the Industrial Master Plan Two which, among other things, encourages the development of manufacturing activities in clusters.

It is not known if the globalizing of SMEs and SMIs like Eng Teknologi will lead to the formation of a Hewlett-Packard, when the industry itself is not indigenous or based on technologies developed from Malaysia. The scenario of Malaysian SMEs and SMIs is that their technologies are invented and patented in the United States or Europe. In the final analysis of these globalization processes, it may not matter if the technologies are foreign or local as long as they can be acquired through the purchase of patents. Yet, lacking global competitiveness, borderless enterprises may be more applicable in the development of existing transnational corporations rather than local SMEs and SMIs. However, of the thousands of enterprises in Malaysia, it is possible that a few may reach international standards or show a cutting edge above others in terms of capital and inventiveness. As it stands, it seems that most of this must still be developed locally with little assistance from outside. Less than 0.3 percent of foreign capital in Malaysia is dedicated to research and technology transfer and most of the research and development centers of transnationals remain in the United States, Europe and Japan. Hence, Southeast Asian rootedness in capitalism can be globalistic only for industries that are resource based rather than dependent on human talent.

Asia's future

A report in the Asia Wall Street Journal in March 1999 by Goad (1999) said that a number of "crash theories" were being formulated by the World Bank, University of Chicago and Hong Kong University of Science and Technology, to define commonalities in Asian economies, which went through similar crises after the baht devaluation and subsequent economic crash in July 1997. It was argued that the private sector had a leading role in contributing to the crises, and that although themes of crony capitalism were too simplistic, declining returns on assets and low productivity growth were some reasons given for the failure of many Asian economies to inspire confidence in foreign investors. An interesting observation that is indirectly related to my own research on "rooted capitalism" was that a common feature to almost all Asian economies was a high degree of family ownership and control of listed companies, supporting the crony capitalism theory. But researchers also observed that the dominance of global players in new emerging Asian markets for construction, banking and information technologies made these economies extremely susceptible to global market trends. There was, however, hardly any observation made in the long-term sustainability of local or self-financial family, ethnic or community-based industries and enterprises that I have referred to as Asia's rooted capitalists (Karim 1998), the backbone of traditional Asian economies and the most sustainable form of businesses that have kept Asia going for the millennium before.

The emerging trend towards globalizing SMEs or SMIs indeed goes contrary to the autonomous multi-networks of enterprises and services maintained by predominantly Asian small players. In Penang alone, it is estimated that more than 1,160 SMEs and SMIs are now busy producing small components of computer parts, while SEAGATE alone has absorbed 600 under its wings. If this trend continues and small local companies are co-opted as vendors for high producers, there will be a loss in autonomy and sustainability as global corporations shop for better and cheaper markets in poorer parts of Asia. If big corporate groups have had a powerful influence in Asia's dramatic fall from grace (Goad 1999: 13), then corporate diversification, rather than dependency on global vendoring may be the next best thing. Companies like Dell became global enterprises because they challenged the global dominance by other computer technologies in the

United States. Asian companies that start off as vendors for global grants can never master the art of global market games since they function as short-term piece rate contractual workers, which survive on the strength of TNC's economic dominance in Asia. The complexity of the problem is compounded by the ethnic and cultural diversities in Asia that in times of economic hardship lead to violent demonstrations of scapegoating and witch-hunting, forcing global players to look towards other regions for investment, triggering off a vicious cycle of poverty and ethnic violence. Transmigration, mostly illegal, have burdened Asia with a multitude of economic and social problems, forcing them to divert spending into welfare, security and rehabilitation. At the bottom end of the heap are indigenous minorities, the new pariahs of modernity and globalization and at the top end are the most favored players, identified to political parties and affiliated to powerful individuals in central and state governments. So Asia's future cannot be as simple as pulling the rabbit from the hat and riding on the neck of the dragon in the last years of the millennium. It requires a concerted effort to remove the grime to expose the clean shining surface of the lamp and a genie is in desperate demand. In granting Asia three wishes, the genie would have to bestow, more equity, accountability and autonomy and if these three wishes cannot be fulfilled, most of Asia will remain defensive of its history and bury its future. A new requiem will be sung.

Sino-indigenous mergers mark the most favored trend of businesses in the future with or without global investors to lend them the competitive edge. As Asian economies recover from the recession, it is likely that these trends will be accelerated, as more contracts and projects are made available in services and manufacturing. The Foo Chow kind of industrial enterprises, rooted in extended clanistic networks, will remain but will be forced to enter into inter-ethnic partnerships to maintain their continuing interests. Eventually, the big corporations will combine Chinese, Malay or foreign acumen. The "rootedness" of the enterprises may not contradict the principles of globalization if capital and markets are extended from other powerful bases globally. But for these enterprises to be sustainable in times of crisis, there must be more inter-ethnic dependency and consolidation of monopolitistic sectors of control.

Bibliography

Beckman, R. C. (1983) *The Downwave: Surviving the Second Great Depression*, London: Pan Books.

Brewer, A. (1980) *Hilferding, Chapter 4, Marxist Theories of Imperialism: A Critical Survey*, London: Routledge and Kegan Paul.

Bukharin, N. (1972) *Imperialism and the World Economy*, London: Merlin (originally published in Russian in 1917).

Chan, K. B. and Chiang, C. (1994) *Stepping Out: The Making of Chinese Entrepreneurs*, Singapore: Prentice Hall.

Chossudovsky, M. (1997) *The Globalisation of Poverty*, London: Third World Network and Zed Press.

Cragg, C. (1995) *The New Taipans*, London: Random House.

Daim Zainuddin (1998) *Key Note Address: The NEAC and Confidence-Building*, 33rd Annual Meeting of the Malay Chambers of Commerce, Kuala Lumpur, *New Straits Times*, May 27, 21; May 28, 12–13.

Goad, G. P. (1999) Roots of Asia, Crash Sought in Corporate Performance, *Asian Wall Street Journal*, 12–13 March, 3.

Gunnar, F. (1998) *Asian Age: Reorient Historiography and Social Theory*, Wertheim Lecture, CASA, University of Amsterdam.

Hilferding, R. (1970) *Finance Capital* (translation from Le Capital Financier), Editions de Minuit: Paris (originally published in Germany in 1910).

Karim, W. J. (1989) Consumption, Status Production and Classes of Goods: The Gender Function, *Samya Shakti*, 4–5, 175–91.

——(1996a) *Conspicuous Consumption and Classes of Goods*, Institute of Asian and African Studies, Tokyo: ILCAA, Tokyo University of Foreign Studies.

——(1998) *Culture as an Interpretation of Destiny*, Paper presented at the Conference on CSEA in the 20th Century, University of Philippines, January 28–30.

——(1998) *Rooted Capitalism and Familism: An Early Development of Finance Capitalism in Southeast Asia*, Paper presented at the ISEAS International Conference on Globalisation in Southeast Asia, 30 July–1 September, 1998.

Khor, M. (1996) Global Economy and the Third World. In Mander, J. and Goldsmith, E., *The Case Against the Global Economy and for a Turn Towards the Local*, San Francisco: Sierra Club Books.

Korten, D. C. (1996) The Failures of Bretton Woods. In J. Mander, and E. Goldsmith, *The Case Against the Global Economy and for a Turn Towards the Local*, San Francisco: Sierra Club Books.

Limlingan, V. C. (1986) *The Overseas Chinese in ASEAN: Business Strategies and Management Practices*, Manila: Vita Dev. Corporation.

London School of Economics Magazine (1998), No. 1. Exclusive Interview by Anthony Giddens with George Soros.

Malaysian Business, New KLSE Listings (1999), March, pp. 32–46.

Mander, J. (1996) Face the Rising Tide. In: J. Mander and E. Goldsmith (eds), *The Case Against The Global Economy and for a Turn Toward the Local*, San Francisco: Sierra Club Books.

Noor Adzman Baharuddin (1999) *Asia Interprise*, Penang, Malaysia, *New Straits Times*, 19.

Preston, P. W. (1998) *Pacific Asia in the Global System*, Oxford: Blackwell.

Rajah Rahsiah (1998) *The Current Economic Crisis and its Effects on Economic Policies*, Paper presented at the Seminar on The Young Generation's Role in Facing the Current Economic Crisis, Kuala Lumpur, July 10.

Suryadinata, L. (1992) *Pribumi Indonesians, The Chinese Minority and China*, Singapore: ISEAS and Heinemann, Asia.

Termin, P. (1976) *Did Monetary Forces Cause the Great Depression?* New York: W. W. Norton and Company.

Veblen, T. (1899) *The Theory of the Leisure Class*, New York: Macmillan.

Wee, H. van der (1972) *The Great Depression Revisited: Essays on the Economics of the Thirties*, The Hague, Netherlands: Martinus Nijhof.

Wu, Y.-L. and Wu, C.-H. (1980) *Economic Development in Southeast Asia: The Chinese Dimension*, Stanford: Stanford University/Hoover Institution Press.

12

FROM A NICHE TO A WORLD CITY

Barriers, opportunities and resources of ethnic Chinese businesses in Australia

Constance Lever-Tracy, David Ip and Noel Tracy

Introduction

Studies of overseas Chinese businesses, what we have called diaspora Chinese capitalism, have long been bedevilled by the area boundaries of academic disciplines and expertise. Country studies or research that stops at the borders of Southeast, East Asia or of China, accumulate. Meanwhile those studied, small owners as well as billionaire tycoons, move their investments, their family members and themselves readily back and forth across these boundaries, facilitated by complex, historically-constructed transnational networks.

Another gulf is that which has for long separated studies of the Chinese in Asia from those in Western countries, the latter was carried out within the tradition of immigration and ethnic small business research. The sometimes-parallel debates never touch, the bibliographies make no cross-references and the key names on one side of the divide are unknown on the other.[1] Here, too, the real world ignores the boundaries. Immigrants and refugees have come in growing numbers to the Americas and Australia; children are sent to study and sometimes to settle and set up businesses; returnees bring back high-tech skills and trade and investment linkages; *astronauts* travel to and fro.

The division of academic labour was, in part, justified by an assumption that there could be no commensurability between the situation of *traditional trading minorities* in *developing countries*, and the activities of *ethnic minorities* seeking a place in *developed societies*. The academic walls become increasingly irrelevant, however, as Asian countries have developed and the developed countries in turn discover in their midst an entrepreneurial sector of small and medium businesses (Piore and Sabel 1984; Storper and Scott 1992). At both ends, and through their transnational interconnections, Chinese businesses have flourished, in *ethnic enclaves* in Western cities and as the most dynamic group in emerging new Asian capitalist classes.

A bringing together of studies of Chinese businesses in Asia and in Western countries would show that they have much to contribute to each other. Both have often been concerned with similar problems: the importance of networks and trust based solidarities and the extent to which these may facilitate economic activity or restrict it; the nature of relations with other groups in the society and whether ethnic ties are necessarily exclusive; issues of identity, assimilation and intergroup prejudice and hostility; tradition and modernity and, incorporating all these, the analysis of the interaction between the structure of obstacles and opportunities facing a group and their ethnic cultural and class resources.

In North America, Western Europe and Britain there is an established and substantial literature on ethnic enterprise, past and present (for overviews see Waldinger et al. 1985; Boissevain et al. 1986; Min 1987; Light and Karageorgis 1994; Portes 1997; Light 1998). Much of this is to contrast the very different levels of business success of diverse ethnic minorities with those in the mainstream. A major theoretical and empirical focus was on conceptualising and documenting the *social capital* provided (at different levels in different groups) by networks and community solidarities. In this context, substantial work was done on social capital and networks in Chinese business communities in America (e.g. Waldinger 1984; Chan and Cheung 1985; Wong 1988; Zhou 1992; Tseng 1997).

There was initially much argument concerning the relative importance to this outcome of the *structure* of the mainstream society versus the *culture* of the minority. In the mid-1980s, Light argued for focussing on the additive power of multiple factors, including the reaction of alien groups to blocked alternative opportunities, and their consequent concentration in fields that remain open, the use of cultural resources (including skills, values, networks and solidarities), both those transmitted intact from the country of origin and the *reactive resources* developed within the country of settlement (Light 1984: 201). Waldinger et al. also argued for an interactive approach to assess the congruence between the economic environment and the resources of the ethnic population (Waldinger et al. 1985: 591). Since then such *interactionism* has become the *dominant movement of thought* in the field (Light and Rosenstein 1995: 333).

Such an interactive approach raised wider questions. Discrimination had demonstrably often left immigrants with only restricted channels of escape from menial or working class jobs, into a narrow ethnic business niche, the most obvious being the provision of goods and services to co-ethnics (themselves employed in undesirable jobs in the mainstream economy). Others might satisfy onerous or unprofitable mainstream demands, unattractive to native business, or provide specialised ethnic products. However, while an ethnic group may be shown to have been herded into a particular narrow niche, it was still possible to explore how far and how they had been able to make that territory their own, to fill it and to exclude others by exerting closure.

Some authors argued that where such a monopolised niche was established, it might constitute a distinct segment of the labour market in that industry. While employers benefited from access to cheap and loyal co-ethnic workers, the latter enjoyed some advantages from paternalism, in particular, access to training and other support, which would, in time, give them realistic access to independent status themselves. While such jobs may be low paid, they could form the bottom rung of a career ladder (Bailey 1985; Waldinger *et al.* 1985; Waldinger 1986; Kaplan 1998).[2]

Portes reported on a study comparing Cubans, Mexicans and Haitians arriving in America in the 1970s and 1980s. It found that over a third of the Cubans were employed by co-ethnics, compared with only a sixth of the Mexicans and 1 per cent of the Haitians, and he links this to the fact that within six years many more of the Cubans, than of the other two groups, had become independent business owners (Portes 1987: 351–2).

The questions did not end with the establishment of such an ethnic niche, for in some circumstances its occupants may be able to reshape and enlarge it, accumulate capital and experience and use it as a base for successful sorties. Waldinger sought to identify the circumstances in which some firms, using ethnic finance and labour and servicing community needs, could 'emerge over time as established businesses ... in the wider business environment' (Waldinger *et al.* 1985: 593).

Whether the starting point is a narrow co-ethnic clientele or a narrow product sold in the mainstream, growth and higher profits are normally conditional on being able to break out of the limitations, by expanding either the market or the product or both. Razin and Light (1998) were able to demonstrate quantitatively the advantages of such diversification. Success depended on the relative strength of constraints and opportunities, and of the individual and collective resources of the ethnic business sector. Wilson, Martin and Portes had argued that where an ethnic niche could be developed into a more complex enclave, with its own inter-linked manufacturing, wholesaling, retailing and business service networks, small firms within it could control competition, gaining some of the advantages of *primary sector* firms, while retaining *secondary sector* flexibility. They demonstrated that the successful development of such a vertically and horizontally integrated *enclave* among Cubans in Miami, led to growth in jobs and new business start ups and to higher profits (Wilson and Portes 1980; Wilson and Martin 1982).

A comparable picture of internal integration and external competitiveness was presented in accounts of Asian (Indian and Pakistani) enterprises in Manchester, in Britain, where the retailing of cheap clothes from market stalls was able in time to generate, upstream, its own wholesaling and then manufacturing activities, strengthening the whole ethnic business community in the process, and providing it with internal ladders (Nowikowski 1984; Werbner 1984). Ward (1984) saw the particular strength of the Manchester Asians to lie in the *middleman minority* characteristics of the area, where the final consumers of the products of a large ethnic enterprise sector were mainstream customers.[3]

Studies of Chinese ethnic business concentrations in California, in San Gabriel valley by Tseng (1994) and Li (1998), and in Monterey Park by Fong (1994), give just such a picture of expansion and diversification, moving out of the city centre Chinatown into what Li calls an *ethnoburb* and developing a much wider range of activities and producer services. What is most striking about these studies is their stress on the importance of transnational activities and the insertion of the *ethnoburb* not only into a mainstream national economy but also into a global economy.

Such a transnational perspective has only recently been theorised or gained a significant place in ethnic small business studies. Seldom did earlier studies pay much attention even to continuing links with the country of origin.[4] Rogers (1992) had distinguished between small-scale ethnic economies that functioned as *ports of entry* for aspiring newcomers, and the far more complex and prosperous *transnational business enclaves* into which some of these could in time develop. The main breakthrough came, however, with the publication of *Nations Unbound* (Basch *et al*. 1994: 7), which proposed a conceptual framework for the study of contemporary *transmigrants* involving *transnational projects and social fields* defined as 'the processes by which immigrants forge and sustain multi-stranded social relations that link together their societies of origin and settlement', forming what they called *Transnational Communities*. Within a short time these came to be acknowledged as one of the main neglected themes of ethnic business studies (Portes 1997: 812; Portes 1999), frontiers for further development and research, which would investigate their potential to generate entrepreneurship and to provide the kind of 'international social capital that supports international business' (Light 1998: 579).

A new field of studies is now also focussing on the *capital-linked-migration* (Wong 1996) of *transmigrant* entrepreneurs from places like Hong Kong and Taiwan. These have destinations that straddle the old divide, involving not only Vancouver, Los Angeles and Sydney, but also places around Southeast Asia. Far from developing progressively from local to global operations these often bring, already well-established transnational activities with them, which can link up with and transform the established ethnic and even national economies (Lever-Tracy *et al*. 1991; Wong 1996; Chiu and Wong 1997; Chen 1998; Tseng 1998).

Research on ethnic business in Australia is only recent, and far less developed than that in America (Castles *et al*. 1989; Lampugnani and Holton 1989; M. S. J. Keys Young Planners 1990; Collins 1995, 1996). Studies of Chinese businesses in Australia are, however, potentially of particular interest because the development of transnational projects and social fields by immigrants from Asian countries, seems likely to be more advanced than in America or Europe. This is because of the proximity of Asia and its growing importance for Australia's trade, and because of Asia's much greater weight relative to the domestic ethnic and mainstream economies. These recently growing opportunities demand not only a study of their interaction with ethnic resources, but also an attempt to trace the evolution of this relationship over time.[5]

This chapter is based on a study of 68 ethnic Chinese enterprises in Brisbane, Australia. In depth interviews were carried out with 73 working owners, 60 men and 13 women,[6] in 1989 and 1990, with a follow up a year later. The study was carried out by a team of mainstream and Chinese researchers, using snowballing introductions. The method led to enterprises of diverse types, established at different dates throughout the city and suburbs, and to people of different ages from different religions, countries of origin and ancestral dialects. Its broad concurrence with the profile provided by census data gives confidence that it covers much of the range of variability to be found in the community.

This chapter takes an interactive approach, but seeks to avoid the counterposing of *structure* and *culture*. Rather, it seeks to trace the historically changing interaction between, on the one hand, the patterned obstacles and opportunities presented by Australian society and, on the other, the resources, or lack of them, of the Chinese in Australia. Each of these, of course, includes both cultural and structural elements. The study shows how a small ethnic business community, surviving in a narrow *niche*, was able to diversify, grow and prosper and move towards the kind of *ethnic enclave*, or *middleman minority area* described by the Miami researchers and Ward, once obstacles to naturalisation, family reunion and new immigration were lifted, giving access to *ethnic resources*. The chapter concludes, however, by suggesting that before fully establishing itself as an *ethnic business enclave* this business community is already showing signs of becoming a *transnational business enclave* (Rogers 1992) or a *global economic outpost* (Li 1998) whose most dynamic members derive resources from their networks in a flourishing international trading *diaspora*, in a region with rapid economic growth.

The Chinese in Australia

Survival

Ivan Light has said of the United States that 'the classic small businesses of pre-war Chinese were ... monuments to the discrimination that had created them' (1972: 7). Such power of dominant social structures to mould minorities was even more demonstrably true of the Chinese in Australia by the 1940s. In the nineteenth century they had had active and organised communities, thriving in a number of economic spheres (Yong 1977). By the mid-twentieth century the community was decimated and still shrinking, restricted to a tiny, tolerated, stagnant niche.

This was brought about essentially by the White Australia policy (introduced with Federation in 1901), which by banning all naturalisation and family reunion and any further immigration, simply cut off any replacement of their numbers and social resources. Yet the community did survive. This was primarily achieved by exerting ethnic closure on their niche, so that the authorities were induced to allow limited exemptions to the immigration ban, allowing a life sustaining drip of new blood in. When the ban was finally lifted, this surviving niche provided the initial launching pad for the expanding, innovative and prosperous Chinese business communities of today.

271

The Chinese were first attracted to Australia by the gold rushes of the 1850s. The 1901 census enumerated 30,000 people of Chinese *race*. As the goldfields declined, they moved to the major cities, replenishing that population even when numbers fell nationally. Yong (1977: 6, 61) describes laundries and cabinet-making workshops and market gardens, booming until the First World War, and flourishing grocery and fruit shops and import–export merchants. County associations and chambers of commerce were active and organised (with some success) to resist further racist legislation between 1904–7.

As the years passed, the debilitating effects of a declining population were increasingly felt in the cities too. Many associations ceased to function (Yong 1977: 6). Enterprises shrank in size, declined in numbers and disappeared. Between 1896 and 1914 an average Chinese laundry employed two hands. Between 1915 and 1921 there were more establishments than employees (Yong 1977: 61). Most of the laundries and cabinet-makers closed in the 1920s and the market gardens were abandoned in the 1930s (Choi 1975: 53). The Chinese-owned Australia China Mail Steamship Company, set up during the First World War, collapsed in 1924 (Yong 1977: 7).

Initially, the movement of the Chinese to Australia, like much of that to Southeast Asia in the nineteenth century, had been organised by the village-based male lineages, which only sent men and expected them to return. In the 1920s, however, restrictions on family emigration started breaking down at the Chinese end, and large-scale movements of women to the Chinese settlements of Southeast Asia began. The continuing dynamism and prosperity of these business-oriented communities is well attested, as was their dependence on family and community solidarities (Omohundro 1981; Lim and Gosling 1983). In Australia, however, Asian exclusion made permanent a *commuting* system in which the men lived, often their whole lives, in Australia, with their wives and children in China. The community began to age and die out.

It did not, however, disappear completely. The commuting system was perpetuated by the selective administrative manipulation of exemptions to the ban. Certain Chinese activities could be sustained by renewable temporary permits for specified purposes (Choi 1975: 36, 41). From generation to generation, some Chinese enterprise owners in Australia returned to China to marry and conceive children, then came back alone. When a son of the owner of an approved enterprise was old enough (or the son of a relative or friend), he could be brought out as an *assistant* on a temporary permit, which could be made permanent when he became a *substitute* for the retiring older man (Choi 1975: 84). Several of our older respondents had come out thus to *assist* a father or other relative they had never seen.

The *commuting system* not only placed an enormous premium on small enterprise ownership, for only they had permanent residence and the right to bring out a family member, but also enabled the authorities to decide, through the manipulation of immigration exemptions, which kind of Chinese enterprises, not in competition with mainstream workers, should be allowed to survive. Laundries and cabinet-makers were progressively starved of new blood. Merchant houses, on the other hand, had always been encouraged and were exceptionally favoured (Yarwood 1968: 77). One of our respondents had even arrived as a child, in the 1930s, with both parents, who came to set up a local branch of their family's large trading company.

The main exemption was for Chinese Restaurants. The taste for Australian–Chinese food goes back to the gold rushes, when women were scarce but men of British origin preferred to avoid female tasks, and it extends to the working class and to small town areas. For the first half of the twentieth century Chinese food was, in many places, the only kind of non-British cooking, which was incorporated into standard Australian culture. Although it was a highly Australianised version of the original, Chinese restaurateurs were successful in establishing closure on their skills by sustaining the belief that only they could provide this requisite commodity.

Despite often-serious staffing crises, the community has resisted for a century the temptation to train non-Chinese in the mystiques of the kitchen. While a few of the twenty restaurant owners in our survey had employed non-Chinese waiters, kitchen work was something else, even today. 'We have employed European boys in the warehouse', said one, who combined the restaurant with a wholesale business, 'but it would be ridiculous to have them in the kitchen. It is hard to imagine Europeans chopping in a Chinese way'. The only exception had recently bought an existing Vietnamese Chinese restaurant where, to his amazement, he found mainstream Australian students (friends of the old owner's son) on the payroll as kitchen hands. He had never seen such a thing in 30 years in Australia.

Faced with such an effective ethnic monopoly the structures of White Australia were bent to replenish these scarce and valued skills. In 1934 the ad hoc exemptions system was formalised, and chefs, assistants and substitute *managers* for restaurants and cafes, were listed as exempt categories (Choi 1975: 41). One old timer in our survey had been brought out in 1959 as a chef for an aging, overworked childless commuter in a provincial town. The exemption papers were arranged by a local senator who did not want to see his favourite restaurant close down. After a few years he bought out his retiring employer.

Even illegal entry could be tolerated for a good cook. There is a well-known incident from the 1950s when a country town branch of the Returned Services League (determined supporters of the White Australia policy), conducted a public campaign in defence of their Chinese cook, an illegal immigrant liable to be deported. Another of our respondents, a trained ship's cook, had jumped ship in 1971 in Sydney. He had found work at once and, with the help of an influential regular customer, had been able to regularise his status within a year as a *special case*.

Restaurants thus became, more and more, the main effective and sustainable form of Chinese activity. The 1947 census found 10,000 Chinese remaining in Australia (ABS 1947). These were now heavily concentrated in small cafes. In 1964 Huck found 61 per cent of Chinese men in Victoria working in cafes

(Huck 1967: 21).[7] In 1968 Choi found that of 165 surveyed Chinese men in the Melbourne work force, 27 per cent were self-employed cafe owners, 8 per cent were cafe owning employers and 23 per cent worked as chefs or waiters in Chinese cafes (1975: 87). Over three quarters of these small proprietors thus had no employees while the remainder employed an average of only three each.

The ice cracks

After the Second World War, despite policies of mass immigration from Europe and later the Middle East, the White Australia policy was reaffirmed. Some changes, however, began to crack the ice in which the community's resources had been frozen. In 1956 assistants, as well as owners, were allowed permanent residence, giving them a legal freedom to change jobs and set up new enterprises. At the same time naturalisation, allowing family reunion, was granted to those with 15 years residence. The following year men, whose fathers and grandfathers may have been living in Australia for 70 or 80 years, at last began to bring in their wives and children. In Victoria, in 1964, Huck estimated that half the married men now had their wives with them (1967: 20) and by 1968 Choi found this to be so for 80 per cent of them (Choi 1975: 96).

The arrival of such family resources transformed many Chinese enterprises. One respondent had become the wife of such an owner, who had gone back to Hong Kong to marry as soon as his naturalisation papers were through. She had completed high school, worked as a bank clerk and spoke good English (which he did not). She took over much of the management, the accounts and the relations with the public, and the business grew and prospered. Another development was an influx, after 1950, of Asian students, under the Colombo Plan. These willingly sought casual jobs in the Chinese restaurants. Some overstayed their visas and disappeared into the community.

In 1966 *racial* restrictions on immigration were much loosened, and in 1973 the White Australia policy was formally terminated. The decline in numbers was now reversed, first slowly and then fast. By the 1986 census 186,000 people gave their *ancestry* as wholly or partly *Chinese*. Some 85 per cent of those in the workforce had been born overseas, four-fifths of them in China, Hong Kong, Vietnam or Malaysia. These migrants were often well educated, with a quarter working in professional or para professional occupations. Twenty per cent of men were *independents*, self employed (8 per cent) or employers (12 per cent) and 15 per cent of women were *independents*, 7 per cent self employed and 8 per cent employers (Jones 1992: 121–3). These are rates of *independence* considerably higher than the national rate of 12 per cent and with a higher ratio of employers to the self-employed. Although the ancestry question was not asked in the 1991 census, a calculation multiplying the 1986 proportions by the growth in numbers of those from the main Chinese birthplaces would suggest there were, by then, some 300,000 people of Chinese ethnicity in Australia (ABS 1986, 1991).

Brisbane: structures and resources

From survival to success

Choi's portrait of Melbourne's narrow and impoverished Chinese business sector in the 1960s is echoed in the memories of some of our Brisbane respondents. The census data for 1986 and our survey of 3–4 years later, however, confirm that the Brisbane Chinese are now very different in their diversity and prosperity. The fortuitous opening up of facilitating opportunities, combined with the unblocking of very considerable ethnic resources, are leading to the development of a complex, dynamic and successful ethnic business enclave.

Brisbane, an expanding city of around 1.3 m people, is some 1,000 km north of Sydney, and thus relatively close to Asia. It is a major regional centre serving a large hinterland containing important rural and mining industries, and with major holiday centres and large tourist developments to its north and south.

Brisbane's Chinese population has grown even faster than the national average, from 400 in 1947 to over 12,000 in 1986.[8] They were by then by no means a generally depressed community (ABS 1986). Over 17 per cent of adult men (over 15 years of age) and over 10 per cent of women held a tertiary qualification. Only 14 per cent of men and 17 per cent of women were classified as having *poor English* and *no qualifications*. Although unemployment rates were high at near 15 per cent, the labour force profile of the employed was not disadvantaged, with 26 per cent in managerial and professional occupations, 33 per cent para-professionals, clerks and trades-persons and only 41 per cent working as sales-persons and personal service workers, plant and machine operators, drivers or labourers. Only 15 per cent of the workforce was working in the restaurant sector, with probably another 10 per cent in *take away* hot food shops.

The rates of business ownership were very high. Twenty-three per cent of men were independents (10 per cent self employed and 13 per cent employers) and 19 per cent of women (11 per cent self employed and 9 per cent employers), considerably higher than the national average.[9] Independence rates varied with country of origin and length of residence, but were high for all groups.[10] Eleven per cent of census independents had an occupation as independent professionals. An industrial breakdown shows 22 per cent in the census to be restaurants, 42 per cent to be in retail trade (which includes take-aways), 10 per cent to be wholesalers, property and business services, with 26 per cent in other categories.

There is no Chinese *ghetto* in Brisbane and only limited residential concentration. Thirty-one per cent of all Chinese lived, in 1986, in the 20 Statistical Local Areas (SLA) of their greatest ethnic concentration, where they constituted nearly 4 per cent of the total population. The remaining 69 per cent were scattered throughout the city. Out of 223 SLA only 23 had no Chinese living in them in 1986. Since then some areas of increasing concentration, mainly in middle and upper class suburbs, have become apparent. The enterprises are also scattered. Most of our initial contacts were in the visible but small Chinatown area where

10 of our first 20 interviews took place. Snowballing introductions soon led us away and four-fifths of subsequent interviews were elsewhere, 10 per cent in other parts of the central business district and the remainder in a wide range of inner and outer suburbs.

The survey, carried out 3–4 years after the census, included 73 owners in 68 enterprises. In addition to 15 restaurants and five *take-aways* (included with restaurants in the discussion below) there were 14 traders (wholesalers and import–export merchants and agents), seven independent professionals (five medical, an accountant, and a university trained software developer), eight manufacturers and artisans (a furniture manufacturer, a pallet maker, a maker of plastic containers, a baker, a jeweller and three printers), seven in other services (a hairdresser, a driving school, an English language school, an estate agent, life insurance agent, TV repairer, car hire and repairs), five retailers (Chinese food and herbal medicines, books and gifts, art and newspapers, fruit and vegetables and a mainstream grocery), three were involved with property and investment, one in primary production (market garden and nut plantations), one was a building handyman and one a bread delivery driver.[11]

A thin line of continuity links this much larger business group back to the narrow restaurant niche of earlier times. Fifteen of the current restaurants, for example, had at least one active partner who had gained experience and worked their way into ownership through earlier employment in Chinese restaurants in Australia.[12] Nearly two-fifths of those respondents who were not restaurateurs had been closely associated with the restaurant sector in some way, being children of restaurateurs or their suppliers, ex-employees or ex-owners. Others had relatives or friends in the sector.

These Chinese enterprises in Brisbane are, however, a largely new phenomenon. Only five respondents were Australian born and some two-thirds had arrived since 1975. Most of the enterprises were under 5 years old. More crucially, the constraints and opportunities facing them and the resources at their disposal have changed dramatically from the earlier period.

Barriers and opportunities

Immigration policy and practice had set narrow boundaries in earlier times. Now changes in those policies not only allowed family resources and a growing co-ethnic workforce, but also facilitated the entry of other entrepreneurial resources. In the third quarter of the twentieth century policy had continued to exclude Asians, but had encouraged mass immigration of skilled and unskilled manual workers from Eastern and Southern Europe and then the Middle East. This was then replaced, with the decline in manufacturing, by one which renounced race as a criterion but which set much stricter requirements in terms of knowledge of English, education and qualifications (with some credit for sponsorship by close relatives, and a quota for refugees) and which in the 1980s started actively seeking business migrants with capital and experience.

For the new Chinese middle classes around the region, often educated in English and already playing the role of minority entrepreneurs, the gates of Australia opened, as they did to refugees from Indo–China. Immigration is, however, never simply a reflex reaction to admissions policies, but must be understood also in terms of the motivations and initiative of the migrants, and the resources of chain migration and family sponsorship.

Inside the country, institutionalised barriers posed fewer obstacles and less channelling for the Chinese than they did for the South and East Europeans. So effective had been racism at the borders that structures of systematic racial discrimination against Asian entry into occupational or business fields largely lapsed in the twentieth century. In its place were established, in the postwar period, a formidable battery of obstacles to non-British overseas qualifications and educational credentials that ensured that first generation non-Anglophone immigrants, mainly from Europe, did not compete for white collar jobs or in professional practices (Quinlan and Lever-Tracy 1990).

The major Greek and Italian immigrant groups have indeed been channelled by such blockages into small enterprises, providing goods and services initially to their own large co-ethnic working class communities, as the only escape from the factory (Campbell *et al.* 1989; Lampugnani and Holton 1989). Less than a quarter of our respondents, however, had turned to self-employment because of a closed access to the kind of employment they desired.

Eight of these felt they had been blocked and lost the use of their skills (in the same way as had many Europeans) by non-recognition of overseas qualifications.[13] These included two fully qualified doctors, restricted to the private practice of Chinese acupuncture and herbalism, two tertiary trained and experienced social workers, who are now running a shop and a wholesale business, an agronomist, now partner in a fruit and vegetable shop, a male nurse now a jeweller, the principal of a school, now a restaurateur and a qualified beautician now owner of a take-away. Unlike the Europeans, only one of these had escaped from factory work, while three of them had climbed to ownership through working in restaurants. Another 10 per cent had taken to business because they believed discrimination (on grounds of race, age or gender) had blocked them from finding work or work that was suitable or at the appropriate level or from obtaining promotion.

Some of these blocked people still feel a deep bitterness at their wasted talents and loss of status, and may have little attachment to their business. Most of the blocked, however, found some satisfaction in 'being your own boss' and a number of them had thrown themselves into a life they would not voluntarily have chosen, finding unexpected resources of courage and initiative within themselves, and had not looked back. *I thought all I wanted to be was a social worker, but now I feel I can do anything.*

While some have thus been trapped by recognition procedures, designed to include the British but to exclude non-Anglophones from Europe, others have been able to by-pass them because of a linguistic heritage derived from historical connections with the British Empire and shared with Australia. In Hong Kong, Malaysia and Singapore, for example, the use of the English language is prevalent among the educated and the educational systems are influenced by a British model. While some institutions in those countries are affiliated to British ones and provide recognised British qualifications, their secondary schooling in general has for long prepared a proportion of students to enter recognised tertiary institutions around the commonwealth. Australian government policies facilitated the coming of overseas students to schools and colleges, even before the White Australia policy was ended. The influx of Asian students began after 1950. Choi (1975: 63, 65) calculated that by 1966, when the number of full Chinese permanently resident in Australia was still only 7,400, there were 8,500 Chinese with temporary residence permits, almost all students.

Fifteen respondents held an Australian university degree or higher qualification (obtained after migrating or on a previous student visa). Others had trained in Britain or New Zealand. A number of them had met some discriminatory obstacles in employment that motivated moves to independence. There seemed, however, to be no barriers for those with such recognised qualifications setting up successfully in private practices. Included in our survey are three medical general practitioners, a gynaecologist and a psychiatrist, an accountant and a computing professional, all in private practice and almost all trained in Australia.

What is striking is that none of these independent professionals has had any difficulties with obtaining patients and clients. Almost all claim to be experiencing growth and prosperity, and none are *struggling*. Most of them are providing straightforward, mainstream, professional services to almost entirely Anglophone, Australian customers, sometimes in partnership with mainstream Australians. It is clear that as independent professionals they are not blocked by any institutionalised racialism. Individual racialists presumably go elsewhere, unsupported by communal norms. Here too we must note that mere access to education and accreditation is not sufficient to explain success. Major personal and familial efforts have been required to achieve such credentials in a foreign country.

An ambiguous support for ethnic enterprise, sometimes cited, is a role as subcontractors and middlemen, enabling mainstream businesses to exploit their co-ethnic workers indirectly, in sweated workshops and as outworkers (Bonacich 1980). We found no outworkers, and the 1986 census, for Australia as a whole, gives a figure of only 2 per cent of migrant Chinese men and 4 per cent of Chinese women as *working from home* (Jones 1992: 122–3). There were also none subcontracting from mainstream firms.

Mainstream markets, rather than co-ethnic ones were central to Chinese business activities and the expansion of these was crucial to their success. Two-thirds of the survey enterprises did over 70 per cent of their business with mainstream customers and clients. The take off of the Chinese business sector occurred in a period when the demand for services, including restaurant meals and health services, was growing fast, proportionately and absolutely.

Between 1976 and 1986 the employed population of Brisbane grew by 20 per cent but the workforce in *restaurants and cafes* grew by 116 per cent. The Brisbane business telephone directory listed 238 restaurant outlets in 1976. Ten years later this had risen to 813, up nearly three and a half times. In the next 3 years growth continued, but much more slowly, with 844 listed by 1989.

Australians have recently developed a passion for exotic cuisines, especially Asian ones, in a society of diversified mass immigration and increasing regional travel where *multiculturalism* has become a cult. Chinese restaurants not only responded to this opportunity but also outpaced it. In 1976 restaurants in the directory with Chinese names had already represented a substantial proportion, with 31 outlets, 13 per cent of the total, but these grew even faster over the next 10 years, to 132, 16 per cent of the total.[14] Since then there has been only negligible increase, although our survey shows that other kinds of Asian restaurant have also been more recently opened by Chinese restaurateurs.

The Chinese have certainly profited from expanding restaurant markets, but their success clearly also depends both on the advantages given by their prior achievement of ethnic closure and by their willingness to respond to more sophisticated tastes by developing and modifying the original narrow and bastardised product. Our respondent's premises have become larger and more luxurious with a wider range of dishes and more authentic ingredients, regional specialities and live crustacean tanks. Professional chefs are recruited from overseas and several respondents had gone back to upgrade their skills. Increasingly the more successful restaurants need to offer a more international Asian cuisine, including elements of Thai, Malaysian, Korean or Japanese cooking as well, with elaborate presentation or cooking at the table and entertainment. Even small take-aways in working class suburbs are beginning to introduce Chinese vegetables and seafood dishes and boiled (rather than just fried) rice. One respondent was a baker from Vietnam, whose skills in making French bread induced continuous, long queues.

A growing interest in holistic and traditional medicines has also created an advantage for Chinese doctors. Two practising doctors as well as one who is blocked (and speaks little English) offer acupuncture and attract mainly mainstream patients. It is significant that the doctor who lays most emphasis on this aspect of his work and on other *traditional* elements, incorporated into a hard sell *holistic medicine* package, attracts almost entirely Australians while the other two, who convey either a more orthodox medical image or a more authentic presentation of acupuncture, have between a third and a half Chinese patients as well. All three, however, are very busy and have clearly been able to get advantage from the credibility provided by their ethnicity, even though there is no ethnic closure on acupuncture.

Around a third of our respondents were involved in some way in international trade in goods or services or had active plans to that end, and for most of the fourteen merchants, wholesalers or import–export agents this was a central activity. These were, generally, the most recent and fastest growing enterprises and a follow up survey in 1991 found that they had done better than the others, with two-thirds having expanded and none closed over the 12–18 months since the interviews.

At first sight, structural factors would seem to be paramount in these developments. The centre of gravity of Australia's trade has been shifting, from Europe and the United States first to Japan and then to Asia in general. The traders were very conscious of the existence in Australia or the potential for development of rural commodities, minerals, technology and medical and educational services that were in great demand in the expanding economies of Asia.

Within Australia, however, they faced an uphill battle to obtain supplies and competitive quotations. Australian producers, long used to the bulk shipment of raw commodities to familiar Western destinations are only beginning to overcome apathy towards new markets, especially in Asia, and to the small quantities that those outside Japan often require initially. The scepticism of large bureaucratised organisations towards small agents and customers was profound. Neither government bodies, set up to assist exporters, nor the shipping and handling cost structures, were geared to their needs.

The successes that were being achieved by the traders were those of pioneers against the stream and owed far more to their own personal and ethnic resources than to supportive mainstream structures.[15] For other groups too, the expanding opportunities or blocked alternatives were only a part of the explanation for the growth, diversification and success of Chinese business in Brisbane. Their own resources, which had had little opportunity to function in the earlier period, were now acting vigorously.

Resources

Ethnic resources, in addition to the ethnic products and skills that met mainstream demand, included for some a privileged position in supplying the needs of their own community. For many there was a personal and family background in small and medium business, providing experience, entrepreneurial values and often capital. Family solidarities provided committed workers and a reliable managerial layer available for expansion and diversification, while community networks in Australia also provided trusted employees and suppliers. Overseas networks were the basis for the traders' activities.

A readily accessible market in their own community is often cited as the starting point of ethnic enterprise, one that they must use as a launching pad into the mainstream if they are to prosper. For the Brisbane Chinese the movement had largely been in the opposite direction, with an orientation to co-ethnic custom as a relatively late, but profitable development. With the growth and prosperity of an ethnic business community supplying the mainstream, a minority were coming to see greater prospects there and choosing to focus on it, sometimes abandoning their mainstream custom in the process.

Only one in six of our respondents depended on Chinese custom for *all or most* of their business and only a third for more than 30 per cent of it. Few of our restaurants ever saw a Chinese customer. Those who were thus focussed included those providing authentic products, in demand by Chinese customers and unobtainable elsewhere, such as Chinese groceries, yum cha meals, books and newspapers in Chinese script, herbal medicines, distinctive types of jewellery and also repairs and adaptations to advanced media multi-systems that newcomers had brought with them.

Others provided mainstream products suitably modified for ethnic needs, presented, for example, in a Chinese language. These included a hairdresser, trained in Australia who had gone to Hong Kong for further training, an accountant and an estate agent aiming at new immigrants, who employed Chinese-speaking staff and made frequent trips overseas to contact potential clients[16] and a driving school aiming at the needs of recent arrivals, often older people, lacking in both English and road sense, for whom *different teaching strategies are needed*. The school trained its own instructors, Chinese speakers had 90 per cent Chinese students, recruited by word of mouth and was confident it had no competitors in its niche.

Although some mainstream customers appreciated authenticity, most wanted ethnic products in a modified form and few had any interest in modified mainstream products. On the other hand, deep fried *dim sums* and holistic jargon are of little interest to Chinese customers. Mixing of clienteles thus often required a degree of segmentation, as with the bookshop, which sells books and newspapers exclusively to Chinese customers, and oriental curios and gifts exclusively to mainstream customers, or a Chinatown restaurant, which serves morning *yum cha* mainly to Chinese and evening dinners to the mainstream.

The immigrants had brought major class resources. Many respondents were already a second if not third generation of urban minority business-people. The parents of over three-fifths of them had themselves been enterprise owners or self-employed (almost all urban) and two-fifths had themselves gained experience working in the family business or in a business or practice of their own, overseas, before setting up in Australia. A substantial majority had expected and aimed to become independents in Australia. Some enterprises were direct offshoots of a family business overseas and many others had received help in establishing themselves, from other family members already in business.

The classical literature on immigrant small business in America often suggested that such businesses were a temporary phenomenon, which would fade as the education of the second generation gave them access to better jobs in the mainstream. Our survey suggests that increasing education may now be drawn on as a business resource. The desire for education for the children, which almost all expressed, had clearly already been established in their parents generation, for nearly two-thirds of them had done at least some tertiary studies and less than a fifth had not completed secondary school.[17]

There was a continuing nexus between business and higher education, often mediated through familial business ties. While some blocked professionals do feel demeaned by being obliged to turn to profit making, many Chinese do not see any status gulf between professional and business activity and while some combine both, others have voluntarily abandoned or downgraded their professional work to take on what they see as more exciting and profitable business opportunities.

We found one doctor who had also initiated a partnership to set up an innovative restaurant, and another who also ran a market garden and was developing a plantation for a new export crop, together with several brothers. An engineer, bored with his job and discontented with a fixed salary had opened a city centre restaurant, and an accountant was developing import–export ventures. When we first came across such cases we found such career paths a little bizarre. To our respondents they seemed entirely normal. We asked those who had a professional training and identity (whether blocked or not) what they would prefer, if obliged to choose between employee status in their profession or an independent status outside the profession and the replies were evenly divided. While many wanted their children to avoid restaurant ownership because of the long hours, they generally hoped for some other kind of independent activity or practice for them. Quite a few of the next generation reaching adulthood were choosing business subjects, accounting or law/commerce and some were moving back with new expertise into the family firm.

Almost all writers on ethnic small business have emphasised the resource of family members inputs, but there are significant differences in interpretation. While some see in this the advantage of access to a docile and super exploitable workforce (Bonacich 1980; Aldrich *et al.* 1984; Sanders and Nee 1987; Westwood and Bhachu 1988) others (Wilson and Portes 1980; Waldinger 1984, 1986; Bailey 1985) emphasise the loyalty and commitment of those who expect, in return, to receive training and later help in access to independence. Our study confirms the importance of family labour but sees its main advantages lying in its contribution to management, facilitating growth and diversification, rather than in exploitable labour power.

In only a little over a fifth of our survey enterprises, was no labour of family members of the respondent used. In 24 cases both husband and wife worked full-time and in another 14 the second spouse (most often the wife) worked part-time in the enterprise. In 9 cases children in full-time study put in some part-time work and in 26 cases extended family members (involving two or more adult generations, adult brothers and sisters and their spouses or, in 2 cases, cousins) were involved.

Only rarely, however, did our respondents speak of the value of family workers in terms of cheap labour, preferring to emphasise reliability, commitment and trustworthiness. Indeed, the opportunity cost of their lost wages that could have been earned outside, and put into the family budget, would cast doubt on the logic of the cheap labour motive. Spouses and other relatives engaged full-time in the enterprise were nearly always partners, with a share in the profits and the equity. Children (of either gender) working casually for a few hours, even if unpaid, were often beneficiaries of a family strategy that was devoting a substantial part of its resources to their education.

In general, the family was seen mainly as a contributor to management resources. Although most also employed non-family labour, only a handful employed non-family managers, and several had cautionary tales warning of the dangers of doing so. There was a clear positive correlation between the number of family members involved, especially full-time, and the number of non-family employees, branches and the range of activities. In one case a newsagency and gift shop, with a gold lotto agency, was in the charge of the wife, while the husband ran an estate agency (both under joint ownership). In another the husband, with several employees, operated a bakery while the wife, also with employees, ran the shop that sold the products. References to family members as *the management,* to the possibility of leaving any of them (but only them) in charge of the till or the premises or in a supervisory capacity were common.

In a couple of cases several brothers, with active wives and adult sons and daughters, were engaging jointly in quite major projects and combining a range of diverse activities using a common strategy and mutual financing. In one case several restaurants and an engineering firm are thus linked, in another four brothers and their families run separate medical practices and market gardens but engage jointly in a large, long-term plantation project.

Trust and reputation-based, personalised networks were the preferred (although not the only) basis for wider business dealings, used in getting advice and information and finding labour, suppliers or customers. Where they were absent, attempts were made to establish such continuing personal ties with those with whom they dealt.

While eleven Chinese enterprises had turned for advice and information, when setting up the enterprise, to government bodies, banks and to professionals such as accountants, lawyers, migration agents and consultants, thirty had obtained advice and information from relatives, friends and co-ethnic acquaintances and another six from non co-ethnic friends. While a variety of means for finding labour were used, including government labour offices and advertising, personal recommendations were not only by far the most common, used at least sometimes by three quarters of those who employed labour, but were considered by almost all to be the best or, for many, the only way to find reliable employees. One suggested that the same person would feel under pressure to do a better job if they had come through a personal introduction than if they had replied to an advertisement.

For those engaged in international trade there can be no doubt that their transnational networks among the communities of Chinese trading throughout much of Asia, were the foundation of their business opportunities, providing for the acquisition of local knowledge abroad and substituting for a legal enforcement of contracts at a distance.

In some cases extended or multi-generational business families, with branches in different countries could leave local decisions to the members on the spot, retaining formal links through a loose family trust or interlocking partnerships or even dispense with these altogether, secure in the continuing trust and cooperation between offshoots that have been given autonomy and retain their own profits. A variety of loose transnational networks of family, friends, old school mates and other trusted contacts provided most of the starting points for the trading activities.

One respondent had been running a trading company in Taiwan and had also had a factory there, from which he had been exporting clothing to large Australian retail chains, for some 15 years. Moving to Brisbane, he took up the import side of the same operation, but was also looking into a range of potential exports. Meanwhile the Taiwan trading company was in the hands of his sister, while the garment factory had been shifted to Indonesia, where labour was cheaper, and was being run by an old school friend who is a long-standing partner.

Another respondent, together with his father and three brothers-in-law, had been manufacturing travel goods and electrical items in Hong Kong and China, exporting to Japan, the United States and Europe. He had recently come to Australia with two sisters and their families, and they had started an import–export agency, which can be seen as an extension of the family business in Hong Kong, but is totally independent. It was concerned first with finding markets in Australia for the family's products, but they were also actively seeking exportable goods. Herbalists, restaurants, food and newspaper shops and wholesalers, which purvey ethnic products, often find it easier to obtain supplies directly from contacts over-seas, and local wholesalers may also readily dabble in such trade when they have a surplus or a shortage.

In the context of the structure of opportunities described in the previous section, these personal, familial and communal resources had produced what continued to be successful and dynamic enterprises, even in what were now undoubtedly hard times, with high interest rates and looming recession. Many more described themselves as *growing and prospering* than as *struggling*. A very high proportion of firms were innovative in minor or major ways, and were will-ing to respond to openings in new and unfamiliar fields, or were developing ambitious, long-term strategic plans. The follow up, a year later, showed their failure rate was well below the national average for firms of similar age and size, and that nearly twice as many were still expanding and diversifying as were fail-ing or contracting. While restaurants were manifesting themselves now as clearly in relative decline, doing less well than the community average, the professionals and especially the traders were doing well.

Ethnic enclave or global city?

We have seen how the permissive or facilitating effects of reduced constraints and growing opportunities have interacted positively, in recent decades, with the expanding resources of Chinese business people, to produce a strong upward spiral. The relationship and the balance between mainstream pressures and ethnic resources are quite different now from what it was while the bar remained on Asian immigration. It is not certain, however, whether we can best conceptualise these developments exclusively in terms of the emergence of the kind of dynamic ethnic business enclave hypothesised by Wilson and Portes (1980), Wilson and Martin (1982) and Ward (1984), drawing its strength from its *social capital* in the form of *bounded solidarity* and *enforceable trust* (Portes and Sensenbrenner 1993).

Much would certainly seem to point in this direction. In simple statistical terms Brisbane, qualifies easily for Ward's regional category of a *middleman minority area*, having a high proportion of Chinese independents, a low proportion of manual employees and mainly mainstream final customers. Ethnic businesses in such an area were, he argued, particularly advantaged by enclave characteristics.

Particularly striking is the extent to which the economic activity of the Brisbane Chinese was concentrated within Chinese owned enterprises. The census counted 21 per cent of the Chinese workforce as employers or self-employed. Our survey found (after subtracting non-Chinese working partners and employees) a ratio of approximately 2.2 Chinese employees for each Chinese working owner. Insofar as the survey is representative, this would indicate that as much as two-thirds of employed Chinese in the labour force were working in such firms. The prevalence of recruitment through personal introduction indicates the relevance of Chinese networks to this outcome. This concentration also gave Chinese enterprises some historical continuity, despite the transformation of the group in numbers and attributes. Many current independents gained experience as employees in earlier ethnic enterprises.

A connecting core of the ethnic economy has continued to be provided by restaurants, the original niche, despite diversification and a current stagnation. They have functioned as the major conduit into employment and into independence (for many who will end up in quite other kinds of employment or business) and as a means for mobility (from kitchen hand to chef, from owner of a take-away to owner of a large city restaurant). They are internally articulated, with their own training mechanisms, ladders and hierarchies and their own norms and channels of information. They put in contact with each other otherwise unrelated individuals and groups and they are a focus for new forms of vertical integration capable of generating new supplier activities.[18]

The clearest indication that the diversification is tending towards an ethnic enclave would lie in the growth of firms mainly devoted to supplying ethnic business. In Brisbane there were seven of them, indicating some development of vertical integration. They included the accountant and the estate agent who focussed on providing for new business immigrants, and a market gardener, a seafood wholesaler, a grocer, a plastic container manufacturer and a distributor of containers, all of who supplied Chinese restaurants and take-aways as the main part of their business.

There are, nonetheless, some reservations about whether an ethnic enclave may be said to be actual rather than incipient. It was, for example, not visibly integrated by either location or formal organisation. The old Chinatown area is badly located, in a decaying inner area, a long walk from the central business district, and is in decline. Only a small proportion of Chinese enterprises are to be found here. Most are scattered, but a new Chinese centre is beginning to emerge in a suburb of heavy Taiwanese settlement (reminiscent of Li's *ethnoburb*). It is not clear yet if this will subdivide the community, as the Taiwanese are perhaps the most distinct of the subgroups, not speaking Cantonese and tending to stick together.

Although there were a number of business and community associations and a trans-denominational Chinese church, and over half of respondents were active in some mainstream, or community organisation (business, community, religious, sporting etc) there was no unifying body.[19]

The notion of an enclave's exclusive nature is problematic. We have indeed scarcely found anyone in Brisbane who can be classified as completely enclosed within an ethnic enclave, in terms of product, sources of finance (which are frequently banks) and expertise, employees and customers or clients. On the other hand there are few for whom ethnicity is completely irrelevant, and for most it is significant in a number of ways. In most cases, strong co-ethnic or overseas links are shown, either in the product or expertise provided, or in the customers, clients or source of the labour force.

A *bounded solidarity* is also problematic. Many placed great emphasis on the value of networks and of personalised trust. Shared history, common experiences, ease of communication and shared membership in social and other organisations of course provide the soil from which such personal knowledge and liking will grow. Nonetheless they are not restricted to people from the same region of origin in China or country of last residence or to co-ethnics even in the broadest sense. It was often asserted strongly that both mainstream Australians and Chinese may prove worthy, or not, of such trust. Some, indeed, claimed with pride that they had established such a relationship, in some cases leading to a partnership, with non-Chinese Australians. Expressions of *us and them* attitudes were very rare, even when the interviewer was Chinese. The strength of Chinese business networking lies not in its boundedness but precisely in its flexible and pragmatic extensibility. *Enforceable trust* on the other hand is certainly a relevant concept, and loss of reputation, for Chinese in Brisbane as elsewhere in the world, remained a significant sanction, although it was more likely to be enforced within networks than pervasively through and by the community as a whole.

Little of this discussion on *ethnic enclaves* has been of much relevance in understanding the strength and growth of the international traders. The problems here point to limitations in the concept, which fails, despite its many strengths, to direct attention to key features of Chinese ethnic business. Within Australia the traders' dealings, whenever they go beyond very small-scale importing, are mainly with mainstream enterprises. Some are engaged continuously in trawling the whole economy for suppliers of marketable commodities, and when they find them they attempt to establish long-term and if possible trusting relations with them. They rarely employ many people and may have only limited contact with the other Chinese in Brisbane. On the other hand, their transnational networks, and their social capital in the Chinese diaspora, are the very foundation of their business.

Notes

1 Among a few exceptions are Wickberg (1988) and Y.F. Tseng (1994), who have studied Chinese businesses in Los Angeles and Taiwanese as foreign investors in Indonesia (1998).

2 Omohundro (1981) gives a very similar picture of assisted access to self-employment for Chinese employees in the Philippines.

3 Ward divided Britain into five types of area. The *middleman minority area* was one where Asians had independence rates for household heads of over 15 per cent, with largely mainstream customers for final products, and where only a minority were manual employees. In Britain only Manchester and Newcastle fitted these criteria, and he contrasted the dynamism and prosperity of their Asian businesses with those in areas where they were mainly supplying large numbers of poor working class co-ethnics.

4 One exception here was in the work done on Cubans in Miami. Portes (1987: 340) described how this city had replaced New Orleans and become an *emerging commercial and financial capital of the Caribbean region* through the interaction of the exiles' economic activity with the geographical position of the city and the evolution of Caribbean Basin economies (p. 3a, 1). Portes and Zhou also discussed the way Dominicans had reinvested back in the Republic the profits of ethnic enterprises in New York. However, their primary stress remained on the explanatory power of *bounded solidarity* and *enforceable trust*, as *reactive responses* developed by an immigrant group within the country of settlement (Zhou 1992: 514; Portes and Sensenbrenner 1993).

5 The trend in American research away from case studies and toward large-scale quantitative data analyses (Light 1988) necessarily eliminates the possibility of tracing the path of historical change.

6 These numbers seriously under-represent the working female partners in these businesses. Male partners often present the public face, and are the ones to whom snowball introductions normally lead, but it was clear that in very many other cases female partners had important or equal responsibilities and were involved in major decisions (for more detail see Ip and Lever-Tracy 1998).

7 This is surprisingly similar to the *more than 60 per cent* of China born entrepreneurs in Minneapolis, Dallas, Miami, Seattle and Cleveland that Razin and Light (1998: 352) found still working in the restricted *ethnic niche* of restaurants in 1990.

8 The 1986 census data on the ethnic Chinese in Brisbane was commissioned as special runs for our study.

9 These percentages are rounded. They are not directly comparable to the national figures cited earlier, since those referred only to the overseas born, but the Brisbane figures are clearly higher than the national average. Comparable figures for Sydney give only 15 per cent of men and 9 per cent of women independents.

10 For those resident under 5 years the independence rates ranged from 5 per cent for Chinese born in Vietnam to 18 per cent for those born in Hong Kong and Macao and 27 per cent for those born in China and Taiwan. (Very few of these were Taiwanese in 1986. Since then several hundred Taiwanese business immigrants have arrived in Brisbane). For those resident over 10 years they ranged from over 11 per cent for those born in Vietnam to 38 per cent for those born in Hong Kong and 51 per cent for those born in China and Taiwan. For the Australian born the rate was 15 per cent.

11 The list mentions what seemed to be the primary business interest of the respondent, but does not exhaust the range of their activities and interests, the diversity and multiplicity of which was often striking. We found no garment firms in Brisbane, although they are often recorded as important among the Chinese in America. The census also

indicates that less than 1 per cent of Chinese employers and self-employed in Brisbane were in the clothing and footwear sector.

12 The old timer, who had joined an already long established restaurant in a smaller town in 1959, explained that he had taken on staff and expanded as the Chinese grew in number in the 1970s and 1980s. With this experience they had rapidly moved on. *There are now 22 Chinese restaurants in that town and 19 of their owners used to be cooks in my restaurant.*

13 Only five of the twenty-five with such qualifications had received full accreditation in Australia, two accountants, two engineers and a teacher. Others had abandoned the field voluntarily before or since migrating.

14 In 1987 there was one restaurant for every 1,700 people in Australia (ABS 1989: 1). On the basis of co-ethnic custom alone, eight restaurants should have satisfied the needs of the Brisbane Chinese.

15 For a fuller account see Tracy and Ip (1990) Asian Family Business in Australia: A New Export Base? *Current Affairs Bulletin*, Vol. 67/2, July.

16 The estate agent was third generation Australian, with over thirty years successful experience in the mainstream, who had spotted an opportunity for an intermediary between newly migrating buyers of homes and businesses and mainstream sellers. He joined a national franchise to obtain access to listings of the latter, moved to Chinatown, recruiting eight new, Chinese speaking staff and aimed to create his own market by contacting buyers before they arrived, with frequent trips to Hong Kong and Taiwan.

17 A level of education considerably higher than for the Australian population as a whole or for its business class.

18 For example, future professionals worked there when they were students and they were meeting places for other Chinese business people. For a fuller account of the role of Chinese restaurants in the Chinese community in Australia see Lever-Tracy and Kitay (1991) Working Owners and Employees in Chinese Restaurants in Australia, *International Contributions to Labour Studies*, 1.

19 Since completing the study, a Brisbane Chinese Chamber of Commerce has been established. Other Australian cities also have recently established and increasingly effective Chinese Chambers of Commerce.

Bibliography

ABS (Australian Bureau of Statistics) (1947, 1986, 1991) *Census of Population and Housing* (including microfiche data and special tape produced for the authors).
——(1989) *Cafes and Restaurants Industry Australia*, Cat. 8655, Canberra.
Aldrich, H., Jones, T. P. and McEvoy, D. (1984) Ethnic Advantage and Minority Business Development. In R. Ward and R. Jenkins (eds), *Ethnic Communities in Business: Strategies for Economic Survival*, Cambridge: Cambridge University Press.
Bailey, T. (1985) A Case Study of Immigrants in the Restaurant Industry, *Industrial Relations*, 24(2), Spring.
Basch, L., Schiller, N. G. and Blanc, C. S. (1994) *Nations Unbound: Transnational Projects, Postcolonial Predicaments and Deterritorialised Nation-States*, Amsterdam: Gordon and Breach.
Boissevain, J., Blaschke, J., Joseph, I., Light, I., Sway, S. and Werbner, P. (1986) *Ethnic Communities and Ethnic Entrepreneurs*, Euromed Working Paper, No. 44, November.
Bonacich, E. (1980) Middlemen Minorities and Advanced Capitalism, *Ethnic Groups*, 2.

Campbell, I., Fincher, R. and Webber, M. (1989) Job Mobility in Segmented Labour Markets: The Experience of Immigrant Workers in Melbourne, Paper presented to The Australian Sociological Association Conference, Melbourne, December.

Collins, J. (1995) *A Shop Full of Dreams: Ethnic Small Business in Australia*, Leichhardt: Pluto Press.

——(1996) *Cosmopolitan Capitalism: Ethnicity, Gender and Small Business in Australia in the 1990s*, Working Paper Series No. 68, School of Finance and Economics, University of Technology, Sydney.

Castles, S., Collins, J., Gibson, K. and Tait, D. (1989) *The Global Milkbar And The Local Sweatshop: Ethnic Small Business And The Economic Restructuring Of Sydney*, Canberra: Office of Multicultural Affairs, AGPS.

Chan, B. L. and Cheung, Y. W. (1985) Ethnic Resources and Business Enterprise: A Study of Chinese Business in Toronto, *Human Organisation*, 44(2).

Chen, J. Y. (ed) (1998) *Taiwanese Firms in Southeast Asia: Networking Across Borders*, UK: Edward Elgar.

Choi, C. Y. (1975) *Chinese Migration and Settlement in Australia*, Sydney: Sydney University Press.

Chiu, Y. T. and Wong, S. L. (1997) *Moving Back and Forth: A Conceptual Discussion of Hong Kong Returnees*, Paper presented at Second Asia Pacific Regional Conference of Sociology, Kuala Lumpur, September.

Fong, T. P. (1994) *The First Suburban Chinatown: The Remaking of Monterey Park*, California and Philadelphia: Temple University Press.

Huck, A. (1967) *The Chinese in Australia*, Croydon: Longman.

Ip, D. and Lever-Tracy, C. (1998) Asian Women in Business in Australia. In G. A. Kelson and D. L. DeLaet (eds), *Gender and the Status of International Female Migrants*, Houndmills: Macmillan.

Jones, F. L. (1992) Labour Market Outcomes Among the Chinese at the 1986 Census. In C. Inglis (ed.), *Asians in Australia*, St. Leonards: Allen and Unwin.

Kaplan, D. (1998) The Spatial Structure of Urban Ethnic Economies, *Urban Geography*, (19)6.

Kotkin, J. (1993) *Tribes: How Race Religion and Identity Determine Success in the New Global Economy*, New York: Random House.

Lampugnani, R. and Holton, R. (1989) *Ethnic Business in South Australia. A Sociological Profile of the Italian Business Community*, Adelaide: Centre for Multicultural Studies, Flinders University of South Australia.

Lever-Tracy, C. and Kitay, J. (1991) Working Owners and Employees in Chinese Restaurants in Australia, *International Contributions to Labour Studies*.

Lever-Tracy, C., Ip, D. and Tracy, N. (1991) *Asian Entrepreneurs in Australia: Ethnic Small Business in the Chinese and Indian Communities of Brisbane and Sydney*, Canberra: OMA/AGPS.

Li, W. (1998) Los Angeles's Chinese *Ethnoburb:* From Ethnic Service Center to Global Economy Outpost, *Urban Geography*, 19(6).

Light, I. (1972) *Ethnic Enterprise in America. Business and Welfare among Chinese, Japanese and Blacks*, Berkeley: University of California Press.

——(1984) Immigrant and Ethnic Enterprise in North America, *Ethnic and Racial Studies*, 7(2), April.

——(1998) Afterword: Maturation of the Ethnic Enclave Economy Paradigm, *Urban Geography*, 19(6).

Light, I. and Karageorgis, S. (1994) The Ethnic Economy. In N. Smelser and R. Swedberg (eds), *Handbook of Economic Sociology*, New York: Russel Sage.

Light, I. and Rosenstein, C. (1995) *Race Ethnicity and Entrepreneurship in Urban America*, Hawthorne, New York: Aldine de Gruyter.

Lim, Y. C. and Gosling, P. (eds) (1983) *The Chinese in Southeast Asia, Volume 1 Ethnicity and Economic Activity*, Singapore: Maruzen Asia.

M. S. J. Keys Young Planners (1990) *Expectations And Experiences. A Survey Of Business Migrants*, Canberra: Bureau of Immigration Research, AGPS.

Min, P. G. (1987) Factors Contributing to Ethnic Business: A Comprehensive Synthesis, *International Journal of Comparative Sociology*, 253, 3–4.

Nowikowski, S. (1984) Snakes and Ladders: Asian Business in Britain. In R. Ward and R. Jenkins (eds), *Ethnic Communities in Business: Strategies for Economic Survival*, Cambridge: Cambridge University Press.

Omohundro, J. T. (1981) *Chinese Merchant Families in Iloilo: Commerce and Kin in a Central Philippine City*, Quezon City: Ateneo de Manila University Press.

Piore, M. and Sabel, C. (1984) *The Second Industrial Divide*, New York: Basic Books.

Portes, A. (1987) The Social Origins of the Cuban Enclave in Miami, *Sociological Perspectives*, 30(4), October.

—— (1997) Immigration Theory for a New Century: Some Problems and Opportunities, *International Migration Review*.

—— (1999) Conclusion: Towards a New World – Origins and Effects of Transnational Activities, *Ethnic and Racial Studies*, 22(2), March.

Portes, A. and Sensenbrenner, J. (1993) Embeddedness and Immigration: Notes on the Social Determinants of Economic Action, *American Journal of Sociology*, 98(6), May.

Quinlan, M. and Lever-Tracy, C. (1990) From Labour Market Exclusion to Industrial Solidarity: Australian Trade Union Responses to Asian Workers, 1830–1988, *Cambridge Journal of Economics*, 14(2), June.

Razin, E. and Light, I. (1998) Ethnic Entrepreneurs in America's Largest Metropolitan Areas, *Urban Affairs Review*, (33)3, January.

Rogers, A. (1992) The New Immigration and urban Ethnicity in the United States. In M. Cross (ed.), *Ethnic Minorities and Industrial Change in Europe and North America*, Cambridge: Cambridge University Press.

Sanders, J. and Nee, V. (1987) Limits of Ethnic Solidarity in the Enclave Economy, *American Sociological Review*, 52.

Storper, M. and Scott, A. J. (1992) *Pathways to Industrialisation and Regional Development*, London: Routledge.

Tracy, N. and Ip, D. (1990) The Asian Family Business in Australia: A New Export Base?, *Current Affairs Bulletin*, July.

Tseng, Y. F. (1994) Chinese Ethnic Economy: San Gabriel Valley, Los Angeles County, *Journal of Urban Affairs*, 16.

—— (1997) Ethnic Resources as Forms of Social Capital: A Study on Chinese Immigrant Entrepreneurship in Los Angeles, *Taiwanese Sociological Review*, 1, December.

—— (1998) The Mobility of People and Capital: Divergent Patterns of Taiwanese-Capital-Linked Migration, Paper presented at IX Pacific Science Inter-Congress, Workshop on *New Asian Immigration and Pacific Rim Dynamics*, Academia Sinica, Taipei, November.

Waldinger, R. (1984) *Through the Eye of the Needle: Immigrants and Enterprise in New York's Garment Trades*, New York: New York University Press.

——(1986) Immigrant Enterprise. A Critique and Reformulation, *Theory and Society*, 15.

Waldinger, R., Ward, R. and Aldrich, H. (1985) Trend Report. Ethnic Business and Occupational Mobility in Advanced Societies, *Sociology*, 19(4), November.

Ward, R. (1984) Minority Settlement and the Local Economy. In R. Finnergan, D. Gallie, and R. Roberts (eds), *New Perspectives on Economic Life*, Manchester: ESC and Manchester University Press.

Werbner, P. (1984) Business on Trust: Pakistani Entrepreneurship in the Manchester Garment Trade. In R. Ward and R. Jenkins (eds), *Ethnic Communities in Business: Strategies for Economic Survival*, Cambridge: Cambridge University Press.

Westwood, S. and Bhachu (eds) (1988) *Enterprising Women. Ethnicity, Economy and Gender Relations*, London: Routledge.

Wickberg, Edgar, (1998), Chinese Organisations and Ethnicity in Southeast Asia and North America Since 1945: A Comparative Analysis. In Cushman, Jennifer and Wang Gungwu (eds), *Changing Identities of the Southeast Asian Chinese Since World War II*, Hong Kong: Hong Kong University Press.

Wilson, K. and Martin, W. A. (1982) Ethnic Enclaves: A Comparison of the Cuban and Black Economies in Miami, *American Journal of Sociology*.

Wilson, K. and Portes, A. (1980) Immigrant Enclaves: An Analysis of the Labor Market Experiences of Cubans in Miami, *American Journal of Sociology*.

Wong, L. L. (1996) *Chinese Capitalist Migration to Canada: a Case of Transnational Migration*, Paper presented at the first Asia Pacific Regional Conference of Sociology, Manila, May.

Wong, S. L. (1988) The Applicability of Asian Family Values to Other Sociocultural Settings. In P. L. Berger and H. H. Hsiao (eds), *In Search of an East Asian Development Model*, New Brunswick: Transaction Books.

Yarwood, A. T. (1968) *Attitudes to Non-European Immigration*, Melbourne: Cassell.

Yong, C. F. (1977) *The New Gold Mountain*, Richmond S. A.: Raphael Arts.

Zhou, M. (1992) *Chinatown: The Socioeconomic Potential of an Urban Enclave*, Philadelphia: Temple University Press.

Part V

TOWARDS A COMPARATIVE PERSPECTIVE OF ETHNIC (CHINESE) ENTREPRENEURSHIP

13

INDIVIDUALISM AND COLLECTIVE FORMS OF BUSINESS ORGANISATION

Rural capitalists in India, Malaysia and Indonesia[1]

Mario Rutten

Introduction

In the recent past, studies on entrepreneurship in Asia emphasised the individual background of the businessmen concerned. This was often based on the notion that industrialisation in Europe was mainly achieved by self-made men, whose entrepreneurial behaviour was supported by specific religious and cultural values. Entrepreneurs in Asia, on the other hand, were generally thought to be culturally more inclined to operate along collective forms of business organisation. The predominance of joint-family enterprises in India and of business networks among Chinese entrepreneurs in East and Southeast Asia were held responsible for the lack of economic development in Asia because they hindered Asian entrepreneurs to become large-scale productive industrialists who are able to compete with their Western counterparts.

Following the rise of East Asian economies over the past few decades, these notions about Asian entrepreneurs have been widely challenged. More and more studies started to turn around the argument by emphasising the aspect of co-operation as one of the key factors to explain the economic success of Asian businessmen. Family enterprises and business networks among successful Chinese entrepreneurs quickly became a popular research theme, while the leeway of Muslim businessmen in Southeast Asia has often been explained in terms of their lack of organisational skills to mobilise capital in such a way as to exploit existing market possibilities.

More recently, this view has been challenged again. Although it is still too early to judge, it seems that the recent crisis in Asia is already setting the stage for a return to the notion that collective forms of business organisation do not go together with the growth of industrial capitalism in the long run and eventually result in economic stagnation. In these analyses, the origin of the Asian crisis partly lies in the inability of Asian businessmen to organise their enterprises on principles of autonomy, individualism, independence and universalism; instead their forms of business organisation are based on collective identity, dependency and particularism.

The major drawback of both the earlier and the recent approaches to entrepreneurship in Asia is that they are one-sided. They often discuss entrepreneurial behaviour in terms of individualism versus collectivism, assuming that some groups are culturally more inclined towards co-operation than others. My findings on rural entrepreneurs in South and Southeast Asia indicate that both types of entrepreneurial behaviour are present within one group. It is not so much collectivism or individualism, which explains successful or unsuccessful entrepreneurial behaviour, but the flexibility to adjust social and economic forms of organisation to changing circumstances in terms of space and time. This is illustrated by three case studies of rural entrepreneurs in three different countries in Asia, belonging to three different communities: (1) small-scale rural industrialists in central Gujarat, west India, almost all of whom belong to the middle and upper castes within the Hindu community; (2) Chinese and Malay owners of combine-harvesters and workshops for agricultural machinery in the Muda region of north Malaysia; and (3) Muslim owners of small and medium-scale iron foundries in rural central Java, Indonesia. The findings of these three case studies in Asia are in line with studies on European entrepreneurs which show that both individualism and collectivism have been important in the rise of industrial entrepreneurs in Europe, both at present and in the past, as a result of which the notions of differences in entrepreneurial behaviour between Asia and Europe have to be reconsidered.

Individualism and entrepreneurial behaviour

For a long time, it was generally believed that capitalism breed best in a ground of individualism. This was often based on the notion that industrialisation in Europe was mainly achieved by men of common origin. It was from the social stratum of independent self-sustaining peasant-kulaks and small and middle-scale craftsmen that the early European industrialists are usually held to have originated. This idea of the 'common' origin of the early European industrialists, as defended most prominently by Maurice Dobb (1976), is closely connected to a more general belief that the chief agents of productivity in the early stage of European industrial development were mostly self-made men. This belief was widely prevalent in the nineteenth century. It is clearly shown in the writings of contemporaries such as Samuel Smiles, in his best-seller Self-Help, published in 1859, and P. Gaskell who maintained in his detailed account Artisans and Machinery (1836) that those 'who prospered were raised by their own efforts – commencing in a very humble way, generally from exercising some handicraft, as clock-making, hatting, etc. and pushing their advance by a series of unceasing exertions'. He added that 'many of the first successful manufacturers, both in the town and country, were men who had their origin in the rank of mere operatives, or who sprang from the extinct class of yeomen' (quoted in Crouzet 1985: 40).

For their financial requirement these early European entrepreneurs are generally held to have operated independent of banks and other financial institutions. Most of the initial capital for their industries 'did not come from institutional sources'.[2] When they had to look outside for the capital they needed to expand, some of them took new partners into the firm. This '... was the simplest way but it had serious disadvantages, especially for individualists whose dispositions were autocratic, like most entrepreneurs of the Industrial Revolution, as it could lead soon to disputes about the management of the firm and the distribution of profits. There are actually very few examples among the larger concerns, whose owners usually wanted as few partners as possible, so that one more often sees them manoeuvring to oust irritating associates' (Crouzet 1972: 191).

It is this belief of the 'self-made man' who sprang from a 'humble origin' of peasant-kulaks and craftsmen, which has strongly influenced the notions on the early European industrialists. In this view, the early European industrialists are held to have been independent businessmen. Whatever profits they accrued were due to their own hard work. There was no government assistance; all of them had to survive in an open, free market economy with fierce competition. 'Born "in humble circumstances" (this is a standard expression), that is, from modest or even poor families, they had started life as wage-earners, often working with their own hands; but, thanks to hard work, thrift, mechanical ingenuity and character, they had been able to set up their own business, to develop it and eventually to become wealthy and powerful' (Crouzet 1985: 37).

Following this notion of the early European industrialists as independent, self-made businessmen, '... scholars, including Weber, have argued that the importance given to caste in India and to clan in China placed inhibitions on the development of "capitalist" activity which was said to depend upon bureaucratic (that is, essentially non-familial, non-nepotic) organisation allied with an individualistic approach to entrepreneurship' (Goody 1996: 138). With regard to entrepreneurship in India, authors used to indicate that the joint family militates against efficient industrial development in a number of ways. It was said to lower the level of competence by encouraging the employment of persons in industry on the basis of family connection rather than merit. Moreover, it was alleged that the joint family acts to lower the incentive of the more capable members of the family because it supports all members of the family who make claim of it, some of whom may make no economic contribution. Another handicap is that it restricts the freedom of endeavour of family members and encourages the personality trait of passivity, because subservience to authority and conformity to tradition were seen as functional requirements of the joint family. Overall, this earlier notion argued that the structure of the joint family is functionally adapted to an agricultural society but dysfunctional in an industrial society. Within this framework, family, kinship and caste still represented the most important organisational basis for entrepreneurship in India, and the idea was that the predominance of these social factors held back economic advance.[3]

In a similar line of reasoning, the predominance of family enterprises and business networks among Chinese entrepreneurs were held responsible for the lack of economic development in most of East Asia up to the early 1970s. These authors called attention to the uncertainty of investment when a business cannot transcend the person of the entrepreneur and the resultant identification of the family with the business operations of its head. They argued that the family component of overseas Chinese enterprises implies that these enterprises have to remain small. The reasons given were partly organisational, partly because of the tensions within families which lead them to split and partly because over the longer term direct family lines die out owing to the absence of heirs or their lack of interest. Moreover, modern industry and the Chinese family business were considered to be mutually subversive, because this form of family organisation encourages particularism, which results in nepotism (Levy 1949). Others argued that the extended Chinese family has negative economic effects because it cares for 'indolent' members and its pooling of income discourages individual savings and 'dilut[es] individual incentives to work'.[4] Some have seen these elements '... as linked to Confucianism which holds "familism" as a central tenet, just as Weber and his followers have seen ascetic Protestantism as doing a similar job for individualism in the West' (Goody 1996: 153). They argued that the ownership of property by a family or clan gives protection in hard times but is a deterrent to economic progress, while on the other hand individualism, which encourages experimentation, is a great advantage. It is this emphasis on collective forms of business organisation among the Asian entrepreneurs, which was often seen as one of the key factors to explain economic underdevelopment in this part of the world.

Co-operation and economic success

Over the years, various scholars working on India started to challenge the earlier view of the joint family as a deterrent to industrialisation. Already in the 1960s and 1970s, historians emphasised the prominence of several hereditary business communities in the formation of the modern business class in India. They pointed out that the rise of business corporations and corporate management in India indicated that Indian businessmen were capable of perceiving new opportunities and developing a distinctive style of management consistent with their needs and social structures. The tight organisation as a commercial community that characterised such groups as the Marwaris and the Parsis, for example, helped the members of those communities to compete on more than equal terms with the rest of the population (Kennedy 1965; Timberg 1978).

This was confirmed by contemporary studies on Indian entrepreneurship in the 1960s. Milton Singer was among the earlier scholars who argued that joint family businesses often played a critical role in commercial and industrial activities in India. Far from inhibiting the growth of the economy, he argued that the joint family and the wider caste and kinship groups provided a nucleus of capital which was used for the technical and specialised education of its members, for starting new ventures, and for operating or expanding existing industries (Singer 1968). Since then, the emphasis on the positive effects of the joint family business system to industrial success has been one of the issues for discussion in studies on Indian entrepreneurship (see, e.g., Deshpande 1984; and Rao 1986). A recent study on family business in India even argues that the family-dominated Indian business community will further flourish in the current atmosphere of globalisation and free-market economies. The reason given for this is that the universal trend of networking and relational contracting is said to reinforce the Indian style of doing business (Dutta 1997).

Following the economic rise of East and Southeast Asia over the past few decades, the number of studies that challenged the earlier notions on Asian entrepreneurs increased quickly. With regard to the Asian entrepreneurs of Chinese origin it is often argued that the predominance of family enterprises and business networks has contributed to their economic success. Having a Chinese or Confucian cultural tradition, these authors emphasise, has shaped the characteristics of these entrepreneurs, such as a strong emphasis on personal advancement through hard work and self-sacrifice with the purpose of gaining honour for one's family, community and ancestors.[5] It is especially the emphasis on extended family households and the development of the family business that is seen as a very important factor in promoting capitalist behaviour among the Chinese entrepreneurs in Asia. Staying together as one family for a large number of years and dividing the property among a relatively small number of children (only sons), has given them the possibility to increase the scale of their business operations and the opportunity to diversify their economic interests. Moreover, these family firms are usually embedded in networks, which rest on trust and reciprocation. These *guanxi* networks add scope and depth to the family firm. In fact, both sides work in tandem, each being dependent on the other for economic success. 'By being part of such *guanxi* networks, family firms are tied to other family firms so that, by combining, they reach beyond the limitation imposed by their size, both geographically and economically' (Hamilton 1996: 17). In sum, many authors argue that it is the family firm and business network as cultural artefacts – based on closeness, paternalism, intense managerial dedication and a work environment which matches the expectation of employees from the same culture – that have been instrumental in the recent accumulation of wealth by Chinese businessmen in Asia.

While family enterprises and business networks have become important factors to explain the recent economic success of Chinese entrepreneurs, the leeway of Muslim businessmen in Southeast Asia is often explained in terms of their lack of collective forms of business organisation. These authors argue that the Muslim background of entrepreneurs has shaped their characters, such as being hard working, untiring, independent, industrious and accurate in calculating; ethics that are thought to support rational capitalist entrepreneurship. At the same time, however, they emphasise that Muslim businessmen combine their formidable drive and frugality with an individualism so fierce that it is almost impossible for them to co-operate even in pursuit of clear common interests. This lack of co-operation is first of all reflected in their difficulty to maintain sufficient unity within their own families to ensure the continuity of their enterprises. The decision to set up a new enterprise among Muslims is often not based on market opportunities, but is the result of the break up of a family in line with the right of succession practised within the community. The lack of co-operation is further reflected in the failure of Muslim entrepreneurs to make use of advanced organisational forms to accumulate capital in order to further develop their business. Authors emphasise that business partnerships and entrepreneurial associations often take very loose forms which protect the autonomy of each partner as much as possible. As a result of the prevailing ideal of independent entrepreneurship and the lack of organisational skills among Muslim businessmen, their enterprises tend to be short-lived and are often unable to expand.[6]

In sum: in contrast to the earlier views that emphasised the predominance of co-operation as the key factor to explain Asia's backwardness, more recent notions have stressed the predominance of family and other collective forms of business organisation as one of the key factors to explain Asia's economic rise over the past few decades. While the leeway of Muslim businessmen is often described in terms of their emphasis on individualism, the success of Chinese businessmen is usually associated with their strong sense of family and clan solidarity. To be able to make this 180° swing in reasoning, views that were earlier embraced are now being reversed. An example of this is the 'Confucian culture' argument (see, e.g., Wong 1989; Redding 1990). While family enterprises and clan networks were first used to explain why Chinese businessmen were unable to develop corporate businesses and thereby to become successful capitalists, the same argument was later turned around to explain the recent rapid development of East and Southeast Asian countries by emphasising the contribution of traditional Chinese 'values' and modes of social organisation to entrepreneurial behaviour.[7]

Together, these recent notions have added to the rise of the notion of an alternative, collectivist form of capitalism in Asia, which is distinguished from the individual spirit held to obtain in the West. In contrast to the earlier views, these scholars emphasise the aspect of collectivism as one of the key factors to explain Asia's business success. In these analyses, it is generally believed that a social or family environment, combined with a keen sense of personal obligation to group welfare and family loyalty, all of which strongly influenced by traditional values and practices, has contributed to the recent accumulation of capital and development of entrepreneurship in Asia.[8]

A common feature of both the earlier and more recent approaches to entrepreneurship in Asia is that they discuss entrepreneurial behaviour in terms of individualism versus collectivism, assuming that some groups are culturally more inclined towards co-operation than others.[9] My own findings on rural entrepreneurs in South and Southeast Asia indicate that these approaches are rather one-sided and that both co-operation and individualism are usually present within one group of businessmen or even within one and the same entrepreneur, although the emphasis might change over time. In order to substantiate this argument, I present below some of my empirical findings on rural capitalists in India, Malaysia and Indonesia.

Joint-family enterprises and partnerships of Hindu industrialists in India

My research findings on the fifty-nine owners of small-scale industries in two villages of central Gujarat, west India show the predominance of the joint-family as a form of economic co-operation.[10] There are only eight nuclear families among the total of fifty-nine; all the others may be characterised as joint families, consisting either of members of three or more generations or of two or more married brothers and their unmarried children. The members of these joint families share a common property and pool together their resources for common consumption. Almost half of these joint families, however, consist of several households, each using its own kitchen; in many cases the family even occupies a number of houses.

This institution of the joint and extended type of family has made it possible for these families to diversify their economic interests. Being part of a joint family enabled them to mobilise financial and managerial resources needed for their different types of business operations in agriculture, trade and industry. It is therefore not uncommon to find that within one family, one member manages the family lands, while another is a trader or industrial entrepreneur. By systematically diversifying their interests, these families create employment outside farming with the aim of slowing down further partition of the family's landed property. Although in the end, these joint families are bound to break up, delaying this process often gives them time to expand their enterprises both in type and variety.

The predominance of the joint family organisation among the entrepreneurs in this region of India is not based on economic considerations only, but is at the same time strongly related to, and based on, an extended and inclusive notion of the concept of family. This notion of family involves a recognition of mutual kinship obligations and expectations, which often includes a large number of (distant) relatives. For most of the entrepreneurs, the kutumb – the local term for family – means an extended joint family which includes parents, married sons and their wives and children, and often also other relatives along the male line of descent, such as the family of the father's brother and father's sister.

This highly developed sense of jointness and family feeling is strongest among those thirty-four families that belong to the Patidar community. For a long time, agricultural land has played a great emotional role in tying the family members of this community together, as a result of which 'family-centrism' has become an

301

important characteristic of the behaviour and attitude of the members of this caste. Among the Patidar entrepreneurs in the two villages, there are many who idealise the advantages of joint ownership of property by relatives. For practical reasons, however, joint families are bound to break up eventually. Whenever the male members of the entrepreneurial families in these villages refer to the break-up of the joint family, they do their utmost to maintain their ideal of jointness to the outside world. In many cases the 'blame' for destroying this state of jointness is placed on the women, for not being able to get on well with their husband's mother, with their husband's sisters, or with their husband's brothers' wives.

Another recurrent phenomenon among the men of these families is their insistence that the division of property in the past took place with entire agreement between all the different parts of the family. In reality, however, the actual division of the family property was often the final outcome of disagreement and conflicts that had already been going on for some years. In many cases, these conflicts are related to the strongly authoritative relationship, which develop between the eldest and some of the younger brothers. After their father's death, the eldest brother (motabhai) becomes the head of the family, something that is not always accepted by the younger brothers in relation to the economic activities of the family. This often leads to tensions among the different family members and finally to a split between some of them.

Co-operation in establishing and running an industrial enterprise is not something limited to members of the same family unit. More distant relatives and members of the same caste may also be involved. All such relations play an important role in the running of the fifty-nine businesses established in the two villages. A large number of the present owner-managers profited from the assistance of relatives and others of their caste at the time of setting up their business and in the first few years of running it.

The highly developed sense of jointness not only explains the predominance of the joint family structure and the support by caste members in establishing and managing small-scale industries, it also partly explains the popularity of partnership as a form of business-organisation among these entrepreneurs in central Gujarat. Of the 59 enterprises, 11 have one owner each, the remaining 48 being owned by partnerships, in which a total of 166 individuals are involved, that is, an average of almost 3.5 partners per company. In 23 cases these business partners belong to the same family; the assets are divided up legally – largely with a view to gaining tax benefits – with virtually no consequences for the management of the enterprise. In the other 25 partnerships different families are involved, and in 11 of these there is no blood tie whatever between the partners.

The number of existing partnerships at the present time does not in itself provide an adequate indication of the importance of this form of co-operation for the rise of industry in these two villages in central Gujarat. This becomes clear when one studies the great number of shifts of ownership that have taken place in the course of time, and the ways in which many of the companies are associated through partners and ex-partners. An overview reveals that 34 of the 59 enterprises have ties with one or more of the others in the form of partners or ex-partners. Besides 3 cases in which only 2 companies are involved, there are 3 clusters of 4 companies inter-connected through partners and ex-partners. Particularly striking is a group of fourteen companies, which are all connected with each other through ties between partners and ex-partners, which gives added emphasis to the significance of partnerships and changes within them. Moreover, the preference among a large number of these families for operating in partnerships is not limited to their industrial activities, but also characterises their trade in agricultural produce, their undertakings in other types of commercial ventures and their involvement in industrial firms outside the two villages. To a great extent these partnerships, too, are set up within the group of 59 families.

Simultaneous involvement in diverse business ventures constitutes one reason for many of these families electing to form partnerships. Someone who is running several businesses at the same time, frequently in different sectors, will not be able to work full-time on a newly established concern, and will generally need a trusted business associate. Operating in partnership enables them to pool together large amounts of capital, experience, contacts and management-potential. In most instances, these partnerships consist of families belonging to the same caste or even sub-caste, and in many cases two or more of the partner-families are connected by (distant) family relations.

This aspect of uniformity in the social background of the respective partners and their families indicates that the partnership as a form of business organisation cannot be explained in terms of capital accumulation only. The predominance of partnership is closely related to the strong sense of jointness and the extended notion of family. For most of these entrepreneurs, the establishment and management of trading and industrial enterprises is a relatively unknown activity, which requires co-operation with others from outside the joint family. For reasons of trust and social control, they hold on as far as possible to their familiar way of operating through kinship and family networks, and therefore prefer to operate in partnership with others from their own social background.

Not only do these entrepreneurs choose business partners from the same social background, but they also strongly and explicitly emphasise the kinship ties and family relations that exist between the different partners. To many of them, the partnership is as much a personal and family form of organisation as it is a contractual business arrangement between different parties. Members of the Patidar caste, more than others, tend to form partnerships. At the same time, however, members of this community have a keen sense of status, and prefer to operate without assistance from outside the family. This emphasis on jointness and family feeling in business operations is often carried to the extent that the ambition of most of the entrepreneurs is to have a business owned entirely by members of their own joint or extended family.

This ideal of a family-owned business often leads to distortions when the history of their enterprise is discussed with persons from outside. In many cases, the owners try to conceal the fact that their company had originally been established in partnership with others from outside the family. In order to realise their ambition of a family-owned business-enterprise, some of these entrepreneurs had actually ended an economically fruitful partnership with someone from outside the family, despite sound business reasons for staying together. More often than not, the partner had been one of the original founders of the enterprise, and had brought in the necessary contacts, technical knowledge and/or managerial experience. Because of the irreconcilability between the reality of the past, and their overall emphasis on self-made or family-made achievement in business, these entrepreneurs often try to conceal the fact that there had ever been a partnership in the past, sometimes without being aware of doing so.[11]

Because of the fact that most partners do not view the partnership primarily as a business arrangement and many enterprises are family firms, differences of opinion over issues concerning the enterprise can escalate to personal conflicts more easily. Although the division of property often originates in bitterness between partners and family members, they usually come together again on a new basis once they are separated. The recognition of mutual kinship obligations and expectations of assistance and support still survives in many families and business enterprises today, if only with diminished force. It is often difficult, therefore, to establish the exact relations between the different family members and business partners. This aspect of fluidity and change is characteristic of their family and business structure. The exact organisation of their families and their firms is not a fixed entity but changes over time. It is not the survival of the joint family or business partnership as such which is important but the predominance of a type of family and business organisation that is characterised both by a kind of jointness and conflict, and by change.

Family enterprises and business networks of the Chinese and Malay entrepreneurs in Malaysia

Studies on the recent rural transformation in the Muda area of North Malaysia are revealing the rise of a class of rural capitalists, consisting of large farmers, traders and owners of agricultural machinery and small-scale industries. Most of these studies indicate that there is a division along ethnic lines within this new capitalist class. The economic behaviour of rural capitalists of Chinese origin is reputed to be characterised by a tendency towards economic diversification and economic progress, whereas the activities of the Malay entrepreneurs are confined almost exclusively to the agricultural sector and are often less dynamic in nature. This difference in business strategy between Chinese and Malay entrepreneurs in the countryside of the Muda area is usually explained in terms of the implications of ethnic differences in family structure. It is argued that, compared to the Malay rural entrepreneurs, the predominance of extended family households and the division of property among a limited number of heirs only has provided the rural capitalists of Chinese origin better opportunities to accumulate capital, to increase their enterprises, and to diversify their economic activities.[12]

My research findings on 40 Chinese and Malay owners of combine-harvesters in the Muda area of North Malaysia show that ethnic differences in family structure only partly explain the differences among the rural business class.[13] In terms of ownership, these entrepreneurs usually operate in co-operation with others, primarily with family members. The extended family household is the predominant form of family structure among the 40 main-partners. Seventeen of them live in a nuclear family, which consists of not more than two generations, usually the father, mother and their unmarried offspring. The remaining 23 families have an extended type of family organisation. Out of these 23 extended family households, 13 families do not live together under one roof but in separate houses. These 13 families have set up 36 separate households to deal with the daily domestic affairs such as cooking food, washing clothes, etc. At the same time, however, the members have agreed to continue sharing the responsibility for their incomes as well as their expenditure. Although most of the adult males live separately with their own families, they still operate as a single family as far as their economic interests in combine harvesters, agriculture, trade and other activities are concerned.

Although this type of family arrangement is not based on economic considerations alone, it does enable these businessmen to increase their rate of surplus accumulation and to follow a strategy of economic diversification, or at least facilitates them in doing so. Because they are part of an extended family household they are often able to mobilise the financial and managerial resources needed for their various business dealings in agriculture, agriculture-related activities such as mechanised harvesting, trade and transport and in industry. On the one hand it creates scope for amassing and transferring capital – by delaying the moment at which it is split up – and on the other hand it enables different business activities to be distributed among the adult male members of the family. Where several business ventures are conducted simultaneously it is therefore frequently in the context of an extended family household.

Although co-operation within the family is characteristic of the majority of these rural businessmen, there are differences within the group that partly coincide with ethnic background. In total, the 40 companies are owned by 71 families, of which 51 are Chinese who own 76 per cent of the total property, while the remaining 20 families are Malays who have a total share of 24 per cent. Of the most actively involved family in each of the companies, 28 are ethnic Chinese while the remaining 12 are Malay. The predominance of the extended family households, as discussed above, is stronger among the Chinese than among the Malay families, although this form of family organisation is certainly not absent in the last category. Out of the 23 families, which are of the joint type, 18 are ethnic Chinese while the remaining five are Malay. Twelve of these 18 Chinese families do not live together under one roof, but still operate as one family in terms of income and expenditure, while only 1 of the 5 Malay families lives in this type of extended family household.

Co-operation within the family is therefore of great importance. However, it is only one form of economic co-operation among the Chinese and Malay owners of combine-harvesters in North Malaysia. The establishment of business activities on unfamiliar ground is not usually undertaken by one family on its own, but in partnership with one or more other entrepreneurial families. In terms of ownership, 27 companies are owned by members of one family who share common property and pool together their resources for common consumption. The remaining 13 enterprises operate on a partnership basis. In the case of 5 of them, the partnership consists exclusively of relatives, usually brothers or cousins who operate together in their combine business but form separate families with regard to other economic activities and expenditure. Four enterprises consist of a partnership with non-relatives, while the remaining 4 companies have a mixed partnership involving relatives as well as non-relatives. Characteristic of almost all these partnerships is their informal nature. They are seldom registered officially but exist as oral agreements among the partners.

The number of existing partnerships at present does not in itself provide an adequate indication of the importance of this form of co-operation for the rise of these entrepreneurs. Looking at the business histories of the 40 companies, there have been many changes in partnership over the years. Out of the 40 companies, 13 operate in partnership at present. The importance of partnership as a form of economic co-operation is further shown by the fact that out of the 27 present-day family enterprises, 18 operated with partners in the past. This means that out of the 40 companies, 31 have at one time or another operated in partnership.

In these arrangements of partnerships, co-operation between families of different ethnic backgrounds is not uncommon. Out of the 13 companies that operate in partnership at present, 6 are owned by Malay and Chinese families together. Four of the exclusively Chinese companies and 4 of the exclusively Malay companies had a mixed Malay–Chinese composition in the past. If we take these previous partnerships into account, it turns out that 14 out of the 31 companies that at one time or another operated in partnership, had a mixed Malay–Chinese ownership. In addition, economic co-operation between Malay and Chinese families in the combine business extends to temporary partnerships for harvesting rice outside the Muda area. Especially with regard to tenders for harvesting on a large scale – for example, for semi-government corporations – Chinese and Malay owners often pool together their combine-harvesters in a joint application. Although in some cases the Malay owners are used as front men in order to meet the government condition of Muslim participation, in many other cases economic co-operation between Malay and Chinese owners of combine-harvesters is on an equal footing.

Notwithstanding these various forms of economic co-operation between the rural entrepreneurs in North Malaysia, there are clear divisions in terms of business behaviour between different groups within the entrepreneurial community. These divisions partly coincide with the distinction between the Malay and Chinese entrepreneurs, but they also coincide with differences in life-style within the Chinese community. In fact, it is the close interconnection between economic behaviour, ethnicity, and life-style that is important for understanding the differences in business strategy, not only between the Malay and Chinese entrepreneurs, but also within each community itself. At the risk of greatly exaggerating the differences, I distinguish here three ideal-types of combine-harvesters – one Malay and two Chinese types.

A characteristic feature of the Malay entrepreneurs is that they usually operate through their contacts within the Malay peasant community in their own home areas. All the Malay owners of combine-harvesters reside in their home villages and their evenings are usually spent at home, often in the company of local friends and relatives who are mostly small or middle peasants. Through these friends and relatives the Malay entrepreneurs establish and extend their contacts with brokers in the Muda area and in other states of Malaysia. In Perak, for example, the larger Malay owners were able to establish first contacts with local Malay brokers through Malay farmers from their home villages who had moved to Perak some years ago in search of agricultural land. Starting with these, they were able to extend their contacts to other regions in Perak and beyond. This rural-based social life provides them with various opportunities to invest their surplus in agricultural and agricultural-related activities, but limits their scope for investments outside the agricultural sector.

This interconnection between economic behaviour and life-style is also visible among the Chinese owners of combine-harvesters. The family structure and inheritance practices common within the Chinese community have indeed facilitated capital accumulation by the Chinese owners of combine-harvesters. A characteristic feature of these Chinese entrepreneurs is that they usually operate through their contacts within the Chinese community. A 'homely' life-style is typical of one category among them. These Chinese entrepreneurs usually spend their evenings in their home villages or neighbourhoods in the company of local Chinese friends and relatives, several of whom are also combine-harvesters owners. Although they sometimes drink a glass of beer, imbibing alcohol is not a major part of their leisure activities. Through these friends and relatives, who usually have a similar 'homely' life-style, these Chinese entrepreneurs establish and extend their contacts with Malay brokers in the Muda area and in other states of Malaysia. Although these Chinese entrepreneurs also meet with the Chinese owners of combine-harvesters who have a more 'conspicuous' life-style, this is mainly confined to working hours. It is this rural based social life-style, which provides them with contacts and opportunities to invest part of their surplus in agricultural-related activities, but limits their scope for investments outside the agricultural sector.

The economically most dominant and socially most visible group among the Chinese owners of combine-harvesters show a clear tendency to widen their economic activities and social networks away from their local agricultural base. Most of these entrepreneurs have recently moved from their home villages to the small rural towns in the Muda area, while some families have even moved to the capital Alor Setar. On the whole, their life-style can be characterised as conspicuous and outgoing. They often spend their evenings outside their homes, usually in the company of Chinese friends from all over the Muda region. During these outings they regularly have dinner together, occasionally followed by a visit to a nightclub or karaoke bar, where they consume large quantities of alcohol. Many of these friends are entrepreneurs themselves, either owners of combine-harvesters or of workshops for agricultural machinery, small-scale factories or private trading companies. Through these Chinese friends they establish and extend their contacts within the business community in the Muda area and in other states of Malaysia. A large part of the surplus of these Chinese entrepreneurs is reinvested in their companies through the purchase of combine-harvesters or tools and machinery. A characteristic feature of the economic behaviour of these businessmen, however, is that their more urban-based social life has given them the contacts and opportunities to divert part of their capital to the non-agricultural sector by establishing workshops and small-scale industries. This tendency towards economic diversification indicates a transition from local, agricultural entrepreneurship to regional, industrial entrepreneurship.

In sum, the findings about the owners of combine-harvesters in the Muda area show that the economic behaviour and life-style of the rural capitalist class are closely interrelated, and that differences in business strategy only partly coincide with differences between Malay and Chinese entrepreneurs, but are as much related to differences within the Chinese community. It is the interconnection between economic behaviour, life-style, and ethnicity that is essential to understanding the business strategy of the rural capitalist class in the Muda area today, especially with regard to their specific forms of economic co-operation and patterns of investment.

Nuclear families and economic co-operation among Muslim businessmen in Indonesia

An important theme running through my conversations with the 155 Muslim owners of small- and medium-scale iron foundries in a cluster of five villages in central Java, Indonesia, was the emphasis they place on independence.[14] Many of them stated that they operate their businesses independently of other enterprises, and that they do not make use of partnerships or other forms of co-operation in any field of activity, either with family members or with non-family members, at present or in the past. Many owners said repeatedly that they had started their enterprises from scratch, that is, without any help from others, including parents or relatives. This emphasis on self-made achievement in business is in line with the general view, discussed above, that Muslim businessmen do not make use of forms of economic organisation any more complex than the nuclear family firm. Although there are a few cases of iron founders who do belong to the first generation of industrialists in their families, who came from relatively poor backgrounds, and who did not receive much assistance from relatives or other iron founders when establishing their factories, these cases are clearly exceptions. The co-operation and support of relatives and of other entrepreneurs in various fields of activity, both in the running of the enterprise at present and at the time of its establishment, has been the rule rather than the exception in this cluster of villages.

Co-operation within the family is an important aspect of the economic behaviour of these entrepreneurs. A first indication of this is the fact that more than one-fourth of the owners (43 families) live in a joint type of family structure. The most common type of family organisation among the owners of these iron foundries, however, is the nuclear family. Almost three-fourths of the entrepreneurs (112 out of the 155) live in nuclear families (i.e. husband, wife and their offspring). In most of these cases, the owners separated from their parents soon after marriage, in terms of residence, property, and business. Family property is divided not only among sons but also among daughters, who usually get shares equal to half that of a son. These aspects of marriage customs and the division of family property among Muslim businessmen have contributed to the large proportion of iron foundries owned and managed by nuclear families.

Although this predominance of the nuclear family form of business organisation seems to be in line with the emphasis most entrepreneurs place on independence, it does not mean that the Muslim owners of the iron foundries in central Java are self-made businessmen who did not receive support and assistance from relatives or friends. This is most clearly shown by the fact that most of the present-day owners were able to establish their factories only because they received their shares in the property of their parents or parents-in-law early. Such shares often include a piece of land, with or without a factory building, financial capital and, of great importance, a share in the clientele of the parent's factory. It is common among the iron founders to hand over some of the regular customers of the enterprise to one's children as part of the inheritance. This custom dates back to the colonial period when orders from the sugar factories in Java made up an important part of the business assets of the most prominent iron founders.

In most cases support from the family has not been limited to providing various types of capital to the new enterprise. Many of the iron founders benefited from other forms of assistance from relatives at the time of setting up their businesses by transferring knowledge and experience in regard to the production process and management practices. In addition to providing support and assistance during the initial set-up phase, in several cases family members continued to play a major role for the first few years of a company's life, particularly in sharing orders and product marketing.

In several cases this sharing of orders has turned into more stable relationships that have lasted for many years, often involving other factories also owned by relatives. In most instances these relationships are not between equal partners but are of a subcontracting nature, involving one larger and several smaller foundries. In some cases a whole cluster of factories is interconnected with one another through subcontracting ties. At the top of such a cluster stands one large iron founder who subcontracts his orders among the other factories, provides them with working capital, and decides about the transfer of labourers and machinery among the foundries. The largest of such a cluster in these villages consists of sixteen companies. A major part of the production of the leading company of this cluster consists of contracts for larger-size pipe fittings from municipal corporations in Java. Part of these orders are regularly subcontracted to fifteen smaller iron foundries in the villages. For this, the leading foundry provides the moulds, raw materials and sometimes also part of the labour force. After the pipe fittings are cast in the other factories they are transported to the leading factory for finishing. These contracts are therefore often a convenient arrangement under which a larger iron founder who contracts out part of the production relieves himself of the burden of labour management and absorbs fluctuations in orders.

This largest cluster of sixteen iron foundries also shows that these clusters are often bound together not only by a business relationship. First, most of the smaller iron foundries to which the leading company of this cluster subcontracts some of the orders are owned by relatives of the owner, among them one of his sons, a son-in-law and one of his brother's sons. The other foundries are owned by friends and by two former employees, one having been a supervisor, the other an accountant. Second, for 5 years this cluster has been organising an arisan (rotating slate club) with a socio-religious function. Every month the members come together to contribute a fixed amount to enable two members per year to make the pilgrimage to Mecca. Finally, the smaller iron founders of the cluster have provided support to the political ambition of the owner of the leading company: partly as a result of their loyalty and that of their relatives and friends, this owner was able to occupy the position of chairman of the local co-operative society for 14 years.

Relations of subcontracting do not exist solely among local iron foundries but sometimes also involve large companies or conglomerates at the national and international levels. Several of these relationships are part of the government's bapak-angkat (foster father) scheme, in which large companies are supposed to act as 'foster fathers' to a number of small-scale enterprises by providing them with financial, technical and marketing support. Although several of these relationships have indeed started as part of the bapak-angkat scheme, many of these families had business contacts with companies at the national level prior to the introduction of the government scheme. The local iron foundries are often the smallest business partner in this venture and therefore dependent on the other partners to a large extent, but it would give a one-sided picture of their position to characterise them with the rather derogatory term of anak-angkat (foster child).

In most cases, co-operation in establishing and managing an iron foundry is seen in the form of assistance, advice and subcontracting; in other cases it is formalised in partnerships. Although most of the entrepreneurs emphasise their reluctance to form partnerships, or at least do not want to admit to them, there are several short-term and ad hoc partnerships among the iron founders studied. This include partnerships for the import of cokes from Russia and cokes and pig iron from China, and a partnership to acquire a large order for lamp posts for urban street lighting from the sultans of Solo, Brunei and a Malaysian state. In almost all these cases, the partners involved are related to each other. This again shows that the establishment of forms of economic organisation beyond the family firm is a common practice among the Muslim entrepreneurs in this part of central Java.

These various patterns of co-operation among the iron founders of central Java, both within and outside the family, do not imply that there have been no conflicts among them. The social history of these Muslim entrepreneurs shows the existence of various factions within the business elite. These factions coincide with divisions along family and geographical lines and turn out to be partly related to socio-religious differences. Moreover, it turns out that economic co-operation has always been an important mechanism through which these entrepreneurial families were able to improve their socio-economic position. Those families that belong to the upper stratum of the business community have in fact achieved their dominant position through establishing organisations that took care of both their economic and socio-political interests.

The history of these associations and co-operative societies shows that the activities of organisations of entrepreneurs are not constant, but come and go depending on the need of the elite within the business community. Moreover, the discussions on the organisational forms to support the economic development show that the various forms of co-operation among the entrepreneurs in central Java do not necessarily mean collaboration between equal partners or small businessmen who join forces. On the contrary, most collaboration between the iron founders has been instrumental in the process of differentiation within the industrial community. Through the use of co-operative societies, associations and partnerships, the elite of large entrepreneurial families has been able to enhance and consolidate its economic position and social status *vis-à-vis* the majority of smaller businessmen and at the expense of those working in their factories who often work under extremely dangerous and unhealthy circumstances for very low pay.

The social history of the iron-founders in central Java therefore shows that the image of the independent, self-made businessmen is a myth in the case of these Muslim entrepreneurs. The economically and socially dominant entrepreneurs among this group of Muslim businessmen have in fact made use of a wide variety of different forms of co-operation, simultaneously and successively, at present and in the past, with regard to purchase, production, technology, sales, capital and labour. By establishing co-operative societies, associations and short-term and long-term partnerships with family- and non-family-members and with local and non-local businessmen, the upper stratum of the industrial community of this part of central Java has turned into wealthy, geographically mobile entrepreneurs well-provided with capital and characterised by a luxurious life-style.

Collectivism and individualism

The findings of the three case studies in South and Southeast Asia, as presented in this chapter, show once more the untenability of the earlier view that the presence of family and wider kinship ties inhibits economic growth. Extended ties, of family, kin and caste have obvious advantages, not only in raising private capital, but also in maximising trust, loyalty and in long-term planning over generations, as well as in motivating the entrepreneurs. Far from inhibiting the growth of the economy, family enterprises and wider caste or kinship groups often turn out to play a critical role in commercial and industrial activities in Asia. At the same time, these different forms of co-operation are characterised by changes over time and by conflicts among the entrepreneurs, which often result in divisions of property. Therefore, both collectivism and individualism, and the changes among them, characterise the forms of business organisation in all these three case studies, although the entrepreneurs belong to three different ethnic communities and operate in three different societies.

The emphasis by earlier scholars to seek out evidence of economic individualism among the Asian entrepreneurs as the mark of an emerging bourgeois group was partly based on the then current interpretations of European industrialisation (Henley n.d: 14). But if this view has been '... so wrong about the role of family, caste and kinship in the development of commerce and industry in the East, is it not time to look once again at the empirical roots of these statements in their own political economy? ... Was there an ethnocentric overvaluation of their own achievements leading the West to insist on revolutionary systemic difference and upon categorical distinctions in a situation where the East was much closer to their own practices than they were ready to acknowledge?' (Goody 1996: 161). In an earlier chapter, I showed how our notions about Asian entrepreneurs are partly based on assumptions about the origin and nature of the early industrialists in Europe that are often highly questionable (Rutten 1994). Here I would like to focus on some of these findings in relation to the issue of collectivism and individualism.

On the question of the sources of capital of the enterprises of the early industrialists in Europe, both at their foundation and during their expansion, a large number of data have been collected by various scholars. The idea that many, if not most, industrialists were self-made men – which was a popular view during nineteenth century – was exposed as a myth by twentieth century economic and social historians. The number of industrialists even in the Industrial Revolution who began without capital or connections of any kind was a minute fraction of the whole.

> Economic historians have not denied that, during that period, a number of self-made industrialists rose from poverty to great wealth, but they maintain that such spectacular successes were atypical and exceptional, while a large majority of industrialists came from rather well-to-do families, which could supply them with some capital to start in business and which also had useful networks of connections in their communities.
>
> (Crouzet 1985: 50–1)

Most firms were started with a small initial capital, which had been accumulated through pre-factory system manufacturing or merchant-manufacturing activities, or through the trading of industrial raw materials or finished articles.

In many enterprises, capital from diverse sources was used. Small partnerships were common, consisting of a group of relatives or friends, though sometimes a stranger was admitted as a sleeping partner (Heaton 1972: 416–17; Payne 1974: 18–19). Small artisan entrepreneurs for example often obtained outside help in order to found large factories. 'Of course we can find some which were founded solely on "artisan" or "commercial" capital, but generally speaking an entrepreneur had to rely on various sources to collect enough capital to found a sizeable new undertaking' (Crouzet 1972: 183).

Overall, however, external supplies of capital were 'less important than the personal or family funds which the industrialists scraped together and ventured in the new productive equipment. The power of heredity and the vitality of the family as an economic group stand out whenever we examine the history of the pioneer manufacturers' (Heaton 1972: 416–17). Payne shows that 'although the firms that were limited were by far the most important in their spheres of activity, judged by size of unit and amount of fixed capital, the vast majority of the manufacturing firms of the country continued to be family businesses in the mid-1880s' (Payne 1974: 18–29). He even suggests that

> ... the over-representation of non-conformists among the entrepreneurs who attained prominence may be explicable not in terms of their religious precepts, their superior education or their need for achievement, but because they belonged to extended kinship families that gave them access to credit which permitted their firms, and their records, to survive, while others, less well connected, went to the wall.
>
> (ibid.: 26)

In order to expand, the pioneer 'firms usually borrowed – on mortgage, bond or note of hand – from family and friends, solicitors and attorneys (or through their agency), or from other manufacturers or merchants with whom they had connections' (Crouzet 1972: 191). Charles Wilson emphasises that 'the parochial character of industry seems to me to go on much longer than is usually supposed: perhaps it still goes on. A knowledgeable businessman could write in 1903 as if the spread in industry of limited liability was a recent thing, and about the same time a soap maker could write to a Bristol rival: "personal knowledge of each other is a great factor in the cohesion of the soap trade ...". He was only repeating what earlier makers had said: that "good fellowship" in the trade was worth ten shillings a ton' (Wilson 1972: 380). Taken together, these economic historical studies not only point at the variety of the sources of capital which had been used for establishment, but also the resort by the first industrialists to the resources of their relatives and friends, on a personal basis.

This use of collective forms of business organisation is also confirmed by studies on contemporary European entrepreneurs. An overview of studies on small businessmen in Europe indicates that the most important characteristic of these enterprises is that they are family affairs (Boissevain 1997: 304). Italy's industrial districts are the classic example of the 'flexible specialisation' mode of industrial organisation, in which a large number of very small firms, each engaged in a highly specialised activity, are interlinked by elaborate relations of subcontracting. In these industrial districts, entrepreneurs trust and help each other, both informally and through formal organisations. Although competition between firms is vigorous, it is limited by moral norms enforced by public opinion within local communities.[15] Therefore, collective forms of business organisation such as family enterprises and business networks are also an important aspect of the business strategy of entrepreneurs in Europe today.

The major drawback of both the earlier and the more recent approaches to entrepreneurship in Asia, as discussed in this chapter, is that they are one-sided. They often analyse entrepreneurial behaviour in terms of individualism versus co-operation, assuming that some groups are culturally more inclined towards co-operation than others. In contrast to the earlier views that emphasised the predominance of collectivism as the key factor to explain Asia's backwardness, the more recent notions stress the predominance of family and other forms of business organisation as one of the key factors to explain Asia's economic rise over the past few decades. Although it is still too early to judge, it seems that the recent Asian crisis is already setting the stage for a return to the view that the Asia's development has been impeded by the family and other collective forms of business organisation. In these analyses, the origin of the Asian crisis lies partly in the inability of Asian businessmen to practise impersonal management styles in individual enterprises.

My findings on rural entrepreneurs in India, Malaysia and Indonesia indicate, however, that both types of entrepreneurial behaviour are present within one group. It is not so much collectivism or individualism, which explains successful or unsuccessful entrepreneurial behaviour, but the flexibility to adjust social and economic forms of organisation to changing circumstances in terms of space and time. The case studies also manifest a tacit contradiction between the actuality of co-operation among relatives and an ideology of individualism or collectivism. The Muslim iron founders of central Java, for example, claim to work alone and attribute their success to their own efforts, but deeper investigation indicates that they do in fact engage in several forms of co-operation, both within the family and outside. On the other hand, studies indicate that Chinese businessmen sometimes tend to overemphasise the use of kinship ties and *guanxi* relations while the day-to-day running of the business sometimes resembles little of these traditional ways (Yao 1987). Moreover, it is also important to realise that still '... little is known about contemporary Chinese trading networks, their structural organisation and how they are affected by modernisation' (Menkhoff and Labig 1996: 129). This again indicates that the researcher must be wary of taking such proclamations of entrepreneurs at face value.[16]

These findings are in line with studies on European entrepreneurs, which show that both individualism and co-operation have been important in the rise of industrial entrepreneurs in Europe, both at present and in the past. This implies that the common notion that western economies are fundamentally different from Asian systems, which are based on groups and networks rather than on individual actors, may be misplaced (Biggart 1991: 212). This is confirmed by several studies that emphasise the similarities in entrepreneurial behaviour between Asian and European entrepreneurs (Orru 1991; Goody 1996). As a result, there is every reason to argue that the notion of differences in forms of business organisation between Asia and Europe has to be reconsidered.

Notes

1 This chapter was written when I was a Nordic Netherlands Research Fellow at the Nordic Institute of Asian Studies (NIAS), Copenhagen, Denmark. A previous draft of this paper was presented at the Second Workshop on *Small- and Medium-Scale Entrepreneurship in Asia and Europe Compared: Organisations, Business Behaviour and the State*, 10–11 December 1998, University of Malaya, Kuala Lumpur, Malaysia. For a more elaborate account of this analysis, see my book publication (Rutten 2002).
2 Wolf 1982: 272. Wolf quotes here Perkin, *The Origins of Modern English Society 1780–1880* (Toronto 1969: 80).
3 See for an early overview of this discussion, Nimkoff (1960).
4 Kerr *et al.* 1973: 94 (quoted in Schak 1998: 3). For overviews of the discussions on the Chinese family business firm and Chinese business networks, see for example, Wang (1994), Brown (1995) or Schak (1998).
5 See for an overview of the discussion on the relationship between Confucian tradition and Chinese entrepreneurial behaviour in Asia, for example, Wong (1989), Redding (1990) and Wang (1994).
6 See for exponents of this view, the interesting analysis by Henley (n.d.) in which he refers to the notion of 'excessive individualism' among Muslim businessmen.
7 See McVey (1992, 9–10) for a discussion of this turn-around in the cultural argument in the Chinese case.
8 See for a critical discussion, Goody (1996: 7 and 151). See for an exponent of this view in regard to East and Southeast Asia, Redding (1990), in regard to South Asia, Rudner (1994).
9 For an overview of the more general discussion on 'individualism and collectivism', see Kim (1995).
10 See Rutten (1995) for a detailed account of this study. The main part of the fieldwork for this study took place in 1986–7 and 1992, with follow-up visits in subsequent years.
11 In most cases, concealment of information about previous partnerships does not spring from a fear of giving away information on profits, income, etc. This is shown by the fact that in answering questions, they often did not lower the actual figures on production and volume of trade but gave the impression that the total amount of income had been earned by their family alone.
12 See Muhammad (1988). Another important factor that is sometimes mentioned is the ethnic policy with regard to the agricultural sector. These authors indicate that the tendency towards economic diversification among the Chinese entrepreneurs is also stimulated by the present Malay Reservation legislation with regard to rice-growing land, which restricts the property rights of the Chinese and more or less forces them to divert their economic interests, while it provides ample opportunities to the rural capitalists of Malay origin to reinvest their agrarian surplus in the purchase of additional agricultural land (Hart 1989).
13 See Rutten (1996) for a detailed account of this study. The main part of the fieldwork for this study took place in 1994.

14 See Rutten (1997) for a detailed account of this study. The main part of the fieldwork for this study took place in 1993–4.
15 Piore and Sabel (1984). For a discussion of the flexible specialisation debate and its relevance for the Asian context, see Holmstrom (1993).
16 See also David Schak (1998) for a critical analysis of the Chinese family business concept, and the way the collectivist ideology has influenced research findings.

Bibliography

Biggart, N. W. (1991) Explaining Asian Economic Organization: Toward a Weberian Perspective, *Theory and Society*, 20(2), 199–232.

Boissevain, J. (1997) Small European Entrepreneurs. In M. Rutten and C. Upadhya (eds), *Small Business Entrepreneurs in Asia and Europe: Towards a Comparative Perspective*, Delhi: Sage Publications.

Brown, R. A. (ed.) (1995) *Chinese Business Enterprise in Asia*, London and New York: Routledge.

Crouzet, F. (1972) Fixed Capital in the Industrial Revolution in Britain. In F. Crouzet (ed.), *Capital Formation in the Industrial Revolution*, London: Methuen.

——(1985) *The First Industrialists: The Problem of Origins*. Cambridge: Cambridge University Press.

Deshpande, M. U. (1984) *Entrepreneurship of Small Scale Industries: Concept, Growth, Management*, New Delhi: Deep & Deep Publications.

Dobb, M. (1976) *Studies in the Development of Capitalism*, New York: International Publishers [1st ed. 1947, revised ed. 1963].

Dutta, S. (1997) *Family Business in India*, New Delhi: Response Books.

Goody, J. (1996) *The East in the West*, Cambridge: Cambridge University Press.

Hamilton, G. (1996) Competition and Organisation: A Reexamination of Chinese Business Practices, *Journal of Asian Business*, 12(1), 7–20.

Hart, G. (1989) The Growth Linkages Controversy: Some Lessons from the Muda Case, *The Journal of Development Studies*, 25(4), 571–5.

Heaton, H. (1972) Financing the Industrial Revolution. In S. Lieberman (ed.), *Europe and the Industrial Revolution*, Cambridge, MA: Schenkman.

Henley, D. (n.d.) *Entrepreneurship, Individualism and Trust in Indonesia*, Leiden: unpublished paper.

Holmstrom, M. (1993) Flexible Specialisation in India? *Economic and Political Weekly*, 28(35), M82–6.

Kennedy, R. E. (1965) The Protestant Ethic and the Parsis. In N. J. Smelser (ed.), *Readings in Economic Sociology*, New York: Englewood Cliff.

Kerr, C., Dunlop, J., Harbison, F. and Myers, C. (1973) *Industrialism and Industrial Man*, Harmondsworth: Penguin.

Kim, U. (1995) *Individualism and Collectivism: A Psychological, Cultural and Ecological Analysis*, NIAS Report Series, No. 21, Copenhagen: NIAS Publications.

Levy, M. J. (1949) *The Family Revolution in Modern China*, Cambridge: Harvard University Press.

McVey, R. (1992) The Materialisation of the Southeast Asian Entrepreneur. In R. McVey (ed.), *Southeast Asian Capitalists*, Ithaca, NY: Cornell University.

Menkhoff, T. and Labig, C. E. (1996) Trading Networks of Chinese Entrepreneurs in Singapore, *Sojourn*, 11(1), 128–51.

Muhammad I. S. (1988) *Household Organization and Reproduction of Large Capitalist Farms in the Muda Area, Kedah*. PhD Dissertation, University of Malaya.

Nimkoff, M. F. (1960) Is the Joint Family an Obstacle to Industrialization? *International Journal of Comparative Sociology*, 1(1), 109–18.

Orru, M. (1991) The Institutional Logic of Small-Firm Economies in Italy and Taiwan, *Studies in Comparative International Development*, 26, 3–28.

Payne, P. L. (1974) *British Entrepreneurship in the Nineteenth Century*, London: The Macmillan Press.

Piore, M. and Sabel, C. (1984) *The Second Industrial Divide*, New York: Basic Books.

Rao, V. L. (1986) *Industrial Entrepreneurship in India*, Allahabad: Chugh Publications.

Redding, G. (1990) *The Spirit of Chinese Capitalism*, Berlin: Walter de Gruyter.

Rudner, D. W. (1994) *Caste and Capitalism in Colonial India: The Nattukottai Chettiars*, Berkeley: University of California Press.

Rutten, M. (1994) *Asian Capitalists in the European Mirror*, Comparative Asian Studies 14, Amsterdam: VU University Press.

——(1995) *Farms and Factories: Social Profile of Large Farmers and Rural Industrialists in West India*, Delhi: Oxford University Press.

——(1996) Business Strategy and Life-Style: Owners of Combine-Harvesters in North Malaysia, *Kajian Malaysia (Journal of Malaysian Studies)* 14(1 & 2), 112–50.

——(1997) Cooperation and Differentiation: Social History of Iron Founders in Central Java. In M. Rutten and C. Upadhya (eds), *Small Business Entrepreneurs in Asia and Europe: Towards a Comparative Perspective*, Delhi: Sage Publications.

——(2002) *Rural Capitalists in Asia: A Comparative Analysis on India, Indonesia and Malaysia*, Richmond: Curzon Press/Routledge. NIAS Monographs 88.

Schak, D. (1998) *The Old Gray Mare She Ain't What She Used To Be: Changes in Taiwanese Business Culture and Practices as reflected in labour intensive SMEs and High-Tech Firms*. Paper presented at the second workshop on 'Small- and Medium-Scale Entrepreneurship in Asia and Europe Compared: Organisations, Business Behaviour and the State', 10–11 December 1998, University of Malaya, Kuala Lumpur, Malaysia.

Singer, M. (1968) The Indian Joint Family in Modern Industry. In M. Singer and B. S. Cohn (eds), *Structure and Change in Indian Society*, Chicago: Aldine Publishing Company.

Timberg, T. A. (1978) *The Marwaris: From Traders to Industrialists*, New Delhi: Vikas.

Wang, Y. F. (1994) *Chinese Entrepreneurs in Southeast Asia; Historical Roots and Modern Significance*, Working Paper 34, Stockholm: Center for Pacific Asia Studies, Stockholm University.

Wilson, C. (1972) The Entrepreneur in the Industrial Revolution in Britain. In S. Lieberman (ed.), *Europe and the Industrial Revolution*, Cambridge, MA: Schenkman.

Wolf, Eric R. (1982) *Europe and the People without History*, Berkely: University of California Press.

Wong, S. L. (1989) The Applicability of Asian Family Values. In P. Berger and M. Hsiao (eds), *In Search of an East Asian Development Model*, New Brunswick, NJ: Transaction Books.

Yao, S. (1987) The Fetish of Relationships: Chinese Business Transactions in Singapore, *Sojourn*, 2(1), 89–111.

317

Part VI

LOOKING BACK AND FORWARD

TOWARDS A BETTER UNDERSTANDING OF CHINESE CAPITALISM AND ASIAN BUSINESS NETWORKS

Thomas Menkhoff and Solvay Gerke

Themes such as ethnic Chinese entrepreneurship and Asian business networks continue to be areas of immense interest both within and beyond Asia. In this book, which seeks to understand, broadly speaking, what makes the ethnic Chinese network capitalism tick, we discussed some of the socio-economic, cultural, historical and political implications of ethnic Chinese entrepreneurship and business connections in the age of globalization. We also attempted to re-examine some of the taken-for-granted assumptions about the unique characteristics, strengths and challenges of what has been termed "Chinese" capitalism, networks and business culture. This was done based on solid empirical data and mid-range theoretical constructs rather than on imagination or fiction. Besides identifying and addressing a couple of theoretical and empirical gaps in the literature on the subject matter, the chapters revealed the enormous differences among the ethnic Chinese in East and Southeast Asia in terms of their economic behavior depending on their nationality or land of adoption. This implies that the Chinese overseas cannot be treated all alike and that theses such as the emergence of a sort of Chinese commonwealth are highly questionable. Let us now briefly revisit, discuss and synthesize the various contributions.

We began by illustrating some of the challenges ahead for Chinese entrepreneurs and their networks posed by the consequences of the Asian crisis (Menkhoff and Sikorski) and their minority status in countries such as Indonesia (Low), one of Asia's foremost crisis economies.

While some observers may have doubts whether the negative picture of Chinese business as being riddled by the perhaps unintended consequences of the Asian crisis (Menkhoff and Sikorski), for example, in terms of change imperatives with regard to technology or proactive change management, is conclusive given the relatively large number of firms who are doing quite well, we feel that the forces of change that are currently impacting on ethnic Chinese firms in the region are significant. Many management gurus believe that the changing business environment in the era of globalization requires a reconsideration of traditional business models, strategy, HR policies, entrepreneurial behavior, network figurations, etc. The Asian crisis challenged many well-established businesses in Asia and beyond, including those owned by ethnic Chinese. "Best" corporate governance practices advocated by management gurus in East and West as well as the transformation of traditional brick and mortar firms to IT driven (intelligent) organizations represent crucial forces of change for Chinese businesses in the new millennium. With regard to the latter, Taiwanese Jerry Yang, co-founder of well-known Internet search engine Yahoo.com or Charles Wang of Computer Associates are often quoted role models.

There is some evidence that the response of many Chinese family-owned SMEs to the new wave of economic and technological forces is uneven and sometimes insufficient (Menkhoff and Kay 2000). Many organizations fail to implement, for example, modern quality/productivity management concepts such as Continuous Quality Improvement (CQI) due to lack of management know how, qualified staff and/or the organizational peculiarities of small family firms. Potential change targets such as strategy, people and/or technology (Leavitt 1965) represent challenges for SME owners and are often neglected. A recent survey (Chua 2001) of 158 ethnic Chinese enterprises in Singapore showed that a relatively large proportion of these firms pay insufficient attention to IT skills upgrading, innovation as a source of competitiveness, product customization, customer satisfaction and e-commerce operations. Based on such indicators, the author concluded that many SMEs in Singapore are not yet ready for the new economy. Predictors and key ingredients of entrepreneurial "new economy compliance," however, remain unclear.

Whether ethnic Chinese small enterprises in Singapore are ready for the new economy is a hotly debated issue in the city-state. Representative empirical data and sophisticated theoretical models, however, are hard to come by. SME policy makers in Singapore do hope that new economy related assistance schemes would motivate more local small entrepreneurs to embrace related changes proactively. To increase online transaction capability of local SMEs and to encourage small entrepreneurs to adopt "ready-made" e-commerce solutions, both Singapore's Standards, Productivity and Innovation Board (SPRING) and the Infocomm Development Authority (IDA) have implemented various new economy related SME upgrading schemes during the past few years. The characteristics of those small entrepreneurs who took up the challenge and those who did not have yet to be ascertained by empirical research. Whether cultural traits are important driving forces should be examined in the context of future research projects.

In contrast to culturalists who regard the cultural (Asian) values of the ethnic Chinese as a key driver of their business acumen, others perceive cultural traits in terms of Chineseness as secondary when it comes to an understanding of successful (or failed) Chinese business operations. Economists, for example, may opt for detailed firm-based, intra-organizational analyses over time rather than for a cultural explanatory approach in order to understand the root causes of corporate growth or decline patterns of Chinese firms and the dynamics of their owner-managers.

Perceptions of analysts with regard to the uniqueness of Chinese businesses, real or imagined, vary widely. While some may argue that the Chinese firms, for example, in Malaysia, do differ in many ways from the Chinese firms in other countries, for example, in Australia, others may emphasize corporate, entrepreneurial and managerial similarities rather than differences depending on their ideological outlook. The often-cited lack of corporate transparency in "Asian" firms is also an issue in certain European countries. Discourses on (Asian) values, cultural myths and so forth are sometimes intentionally constructed and maintained by strategic groups. Such processes are not confined to Asian countries. To examine this construction process in the context of a case study, it might be useful to focus on the connection between business, globalization and Chineseness based on the case of the World Chinese Entrepreneurs Convention pioneered by the Singapore Chinese Chamber of Commerce & Industry (SCCCI) in 1991 and the subsequent World Chinese Business Network which was first established on the Internet by SCCCI in 1995. Unfortunately, we do not have the space here to embark on such a journey. What is more important in the context of this book's agenda is to acknowledge that these gatherings and virtual (business) communities of Chinese (business) people should "not be viewed as closed communities existing as an end to themselves but as evolving networks with a global outreach" (Hong Hai 2001: 27).

The development and maintenance of local, regional or international *guanxi* ties based on "tribal," clan, dialect, kinship or other ties has been intensively discussed in the literature on Chinese business. We interpret the significance of such ties in intra- and interfirm business affairs as a survival mechanism as well as a function of the institutional landscapes in which Chinese firms in Asia are embedded, the development stage of the respective (host) economy and other factors. The institutional set-up (structure) rather than culture seems to be one of the key variables in understanding what is often seen as "typical" Chinese business behavior and networking patterns. Traditionally, Indonesia and the country's famous trading minorities represent interesting case studies in this respect (Wertheim 1980; Evers and Schrader 1994).

Whether ethnic Chinese Indonesian business people with their capital, entrepreneurship, networks and proven track record can induce the recovery process in Indonesia and other ASEAN economies as argued by LOW, remains to be seen. In 1999 the chairman of the Chinese–Indonesian Association, Eddie Lembong said that the election of President Abdurrahman Wahid and Vice-President Megawati Sukarnoputri will provide stability in Indonesia. It was hoped then that Indonesian business people would bring back the billions of dollars they deposited overseas as a consequence of the country's economic crisis and political unrest in 1998 (*Straits Times*, 10/28/1999). Experts felt that the return of the money would provide a significant boost to the efforts to end the country's economic crisis. How much of the money deposited overseas returned home during the past two years is not known. What is clear, however, is that Indonesia's situation in August 2001 when this chapter was written is not really stable despite the positive assessments of the country's new President Ms Megawati by analysts. The evolution of Indonesia's current challenges has to be analyzed in the context of the expanding global market system, the dynamics of strategic group formation (Evers and Schiel 1988), the painful built-up of system trust and many other factors. Concerned scholars who study the role and history of the Chinese minority in Indonesia feel that in the past too little emphasis has been put on the functioning and importance of the Javanese connection between members of the former power elite and local tycoons. The networks between Chinese entrepreneurs and Malays or Indians in Malaysia are of similar importance and require attention in addition to the often discussed internal Chinese relationships.

In view of the potentially explosive character of minority–majority relations in certain parts of Southeast Asia and business operations in moral economies, a crucial goal of the monograph was to shed light on what is sometimes perceived as "mysterious" collaborations between the ethnic Chinese in Southeast Asia and Mainland China. This objective was achieved by incorporating a couple of contemporary empirical studies, which described, analyzed and explained the logic of such collaborative ventures. Tracy and Lever-Tracy presented interesting empirical data on the actual investment patterns of the Chinese diaspora in the People's Republic of China. Schlevogt explored the interconnections and synergies between the ethnic Chinese overseas and Mainland China's private entrepreneurs as well as state-owned firms based on recent survey data. Heberer provided ample empirical evidence for his thesis that private (Chinese) entrepreneurship has become a key driving force of socio-economic and political change in both Mainland China and Vietnam while Lindahl and Thomsen examined the changing socio-economic role of Vietnam's *hoa* and their multiple linkages to local, regional and international business partners.

Most of the chapters support the hypothesis that the facets of Chinese entrepreneurship and the formation, cultivation and particular structure of network ties are contingent upon time, historical factors, the institutional framework and place. In plain English: there are many similarities between Chinese entrepreneurs in Asia and beyond with regard to the moral economies in which they are embedded which explain the importance of networking, *guanxi*, *xinyong* etc. but there are also profound differences among them. The latter is often overlooked, as convincingly argued by Chan and Tong (2000) who conducted a study of Singaporean Chinese businessmen doing business in China. They explored the dynamics underlining the various ways in which the Singaporean Chinese modes of doing business coincide with and differ from those of Mainland Chinese. As they read it, being Chinese is a cultural asset, which can act as a sort of bonding agent between the Singaporean Chinese and their counterparts in Mainland China. However, a deeper analysis showed that there are sufficient differences in cultural ethos and business conduct that set the two peoples apart from each other. Unlike the Singaporean Chinese, the authors argue, the Chinese do not separate the social, moral and economic realms of business conduct, seeing all of them as being equally integral to the larger whole. A Mainland Chinese businessman works with a minimum of written agreements while relying on trust, sincerity and goodwill to realize verbal agreements and to orally interpret the written. The spoken substantiates and fills in the written. He also prefers a slow, gradual build-up in his business conduct – his conception of time differs markedly from that of a Singaporean. As far as a Chinese businessman is concerned, this emphasis on the social, moral, oral and temporal realms of his business conduct lends itself readily to the creation, development and maintenance of *guanxi* networks. As social/interpersonal relations, *guanxi* is precarious and thus requires vigilant accommodation and adjustment on the part of both parties. In China, *guanxi* is fundamental to business success, a fact the Singaporean businessman has learned not to ignore. On the one hand, Singaporean and Chinese businessmen, to a certain extent, are united by some aspects of a shared ethnicity and heritage – origin, language, food, kinship, familism and religion. On the other hand, the cognitive and behavioral differences between the two peoples are substantial enough to cause anxiety and discomfort to both parties, now that the Singaporeans have, decades before the Chinese, launched themselves onto the road of development, modernization and globalization. Singaporeans doing business in China, Tong and Chan concluded, have thus found themselves arbitrating cultural sameness and differentness while interacting with the Mainland Chinese – a Singaporean Chinese is like them and not like them; or he is like them now, but not like them later. This ability to oscillate between ethnic and national identities may cast the "hybrid" Singaporean in a new role in a new international order of trade and commerce, that of a cultural broker or "knowledge arbitrator." He is the classical marginal man or the trading middleman recast and renewed for a new world stage, a role Singapore has already begun to play while mediating between China and third-party investors.

The extent to which the "unique" networking style and advantages of Singaporeans doing business in China *vis-à-vis* non-Chinese actors are real or imagined as well as the specific type of capitalism evolving in China and Vietnam are important topics for future research projects. With regard to the latter, it is necessary to debate the conceptual usefulness of Western notions of the state and the market in socialist economies, to explore the different connotations of capitalism such as its morally compromising character and its downside as well as to discuss the question raised by some scholars whether a new type of (moral) capitalism is in the making in these emerging markets.

According to Lever-Tracy and Tracy (1999), there are different kinds of capitalism in operation in the contemporary globalizing, multicentred economic system. Chinese network capitalism is just one of them. They conceptualize three main ways of integrating capitalist operations in Asia – through a hierarchical plan, through free market relations and through horizontal networks. These different modes of integration have different requirements for effective functioning, different strengths and weaknesses and different paths of development and are likely to degenerate or collapse in different circumstances. Although all capitalist groups make use of and are involved with all three, they do so with different priorities and in different combinations – the Japanese and Koreans leaning towards the first, Western operators in the region tending to rely on the second and diaspora Chinese capital giving preference to the third. Although co-existence between these ways of integrating is ubiquitous, Lever-Tracy and Tracy feel that the synergy is unstable. As Asia's malaise has shown, a sudden change in the balance, produced by a very rapid increase of short term, anonymous, market directed flows of "hot money" caused a disjuncture at the interface, which irrupted into an escalating crisis. As they read it, the network capitalism of the Chinese diaspora has been damaged by the temptations of both crony capitalism and of market speculation. It has, however, its own resources, enabling significant sections to survive the crisis and for new winners to emerge.

The debate about the different types of capitalist integration continues. Some analysts have argued that such models might be too static and that they ignore the vast differences between East Asian economies such as China and Korea as well as the significant role of politics in Asian market cultures. Social constructivists may read type three of the model as "the discursively construction of a specific type of Chinese capitalism" in the context of global capitalism, arguing that this has increased the *visibility* of the Chinese community as a whole. This can be particularly harmful in minority settings and times of crisis. Chinese diasporic capital is sometimes perceived as a threat in some Southeast Asian countries which can trigger ethnic problems and even conflicts. The creation of interlocking ties in minority settings can thus be dangerous. As a result, there are limits to the usefulness of networking in capitalism, especially in situations where economic rationality is questioned and predictable frameworks do no longer exist as in the case of Indonesia at times. Such a perspective is seldom followed-up systematically in the literature on Chinese business.

It is hoped that the monograph will stimulate a discussion about the causes and effects of the public (and subsequently academic) construction of a specific Asian (Chinese) capitalism as a sort of "better capitalism" and its various material bases in Taiwan, China, Singapore and elsewhere. Discourses on ethnic capitalisms can be very powerful in creating reality which makes it difficult for academicians, journalists and other concerned observers to question associated images and notions, for example, with regard to cultural differences between East and West in general or the homogeneity of the East Asian development model in particular. New and trendy viewpoints are easily internalized.

This monograph has put particular emphasis on analyzing Chinese business networks, their respective drivers, outcomes and associated challenges. Whether common ethnicity and culture are effective germinating powers for business and cultural exchange among the Chinese and the degree of openness of associated social structures are contested issues not least since the first ever World Chinese Entrepreneurs Convention in 1991 in Singapore organized by SCCCI. The chapter by Gomez is a valuable contribution to this ongoing discussion. Based on detailed case studies of three large Chinese-owned companies in Malaysia, Gomez challenges common-sense assumptions that culture and common ethnicity are the main driving forces of successful Chinese entrepreneurship and network expansion in Asia. Entrepreneurial abilities and competencies, occupational experiences and the use of class resources rather than ethnicity and culture *per se* explain success of Chinese entrepreneurship and the expansion of their networks.

However, some scholars might disagree with the notion of network formation as skillful, individualistic and rational formation of cool strategic alliances. Skeptics might stress that "there must be something going on between the big guys" or that protection by the state has been an important variable in the success stories of some of the largest Chinese-owned firms in Southeast Asia. Some may point to the narrow empirical base of contemporary studies on Chinese business which makes generalizations difficult while others may stress arguments put forward by proponents of the new economic sociology that the world of business is driven by social forces, that network members observe each other carefully, that informal exchange processes are significant and so forth regardless of anonymous demand and supply mechanisms. The literature on ethnic entrepreneurship suggests that the manipulation of ethnic identity for business purposes is often seen as a universally legitimate strategy of ethnic entrepreneurs. There are institutionalized network ties at work in many Southeast Asian countries, for example, in local/regional Chambers of Commerce and Industry, clan associations, religious organizations etc. and it seems that there is a re-emergence of these structures because of promising business prospects with China. Respective empirical studies, however, are rare. Liu's chapter (1998) suggests that respective intra-communitarian and evolving transnational networking activities are economically motivated rather than socially exclusive or primordial in nature, a point also raised by Wong (1988) and Menkhoff (1993). Yeung's contribution to this volume, which provides new and interesting insights into the role, logic, extent and lubricants of transnational Chinese entrepreneurs from Singapore and their globalization efforts, does also support this argument. His rich database is extensive and exceptional in the context of past and contemporary Chinese business research.

Another issue that we want to highlight here concerns the potential dangers of "romanticizing" Chinese entrepreneurship and business networks. Sometimes scholarly work can cause the perpetuation of stiff-necked stereotypes and myths about Chinese business, its imputed uniqueness and power etc., especially when the subject matter is treated with sympathy. Chinese transnational business networks are not always characterized by smooth cooperative ties. Academicians often shy away from analyzing the other side of business issues such as the dysfunctions of *guanxi* and *xinyong*, which are often proclaimed as typical and effective lubricants in Chinese business, conflict, feuds and so forth. Such topics and themes are usually taken up by journalists as exemplified by M. Backman's book *Asian Eclipse* (1999). Chinese business, like other research subjects and objects, is socially (and culturally) constructed. Scholars do actively take part in these processes. More self-reflection might be helpful to increase objectivity and to anticipate potential negative implications of research work on the Chinese overseas (Chan 2000).

Against this background, the piece by Yao is probably one of the most stimulating and provocative contributions in this monograph. Yao introduced a unique interpretation of the famous Chinese *guanxi* tactics, which are often essentialized in the mainstream literature on Chinese business. *Guanxi* exchange among Chinese traders in the small East-Malaysian township where Yao conducted his fieldwork is characterized by a profound "tension" in reconciling objectives such as social (relationship) pleasure (which gives no profit) and individual gains (marked by competitive violence). The dialectic relationship as well as the strategic harvesting of the two typify the cultural model of *guanxi*. Yao's theses are supported by the increasing tendency of business colonizing the private sphere as well as the visible combination of pleasure and profit in slogans and concepts such as "relationship banking" or "gifts as commodity."

In terms of future research, it might be helpful to examine whether the underlying problem of *guanxi* and social capital formation in transactions is somewhat universal since such practices can also be found in European countries such as France or Italy aimed at identifying "what is so Chinese in Chinese *guanxi* transactions." That non-Chinese business partners are important objects of "Chinese" *guanxi* tactics, a sheer necessity in business, is seldom highlighted and systematically analyzed. Others may point out that there are qualitative differences between different ethnic Chinese people in Asia which need to be further scrutinized (one example provided by one of the contributors concerned the foreign manager of a foreign-owned hotel in China who was forced to resign since he did not succeed in getting necessary fittings released from the Customs Department; his Singaporean Chinese successor simply invited the head of the department for lunch and things worked out smoothly ...). Some scholars have stressed that the notion of "*guanxi* as Chinese *guanxi*" is an ideological construct whose emergence is closely linked to the rise of East Asia, a point that deserves further examination. Besides that more emphasis should be put on the importance of gender in understanding and conceptualizing Chinese *guanxi* practices and transactions since women play a significant role in Chinese firms.

In line with the agenda of the monograph, Wazir's contribution has challenged the often voiced socio-economic exclusivity of Chinese business(men) and their networking strategies, by highlighting the potential and increasing numbers of inter-ethnic entrepreneurial collaborations between Chinese and Malay business partners in Malaysia. By putting emphasis on interethnic collaboration in a crisis situation rather than the opposite, her chapter helps to correct the popular image of Chinese businesspeople as being a homogeneous and isolated group of commercial strategists who have no links with other (ethnic) groups. Despite the plausibility of her arguments, only future empirical research can show how far the somewhat idealistic picture of Chinese and Bumiputeras cooperating in business in harmony for mutual benefits is in line with reality. Furthermore, it would be worthwhile to study the social organization of respective business collaborations (including management-labor relations, the role of gender etc.) within the wider socio-political context of Malaysia and to examine the ongoing change from personalistic forms of trust and transactions to a greater reliance on system trust and contractual/legal arrangements.

The new 10-year social economic plan (OPP3), which was unveiled by Prime Minister Dr Mahathir in April 2001, again emphasizes the need to increase Bumiputra participation in leading sectors of the economy and achieving Bumiputra equity ownership of at least 30 per cent by 2010. Whether OPP3 will help "to create a fair and just society" as indicated by Foreign Minister Datuk Syed Hamid Albar (*New Straits Times*, 4/4/2001) has to be analyzed in the future.

The contribution by Lever-Tracy, Ip and Tracy provided interesting comparative insights into the emerging dynamic and relatively integrated Chinese business community in Brisbane, Australia. Like many other authors in this monograph, their chapter convincingly questions the adequacy of conceptualizing these developments, exclusively, in terms of the emergence of an ethnic business enclave, advantaged by the social capital of bounded solidarity and enforceable trust.

Rutten is one of the few authors in this collection who pursued a truly comparative perspective. His chapter clearly illustrated the usefulness of empirical–theoretical research on ethnic (Chinese) entrepreneurship in different communities and countries by highlighting the many similarities between different types of ethnic entrepreneurs in India, Malaysia and Indonesia. We feel that these similarities make any attempt to essentialize Chinese business more than questionable. More empirical, comparative research is necessary to systematize such issues.

To sum up, we hope that the quality of the chapters and the different viewpoints of the contributors (whom we might simply dichotomize into culturalists and those who interpret culture as being contingent upon time and space) regarding the subject matter of the monograph will not only improve our understanding of Chinese entrepreneurship and Asian business networks but also help readers to appreciate the great diversity of "Chinese" entrepreneurs and "Asian" business networks. Notwithstanding conflicting perceptions of Chinese business issues, most observers tend to agree that Chinese capital will continue to play a prominent role in the consolidation and further development of Asia despite the current tough business environment. How ethnic Chinese entrepreneurs, their family businesses, conglomerates and networks – who have played a significant role in the regional economic integration of East and Southeast Asia throughout the past decades (and increasingly in the context of global market expansion) – adjust to the process of globalization and the emerging knowledge-based economy are important topics for further research. Common-sense suggests that the issue of Chineseness, the construction of a Chinese variant of capitalism, the discourse on the Asianisation of Asia, the resurgence of the new Asian consciousness and so forth which surfaced during the pre-crisis years will resurface once the crisis has been fully resolved. Such a development could be interpreted as another powerful argument for more solid cross-cultural comparative research on ethnic (Chinese) entrepreneurship and business networks in East and West.

References

Backman, M. (1999) *Asian Eclipse – Exposing the Dark Side of Business in Asia*, Singapore: John Wiley & Sons.

Chan, K. B. (2000) (ed.) *Chinese Business Networks – State, Economy and Culture*, Singapore: Prentice Hall.

Chan, K. B. and Tong, C. K. (2000) Singaporean Chinese Doing Business in China. In K. B. Chan, (ed.), *Chinese Business Networks – State, Economy and Culture*, Singapore: Prentice Hall.

Chua, C. S. (2001) *The New Economy and Chinese Enterprises in Singapore*, Unpublished Ms., Faculty of Business Administration, National University of Singapore.

Evers, H.-D. and Schiel, T. (1988) *Strategische Gruppen. Vergleichende Studien zu Staat, Bürokratie und Klassenbildung in der Dritten Welt*, Berlin: Reimer.

Evers, H.-D. and Schrader, H. (eds) (1994) *The Moral Economy of Trade. Ethnicity and the Development of Markets*, London: Routledge.

Hong Hai (2001) Networking through the World Chinese Entrepreneurs Convention, *Chinese Enterprise*, March, 27–8.

Leavitt, H. J. (1965) Applied Organizational Change in Industry: Structural, Technical and Human Approach. In Cooper, W. W., Leavitt, H. J. and Shelly, M. W. II (eds), *New Perspectives in Organizational Research*, New York: John Wiley.

Lever-Tracy, C. and Tracy, N. (1999) The Three Faces of Capitalism and the Asian Crisis, *Journal of Concerned Asian Scholars*, 31(3), July–September.

Liu Hong (1998) Old' Linkages, New Networks: The Globalization of Overseas Chinese Voluntary Associations and Its Implications, *The China Quarterly*, No. 155 (September).

Menkhoff, T. (1992) Chinese Non-Contractual Business Relations and Social Structure: The Singapore Case, *Internationales Asienforum*, 23(1–2), 261–88.

——(1993) *Trade Routes, Trust and Trading Networks – Chinese Small Enterprises in Singapore*, Saarbruecken/Fort Lauderdale: Breitenbach Publishers.

Menkhoff, T. and Kay, L. (2000) Managing Organizational Change and Resistance in Small and Medium-Sized Family Firms, *Research and Practice in Human Resource Management*, 8(1), Special Issue, 153–72.

Menkhoff, T. and Labig, C. (1996) Trading Networks of Chinese Entrepreneurs in Singapore, *Sojourn*, 11(1), 130–54.

Wertheim, W. F. (1980) The Trading Minorities in Southeast Asia. In H.-D. Evers (ed.), *Sociology of Southeast Asia*, Kuala Lumpur: Oxford University Press, pp. 104–20.

Wong, S.-L. (1985) The Chinese Family Firm: A Model, *British Journal of Sociology*, XXXVI, 58–72.

——(1988) *Emigrant Entrepreneurs – Shanghai Industrialists in Hong Kong*, Hong Kong: Oxford University Press.

——(1998) *Chinese Entrepreneurs as Cultural Heroes*. EAI Occasional Paper No. 3, Singapore: East Asian Institute.

INDEX

Adidas 136–7, 140–1
anak-angkat 310
An Ha (export processing zone) 132
Angkatan Bersenjata Republik Indonesia
  (ABRI) 57
Anwar Ibrahim 51–3, 163
Asian Competitiveness Report (1999) 25
Asian (financial/economic) crisis 43–4,
  160, 185, 201, 207–9, 295, 314

bamboo network 36, 189
Bancorp Holdings 171
Ban Hin Lee Bank Bhd 160, 179
bang (Chinese business association)
  143–5; speech group *bang* 145–6;
  Teochew *bang* 146–7
Bangkok Bank Group 78
Bank Bumiputera Bhd 169
Bank Central Asia 35, 78
Bank Negara (Malaysia) 171
bapak-angkat 310
Barisan Nasional (National Front) 51, 159,
  161
Barrington Moore 119
Batam 78
Beijing East Suburb Agriculture Industry
  Commerce United Corporation 201
Berjaya Group 69
Binh Hung *Hoa* (export processing zone)
  132
boat people 130
Boon Siew Sdn Bhd 166–7
bumiputera 51, 53, 160–1, 163, 167–8,
  171, 173, 179–81, 257, 260–1
bumiputeraism 258

Camdessus, Michael 52
campaign X1, X2 129–30
CDL Hotels International 200–1
Centre for Information and Development
  Study 52
chaebol 23, 45
Champion Technology 79
Chandler 179
Charoen Pokphand Group 31, 68–9, 78
Chearavanont family 78
Cheng Heng Jem William 165, 168
Cheng Yean 167
China Resources 78
China Strategic Management Company
  73
Chinese business networks 184, 187,
  196–7, 295, 298–9, 304
Chinese capitalism 32, 36, 38, 186, 244,
  250
Chinese diaspora: groups 70; in Hong
  Kong 76–7, 80; investments in China
  65–71; joint ventures 75–6; networks
  71–2; and reform process in China 65,
  73–6; in Taiwan 76–7, 80
Chiwan Petroleum Supply Base Co. Ltd
  195
Cholon 129–31, 136–7, 140, 142–3, 147
Chua, James 204–5
Chua Seng Teck 203
Chua, Thomas 204–6
CITIC 32
Clyne, Ian 34
collectivism 295–6, 311–14
Colombo Plan 274
commuting system 272

compatriot *Hoa* (overseas Chinese): corporation with 140; investments in Vietnam 131

confidence, "culture of confidence" 257–8

Confucian: capitalism 236–7, 244; ideals 31; ideas 108; law 132; principles 94, 97; social theory 233, 251; tradition 218; values 86, 93–4, 96, 236, 244

Confucianism 140, 233–4, 251, 298–9

crony capitalism 45, 51, 53, 57, 264

cronyism 258

cukong cronyism 28

danwei 102

Dao Heng Bank 200, 202

Decree on enterprises (Vietnam) 111

Democratic Party (Thailand) 46

Deng Xiaopeng 66, 98, 118

Dhanin Chearavanont 31–2

Dharmala Group 69

doi moi economic reform policy 130–1, 135, 147

Eastern Europe 136

entrepreneurship in Asia 295–6, 298–9

Estrada 52

ethnic (business) niche 268–9, 271

ethnic enclave 271, 284–6

ethnicization of production 36

ethnoburb 270, 286

European Institute of Asian Studies 26

Eu Yan Sang Ltd 195

export quotas 136–7

familism 93, 255, 258, 298

family-related values 88

First Pacific 37

Foo Chow 259–60, 265

Fujian 31, 66, 69, 73, 75, 80–1, 200, 219

Gaige Kaifeng (reform and opening) policy 91

gang qing 237, 242, 249

Gan Kai Choon 201

Genting Bhd 168

gift exchange (economy, relationship) 244–6, 248

Goh Chok Tong 54, 59

Gokongwei, John 35

Golkar Party 45, 50

government linked company (GLC) 57

Guangdong 31, 66, 70, 73–5, 80–1, 132, 137, 147

Guangdong Model 75

guanxi 23–4, 26–7, 31–2, 45, 59, 89–90, 130–1, 133, 135, 137–8, 140–3, 146, 148, 190, 219, 220, 224, 226–8, 230, 233–52, 299, 314; *fuji guanxi* 236; *guoji guanxi* 236; *jiating guanxi* 237; kinship *guanxi* 31; *pengyou guanxi* 237; *routi guanxi* 236; *sayshangye guanxi* 236; *shangye guanxi* 236

guanxi capital 32

Guoco Group 200

Habib Corporation 262

Habibie 49, 51–2, 54, 57

haoshi 240

hegu (traditional Chinese partnership) 142

HKR International 35

Ho Chi Minh City (HCMC) 129–32; Chinese Business Department of HCMC 147

Hock San Yuen Food Manufacturing 195

Hokkien 160–1, 164–5, 168, 178–80, 260

Hokkien Association 159

Hok Tong Group 220

Hong Kong Chinese Bank 78

Hong Kong group 78

Hong Kong Tin Corporation (M) Bhd 172

Hong Leong Bank 160, 179

Hong Leong Group 69, 166, 168, 200–2, 210

hui (rotating credit system) 142, 144

Hutchinson group 37

individualism 295–6, 311–14

Indonesian Association of Muslim Intellectuals 52

Indonesian Chinese Reform Party 49

Indonesian Democratic Party (PDI) 50

Industrial Association of District Five 130

industrial cluster 94

Institute for Economic Management 113

Institute of Policy Research 52

Interior Pte Ltd 195

internationalization of Chinese business 185, 192, 202, 208
International Monetary Fund (IMF) 26–7, 44, 52–3
Intraco Ltd 195
intrapreneur (manager intrapreneur) 185, 187, 202, 205

jen-ch'ing 233
JGG Finance Company Ltd 170–1
JG Summit Holdings 35
jia 222
Jiangxi Povincial Investment Group 175
Jiangxi Provincial Power Electric Corp 175
Jingji Yanjin (journal) 106
Jurong Shipyard 195
Jurong Town Corporation 195

Kah Motor Co. Sdn Bhd 166
Kamil, Nik Ahmad 169
Kamunting Bhd 161
keiretsu 45
Keretapi Tanah Melayu (KTM) Bhd 175
Khazanah 175
Khoo Kay Peng 160, 165
Khoo Teck Puat 160
Koh, Tommy 26
Kong 133, 137, 147
kuan-shi see guanxi
Kuok Group 69
Kuok, Robert 31–2, 190
Kwek Hong Lye 200
Kwek Hong Png 200–1
Kwek Leng Beng 200–2, 210

lai wang 237–8, 242, 244, 247
Lao Chong 239–42, 245, 249–50
Lau, Datuk Hui Kang 259
Le Dan Doanh 113
Lee Boon Chim 220
Lee Kai Tong 220
Lee Kong Chian 219–22, 226–7
Lee Kuan Yew 25, 45, 54, 251
Lee Mo Tie *see* Riady, Mochtar 34
Lee Phie Soe 219, 221
Lee Rubber Group 219, 220–7, 230
Lee Seng P'ng 220

Lembaga Tabung Angkatan Tentara (LTAT) 173
Lian Hin Group 220
Liem family 69
Liem Sioe Liong 48, 78
Li Ka-shing 37, 78
Lim Goh Tong 168
Lim Nee Soon 219
Lim, T.K. 165
Lion group 166, 168
Lippo Group 34, 78
Loh Boon Siew 165–8, 177–9
Loh Boon Siew Sdn Bhd 167

Mahathir Mohamad 161
Mah Kok Hui 205–7
Malayan Banking Bhd (Maybank) 160, 168–9, 178, 180
Malayan Chinese Association (MCA) 59, 159, 161–2, 168
Malaysian People's Movement for Justice 52
Malaysian Timber Association 259
Marcos 44
Mar'ie Muhammad 52
MBf Holdings 35, 38
Megawati Sukarnoputri 50
mianzi 140, 143, 248
middleman minority 271
mien-tsui 233
minying keji shiye 109
MUI Bank Bhd *see* Hong Leong Bank
multiculturalism 279
Multimedia Supercorridor (MSC) 51
Multi-Purpose Holdings Bhd (MPHB) 161
Muslim businessman 308

Nakornthon Bank 36
Nanchang Zhongli Power Co. Ltd 175
Nanshan Development Company 195
Nasir Tamara 52
National Economic Action Council (NEAC) 53–4, 257
nepotism 133, 225, 298
New Economic Policy (NEP) 43, 48, 51, 55, 57, 160–1, 163, 168, 171, 178–9
New Economic Zones (Vietnam) 130

new taipan 24
Ng family 69
Noor Adzman Baharuddin 262
Nusantara 255, 261

Oei family 72–3
Oei Hong-leong 73
Oriental Assemblers Sdn Bhd 166
Oriental Holdings Bhd 165–8, 179
Oversea-Chinese Banking Corporation
  (OCBC) 160, 168, 178, 221

Pacific Bank Bhd 160
Pangilinan, Manny 37
Pearl River Delta *see* Guangdong
Penang Yellow Bus Company Sdn Bhd
  165, 167
People's Action Party (PAP) 45, 192
Peregrine Investment Holdings 209
Petronas 53
Phung Hung Bank 130
Phung Nam Bank 130
Port Singapore Authority 195
pribumi 48
Private Enterprise Law and Company Law
  131
private entrepreneur: classification 101;
  debate about 104–5, 108; discrimination
  of 102; network 102, 114; social/
  political role 101–4
privatization: and change in values 117;
  and industrial change 117; and social
  change 117
Provisory Regulations for Private
  Enterprises in the People's Republic of
  China 111
PT Steady Safe 209
Public Bank Bhd 160, 168–71, 178–9
Public Finance Bhd 169

Qiyijia (journal) 107
Quek Leng Chan 160, 168, 200–2

race riots (Malaysia, 1969) 160–1
racial riots (Indonesia) 49–50; (Malaysia)
  51
Rais, Amien 52
Razaleigh Hamzah 163

regionalization of Chinese business 192–3,
  195, 202
Registry of Companies and Businesses
  (ROCB) 222, 227
Renmin Ribao (People's Daily) 107–8
renqing 234, 247, 252
Riady family 69
Riady, Mochtar 34
Ricardo 101

Sachs, Jeffrey 25
Salim Group 32, 35, 38, 48
Schumpeter, Joseph A. 101–2, 106, 184
Second Fujianese World Chinese
  Entrepreneurs Convention (1996) 165
Sejahtera Mandairi Foundation 48
self-made (business) man 296
Sembawang Maritime Ltd 195
Shehuixue Yanjiu (journal) 107
shiji 243
Siam Pakthai 220
Sinar Mas Group 68–9
Sino-Bumiputera partnership 257, 261
Smith, A. 101
Soeharto 35, 45, 47–9, 50, 54, 57–8, 209
Soros, George 53, 257
Southern Bank Bhd 160, 168, 178–9
Standard Chartered 36
strategic alliance 34
Strategic Groups 121
Sunwa Construction 195
Syarikat Pembenaan Yeoh Tiong Lay Sdn
  Bhd 171–2, 174

Tan Kah Kee 219, 226
Tan Sri Koh Tsu Koon 262–3
Tan Thuan (export processing zone) 132
Tasek Cement Bhd 168
Teck Wah Group. Ltd 204–6, 210
Teknologi Tenaga Perlis (Overseas)
  Consortium Sdn Bhd 175
Temasek Holdings Pte. Ltd 201
Tenaga Nasional Bhd 173, 175
Teo Chee Hean 54
Teochew *bang* 146–7
thau-ke 223
The Hong Piow 160, 168–71, 177–8
Tiananmen crackdown 66

tiger economies 132, 136
Ting Pek Khiing 165
transnational corporations (TNC) 36,
  184–7, 192, 195–6, 206, 265
transnational entrepreneurship (Chinese-)
  185–9, 190, 196–8, 200, 202, 206–8
transnational networks 267–8
tribal mentality 34

United Industrial Corp (UIC) 35
United Malays National Organization
  (UMNO) 45, 51, 53–4, 59, 159, 161–3,
  169
Urban Development Authority (UDA)
  175

values: Asian 45; Chinese cultural 133,
  218, 234, 300
value system 218
Viet *Hoa* 129–33, 138–9, 140; networks
  135; transnational corporation 136
Viet Hoa Bank 130, 146–7
Viet Hoa Construction Company 130,
  147
Vietnam Father Land Front 147–8
Vincent Tan Chee Yioun 165

Wahid, Abdurrahman 49, 51–2
Wanglee family 37

Web-based Chinese Management (WCM)
  84–98
Weber 297–8
White Australia policy 271, 274
Wong Lum Kong 167
Wong Nai Siang 260
World Bank 112
World Chinese Business Network
  (WCBN) 32
World Economic Forum (WEF) 25
Wu, Gordon 173
Wuxi Teckwah Paper Products Co. Ltd
  (Wuxi Paper) 204–7

xinyong 130, 138, 140, 142, 144, 146, 220,
  224, 227–8, 237

Yap Twee 219, 221
Yeoh Cheng Liam 171
Yeoh, Francis 171–2, 174, 178
Yeoh Seok Kian 172
Yeoh Tiong Lay 171–2, 177–8
YTL Corp group 172–6, 178–9
YTL Corporation Bhd 171

Zainuddin, Daim 25, 51, 53
zao sheng yi 237
Zhongguo Gongshang Bao (journal) 107,
  109

For Product Safety Concerns and Information please contact our EU
representative GPSR@taylorandfrancis.com Taylor & Francis Verlag GmbH,
Kaufingerstraße 24, 80331 München, Germany

Printed and bound by CPI Group (UK) Ltd, Croydon, CR0 4YY
01/05/2025
01858333-0009